FRIENDLY FIRES

*Recollections of a
Diplomatic Family*

VOLUME II

Friendly Fires
Copyright © 2018 by Robert and Barbara Pringle

Published by Piscataqua Press
An imprint of RiverRun Bookstore, Inc.
32 Daniel Street
Portsmouth, NH 03801
www.riverrunbookstore.com
www.piscataquapress.com

ISBN: 978-1-950381-09-8

Printed in the United States of America

Contents
Volume II

10. Papua New Guinea, Solomon Islands, Vanuatu, 1985-1987

A House on the Edge of Heaven   8
Our Friend, CINCPAC   12
Barbara Arrives   14
Exploring Melanesia   17
The Children Come for Christmas   24
A Short Pidgin Lesson   26
The Solomon Islands   29
A Highly Migratory Fish Story   31
Barbara, Her School, and the Big Stone Axe   34
The Myth of a Separatist Movement   38
Exploring the Sepik River   40
The Highlands Show   47
The Crime Problem   49
Vanuatu, or Pure South Pacific   52
A Most Explosive Harbor: Rabaul   56
Why Cargo Cults Make Sense   59
The Big One that Didn't Get Away   62
Revenge of the Wigmen   62
Malinowksi's Islands and the Kula Ring   65
A Missing B-17 is Found   66
Paradise and its Birds, Close to Home   69
Last, Best Diving and a Call from the President   70

11. Ronald Reagan's Man and Wife in Mali, 1987-1990

Getting Confirmed   73
Arriving in Bamako   79
First Visit to Timbuktu   88
Star Attractions of Central Mali   94
     * The Dogon Country   95
     * Mali's Monument Valley   96
     * Desert Elephants   97
     * The Niger's Inner Delta   100
     * The Great Mosque of Djenné 102
US Economic Assistance   103
The Peace Corps in Mali   108
Requirements for a Bush Taxi,
     and a Visit from Maureen Reagan   109
Beads, Ancient and Otherwise   111

Barbara Visits Jamie in Spain,
    or Why Diplomatic Passports are Overrated   112
Annie Graduates and Works for CARE   116
The State Visit   121
A Week on Mali's Great River   128

12. MALI (2): DEMOCRATIC TRANSITION AND DESERT REBELLION, 1987-1990

Bits and Pieces
    * *The Joys and Sorrows of Sahelian Dogdom*   135
    * *Where's My Tux?*   135
    * *The Most Mysterious Bead*   135
    * *Protocol and Polygamy*   137
    * *Bird Watching and Softball*   137
    * *Our Very Own Baobab*   138
    * *An Ecumenical Bridge*   139
Diplomatic Niceties   139
Barbara's Work with AMALDEME   141
The Cattle Crossing at Diafarabé   145
Kankan Moussa's Gold: Not a Myth   148
Our Daily Routine   151
Visiting Tessalit and Dakar, and Back by Train   153
Time Off in Israel   158
A New Look Soviet Ambassador   159
Pax Celebrates the Fourth of July   161
Medevac'd to Paris   163
Finding Islam in Mali   165
A Closer Look at the Tuareg   165
The Pope Visits Mali, as do *les Mamans*   175
A Diplomatic Tour of the North   176
Archaeology in the Niger's Inner Delta   179
Diplomacy, Cultural Artifacts, and Democratization   181
A Postscript on Mali   187

13. CAREER AND FAMILY IN THE UNITED STATES, 1990-1996

Barbara Hunts for a Job, Again   192
Life in a Regional Office: Central Africa (AF/C)   195
A Southern African Interlude   206
The Potomac School   210
The Heart of Central Africa: Congo Kinshasa   214
An English Vacation   218
The Rwandan Genocide   220
Gabon, Equatorial Guinea, and São Tomé-Principe   224
A Family Crisis Intervenes   233

Diplomacy and the Environment (OES/ETC)   235
On the Rivers of Russia   242
A Seaborne Conference on Forest Issues   249
Our Old House Gets a Fix   252
The Senior Seminar   253

14. SOUTH AFRICA (1): PRESENT AT A CREATION, 1996-1999

Bob's Role as DCM, Again   261
US Relations with the New South Africa   263
A Bit of History for Perspective   266
Getting Settled in Pretoria *and* Cape Town   269
The Colored Conundrum   282
Two Big Visits   285
Durban   293
David and Anne Get Engaged   297
The Embassy's Morale Problem   301
Meeting the South African Pringles   305
The Kwa-Zulu Natal Battlefields:
　　Isandlwana and Rorke's Drift   307
Wakkerstroom: Birds, Schools, and Tourism   308

15. FINALE IN SOUTH AFRICA

Bits and Pieces
　　Ancient pre-Humans and their Study   313
　　Opera, Classic and Home-grown   314
　　Two Houses   316
　　The Otenequa Tjoe-Choo   317
　　The Lady of Nieu Bethesda   318
Madiba Stomps on Uncle Sam   319
The Joys of Kruger National Park   321
Almost Everyone Visits South Africa   325
FLOTUS and POTUS at Last   332
Family Milestones   337
Visiting and Helping Neighbors:
　　Lesotho, Swaziland, Mozambique and Namibia   341
A Whiff of Terror: the East African Bombings   348
Even Fidel Visited Cape Town   349
Combining Travel with Reporting   350
Barbara's Two Interesting Jobs and Our Last Visitors   353
Signs of Change, Large and Small   359
Preparing to Say Farewell   361
Always Time for One More Trip, to Madagascar   364
Kalahari-Gemsbok   366

16. Assignment Washington and Retirement

Bob Teaches at the National War College 370
The Area Studies Trips 376
9/11 383
Back at Potomac School 384
Life without Work? 386
Bali and Its History 388
Barbara Retires: from Teaching to Volunteering 395
A New Addition to the Family 398
"Freedom of Information" 402
A Glimpse of the World Bank 404
Democracy in Mali 406
Islam in Indonesia Observed, and a Return to Sarawak 408
The Malay Pirates Strike 415

17. Looking Back, Looking Forward

Globetrotting and Bird Watching 420
Strife on the Alexandria Waterfront 425
Looking Back at the Foreign Service 428
Barbara Sums Up 432
The Trailing Spouse Dilemma 436
How Fortune Smiled on Us 438

10

Papua New Guinea, Solomon Islands, Vanuatu, 1985-1987

I arrived in Port Moresby on September 11, 1985, to become Deputy Chief of Mission at our embassy in that city. It served three countries: Papua New Guinea, Solomon Islands (of Guadalcanal fame) and Vanuatu, once the New Hebrides. Barbara stayed behind while Jamie and Annie were still on school vacation, so I was by myself for almost two months.

Our two-month interlude at home had been a hectic hodge-podge:

. . . the usual home-leave rush through the States—consultations on the new post, inadequate efforts to see friends, a couple of weeks to relax in North Carolina, then departure (for Bob) in order to make it to Port Moresby in time for the tenth anniversary of independence. Barbara stayed on in the US for another month to get the kids settled in school, look after various problems in connection with our house in Alexandria, and visit Wawatosa, Wisconsin (sister school of the Ouagadougou International School), to tell them about their far-away sibling.[1]

My most vivid first impression of Port Moresby was of our new house, which was perched on a hill with a magnificent vista. Although not large, it was the most spectacularly located dwelling we would live in during our Foreign Service career, with the possible exception of the one in Cape Town. A local Australian developer had built it for his own residence, but he soon made himself a bigger place and rented this one to

---

[1] From our annual Christmas letter, dated November 1, 1985.

the US Embassy.[2] I remember waking up in the bare master bedroom with the sun streaming in and the radio playing an American hit pop song, something about "the rebels." I was never able to identify it later, but the memory is visceral, the way sounds and smells can be.

Newly arrived in this alien setting I could not help but worry about Moresby's[3] famous crime problem, and was greatly relieved to have as next door neighbors Colonel John Robbins and his wife Jenny, who soon became fast friends. John was the Australian military attaché and ran the Australian military assistance program on which the infant PNG defense force was totally dependent. Surely, I hoped, John could save me if the notorious "rascals" attacked, and *in extremis* I could hop over my wall into his garden.

I was to discover that in PNG the American and Australian roles were reversed: they were the great power, and we were the incidental ally. This was totally logical; they were both the former colonial power and next-door neighbor, and they were giving PNG more foreign aid, *per capita* in the receiving country, than we were giving to Israel. They were cheerfully gracious about our minor status, automatically letting us buy wine and beer from their "liquor locker." At a bigger post where we were Top Nation and they were the small fry, we could not have granted such a privilege to their diplomats without endless bureaucratic hassle, if at all.

A House on the Edge of Heaven

Our house was near the top of Tuaguba Hill and looked down, depending on one's vantage point, at a kaleidoscopic series of exotic views:

(1) Slightly to the southwest was downtown Port Moresby, with its modern harbor and scattering of office buildings, and,

---

[2] Bob and Barbara letter to Dear Family, March 3, 1986. At the time of our arrival the State Department was paying him a yearly rent which amounted to about one-eighth of the sale price of the house, because although there was plenty of money for rentals, the capital budget was starved. Eventually we persuaded Washington to find the money to buy it, and it is still the DCM residence at this writing.

[3] The "Port" is often dropped in everyday usage.

just below us, the Royal Papua Yacht Club.

(2) Almost below us lay a village of houses on stilts over the water, Hanuabada,[4] which had already existed when Port Moresby was founded in the 1880s. Unaccompanied, unintroduced foreigners were generally not welcome there even a century later. These were Motu people, who had once lived by making pottery. Every year they had taken their pots up the coast in large fleets to the Gulf of Papua to trade them for sago. They had long ago abandoned this practice, but they were still great sailors.

(3) Slightly further out was the large, shallow "inner harbor," including the wreckage of the *Macdhui*, an Australian steamer sunk in a Japanese air raid in June, 1942, when the Pacific war still hung in the balance. Near the *Macdhui* was a small, uninhabited island, connected to the mainland by a causeway built by an American engineering unit during the

A traditional Motu trading and fishing village, Hanuabada, lay in the harbor just below our house.

---

[4] Hanuabada is also illustrated in a painting by Jenny Robbins which currently hangs over Barbara's desk in our bedroom.

war. Its builders were still remembered for having been black.

(4) Beyond the harbor we could see an enormous barrier reef, structurally similar to Australia's Great Barrier Reef, which runs along much of the southern coast of PNG. All watercraft regardless of size going to or from Port Moresby's harbor must pass through a narrow passage, maybe half a mile wide, in this reef. Beyond it is the Coral Sea, often adorned with glorious sunsets. The house had a terrace with a small swimming pool looking in the direction of Hanuabada and the wreck of the *Macdhui* and the reef and beyond; from that area and from our bedroom we appreciated those sunsets, evening after evening.

(5) Looking toward the interior, there were layers of mountain ranges covered with roadless tropical forest stretching back toward the Owen Stanley Range, the spine of New Guinea.

(6) Interrupting our view toward the interior was the back of Tuaguba Hill, an arid, sandy promontory against which our house was built. When we arrived the lot line was not fenced, a real hazard in view of the crime problem.

Put another way, we lived in a setting of almost bizarre environmental variation as well as ethnic and linguistic diversity, saturated by memories and relics of World War II. We were not far from the equator, but although we looked out at tropical forests and coral reefs, Moresby is in a "rain shadow" and our immediate surroundings were sere and brown. In the forested mountains just behind us, rainfall was three or four times higher. Rain came mainly with the monsoon, during our winter months, and along with it powerful winds. Normally scuba diving was excellent on the seaward side of the big barrier reef, but during the monsoon months enormous waves crashed against it. Inside the reef windsurfing was popular, and from my office window I could see hardy fanatics careering along like mad water bugs over the wind-whipped waves.

Before long we began to feel nautical ourselves and acquired a seventeen-foot boat with a 40 hp Evinrude outboard motor and a second small motor for backup. We opted for this instead of a sailboat because we wanted it primarily as a dive boat, able to visit nearby islands in the harbor and get outside the big reef when the weather was good. I soon learned how to trail it behind our new Subaru (driving on the right again) down to the harbor and back up our steep hill with its sharp turns.

The house did have a few drawbacks, including the servant situation. We inherited a maid, Melata, who unfortunately had no cooking skills, and her unemployed, ne'er-do-well husband who, like many of his compatriots, had a drinking problem. I wrote Barbara, "They live in the property [in a small yard slightly downhill] with a herd of dogs to make noise in case of 'rascals.' This is supposed to wake up our security guard who then calls his agency with his two-way radio."[5] This protection was not very reassuring, nor was the fact that the Port Moresby fire truck couldn't reach the upper elevations of Tuaguba Hill where we lived, a problem because the dry grass which covered it often burned.

Our embassy occupied a tall, narrow office building, "like a match box on end," about a ten-minute drive from where we lived, down the steep hill and around hairpin curves.[6] We had seven Americans to cover our three countries: Ambassador, DCM, Consul, Political/Economic Officer, Admin Officer, Information Officer, a lone secretary, plus several local employees. Everyone had multiple functions (I, for example, administered our tiny military training program) and some of us traveled occasionally to our other two posts, Honiara (Solomon Islands) and Port Vila (Vanuatu), where we had no permanent facilities or staff. We had a very small aid (USAID) program administered from Fiji, and its small size and non-resident status greatly limited our influence.

Even the ambassador, Paul Gardner, often typed his own cables. Perhaps for this reason we were among the first embassies to receive an electronic word processor, a great boon. For personal mail, we depended mainly on international mail and the diplomatic pouch, which came, very slowly, via Canberra. E-mail was still in the future. Most of our administrative needs were covered by our embassy in Canberra, as I discovered when I filed my claim for travel

---

[5] Bob letter to Dear Family, September 15, 1985.
[6] The embassy has moved twice since we were there.

expenses immediately after arrival, only to have Canberra take weeks to process it, resulting in complaints blaming me from our travel department in Washington.

The basic problem was that the State Department's Bureau of East Asian and Pacific Affairs, under whose aegis we fell, served mainly large, orthodox embassies like Tokyo and Jakarta, and simply did not know how to handle the small, weird ones like us. I thought we should be transferred to the Bureau of African Affairs, which dealt with pint-sized customers all the time.

American interests in our three countries were almost as sparse as our staffing. The countries were small (total population less than five million) and poor. Vast natural resources were just beginning to be exploited, and US companies were not heavily involved. US tuna fishermen were expanding into the area, creating headaches described below. We were interested in friction between Australia and Indonesia over the Free Papua Movement in the Indonesian half of New Guinea, but not (with reason) greatly concerned about it. There were about 1,500 American missionaries and a smattering of hardy tourists and scientists, bird watchers and scuba divers in our countries.

Our Friend, CINCPAC

None of this was attention-grabbing from a Washington perspective, and the only high-ranking US government entity that paid much attention to us (or could easily find our countries on a map) was the Commander-in-Chief Pacific, or CINCPAC, always headed by a four-star admiral. For his attention, and for other reasons, we were very fond of him. (CINCPAC was both a person and a military command.)

CINCPAC had never forgotten where the Great War in the Pacific had been fought. CINCPAC cared about broad strategic interests in the vast Pacific region, which to many were beginning to seem obsolete. (At this writing, a quarter century later, they are once again in vogue, thanks to China.)

My arrival in Port Moresby coincided with the tenth anniversary of PNG's independence, and there was a big celebration. The British High Commissioner, representing

Queen Elizabeth, appeared in white pith helmet and plumes, but his feathers weren't as colorful as those of the dancers from all corners of the country who performed all day Sunday in the football stadium. There was a dawn ceremony at the hilltop memorial for war dead, including Papua New Guineans, where I again heard the moving lines of the poem always recited at British and other Commonwealth remembrance days:

> Age shall not weary them, nor the years condemn.
> At the going down of the sun and in the morning,
> *We will remember them.*[7]

We were represented at this ceremony by CINCPAC in the person of his deputy, an Air Force three-star general who headed our Pacific Air Force under the admiral. In addition, the Navy provided a ship visit, in the shape of a freighter which serviced the culinary needs of the Seventh Fleet, a kind of gigantic floating grocery store. I never figured out whether anyone at CINCPAC was aware of the delicious appropriateness of this. The ship was of course the quintessential *cargo* vessel, celebrating the independence of a country famous among other things for its *cargo cults*. More about them later.

Embassy staff were invited to visit the ship and do a little shopping. The only limitation was that we had to purchase at least fifty pounds of whatever it was. This was a bit daunting, especially without Barbara's advice, but I finally decided we could use fifty pounds of whole stewed chickens, in big cans and at a bargain price. Surely our Navy could not be delivering inferior chicken to its sailors?? Wrong. It turned out to be uniformly tough and stringy, but we got through it eventually, primarily via lots of casseroles. The captain told us that his cargo included 70,000 eggs en route to the fleet. "If we ever get hit by a torpedo we'll be the world's biggest omelet," he told me.[8]

Later CINCPAC himself, Admiral Ronald J. Hays, would pay us a visit. His personal plane rolled in past the moldering revetments lining the runways at the Port Moresby airport,

[7] Robert Lawrence Binyon, "For the Fallen," 1914.
[8] Bob letter to Dear Family, September 15, 1985.

built to shelter American B-17s from Japanese air raids, and pulled up to the terminal. Then, perfectly timed, his blue, four-star Admiral's flag popped out of its nose, no doubt amazing the natives as well as us, as did his personal satellite communication specialist, who accompanied him with a black suitcase on all his calls.

Hays wore his rank lightly; the Navy had a way of sending its smartest, most affable admirals to the senior Pacific Command, and he was no exception. He had a son in the Foreign Service who had been the head of our professional association and was at this time posted as DCM to Bujumbura, another major world capital. The natives were definitely friendly to him. One of our more colorful politicians, a typical Highlands "Big Man," having heard that the Philippines wanted to get rid of the US bases there, announced that we would be welcome to move them to PNG.[9]

Barbara Arrives

I arrived early in November, having gotten the children installed in their respective schools, Annie at Madeira and Jamie at Milton. I followed the same route Bob had: from the East Coast to Hawaii, which allowed a leisurely stroll on the beach and the purchase of a much treasured necklace and earrings set made of real pink coral, which was still affordable then; next deep into the Southern Hemisphere to Sydney, Australia; then, after visiting with various friends from Cornell, north to Brisbane, where our friend David Kenney was Consul; and finally north again to Port Moresby, almost on the equator.

A more direct route would have taken me directly southwest from Hawaii to Port Moresby, or at least to northern Australia, but there was no such service. The whole trip at that time required roughly 30 hours flight time plus at least two overnight stops, one in Hawaii and one in Australia.

Although Bob had taken care of certain chores of being in a new post, like the important one of beginning the process of buying a new car, he had saved most of the settling in duties

---

[9] Bob and Barbara letter to Dear Family, March 3, 1986.

for me. I arrived on the same plane as our air freight from North Carolina, which included our scuba gear, and so a top priority was to get back underwater again as fast as possible. I wrote in my first letter home that . . .

. . . we've dived four times since my arrival. That is partly due to the fact that we signed up for a refresher course which, to our surprise, turned out to take place both days last weekend, plus yesterday evening—but now we are definitely at home in the water again.[10]

Diving was to become our most important recreational pursuit in PNG, one in which Jamie and Annie could soon share.

In that same letter I observed that our new post was unlike Ouagadougou in many ways. Although dark skinned, the inhabitants did not resemble Africans. They behaved, for good reason, like people who had never been subjected to extended colonial rule, or to the constraints of a shared religion like Islam, although they were becoming thoroughly Christianized fast.

The consequences are many—difficulty in getting local service people, like plumbers and electricians; a work-to-rule attitude in offices and stores—all of which close on the dot; chaos . . . in parliamentary debates, and, at home, problems getting help for entertaining. . . . I'm going to miss faithful Duna and Prospère. . . .

In trying to redecorate the house to our taste, manage the constant entertaining, which though informal still required a lot of food preparation, and later, combining a teaching job with my spousal duties, I was to encounter this aspect of PNG society constantly. I finally found an excellent caterer who could arrive with prepared dishes that needed only heating or last-minute cooking to take some of the pressure off preparing food for large gatherings, but issues of service and shopping for drinks, rounding up sufficient cutlery and dishes, etc., still remained annoying chores.

---

[10] Barbara letter to Dear Family, date lost.

*Shopping in Port Moresby was not done in your average supermarket,
although Mila Mala was Australian owned and fairly large.*

On one occasion, as we set out trailing our boat for a
scuba expedition in the harbor, we noticed a car perched
precariously, engine and front wheels pointing down off
a curve of the steep downhill road leading away from our
house; later we learned it belonged to the woman who had
catered our dinner the evening before. How she got it back
on the road relatively undamaged we don't know, but she did.
And she didn't even drink.

Getting settled in was not helped by the vagaries of Foreign
Service shipping of household effects. We had already come
back from our first trip outside Port Moresby and were trying
to prepare for the children's Christmas visit when I wrote:

*We are delighted finally to have our sea freight shipment. .
. . When the shipment first arrived, we received two of our
three crates. The one that was missing was by far the most
important, with almost all our African art, our shell collection,
and our books and records in it. . . . The ship's second mate
said he could remember only two crates. . . . Antwerp swore
they had put three crates on the ship. Evaporated! Finally, the
administrative officer found it on the container dock—wet, and*

with one bottom corner so rotten that the floor was separating from the rest of the crate. Given all this, we were extremely lucky that there was virtually no damage to the contents. . . .

I also noted the extraordinary, continuing Australian presence:

The French in West Africa were never like this. It's not quite the pied noir *situation that I studied when I wrote my thesis on Algeria; the bus conductors are not white. But top management everywhere is; as are the heads of all major commercial ventures, of which there are many more here than in Burkina. That's not to say that there is not a thriving local sector—there is, but on top of that is still a huge Australian frosting. There are seven international (i.e. Australian system) primary schools and although there is only one international secondary school [where I would soon be teaching] that, I have discovered, is due to the fact that most expatriate teenagers return to Australia for boarding school.*[11]

One similarity with West Africa, I noted, was the rich traditional art scene, with marketing helped in some cases by missionaries and Peace Corps volunteers, so that the products of distant valleys and islands were often available in Port Moresby and other major cities.

Exploring Melanesia

As in Ouagadougou, Bob's job as DCM in Port Moresby was primarily to back up Paul Gardener in his ambassadorial duties and to exercise his analytical skills as needed, meaning that travel was essential. There was much to learn about our three countries, but Port Moresby had no road connection with any other part of PNG, much less the other two countries, and myriad islands in PNG itself were beckoning. We soon discovered that Air Niugini was a little gem of an airline, albeit expensive; its staff loved wrapping and caring for large carvings

---

[11] Both quotes are from Barbara letter to Dear Family, November 6, 1985, slightly edited for clarity.

and charged nothing for scuba tanks.

The human scene we would explore was, to understate the case, extraordinary. Papua New Guinea is the heart and largest component of Melanesia, a term meaning roughly "Land of Black People," and used to describe ten million people, somewhat more now than in 1985, living in "our" three countries plus the western half of New Guinea (now part of Indonesia), Fiji and New Caledonia.

The Melanesians are characterized by almost stupefying ethnic and linguistic variety. There is no precise explanation for such diversity, beyond the fact that even in recent times many of them lived in narrow mountain valleys or on small islands, either very isolated or constantly at war with each other. Despite their small population, they speak something approaching one-third of the world's languages—real languages, not dialects. Their ancestors came in migrations from the north and northwest that began at least 40,000 years ago and included the ancestors of native Australians. The aquiline facial features of many modern Melanesians resemble those of the Australian aborigines, although they are generally darker skinned.

(Have a world map handy as you read what follows.) New Guinea is the second largest island on earth, after Greenland. On a map it looks like a giant reptile draped over the Australian continent, with its head and shoulders on the west (the Indonesian portion) and its torso and tail slithering southeastwards (Papua New Guinea), finally petering out into a long string of islands which includes the Solomons, Vanuatu and Fiji. There are many more islands north of the eastern half of New Guinea, belonging mainly to Papua New Guinea. The big island has a mountainous spine with peaks of up to 16,000 feet on the Indonesian side. The highest mountains even have a few glaciers, but they are rapidly melting. Interiors throughout New Guinea are mainly mountainous with some big interior valleys, rivers and wetlands and scattered but intense volcanic activity, especially in the islands to the north.

Despite some early exploration, Europeans generally ignored Melanesia until late in the nineteenth-century scramble for colonies. By World War I, the western half of New Guinea was part of the Dutch East Indies. The eastern half of the great island was divided, the Germans controlling the northern half (resulting in geographic names like "Bismarck Sea" and "Finschafen") while the southern half was administered by Britain. After World War I, German New Guinea was added to the British, later Australian, holdings under a League of Nations mandate. The island chain stretching southeastwards was divided between Britain (Solomon Islands, Fiji) and France (New Caledonia, Tahiti). The New Hebrides (now Vanuatu), caught between imperial rivals, had become a "condominium" in 1906, jointly ruled by France and Great Britain.

All of this was unimportant until World War II, when the Japanese planned to attack Australia and the region suddenly became a critically important combat theater. In May, 1942, the Australians, with American help, turned back a Japanese fleet which was bringing troops for a landing at Port Moresby in the Battle of the Coral Sea. New Guinea and the adjacent islands became the scene of grinding combat, the first stage in MacArthur's island-hopping campaign toward the Philippines and eventually Japan. American Marines fought for months at Guadalcanal, and what had been their headquarters eventually became the new capital of the Solomon Islands. The island of Espiritu Santo, part of Vanuatu, was a rear base area for the Guadalcanal campaign, and became the setting for the musical *South Pacific*. "Bali Hai" was a little island just off Espiritu Santo, nowhere near the real Bali in Indonesia.

Colonial rule over the future Papua New Guinea was initially penny-pinched, but eventually quite enlightened. At first the Australians traveled into unexplored areas by foot patrols, with plenty of armed police and bearers carrying their gear in big metal trunks known as "patrol boxes."[12] The natives regularly attacked them, if only because they usually appeared from the direction of enemy tribes.

In the 1930s explorers seeking gold used light aircraft to reach the highland interior of New Guinea. There they discovered broad valleys with tens of thousands of people, hitherto unknown to outsiders, practicing intense

---

[12] Patrol boxes were readily available in Port Moresby, and we bought one which is now used for storing archives in the basement of 216 Wolfe Street.

horticultural agriculture.[13] (These people were similar to the Dani people of Indonesian New Guinea that I had visited with Ambassador Galbraith in 1970—see Chapter 5.) A famous documentary entitled *First Contact* shows an Australian shooting a pig in front of amazed villagers, to persuade them not to consider being unfriendly.

After World War II, the Australians employed Eastern European refugee doctors, some of them quite brilliant, but unable to find work elsewhere due to their "foreign" medical degrees, to extend basic medical care to the remote interior. Soon there were towns, schools, more missionaries and a few major roads. But colonialism rapidly became highly unfashionable in the Cold War era. Although Papua New Guinea could have used a few more years of enlightened colonialism, independence arrived, ready or not, in 1975.

Our first travel together was a ten-day, 900-mile trip in late November, 1985, to three of PNG's four highland provinces (Western Highlands, Chimbu, and Eastern Highlands). We flew to Goroka, one of the major towns, then drove down the Highlands Highway to the important port of Lae, from which Amelia Earhart had departed on her fatal last flight across the Pacific in 1937. Then we continued by road to Madang, another important coastal town in the old German area and then returned by air to Port Moresby. Note that while the recently discovered Highlands were linked to the north coast by a modern highway, there was no such thing, and still isn't as of 2017, connecting Moresby to anywhere important. I wrote:

The Highlands Highway . . . is only just beginning to unite this highly fragmented region. The completed portion of the road links the provincial capitals of Mt. Hagen, Kundiawa and Goroka, threading through magnificent scenery all the way. Finally, at Kassam Pass, it drops thousands of feet into the broad Markham Valley; from there it is a straight, flat dash of about 200 kilometers into Lae, which is PNG's second city by virtue of its role as port and processing center for the Highlands.

---

[13] Hank Nelson, *Taim Bilong Masta: The Australian Involvement with Papua New Guinea*, Australian Broadcast Commission, 1982, esp. pp. 133-193.

The three highland towns we visited, averaging about fifteen thousand in population, are all prosperous, bustling centers of coffee processing,[14] government and missionary support services, vegetable production and retail trade. Each has regular commercial air service, and airports (except for Mt. Hagen) are in the middle of town, appropriate for a region whose inhabitants first encountered the wheel only fifty years ago, on an airplane. Each of the towns has at least one Australian-run hotel. There is plenty of economic activity— Goroka has five supermarkets, and there is constant truck traffic on the highway—but also ample evidence of un- and under-employment in the form of crowds of youth hanging around crossroads and town centers.[15]

We saw plenty of evidence of the country's crime problem, which covered a spectrum from purely traditional to painfully transitional:

About thirty kilometers out of Mt. Hagen, crowds of obviously excited people on a side road stopped our car. Our driver was about to turn around and beat a hasty retreat when he learned that these were only spectators. They were watching a tremendous inter-clan rock fight in progress along a dry streambed to the north. As is well known, spears and arrows are still commonly used. Several of the casualties in a recent "war" in Enga Province [east of our travel area] died of multiple arrow wounds in the buttocks. . . . This is the cultural equivalent of posthumous decoration, because it means the victim was especially courageous in demonstrating disdain by waggling

---

[14] We had heard that the PNG Highlands produced excellent coffee, much in demand in the discriminating German market, yet the coffee we bought in Port Moresby's supermarkets was awful. The problem was that it was not roasted enough, as we learned from the Australian-run coffee cooperative in Goroka. From then on to the end of our stay, we bought coffee directly from them, dark roasted to our taste, and we have been drinking PNG coffee ever since. It is grown almost entirely by the same smallholders who also run for Parliament and sometimes have tribal fights with each other.

[15] Robert M. Pringle, DCM Port Moresby, "Report on a Trip to the Highlands of Papua New Guinea, November 30 to December 10 [1985]".

his posterior in the direction of the enemy lines.[16]

The culture-crossing interplay between modern commerce, crime, and efforts to improve matters was something to behold. Further along the road we had another taste of it:

Our second stop on that day was to visit several projects . . . that had been implemented by the hyperactive wife of an expatriate judge in Goroka to employ "rascals" who had been robbing the cargo trucks lumbering up the narrow pass from the seaport [at Lae] to the Highlands. They used to jump on the backs of the slow-moving trucks and throw the cargo out as the terrified driver just wanted to keep going and get out of there. Now this lady has introduced a scheme to have them ["rascals" who had been arrested] cut timber in the local forest for use in construction and use the proceeds to buy tools and other equipment to start gardens. This is all part of a scheme to grant probation to the offenders in order to cut down the cost of having so many men in jail. . . . The project now has the help of two Canadian volunteers experienced in probation work with Eskimos, so it looks promising.[17]

Further along the Highlands Highway we came to Ukarumpa, base of the Summer Institute of Linguistics, better known as SIL, and home to the largest US presence by far in PNG. SIL is a specialized missionary operation, an outgrowth of the Wycliffe Bible Translators. Their mission is to translate the Bible into as many languages as possible. At the time of our visit they had worked on 175 of PNG's roughly 700 languages, completed 45 Bible translations (some of them only the New Testament and Psalms), and were employing roughly 700 professional staff, half of them Americans, with translation teams at work in more than 100 locations. The Ukarumpa base, established in 1957, had a primary and a secondary school for SIL dependents, a sophisticated computer capability which had cut in half the time required to translate the Bible, a printing plant, and a fleet of four fixed

---

[16] Ibid.
[17] Barbara letter to Dear Family, December 15, 1985.

wing aircraft and one helicopter used to transport translators to their field locations.

Most educated observers, especially the Australians, were convinced that Ukarumpa was a CIA base. I am quite sure it was not, if only because the places they sent their translators were of no earthly interest to the US Government, but if you tried that line with an Australian you would get an "Aw, C'mmon Mate!!" response every time.[18] The belief was no doubt encouraged by allegations of past SIL involvement with the CIA[19] in parts of Latin America.

Other highlights of the trip included encountering Dr. Carlton Gajdusek at the Institute for Medical Research, a high-powered PNG government laboratory. We wondered whether a poor country like PNG could afford such an expensive facility, even though it was doing locally relevant work, including research on pneumonia, and had developed a possible vaccine for *pigbel*, "a curious and often fatal disease associated with overindulgence at traditional highland pig feasts."[20]

Gajdusek, by then head of the HIV laboratory at Ft. Dietrich, Maryland, was still visiting New Guinea to do research and was as fascinating and talkative as ever. Since Bob had met him in Jakarta he had received his Nobel Prize for work on *kuru* leading to the discovery of retroviruses (see Volume I, Chapter 5). He loved talking about his virtuoso knowledge of New Guinea languages and later told us that he had been the one who told SIL that they should locate at Ukarumpa, because it was in an area particularly rich in languages, even for New Guinea.

Finally, after a week of travel and work (well, sort of), we celebrated by diving on the wreck of a coral-encrusted US B-25 bomber sitting on one of Madang's offshore reefs. Sadly, the crew had ditched the plane right off a small island which

---

[18] In addition, Ukarumpa invited visitors, something CIA bases rarely did, and had a nice printed brochure describing the facility. For SIL as it is today, see http://www.sil.org/sil/.

[19] Obliquely referred to in the Wikipedia article on SIL at http://en.wikipedia.org/wiki/SIL_International.

[20] "The Institute for Medical Research: High Class Medical Research in the Highlands (and Lowlands Too)," in Pringle, "Report on a Trip to the Highlands of Papua New Guinea [1985]".

turned out to be a Japanese outpost, and all but one of them were killed. We never heard what had happened to him.

By the time we flew back to Moresby, the embassy had, after months of hassle, installed air conditioning in the bedrooms our children would use during their all-too-short Christmas visit.

The Children Come for Christmas

We had no trouble keeping them amused. Jamie helped me set up a salt-water aquarium and collect specimens, including a Nemo-style clownfish, from Ela Beach in Port Moresby, which still had a pretty good fringing coral reef. He also helped collect a sea anemone so the clown fish would feel at home, to which we observed the clownfish feeding bits of fish. Our neighbors, the Robbins, took us all sailing along the big barrier reef—the same one we could see from our house—and the children enjoyed snorkeling along the spectacular dropoff on its seaward side. They had not yet taken scuba diving lessons; that would come on their next and longer visit, but Annie managed to go windsurfing with one of her new friends.

The high point of their all-too-short stay was Christmas at Kiap Orchid Lodge in Enga, the westernmost of PNG's highland provinces. We went at the invitation of Gordon and Jackie Morgan, friends from New Zealand. He was running a construction company in PNG, and they had children the same age as ours. The lodge, an eco-tourism initiative assisted by a British VSO volunteer, was perched on a 9,000-foot elevation ridge, 2,000 feet above the provincial capital of Wabag. It had rough edges, including at least one bedbug (which nailed Bob), but our visit was unforgettable for other, better reasons. For Christmas dinner we had a full scale *mumu*—pork, greens, and sweet potatoes cooked in a giant, earth-covered pit.

Guests walked out through the door of the lodge into a potpourri of highland life: views of the ranges[21] stretching into the distance, the longhouse-like houses of the locals (mat walls and grass roofs, no windows or chimneys, very smoky!), groups

---

[21]"Ranges" (plural) is common New Guinea usage, appropriate for the landscape.

Annie and a new friend display their bilums (net bags woven using local plant fiber) near Kiap Orchid Lodge, in Enga province in the Highlands, where we spent our first Christmas in PNG.

of women with children hanging on their hands and *bilums* (net bags) hanging on their heads, and men out walking their hand-fed prize pigs on leashes. Everyone was very friendly and no one objected to photography—not something that one could take for granted in PNG—perhaps because they knew that the lodge was meant to help the local economy.[22] (Since we were there, an enormous gold mine has opened near Enga, and I suspect that the largely unchanged highland lifestyle we

---

[22] According to an entry in the 2008 *Lonely Planet Guide to Papua New Guinea and the Solomon Islands*, the lodge was already very run down.

saw is long since gone, at least its physical aspects.)

The high point of our visit was a *singsing* (dance festival) in nearby Wabag, at the invitation (which was addressed to Sir John and Mrs. Pringle) of the local member of Parliament and Minister of Administrative Affairs, Albert Kipalan, a well-educated and prominent politician. The music and dance performance was intended as a fundraiser to benefit the expansion of Wabag's primary school. Three other MPs and the Deputy Prime Minister, Sir Julius Chan (a Melanesian Chinese from one the islands north of New Guinea proper) also attended, not to mention half the local population.

The big shots, local and national, began the celebration by advancing, half a dozen abreast, through a crowd of almost equally picturesque spectators toward a reviewing stand, where we were already seated. Wearing ground-length, woven grass skirts, they swayed to the rhythm of long, *moka*-style drums, their faces decorated with black paint, wearing big pancake-like hats made of human hair and decorated with black bird-of-paradise plumes. We learned that this formal Enga dress style is quite disciplined, not allowing for the degree of improvisation found in other provinces.

We sat in the reviewing stand right behind Minister Kipalan, staring into a big bunch of *pandanus* leaves tied behind his waist, a common sartorial touch in New Guinea referred to by our irreverent Australian friends as "ass grass." After the spectacle of the entrance procession, the speeches were quite ordinary small-town fare. Perhaps because of the diplomats present they were mostly in English, not Pidgin. There followed lots of dancing by the local crowd.

A Short Pidgin Lesson

Melanesian Pidgin, often referred to as Pidgin English or just Pidgin, is PNG's *lingua franca*, especially among the less educated. It was developed by Melanesians during the colonial era, when local workers from differing language groups found themselves living together far from home for a long time. In the 1980s, it was commonly used in parliamentary debates on everything from the budget to national defense, and there was at least one Pidgin-language newspaper, *Wantok*, from "One

The scene outside a small food (and beverage!) stall after after the singsing in Wabag during Christmas vacation.

Talk," best translated as *The Nation*. [23]

A cursory glance reveals a language based largely on English vocabulary but having a very different structure; often several English derivatives are used to describe an object or action conveyed by one English word, as in *mixmaster bilong Jesus*, which refers to a helicopter. (It should be mentioned that some of the more unlikely pidgin phrases, like this one, may have been faked by foreigners.) Largely because of this characteristic, Pidgin is very difficult to understand when spoken fast, and when we took lessons we discovered that it is no picnic to speak either. Annie joined our lessons for a time when the children came out for their 1986 summer vacation and was pronounced best (*namba wan*) student in our class, which no doubt helped her to get into the University of Chicago later!

Here is a sample of how Melanesian Pidgin works, based on the first two lines from Little Red Riding Hood (*Liklik Retpela Hat*). The first line is *"Bipo tru igat wanpela liklik meri, nau nem bilong em Liklik Retpela Hat."* Translation: A long time

[23] It has a very interesting style guide: Frank Mihalic, *Stail Buk bilong Wantok Niuspepa*, Port Moresby, 1986.

ago, there was a little girl named Little Red Riding Hood.

Explanation:

--**Long ago** (*Bipo tru* = before true; *tru* meaning "really," as in "a really long time before")

--**there was** (*I gat* = he got, which can also mean "there was" or "there is")

--**a little girl** (*wanpela liklik meri* = one little female; *mary* meaning "woman" or "girl") *liklik* meaning "little", thus making *mary* mean "girl"; *wan* is "one" and *pela* is "fellow," a counter used with people and objects. (We have some counters in English, as in "two head of cattle," but Pidgin is full of them.)

--**named Little Red Riding Hood** (*nau nem belong em Liklik Retpela Hat* = now name belonging to her Little Red Hat; *bilong* (belong) makes the next word possessive, *em* means "him" or "her," *retpela* is "red" plus a counter and *Hat* substitutes for "hood").

Now you should have no trouble with the second sentence:

Ol I putim dispela nem long em bilong wanem dispela liklik meri i save putim kain hat i retpela hat long het bilong im.

Clues: *Ol* is from "all," *I* is "he" or "she", so *Ol I* is "Everyone"; *putim* is from "put him" and in this sentence works roughly as "called" [her this name]; *long* is an all-purpose preposition meaning "at," "on", and much more (but *long long* means crazy); *het* is head, *save* is from "savvy" but in this case means usually or accustomed to, and *kain* is "kind" as in "a kind of hat."

Translation: Now she was called that because she was in the habit of wearing a little red hat (hood) on her head.[24]

What makes Pidgin frustratingly difficult is the absence of punctuation, multiple meanings for one word leading to numerous false cognates, and a subtle but critical rhythmic pattern. Here is a test: *Lukim yu bihain* means which of the following: (a) "See you later," (b) "Someone is looking at your posterior," (c) "Look behind you!"[25] When Red Hiding Hood knocks on grandmother's door, the word for knock is *pait*, from "fight." Hence one of our favorites: a piano is *bigpela*

---

[24] We can't locate the source of "Little Red Riding Hood" in Pidgin, but suspect it might have been instructional materials, now lost, for our Pidgin lessons. One thing is sure, we couldn't have produced it ourselves; we never mastered the language to that extent.

[25] The answer is (a) "See you later."

bokis yu paitim tit (teeth) em i singaut. Pidgin is shot through with anachronisms and political incorrections; an excellent oral history of the colonial era, mentioned earlier, is entitled *Taim Bilong Masta*, and Prince Charles is *namba wan pikinini bilong missus kwin. Pikinini* is the standard word for "baby" or "child" and no one, as of 1985, seemed to object.[26]

The Solomon Islands

We were anxious to get to see our other two countries before Barbara found a job. Vanuatu was off limits because its premier, Father Lini, an Episcopal priest, was in the official US doghouse for his support of radical causes (more on him below), but the Solomons was OK. En route we spent a weekend on Bougainville Island, a part of PNG and site of one of the world's largest copper mines. The mine was still recovering from a long struggle by the inhabitants against both Australia and PNG, which had resulted in its closure and years of political turmoil.

The dispute was partly the result of racially-tinged friction. Ethnic Solomon Islanders, including those living on Bougainville, tend to be blacker than the majority of Papua New Guineans (some so black they seem almost purple) and better educated, thanks to early missionary work in the region. They particularly resented the numerous and much less couth highlanders of the mainland, sometimes referred to by them as "redskins," and feared that they would eventually dominate PNG once its multi-ethnic pot began to melt. We heard all about that, viewed the enormous pit of the mine, met the American representative of a company selling trucks and other mining equipment, and went diving (of course) in our spare time.

Continuing to Honiara, the capital of the Solomon Islands, we regretted not using SolAir (the Solomon Islands Airline), which would have allowed us to visit some of the

---

[26] There are regional variants of Pidgin and one of the better short introductions is about the Vanuatu version: Darrell Tryon and Allan Longoulant, *Everi Samting Yu Wantem Save Long Bislama* [as the Vanuatu version is called] *be Yu Fraet Tumas Blong* [sic] *Askem*, Media Masters (South Pacific) PIDGIN POST publication, no date.

intermediate islands along our route, instead of Air Niugini. We were flying down "The Slot," a corridor between a twin row of islands, famous during world War II as the pathway for Japanese warships heading southeast to attack US Marines on Guadalcanal. It is also the area where John F. Kennedy's PT Boat was destroyed.

Barbara's letter summed up our stay in Honiara and captured the essence of Foreign Service life at its most interesting:

Bob's job here is not more demanding than the one in Ouaga, but his extracurricular activities (the garden, the aquarium, the newly gathered shells that have to be cleaned, the diving) are, and so the letters are increasingly falling to me....

The [Honiara] airport is the old Henderson Field, the objective of the first man-to-man ground combat between Americans and Japanese.[27] Later in the war, nearby Honiara was developed as a major supply and repair base for operations resulting in the retaking of the north coast of New Guinea and then the Philippines. We took a tour of the battlefield.... Plus we dived together on a couple of Japanese transports that had been unloading when American planes sank them just off the beach; one day when Bob was making official calls, I dived on a B-17 bomber which had soft coral festooning both its wings. I liked it the best, because I could see what was what, in contrast to the ships, which are just damaged enough so that I can't tell where I am.... I tried my hand at using the underwater camera (usually monopolized by guess who) and produced some not bad results; it was fun.

On land, Bob had a heavy schedule of calling on everyone from ministers of the local government... to local bankers, to volunteer agencies that administer USAID funded projects. I

---

[27] US Marines arrived on Guadalcanal in August, 1942, and captured the lightly defended airfield (later Henderson Field) which the Japanese had just built. The Japanese then mounted an all-out offensive to recapture Guadalcanal, which they almost did. The campaign, complete with massive naval battles just offshore and in "The Slot", lasted months and marked a turning point in the Pacific War. Our Navy was using the infamous torpedoes made at the Alexandria Torpedo Factory, close to where we now live, and far too many of them were duds.

visited several of the development projects (gardens, piggeries, chicken raising projects, water pumps) with him, as well as making an interesting trip, in which we forded a river in flood, to visit a Peace Corps couple at their site (more chickens, a kindergarten, water seal toilets, roof and gutter water collection. . . .)

We made a one-day trip to one of the other islands, on which is found the second-largest town in the Solomons— Auki, population 2,500. It has a six-bedroom guest house, one street with six Chinese shops, a market and a dock. The visit was interesting, especially because we visited a village in the lagoon and saw shell money being made; it is still being used in ritual transactions like payment of bride price, The villagers who make it, however, are now Bahais. Our visit ended with a swearing-in ceremony for twenty-nine newly trained Peace Corps volunteers. Bob, representing the Embassy, made a speech, but was outclassed by the local Deputy Prime Minister, a traditional story-teller of the first rank. I had food poisoning from something the hotel had served at lunch, so sat on the sidelines and didn't get to meet as many people as I would have liked to.[28]

A Highly Migratory Fish Story

The only real issue we had with the Government of the Solomon Islands was a nasty dispute over tuna fishing rights. An international Law of the Sea treaty[29] had been adopted in 1982, establishing 200-mile Extended Economic Zones (EEZs) within which each nation has the right to regulate fishing. Scattered-out archipelago nations typical of the Pacific, including the Solomons, often have tiny populations—in their case, about 200,000 in 1982. But if you connect all their EEZ boundaries, from island to island, they are authorized to regulate fishing over huge areas of the ocean. The US Congress has never ratified the Treaty, but for most other countries,

---

[28] Barbara letter to Dear Family, March 3, 1986.
[29] For the basics of this very complex treaty, formally the United Nations Convention on Law of the Sea (UNCLOS), and still detested by many American conservatives, see http://en.wikipedia.org/wiki/United_ Nations_Convention_on_the_Law_of_the_Sea.

especially those in the Pacific, it was the law.

This upset the US tuna fishing fleet, which was just moving into the Western Pacific as tuna stocks declined elsewhere. Some of the boat owners were new American citizens who were recent arrivals from Yugoslavia. Many had invested in expensive, high-tech fishing boats equipped with search helicopters to locate schools of tuna. But the price of tuna had been declining and many of the boat owners were deeply in debt. Senator Warren Magnuson, Democrat of Washington, came to their rescue by passing legislation which decreed that because tuna was a "highly migratory species" they could be caught within other countries' two hundred-mile Extended Economic Zones without their permission, contrary to the interpretation of countries which had signed the treaty.

Magnuson's law specified that if any country seized one of our boats within its EEZ, the US Government was required to implement economic sanctions against it, the most serious hostile measure any country can take against another short of war. Known as the Magnuson Act, the law went on to require the US Government to reimburse the owner for the loss of his highly-leveraged boat, meaning that our tuna fisherman could operate wherever they wanted to without risk. The Australian and regional press was already condemning the US as the bully of the Pacific when a Solomon Islands patrol boat seized the *Jeanette Diana*, one of our tuna boats, in June, 1984. It sat in Honiara for months while we demanded its release, to no avail.

This kind of thing might have gone on indefinitely if the tuna canners—StarKist, Bumble Bee, *et al.*, hadn't come to the rescue. The often recently naturalized American fishermen tended to be super-patriots, aggressively demanding their rights under US law. The canners, sophisticated big capitalists, saw that we would risk losing a new and promising fishing ground unless something was done. With their support, negotiations eventually got under way.

The result was elegant. Repealing the Magnuson Act would have been politically difficult, if not impossible. So instead, with the support of the canners, countries that were parties to the dispute forged a new international agreement. It not only recognized the right of each country to regulate tuna fishing in its EEZ, just as it did for other species; it also provided financial assistance to help the small island countries develop their own tuna fishing fleets. Because treaty law trumps domestic law, one reason why the US Congress is typically suspicious of treaties, the troublesome provisions of the Magnuson Act were thus overruled. US relations with the nations involved reverted to cordiality, and US tuna boats remained free to fish for tuna in the western Pacific, provided they followed local regulations. The treaty was signed in Port Moresby in 1987, just before the end of our tour of duty there. We all got Charlie Tuna wristwatches from StarKist as souvenirs.

At the beginning of the *Jeanette Diana* affair and in the absence of any official US presence in the Solomons, our ambassador, Paul Gardner, had sent our consular officer, Peter Kaestner, to Honiara to open a dialogue with the government. As the crisis dragged on, Peter visited some outlying islands, but after one such trip he failed to return on time. Meanwhile the mimeographed "newspaper" in Honiara, run by and mainly for the expatriate, largely British community, reported in tones of amusement that the American Consul had gone missing on a certain remote island peak while bird watching. (In the small town of Honiara, the British, being themselves great bird watchers and no doubt aware of Peter's proclivities, would have had no trouble figuring out what was going on.)

Paul was getting more and more worried, but just as he was about to call in the US Air Force to mount a search effort, Peter emerged from the wilderness claiming that he had been on legitimate official travel hunting down some remote missionaries to update their passports and make sure they were OK, under the rubric of Citizen Services.

Kaestner is from an extraordinary Baltimore family. He is one of ten siblings, and both he and an older brother became avid amateur ornithologists. Both decided to seek careers that would facilitate affordable bird watching in exotic areas. His brother chose the Baltimore-based McCormick Spice Company, whose operations are global. Peter did him one better, and joined the US Foreign Service. As we became birdwatchers ourselves, we realized that he was a champion of international birding, a highly completive avocation in which a birder is ranked by the length of his "life list" of birds

seen. The mountain where he later admitted getting lost had
several endemic birds, meaning they are found nowhere else
in the world. Enough said about why he was there.

We would later see him in action, a Bat Masterson of the
spotting scope. See that yellow speck at the top of yon tall tree?
Boom, and Peter's tripod-mounted spotting scope would be
positioned, a gorgeous, tiny warbler filling up its viewfinder.
In 1993, when I joined the State Department's Office of Oceans
and International Environmental and Scientific Affairs (OES),
negotiating environmental treaties among other things, I was
able to land him as my deputy, a round peg in a round hole
for a change.[30] Peter had continued to prove himself adept
at combining diplomacy with ornothology. In 1992, while
assigned to Columbia, he had discovered a species of ant pitta,
a bird hitherto unknown to science, in the eastern Andes. The
bird was named after him in Latin: (*Grallaria* [the Ant Pitta
genus] *kaestneri*).[31] Unfortunately for those who love puns, it
could not be **Pitta** *kaestneri.*

Barbara, Her School and the Big Stone Axe

Upon our return from the Solomons, Barbara found a
communication from the International High School in Port
Moresby, or PMIHS, where she had substituted occasionally
since her arrival, offering her a full-time position for the school
year beginning in February, 1986. Of course, the principal had
waited until the last minute to make that decision, and I have
always been irritated that I had to scratch going to Vanuatu
with Bob later in order to take the job.

In the event, it was, like my previous overseas teaching gigs,
an excellent window into local culture, the more so because it
had a large contingent of local pupils and teachers, although
it followed the Queensland curriculum from Australia.
However, that program was not ideally suited to the needs
of teen-agers in Papua New Guinea; very few Australian
dependents remained in Port Moresby past grade six; and
the expatriate students were mostly from other developing

---

[30] See Chapter 13 for more on this.
[31] Pitta will eventually tell this story himself; he has a book in draft.
Meanwhile, see the excellent Wikipedia entry about him.

countries of the Commonwealth. This geographical chaos in administration, teaching staff, and curriculum made Port Moresby International High School the weakest, academically and socially, of all the schools in which I taught.

Two of my history teacher colleagues remained friends for years. Carol Kidu, an Australian married to Sir Buri Kidu, the first Chief Justice of PNG, was mother not only to her own children, but to a large number of others in his family, for by custom those who can do so take care of less fortunate relatives, and Sir Buri definitely was the best off of that family. Besides, his base was a Papuan coastal village near Port Moresby, which was the reason he had gotten a good education during the Australian period. After his untimely death, Carol remained the matriarch of the large family, and she even entered local politics, serving in Parliament for at least one term. Less colorful, but an equally good friend, was Joan Howell, wife of the British Ambassador, who, like me, was teaching more for personal satisfaction than for the paltry salary paid to locally hired expatriates.

Physically, the campus of the school, like much else in the city, rippled down a hill, a conglomeration of long, low classroom buildings on stilts, overlooking large athletic fields. Classes were scheduled on a large magnetic board on which the principal arranged and rearranged teachers and the many sections of each course that needed to be taught until all classes were covered. The result was illogical and chaotic teaching assignments. For example, for a few months yours truly, she of the tone-deaf ear, taught a section of grade seven music. A generous and musically more sophisticated local colleague explained to me how to get through that one by using a recording of *Peter and the Wolf*, with its different instruments signifying different characters in the tale.

When I was assigned a gym class, at midday in eighty-five plus degree heat, but no possibility of a shower before teaching my next class of history, I sat in the bleachers watching the students run around with hockey sticks and being sure no one got hurt, or if someone did, I was there to help. Finally, the principal wised up and assigned grade nine Home Economics as that extra class for me. I do know how to sew, and then at least I had some useful knowledge to pass on to my pupils.

History classes were, in general, more appropriate. The one that was most fun was "History through Film," which I invented and taught all year to tenth-grade school leavers; these were the students who did not intend to finish the final two years of high school, but rather to go straight to work (if it could be found). They were not interested at all in another conventional history course, and no one in the administration cared what I included in my course. So I raided the embassy's and friends' videotape collections, and built weekly units around whatever suitable films I could find. *Casablanca* and other war films were popular, as were any with western US themes. *Gandhi* had just come out, and *Lawrence of Arabia* was available, and this course was a huge success.

One of the most interesting and satisfying results of my experience at PMIHS was the course in Melanesian Prehistory which I took at the University of Papua New Guinea in order to teach it. Given the school's inept course scheduling, many expatriates had to teach a seventh-grade course in this subject, with which none of them was remotely familiar, certainly not me. I also calculated that this university course would count toward renewal of my teaching certificate back home in Virginia.[32] It was taught by Dr. Les Groube, an eccentric Briton who had emigrated to New Zealand and was teaching in PNG under the auspices of the Colombo Plan.

At one point Dr. Groube invited me to accompany him to the Huon Peninsula on the north coast to look for waisted stone axes, that is, large stone axes with indentations near the top in which to secure the strings that held the axe itself to a haft. These axes are evidence that people arrived in New Guinea at least 40,000 years before present, because some have been found between layers of volcanic ash, which are accurately datable.[33] They suggest a very early form of agriculture on New Guinea, in which a clearing was cut in the forest to allow edible plants requiring full sun to flourish along its edge.

This was supposed to have been a university class trip,

---

[32] I was correct; the officials at the Virginia State Department of Education didn't bat an eyelash in giving me full credit for a course in a country that they had most likely never heard of.

[33] For this date see Peter Bellwood, *Pre-History of the Indo-Malaysian Archipelago (rev. ed.)*, University of Hawaii Press, 1997, p. 190.

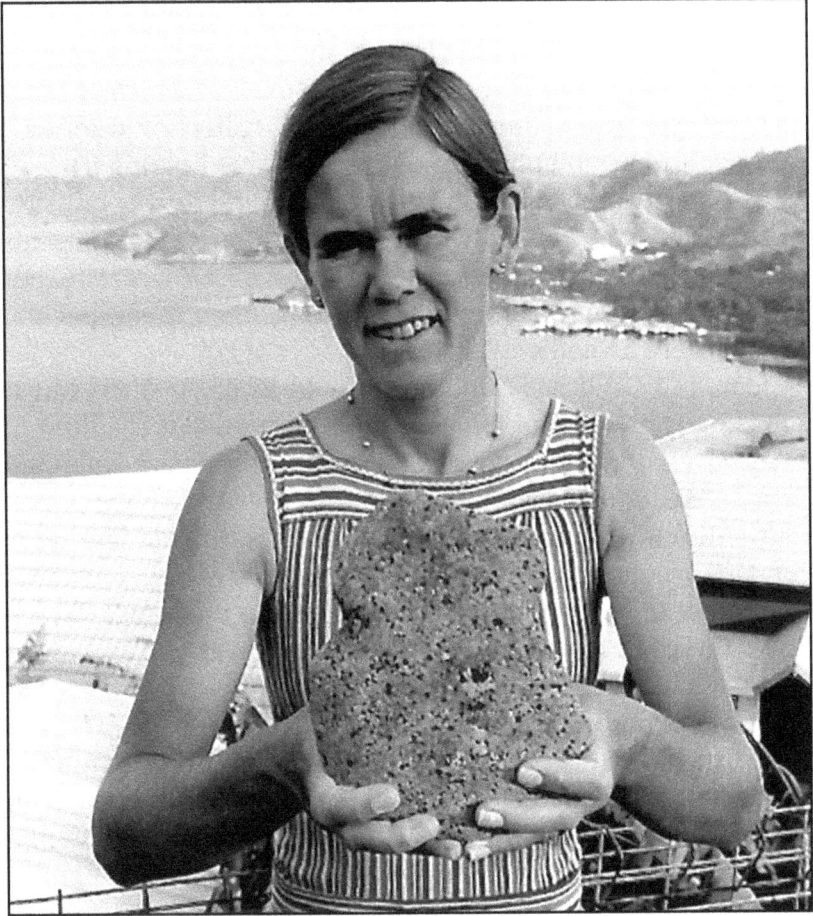

Barbara shows off the ancient stone axe, of a type providing evidence that people arrived on the island of New Guinea at least 40,000 years ago, which she found while on a university field trip to the Huon Peninsula. It is now in the PNG National Museum.

but financing had not been forthcoming. However, Dr. Groube wanted to show off this subject of his research, and I could pay my own plane fare. For me the outcome was spectacular. The north-facing coast of Huon is covered with ancient, uplifted coral terraces, clearly visible from a boat offshore, and it is here that these axes are typically found, in the rubble of runoff channels. As we walked on these terraces, I was looking for the shape of an axe (about the size of a dinner plate) but Dr. Groube, who was in the lead, later told me that he was looking for color variations below his feet. He was expecting an axe to be brownish, as some indeed are. But I spotted the only one we found, and it wasn't brownish; it was more dark gray. We had to give it to PNG's National Museum, which already had plenty of them, but we still have the collection reference number and a good photo of the axe with me holding it.

The crime situation didn't affect the school during our stay in Port Moresby, but sadly, about a year after we left, rascals assaulted two girl students after an evening dance party. Their brothers had come in a vehicle to fetch them, but the rascals were armed and chased the boys away.

Joan and I did have one brush with local violence, but it turned out more than all right for us, because it resulted in one and a half days of unexpected holiday time. As I explained in a subsequent letter home, "In traditional society, which was without a system of hereditary chiefs, the leaders were Big Men who managed to be the bravest warriors, have wives who grew the biggest yams and raised the most pigs, which could then be traded for prestigious shell jewelry or sacrificed in great feasts. . . ."

The funeral of a Highlands Big Man, Sir Iambacky Okuk, a parliamentary representative from Chimbu, drew hundreds of his supporters to the capital, where they showed their grief by rioting (perhaps because his demise signaled the end of a flow of largesse that had bestowed great benefits on them). I observed, "Anyway the sooner the body is out of Port Moresby, the better." But first, Joan and I, who lived across town from the school, had to find a way to navigate its hilly roads and avoid the riots; we did, and enjoyed the following day off too, "because school certainly didn't want responsibility for 800 children while the body is being moved to the airport." [34]

The Myth of a Separatist Movement

In March, Bob went to Melbourne, where the Australian equivalent of the US Council on Foreign Relations was holding a conference on the Australian-Indonesian-PNG

---

[34] All three quotations are from Barbara letter to Dear Family, n.d. but would have been sometime in 1986.

relationship. It was a topic of some interest to Embassy Port Moresby because we realized that the Australian-Indonesian relationship was strategically important, and New Guinea, divided between Indonesia and PNG, was a much talked-about point of friction between the two countries.

There were lots of old friends there from various US embassies and from Indonesia, including Sabam Siagian, editor of the *Jakarta Post* and brother of Toenggoel, with whom I used to room at Cornell (and through whose Indonesian cooking I had met Barbara). It was Sabam's job to present the Indonesian case to the Australians who, especially on the Left, tend to fear that the Indonesians are oppressing the population of West Irian (the Indonesian half of New Guinea), are about to invade PNG, etc. There is some truth in the former, none whatsoever in the latter, and much of the Australian concern is, I'm afraid, a result of their tendency to have "yellow peril" phantasms about the Indonesians.

I have been surprised since arriving [in PNG] to find that the issue is not nearly as heated among the Papua New Guineans themselves as I had expected. They do sympathize with their Melanesian brethren in West Irian but they are also determined to get along with the Indonesians and regard the border-hopping rebels [of the Free Papua Movement—Organizasi Papua Merdeka] as more a nuisance than anything else. As for the Indonesians, they seem, if what Sabam told us is correct, to be waking up to the fact that they have behaved with little sensitivity toward the Irianese, whom they do tend to regard as savages, including much ballyhooed plans to send huge numbers of Javanese "transmigrants" (settlers) to West Irian, sufficient to swamp the indigenous population. Since these plans are in any case wildly beyond their capacity to implement, everyone is agreed they should stop advertising them.[35]

As things have turned out since then, the threat of Indonesian-government sponsored Javanese migrants has proved much less problematic than spontaneous (unsponsored) migrants, who at this writing (2016) have for some time been a source

---

[35] Bob letter to Dear Family, April 20, 1986.

of growing ethnic friction in Indonesian Papua (the current term for West Irian). The problem *du jour* at the time of the conference, pan-Melanesian nationalism creating problems between Indonesia and Australia, has not yet materialized and still seems unlikely to do so.

I came home via Bangkok where the State Department was holding a conference of all its embassy narcotics coordinators, one of my numerous roles as DCM Port Moresby. In fact, we didn't have much of a drug problem in PNG except for marijuana, which was beginning to displace beer among the more with-it urban youth. Given the proven destructiveness of alcohol everywhere in Melanesia, it seemed to me that pot might, if anything, be an improvement.

Exploring the Sepik River

Our next trip, by now sandwiched into a school vacation, was to the 700-mile Sepik River, PNG's longest, famous for its mud, mosquitoes, art and architecture. A documentary entitled *The Sepik: Eater of Men* was showing in the US, and we had to reassure family that this referred to the dangers of navigation; there had been no cannibalism in PNG since 1911. This was technically true, but as late as 1933 the Australians had hanged men for headhunting.

To reach the river you have to drive inland from the provincial capital at Wewak because its lower reaches are uninhabited swamp. One of the largest towns along the way, Maprik, is famous for its spirit houses with soaring peaked roofs, the model for the National Parliament building in Port Moresby.

The Maprik people are also known for the cultivation and worship of yams up to six feet in length. Despite missionary activity, the yam cult was still flourishing at the time of our visit, while the attractive masks made for the yams to wear were also being produced for tourists.[36] Maprik's only hotel was occupied by a Spanish television crew, so we stayed at the agricultural college, in the girls' dormitory which was nearly empty because there were very few girl students, part

---

[36] We have one in the attic; the wicker face mask with the big ears.

of a broader problem of underutilization of PNG's tertiary education resources, about which I wrote a report.

The girls regaled us with tales of conflict with the local Maprik villagers. Apparently the locals have never reconciled themselves to the loss of land when the college located in their midst. Brawls with male students are common, and villagers had just stolen a pig from one of the girls' practice farms. . . . Sure enough, the next morning we discovered a piece missing from our rental car, apparently pilfered during the night by a marauding "townie."[37]

We had another problem with the rental car. It was actually a Toyota Hilux (car-pickup hybrid) and people were forever trying to hitch rides in the back. The custom on any New Guinea road is to take full advantage of any vehicle to transport anyone who is looking for a ride; people were offended that we did not stop for them, and sometimes angrily ran after the pickup as we passed them by. Given the rather obvious rowdiness of the area, transporting just anyone didn't seem like a great idea, and of course it would have upset Uncle Sam, who was paying for the vehicle.

From Maprik we went to the nearest river point at Pagwi, and from there onwards our travel was mostly by small boat. Needless to say, it brought back memories of Sarawak. We arranged transportation as we went. We experienced hordes of mosquitoes, and almost as many outboard motor problems. We cadged a ride upriver with a Department of Primary Industry officer on his way to Ambunti, headquarters for the entire Middle and Upper Sepik districts. En route we passed two launches filled with prisoners arrested for tribal fighting on their way to justice downriver. At Ambunti the proprietor of its small but quite comfortable tourist lodge arranged the rest of our river travel. Bob wrote:

You can see why some patrol officer decided on Ambunti for his seat of government. The town is situated on a hill overlooking

---

[37] "'Town' and 'Gown' in Maprik," from "Report on a Trip to East Sepik Province, Papua New Guinea, April 12-18, 1986."

a bend in the river, the district officer still lives on the hill and there is a local courthouse there modeled on a traditional spirit house, but most of the town is on the riverbank. There is an air strip in classic [gravity-assisted] New Guinea style on a slope, with the hill at the one end, [to begin take-off] and the huge, brown river at the other [to land at, hopefully not in]. Ambunti is theoretically serviced several times a week by Douglas Air, third in the pecking order of PNG aviation after Air Niugini and Talair, and repeatedly grounded for safety violations.

The population of 900 includes government, missionaries, etc., and a substantial settlement of river-dwellers who have moved in to get access to schools, to clansmen [relatives] with paying jobs, and to the excitement of "town" life. The problems of urbanization occur even in places like this, and the Ambunti example could only be described as squalid, with dirty and dilapidated housing and a general atmosphere of depression in the migrant settlement. [38]

There was already plenty of tourism along the river around Ambunti, and with it a flourishing art market. Carriage-trade tourists came via the *Melanesian Explorer*, a small cruise ship based in Madang operated by our friend Jan Barter. She and her husband, a local businessman, were already old timers in PNG, and later he was for a time a member of the PNG Parliament. This ship also went to the islands north of the mainland, a trip we would later take.

All villages along this stretch of the Sepik sold handicrafts, and in some there was virtual mass production. Dealers from Port Moresby and elsewhere roved the river in floating vans, buying in bulk. Some old spirit houses with wonderful art were falling apart, full of dirt, decay and spiders. But at Sasariman, above Ambunti, we saw a new one being built using traditional methods and dyes, and "it was clear that for the old man in charge, this was a genuine effort to preserve tradition—and attract a few tourist bucks at the same time."[39] Crocodile farms were also popular; you learned that if you turn a baby *puk puk* over and tickle its tummy, it will immediately

---

[38] From personal notes on a trip to East Sepik Province.
[39] Ibid.

go to sleep, a trick not to be attempted with adult crocs.

The high point of this expedition was a trip into the Chambri Lakes, a large shallow, water lily-and-rush-clogged body of water connected by open channels to the river. The *Melanesian Explorer* couldn't get into this area and our narrow canoe just made it, through a passage almost blocked by water lilies,

... to a village where the guide had relatives [as in many parts of the country, you didn't just wander into a village without introduction] ... and stayed in the largest [of a four-house complex]. ... It was very traditional—the famous carved hooks were hung from the ceiling with food and other possessions hanging from them. Sago pots with funny faces, for which the region is famous, were actually full of sago.[40] Instead of using my little camping gaz stove, I cooked on a clay hearth over a little fire (noodle soup with canned wieners in it, real gourmet fare). Despite the mosquito net, it was cool, and we slept well.[41]

After dinner everyone listened to the East Sepik provincial radio news in Pidgin—a reminder of the near monopoly sway of rural radio in PNG.

The next morning we visited another village, Aibom, where the sago pots with funny faces were made. One of the elders was sitting on a wonderful carved stool in the shape of a turtle. When we asked him about it, he offered to sell it to us, and we could not resist buying it. Then, as we were leaving, he said something like "Well, too bad, where will we sit to tell stories from now on?" He seemed to be teasing us, and we consoled ourselves with the thought that in the Sepik climate everything rotted fairly soon. It made us feel a little uneasy anyway, but not enough to try returning the stool, one of the really fine pieces we acquired.[42]

---

[40] See the one in the Chinese bookshelf, used to hold matches.

[41] Barbara letter to Dear Family, April 20, 1986, slightly expanded. The best "hook" we have hangs at the head of the stairs at 216 Wolfe Street; Bob bought it in Port Moresby soon after his arrival and has no idea which region of PNG it is from.

[42] The stool is the large, heavy one now in the attic/library/art gallery next to the rear window. The account of buying it is from memory.

The Chambri Lakes, with their mats of floating vegetation, are a maze to navigate, but beautiful to view and dotted with picturesque villages.

On the way back to the main river we ran afoul of Chambri's famous "floating islands." These room-sized (and bigger) chunks of matted vegetation break loose and float around, blocking boat channels. The locals sometimes plant gardens on them, and island rustling can be a problem. When they get in your way, as happened to us three times, you poke the prow of your boat into a crack between one island and another, and push. I tried to help, which alarmed our guide, who thought I was going to fall overboard and vanish into the *puk-puk* filled waters, but we got through and back home.

We were lucky on this trip. A few months later, my embassy colleague, information officer Mike Anderson, was held up by bandits in the Chambri Lakes. Nothing daunted, he continued his touristic trip into the Highlands, where he was again held up by "rascals" at another place we had visited, and this time they took not only his money but his eye glasses.

Despite Mike's misadventure, our trip on the Sepik had been so memorable that when Annie and Jamie came seven months later for Christmas, we sent them on a similar trip, with a reputable guide. They had a fine time, but when, a few weeks later, Jamie returned to Dartmouth, where he was by this time in his freshman year, he came down with malaria. Fortunately it was not a serious case, and the doctors at Dartmouth's research hospital actually listened to him when he said it was probably malaria and treated him for it.[43] Barbara, her sister Kathy and her parents subsequently visited the Sepik, but on the *Melanesian Explorer,* in January, 1987, and nothing bad happened to them. [44]

In May, a month after our Sepik adventures, we headed home for a month of "R and R." It was a mad dash through the US in which we saw only a tenth of our friends in Washington, attended Jamie's graduation from Milton, inspected Aunt Kathy's new house in Medford, near Tufts University, visited Maine and Nantucket (both good contrasts with PNG!), saw Aunt Margot and wild flowers in the Big Horns (Wyoming), and dropped in on Mark and Kate in Carmel before the long series of flights back across the Pacific.[45]

The children were with us in July and August of 1986, our only full summer in PNG. Our first priority was keeping them safe, and we made sure that they never went anywhere unaccompanied. Our second priority, and theirs too, was to get them scuba lessons. After that we did a lot of diving together, including night diving, which was great for shell collecting, most mollusks being nocturnal. In addition to her Pidgin lessons, Annie got a job at the Cheshire Homes, a British-based organization serving handicapped children, while Jamie did clerical and maintenance chores at the embassy.

---

[43] There's more to the story that this. A number of Jamie's classmates had gotten ineffective measles shots as toddlers. As a result, a measles epidemic had hit the Dartmouth campus. When he arrived at the hospital, at first the staff said "measles," but luckily were willing to listen to him when he said, "No, malaria. I haven't got any spots, and besides I have just returned from camping out along a big river in New Guinea." Because he had been abroad as a toddler, he, in fact, had had an effective measles shot much later than his fellow students.

[44] It was on this trip that Barbara bought the tall statue, now in our dining room, which according to the young man who carved it represents a dream of his ancestors. It cost US $100, with which he intended to buy his mother a sewing machine. See Barbara letter to Dear Family, April 25, 1987.

[45] This is almost verbatim from our Christmas letter for 1986.

Barbara and Annie pose behind a barrel sponge on a spectacular reef in West New Britain.

These jobs, Annie's volunteer and Jamie's paid, minimally, were good, because as Barbara observed to their grandparents, "This town is very different for Jamie and Anne than Ougadougou was. There, there were few spectacular activities, but a small group of friends on vacation to do what there was with, and also the famous *mobylette* provided independent transportation. Here, with other-side-drive and precipitous hills, we have not even let Jamie practice on our car, much less would we think of having him drive it alone. . . ." Then there was the fact that boarding-school vacations of southern-hemisphere friends were backwards from theirs, so they had little teen-age company for the first part of the vacation. However, the final three weeks coincided with a term-break for Kiwi and Aussi students, and among other activities, Annie's sixteenth birthday party was a big success "with friends from France, Australia, and New Zealand in attendance."[46] There was also at least one more successful wind surfing expedition with their friends.

The Highlands Show

We went as a family to the biennial Highlands Show in Goroka, a multi-day gathering of performers from all over PNG arrayed in traditional wigs, face paint, Bird of Paradise plumes (there are thirty-nine varieties of Birds of Paradise), leaves, grass, soot mixed with pig fat, dried flowers, hand-made netting, beads, tusks, shells, weapons, etc., etc. The show, which alternates between the two highland capitals of Mt. Hagen and Goroka, is said to have been conceived by Australian district officers (or *kiaps*) as a way of funneling tribal rivalries into peaceful competition. If this is true, it did not work, but these two Highlands Shows certainly were, and still are, one of the great ethno-artistic spectacles anywhere.[47] Yet there is so much variety in personal adornment in PNG that many famous styles (e.g. the Mud Men of Asaro; the Enga dress we had seen at Christmas) were not represented at this Goroka Show. Subsequently, we encountered more of them at the annual Port Moresby Show.

If I had had to pick a winner from the whole spectacle, it would have been a simulated tribal fight between two groups, beginning with a mock land boundary dispute and ending with big clubs thwacking flesh in unnervingly realistic manner, although it was probably no more lethal than the NFL.

Back in Moresby, the kids helped us capture fish for our aquarium. Jamie even caught a lion fish, something we had been striving to do since we acquired the boat, although the southeast monsoon almost prevented that; he got banged up trying to get over the reef with his prize secure in a plastic bag, and Mom, who was supposed to help him by taking his flippers before he climbed into the boat, couldn't do so

---

[46] Source misplaced, but obviously from a letter home from Barbara.

[47] See http://www.gorokashow.com/ for a glimpse of what it was like in 2012.

because of the waves.

Bob took them to visit the magnificent House of Parliament, an independence present from the Australians modeled after a Maprik spirit house and built lavishly from local woods. The session they saw included a debate which ended with the Honorable Members throwing their briefcases at each other, a lesson in Melanesian civics. They saw spectacular sailboat (*lakatoi*) races off Ela Beach, in the middle of Port Moresby, staged by competing teams from nearby coastal villages. The boats were based on traditional designs used in the sago-for-pottery trade mentioned earlier, and had colorful sails advertising Port Moresby car dealerships and other local enterprises.

Anne and Jamie went to the only embassy Fourth of July celebration that we attended in Port Moresby,[48] held at the back yard *cum* amphitheater of the (since replaced) Chancery. It was situated on a steep slope, adding to the problem of coping with inebriated visitors, which was serious at this post. Nothing was more embarrassing than to have two of your honored guests get in a fight with each other at the end of your "diplomatic" reception. The wife of the Japanese Ambassador, at her husband's farewell reception, said plaintively to Barbara, "You know, in most countries it is not polite to close the bar. But here it is very important—you *must* close the bar" (meaning "in order to encourage the most persistent guests to leave").

Timing of the bar closing to maintain minimal politesse while avoiding brawls was the trick. To be fair, at the Fourth of July reception we hosted, the only acute case of disorderly inebriation was "an obscenity-shouting Scottish" [judging from her accent] woman who had to be escorted to a nearby apartment where she passed out. Since she wouldn't tell us her name, we never *did* find out if she was the wife of a guest or a gate-crasher.[49]

Toward the end of our stay, the government of PNG appointed one of the few highlanders in its diplomatic

---

[48] Only one Fourth because we were there from September 1985 to June 1987.

[49] July 20, 1986, Letter to Dear Family, signed *Em Tasol dispela Taim* ("That's all for Now"), *Bab na Barbara*.

service to be ambassador to the US. Kiatro Abisinito was well educated and we all knew and were very fond of him, and were delighted that he was succeeding so well. But not long after his arrival in Washington, he was driving a PNG embassy vehicle while inebriated when he hit four other cars, seriously injuring one of the drivers, who was a newspaper reporter. This resulted in a flood of hideous publicity, and his government had to summon him home in disgrace.

In a memo to my successor, I warned him about some of the other special problems of entertaining in PNG. Not all Papua New Guineans were eager to attend dinners and receptions, especially at the homes of people they didn't know. Except for the most affluent, transportation was a problem, especially after dark. People found it almost impossible to say "no" to an invitation; they just didn't come. Then there were the dangerous few who came for the sole purpose of getting drunk. My second ambassador, Everett Bierman, a devout Christian, discovered that his most valuable and least risky form of contact with Papua New Guineans was his regular attendance at church with his even more devout wife.[50]

The Crime Problem

Of course drunkenness fueled all sorts of misbehavior at home, including crime. The crime situation preoccupied all foreigners, nourished by lurid accounts of burglaries and gang rapes of expatriates. It was understandably a serious deterrent to tourism and to investment. When I wrote a report on PNG's crime problem, I discovered that there were already shelves of studies on the subject, none of which seemed to have accomplished anything.

Obviously the problem was rooted to some extent in the traditional Melanesian habit of tribal warfare, often between very small groups. Was such war "criminal" or even war at all? In some areas, these fights were more like ritual or sport than real war. Among the Dani (highlanders on the Indonesian side of the island), hostilities customarily stopped when someone

---

[50] From "Contacts," a memo from me to my successor (perhaps written from the State Department after our departure), July 8, 1987.

was injured and both "winners" and "losers" went home.[51] But in many areas warriors inflicted real damage on each others' villages and schools. When the Field Force of the PNG police intervened, it would often burn down more houses as punishment.

When we visited the Southern Highlands with Clay and Kathy near the end of our stay, we noticed smoke in the valley below the quite elegant resort, the Ambua Lodge, where we were staying. Oh, someone explained, that's just a Field Force unit, flown in from Port Moresby, burning houses because of tribal fighting. In this region, rival factions practice trench warfare for both offense and defense, and it was a minor tourist attraction to see the trenches under construction. They normally surrounded house and garden plots and acted as secure avenues for moving without being observed. No one minded having pictures taken. The Southern Highlands is a region where tribal fighting is a cherished tradition, and it does not seem to have been affected much by subsequent oil and gas development in the area.[52]

When we arrived, tribal fighting was customarily conducted with traditional weapons. The Danis on the Indonesian side often shot the same arrows back and forth at each other, presumably to reduce their "defense" expenses. More recently, in PNG, there have been reports of warriors using firearms.

In Port Moresby the situation was different. The "rascals" we worried about were second-generation (or more) city dwellers, often the children of low- and mid-level civil servants, a mixed bag of immigrants from many parts of PNG, and here the problem seemed to be at least as much the product of deracination as of tradition. The danger was greatest around the housing developments where these youth and their families lived. In addition, however, it was not safe to wander along the coast without a friendly contact. Foreigners

[51] The classic account of Dani warfare is Robert Gardner and Karl G. Heider, *Gardens of War: Life and Death in the New Guinea Stone Age,* New York, 1969.
[52] In 1995 we revisited the nearby Kikori Valley, by then traversed by a major oil pipeline, partly on official business in connection with Bob's job in OES (see Chapter 13).

had been robbed on the way to one popular nearby beach, and as mentioned earlier it was considered unsafe to visit Hanuabada, the village on stilts that we looked down on from our house, without a host resident there.

Elsewhere in the country, travel into rural areas was usually quite safe. During our time, a Peace Corps program had been running for several years with volunteers scattered across the country. They had experienced only one serious criminal incident, when a volunteer who broke the rule about avoiding night travel was robbed, but not injured, on a rural bus. The program was nonetheless shut down shortly after we left in 1987, perhaps because its director lived in one of the most unsafe areas of Port Moresby and was understandably nervous as a result.

The ineffectiveness of the government's effort to control crime had something to do with the megadiversity of its political base. In the June, 1987, election, which we witnessed, there were a dozen political parties and scores of *ad hoc* groups representing clan-based associations. We watched the results come in from all over the country, displayed on TV monitors at election central on Port Morseby's Ela Beach. Voter turnout in such elections was usually ninety percent or more, and in some districts it seemed as if every adult male and quite a few women were running for parliament. This was especially true in the Highlands, where ballots were often many feet long.

PNG has a one-house legislature, and after the election, the new Parliament chooses the Prime Minister. But despite what was in one sense the purest of pure democracies, multi-party coalitions were inevitable and the same lackluster politicians took turns as the nation's leader year after year. The driving spirit of the whole political system was intense distrust. So-called "Big Men" were acceptable at the local level, but the idea of a strong central leader, or of nationalism on a truly national scale, was still inconceivable. Elections were nonetheless immensely entertaining to all concerned, except perhaps the harried Election Commissioner who was supposed to make the electoral system work.

The results of all this frenzied politicking were of little official interest to the US at the time. There was no danger of a communist takeover, radical Islam was in the distant future, and if PNG's democracy was chaotic and inefficient, that was Australia's problem, not ours.

By the end of 1986, Paul Gardner's tour as ambassador was drawing to a close, and we learned that his replacement would be Everett Bierman, mentioned earlier. He was a political appointee who was retiring from years as the senior Republican staff member of the Senate Foreign Relations committee. Since he would be a neophyte in every respect, I was finally able to persuade Paul to let me visit Vanuatu to prepare for escorting the new ambassador when he went there to present his credentials.

Vanuatu, or Pure South Pacific

Vanuatu was the smallest of our three countries, with a population of about 140,000, scattered across the New Hebrides, a string of islands large and small. Located

Painting presented by a famous local artist and cartoonist to Ambassador Paul Gardner at the end of his tour in PNG. It depicts a fancy bridge built with US Embassy Self-Help funds, which Ambassador Gardner dedicated. The local people did not like the net sides, which interfered with fishing from it. The sign reads "Paul's bridge" in Pidgin.

between the colonies of regional rivals Britain and France, it had become a "condominium" with British and French administrations under a Spanish President. The British and French representatives located themselves on two different hills within sight of each other in the capital of Port Vila, where each was always trying to fly his flag just a tad higher than his rival. The Spanish President was supposed to make sure that they didn't come to blows. It deserved an opera, and it did get *South Pacific.*

Most French residents were planters, mainly of coconut trees, for copra and coconut oil, especially on the biggest island, Espiritu Santo, which became the American rear base for the Guadalcanal campaign. That explains why, in the musical, Ezio Pinza sings in French (*"Dites-moi, pour quoi, la vie est belle-UH?"*)

Later, in the run-up to Vanuatu's independence, there occurred a struggle dubbed "The Coconut War" by the Australian press. Certain people, including a group of French planters on Espiritu Santo, opposed independence because they knew that the resulting government would be Melanesian-dominated and supportive of the Melanesians fighting against French rule on neighboring New Caledonia, as indeed turned out to be the case.

The Espiritu Santo rebels were supported by a mysterious American-based organization called the Phoenix Foundation, which supposedly wanted Vanuatu to become a libertarian tax haven. The anti-independence coalition seized the Espiritu Santo airport in June, 1980, but their uprising ended when Papua New Guinea, the Melanesian superpower, sent in troops.[53] Father Walter Lini, an Anglican priest, became Vanuatu's founding Prime Minister, and he was indeed sympathetic to the anti-French forces. He tried to invoke Libyan support for them, was playing footsie with the Cubans, and doing other things Uncle Sam didn't approve of, such as espousing something called Melanesian Socialism.

When I got to Vanuatu to make the requisite official calls in preparation for an ambassadorial visit, I was quite enchanted with it.

---

[53] http://en.wikipedia.org/wiki/Coconut_War.

Vanuatu is a charming country, also one with considerable economic potential because of its intensely volcanic origin and resulting good soils. The island where the capital, Port Vila, is situated is a pretty mélange of rugged green hills and turquoise lagoons. Vanuatu's peculiar dual franco-anglo heritage, which colors everything, allows the charm of francophonia without the dreadful inconvenience of a place where the people don't understand English. Underlying this modern duality is Melanesian cultural complexity unrivalled elsewhere: more than 100 languages for 140,000 people (compared to 700 languages for 3.5 million people in PNG).[54]

Compared to PNG and Solomon Islands, there seemed to be more successful small businesses, a notable atmosphere of cheerful friendliness, and less apathy and hostility in the face of change. The Vanuatans were fascinated by their own culture and working hard to preserve it. The Vanuatu Cultural Center and Museum, run by an American, Kirk Huffman,[55] was bursting at the seams with wonderful art. Like the Sarawak Museum, it was dedicated to drawing on and enhancing the pride of rural people in themselves. A tourist with deep pockets could buy a hardwood slit drum weighing a ton at its souvenir shop, as well as more practical artifacts.

The government's economic policies were amazingly enlightened, including a system of negotiating long-term leases between customary landowners and modern developers. Australians operating a dive resort near the capital and adjacent to a rich fringing reef had persuaded its traditional owners to accept its transformation into a nature reserve. This meant outlawing destructive but popular fishing methods, including spear fishing, in return for lease payments and employment opportunities—an early example

---

[54] Based on my "Report on a Trip to Vanuatu, December 6-11, 1986." By 2016, Vanuatu's population had approximately doubled.

[55] As of 2012 Huffman was still the Honorary Curator of the Cultural Center; for a recent comment by him see http://www.dailypost.vu/content/land-vanuatu-mother-under-threat.

of eco-tourism.[56]

Father Lini's ruling Vanua'aku political party, which he had formed before independence, was working well across regional and linguistic boundaries. But Vanuatu also had a serious cargo cult named after a mythical American named John Frum who was going to return loaded with canned food and refrigerators.[57] And, as I reported, there was:

No crime. *Well not much anyway. As you drive around Efate, the island on which the capital, Port Vila, is located, you pass "self-service" fruit stands where one is expected to take what one wants and leave the money. Or, as you pass the central jail, you can see ex-rebel Jimmy Stevens, the leader of the losing side in the Coconut War, holding court outside the prison walls under a banyan tree. Certainly there is, as yet, nothing in Vanuatu to compare with the crime problem in PNG, or the obvious symptoms of one developing in Honiara.[58]*

The absence of crime might have had something to do with the fact that the Vanuatans were still drinking *kava*, a traditional drink. Adolescent boys chewed the root of a pepper plant and expectorated the pulp into a communal bowl. Foreigners said it tasted like drinking Novocain, but it didn't seem to be doing as much damage as the beer mainly consumed elsewhere in Melanesia.

---

[56] I did sneak away from a round of official calls to dive at this place. One arrived in late afternoon to see the spiny lobsters emerge from their holes and march up the reef slope through gorgeous coral. My second most memorable dive was on Espiritu Santo, where the *USS President Coolidge*, a luxury liner converted into a troop ship, hit a Japanese mine while entering the harbor in October,1942. Its captain beached it in shallow water and more than 5,000 troops got off the ship safely. Today it is a favorite dive site, not least for the mammoth enlisted men's head over the stern, with hundreds of white toilets cheek by jowl, so to speak, stretching into the underwater gloom. One can imagine what this place must have looked and smelled like after breakfast on a normal day at sea.

[57] James P. Sterba, "Vanuatans Await the Second Coming of One John Frum," *Wall Street Journal*, June 10, 1986. As of 2016, John Frum was still going strong: see Bob Morris, "Hope, Faith, Patriotism and Magic," *New York Times* op-ed, July 2, 2016.

[58] Pringle, "Report on a Trip to Vanuatu, December 6-11, 1986."

I concluded that Vanuatu was the perfect place to see traditional South Pacific culture, without witnessing something akin to the worst kind of American Indian reservation, and tourists were beginning to come, mostly from Australia, despite totally inadequate air service compared to competing destinations like Fiji. I was mystified as to why the Vanuatans did not in general want to be remembered as the setting for Michner's famous musical, although there was something named "Bloody Mary's Fast Food" in Port Vila.[59]

Barbara was most annoyed about missing Vanuatu (that's a teacher's schedule for you!), but in January, 1987, we made a trip to some of the islands north of the New Guinea mainland, including the provinces of East New Britain, New Ireland and Manus (geographically, the Bismarck archipelago).[60] Although home to only about half a million people, about one-seventh of the national total, this region was relatively prosperous for a number of reasons. The population was reasonably well-educated, due to early exposure to missionaries. Also, some areas had benefited from aggressive economic development under the pre-1917 German regime.

There are several ethnic groups. The best known is the Tolai. We called on one of them, Sir Paulias Matane, who had been PNG's first ambassador to the US before achieving a common Papua New Guinean ambition of retiring to his village, in his case a comfortable home in a dispersed Tolai settlement. Very much the elder statesman, he had just completed a study of PNG's educational system, lectured frequently on Christian topics, and had recently returned from a trip to the Holy Land. He was planning a celebration of the fortieth anniversary of his village school, to which the diplomatic corps would be invited.

A Most Explosive Harbor: Rabaul

Not surprisingly, you didn't have to worry much about crime in East New Britain. What we might have worried about was

---

[59] Bob and Barbara letter to Dear Family, March 29, 1987.
[60]"Notes on a trip to the New Guinea Islands (East New Britain, New Ireland and Manus), January 2-10, 1987."

that the whole place, which lies at the intersection of three tectonic plates, would blow up, as indeed parts of it do rather frequently. The Germans had located the capital of their entire New Guinea colony at Rabaul, on the edge of a huge caldera created by a Krakatoa-like blast about 1,400 years ago. Open to the sea on one side, it is a superb natural harbor, and at the beginning of World War II the Japanese turned it into a major naval base. MacArthur's forces bombed it constantly, but eventually "island-hopped" around it.

There are smaller, but often lethal eruptions around the caldera about every fifty years. Landing at Rabaul, we flew in low over a steaming hotspot at the very edge of the city. The PNG Volcanological Laboratory was located not far away, on the rim of the caldera. The laboratory had covered the rim as well as its floor (the harbor) with sensors to measure movements heralding an eruption. Its director, Dr. Peter Lowenstein, told us that four years previously the sensors had showed that the rim was expanding outward, an ominous sign. Volcanologists from the US and many other countries flew in to study it; evacuation planning began, and then . . . nothing, until 1994, when an eruption (one of the fifty-year cycle variety) almost completely destroyed the town. The airport was moved to a new site, but as this is written Rabaul is being rebuilt on the old site.

After diving on the spectacular outer wall, with a drop-off of several thousand feet, we dived in the caldera-harbor, the bottom of which is littered with Japanese ships destroyed by US bombers. The water visibility was much clearer than at the better known Truk Lagoon, which we had visited ten years previously on our way home from Manila. I was having such a good time that on our second dive, I failed to secure the back of my Nikonos underwater camera, which of course meant no more pictures, and no more camera, except for the lens which survived, making it an expensive bit of absent-mindedness.

Annoyingly enough, the second dive was spectacular. The first thing we saw was a small freighter with a huge ray, at least ten feet long, asleep on what was left of its deck. The ship had obviously exploded, scattering wreckage, including lots of new-looking truck tires and artillery shells, in every direction. Irked by my mistake, I decided to take home a brass artillery shell casing—a shameless violation of diving etiquette, but our guide didn't stop me.

Back in Moresby I noticed that although the warhead of the shell was missing, which was why I had picked it up, its base showed no evidence that the detonator had fired, and the inside of the casing was filled with what seamed like slivers of wood. I assumed that some Japanese officer on the ship had been using it as a container of some kind. I thought nothing more about it until we were packing out to go home, when Barbara persuaded me that I'd better have an expert make sure the shell was really dead.

Now, if there was anything the Papua New Guinea military knew thoroughly, it was how to dispose of World War II munitions safely. They were constantly being discovered and played or tinkered with, often with fatal results, and there happened to be a unit that specialized in this kind of work just down the hill from us, so I took it to them. They discovered that a live detonator was still in my shell, and when they set it off the explosion was sufficient to blow pieces out of the brass casing. The slivers of wood were actually cordite, a kind of gunpowder used in artillery shells. I wrote a thank-you note on embassy stationery to the unit commander:

Captain John Kari
EOD Unit
Papua New Guinea Defense Force   *June 5, 1987*

Dear Captain Kari:

Many thanks for your help in taming our "souvenir." It would certainly have been unfortunate if it had gone off in our baggage on the way home! It is amazing that after 45 years under water it could still behave like that. You have a very interesting job, and we greatly appreciate your help. [61]

Robert M. Pringle
Deputy Chief of Mission

---

[61] A copy of the letter is inside the shell casing, which we still have.

In PNG, the lingering shadow of World II had many aspects, political, physical, and religious. Politically, the loyal support of many Melanesians had created a durable bond with Australia, which counterbalanced the frequent frustrations of dealing with PNG's chaotic, post-independence democracy. Memories of the "coastwatchers," who, from deep in Japanese occupied territory, warned Allied troops of approaching Japanese warships, contributed to this political tie. So did a single photograph showing a Papua New Guinean leading a blinded Australian soldier, his face covered with bandages, back from the front lines, up and over the Owen Stanleys on the infamous Kokoda Track. It inspired a poem entitled "Fuzzy Wuzzy Angels":

> From mortar or machine gun fire,
> Or a chance surprise attack,
> To safety and the care of Doctors,
> At the bottom of the track.
> May the Mothers in Australia,
> When they offer up a prayer,
> Mention those impromptu Angels,
> With the Fuzzy Wuzzy hair.[62]

For us, the physical relics included that shell casing, and also a quart beer bottle we found while diving inside the Port Moresby reef; it had a lovely sea-glass patina from forty years of rolling around in the ocean and the date 1944 on its base. Unfortunately our maid, Melata, threw it out after a party, thinking it was just another beer bottle.

Why Cargo Cults Make Sense

On the religious side there was, of course, the cargo cult phenomenon. Cargo cults manifest the desire of hitherto profoundly isolated people to acquire the physical paraphernalia of their conquerors by the use of magic or religion. It all seemed very primitive and unsophisticated

---

[62] Last verse only quoted: http://www.anzacday.org.au/anzacservices/ poetry/fuzzywuzzy.htm.

until we got to New Guinea, where, in the mid-1980s, it suddenly made sense. The war had brought a flood of foreigners loaded with *stuff*: boats, airplanes, vehicles, weapons, fuel, and supply dumps without end. The weirdness of all this apparition-like reality was aggravated by the fact that even though MacArthur's forces had moved away from New Guinea well before the end of World War II, we (the Americans) didn't stop building and extending our bases there. More than one million Americans served in these bases before the war ended.[63]

When the war did end, the American troops, often by this time in rear areas far from the fighting, were faced with a choice: account for all left-over equipment and prepare it for shipment back to the US, which would take months, or declare it all "inoperable" and push it off the nearest reef, or into a forest. Such cargo is still everywhere. During our stay, an entire motor pool was found under a beach where the departing Americans had dug a trench and buried it. Marsden matting, steel plate with holes in it, once used to pave roads and airstrips and still useful today, is ubiquitous. Much more no doubt awaits future archaeologists.

Cargo cults continued after the war. One of the best known was the Lyndon Johnson Cult. It started on the small island of New Hanover, just off New Ireland. In an early election, before full independence, the New Hanoverians decided they would like to have the Americans come back, and voted for Lyndon Johnson. The Australians called it a cargo cult, but it may have been veiled criticism of the government for being so comparatively stingy. The cult, if it was one, was still alive in 1986.

On a map, New Hanover looks like an egg being swallowed by a long Pollywog, which is New Ireland, 220 miles long by, on average, only fifteen miles wide. We drove along part of the road which runs the length of New Ireland, visiting some interesting American Catholic missionaries before continuing on to Manus.

Manus is a big, oblong island west of New Ireland, a

---

[63] James Griffin, Hank Nelson and Stewart Firth, *Papua New Guinea, A Political History*, Heinemann Educational Australia, Richmond, Victoria, Australia, 1979, p. 83.

place where Margaret Meade did some of her best-known research. At the time of our visit in 1986, it had a population of about 30,000 energetic, well-educated people. Because they were ambitious, many went to Port Moresby, where they cut a swathe in national affairs. There was talk of various big projects on Manus itself, including a tuna cannery, but island development was hampered by the chronic outflow of talented people.

During the war Manus had been yet another US base, which included a long road running parallel to a fringing reef, one of those over which US stuff, still visible, had been pushed at the end of the war. We decided to go diving along it, having, as always, brought our scuba gear along. We did see more of the equipment, but it was a short dive due to a number of large, overly inquisitive Grey Reef Sharks. This was one of the few times we had shark concerns in all our New Guinea diving.

Early in the New Year, we learned that I had been nominated as ambassador to Mali. That meant we would be departing PNG before my two-year assignment was fully completed. Soon there were forms to be filled out, including one that asked me whether I was registered to vote as a Democrat or Republican. I really couldn't remember, but thought Democrat was probably more accurate. I was worried that this honest reply might endanger my appointment by the Reagan White House, but it didn't. The White House had long ago decided which ambassadorships, among those coming open in 1987, it wanted for political appointees, leaving the others for unimportant career Foreign Service Officers.

Barbara and I had to go to Manila for physical exams, requiring a trip via Sydney, because the nearest US Government doctors (no others would do, not even Australians) were in the Philippines. It seemed like a waste of government money, but we enjoyed going back, and we were able to stay at the newly refurbished Manila Hotel. We thought Manila looked run down compared to when we were there. "When it comes to quality of life (and air) Port Moresby looks great by comparison."[64]

---

[64] Bob and Barbara letter to Dear Family, March 29, 1987.

The Big One that Didn't Get Away

As our time for departure drew nearer, Barbara's parents and sister Kathy came for a visit. We had a small problem in preparing for this visit. Clay, hearing stories of excellent fishing in New Guinea waters, had given Bob a handsome Christmas gift of tackle, including big silver lures, wire leaders to resist sharp teeth, and more. The problem was that we always spent so much time diving that we never had time for fishing. All Clay's tackle was still sitting unused as his arrival date approached.

So next time we went diving, as we were returning through the reef passage into the harbor, I threw one of Clay's big silver lures over the stern on a hand line, which was all we had. I never imagined anything would bite. When I felt a curious drag on the line, I assumed the line had gotten tangled with some seaweed. I had let out a lot of line so it took some time to get whatever it was anywhere near the boat. Then suddenly this very big fish jumped clear out of the water! Barbara's reaction was, "Just like Hemingway, *The Old Man and the Sea.*"

Soon we could see silver sides flashing deep in the clear water. How on earth to get this large fish into our small boat, since we had no proper gaff? Luckily, we did have a couple of cargo hooks which we used to turn over slabs of dead coral while looking for shells, and one of them did the trick. The fish was a forty-eight inch Barred Mackerel (aka Narrow-barred Spanish Mackerel), a Pacific species similar to the King Mackerel of the Atlantic, and cut into steaks it was very edible indeed.[65] From then on, we always trolled when coming to or from the harbor, and although Jamie and I caught a few smaller fries, there was never another to rival our big one.

Revenge of the Wigmen

The parents' visit, which took place early in 1987, turned

---

[65] And, yes, there is a picture of me holding the fish by the tail on our terrace, and you can estimate its length by my height, 5'10". Our friend, Jenny Robbins, wife of the Australian Naval Attaché, identified the fish for us, and told us that the best way to prepare it for eating was to cut it into steaks.

out to be a great success. After exploring Port Moresby (quickly accomplished) and enjoying its offshore islands and reefs, Clay, Kathy, Barbara and I went to the Southern Highlands, home of the famous Wigmen. Char did not come along on this part of the trip because she had recently been diagnosed with macular degeneration and had to be cautious about cabin pressurization, or lack thereof, in small planes.

After some typical PNG aviation, poking around in the clouds looking for Mendi, the provincial capital, we landed and had a good time exploring the local cultural scene, with its picturesque tribal fighting, including trench warfare (see above). The very nice Ambua Lodge, perched on a mountainside above the town, also featured bird watching. A young local guide took us out one morning, but craning our necks to see various Birds of Paradise,

Bob shows off the surprise Narrow-barred Spanish Mackerel that he caught with tackle sent by his father-in-law. It provided many delicious meals.

we had only so-so luck spotting them way up in the canopy of the tropical forest.

In the *de rigeur* category was a visit to the professional Wigmen, who put on their finest wigs and face paint and gave dance performances for visitors. Most Southern Highlands men wore wigs, really oblong hats, but the everyday ones were quite modest, made of dried flowers and twigs,[66] or

[66] For an example of every-day wiggery, see the photo of an old man on my study wall, snapped out the window on our way to Ambua Lodge from the Mendi airport, and one of the best pictures I ever took in New Guinea.

Near Mendi in the Southern Highlands, Barbara's father, as the respected elder, was honored by smoking a pipe in the Men's House with the Wigmen who had earlier demonstrated to us their techniques of face and hair decoration.

maybe a bunch of grass adorned with the red and yellow label from a tin of mackerel (*tinfis* in Pidgin). However, the ones we visited had dress-up wigs with real Bird of Paradise plumes, and they demonstrated every step of putting on face-paint and their wigs before dancing. Then they invited us to see the men's house. The only hitch (or itch) to all this came when our hosts invited Clay, as the senior male present, to join them on a bench for a ceremonial smoke. In the resulting photo, it is clear that our patriarch was enjoying all this.

Well and good, but after their return to the US, both he and Char came down with an acutely itchy rash, which at first defied diagnosis, but turned out to be scabies. Barbara wrote: "Well, well, you come to the wilds for three weeks and manage to pick up something we've avoided for two years."[67]

On the way home from Mendi, our plane circled so long trying to find a break in the clouds at an intermediate stop (where it finally could not land) that it ran low on fuel, so we

---

[67] Barbara letter to Dear Mother and Daddy, May 12, 1987. Actually, we were in PNG just short of two years.

made an unscheduled side trip to Mt. Hagen to buy more. However, the pilot had not directly asked whether that airport had any fuel, and after we landed, it became clear that it didn't. More culture shock for Clay, who shook his head in disbelief, but he certainly was getting a grand tour of the New Guinea Highlands. Fortunately, the plane still had enough fuel to make it to Lae on the north coast, where, finally, enough fuel to get home was available. To end the visit Barbara, her parents and Kathy went up the Sepik on the *Melanesian Explorer*, and that trip, with all its interesting riverside villages and amazing spirit houses, was a great success also.

Malinowski's Islands and The Kula Ring

In April we visited the Trobriand Islands and others (Woodlarks, D'Entrecasteaux chain, Marshall Bennetts, and more) at the eastern end of New Guinea, a region made famous by Bronislaw Malinowski, the father of modern field anthropology and a truly great social scientist. Malinowski had started his fieldwork in Australian New Guinea when World War I broke out. He was Polish and therefore technically an enemy alien, since his home in Poland was part of the Austro-Hungarian Empire. The Australians were going to intern him, but he talked them out of it, pointing out that he could hardly do any harm in such a remote area.

The result was a stream of anthropological classics with attention grabbing titles and profoundly scholarly text. One of our favorites is *Argonauts of the Western Pacific*, in which he wrote of a ritual trading cycle, known as the Kula Ring. Islanders traded shell necklaces in one direction, clockwise, and shell arm bracelets in the other, counterclockwise. These items, each with its own history, were passed from island to island in elaborately decorated canoes, as means of keeping peace and enhancing communication. The Kula Ring is famous as an early example of regional peacekeeping in a setting where war was often the norm.

We went on the *Melanesian Explorer*, the same little cruise ship in which Barbara and her family had just visited the Sepik. We were astonished to discover that the Kula Ring still existed, and we were lucky enough to see it going on, by means of big, brightly painted outrigger canoes with woven *pandanus* sails, just as Malinowski had described. We visited several other isolated island groups, where bare breasts and grass skirts were the everyday fashion, not worn to attract tourists. The water visibility at some of our anchorages was well over 100 feet, the clearest we have ever seen. Despite its small size—we had nine passengers—the *Explorer* (since replaced by larger vessels) was comfortable, but quite bouncy, and traversing the strait between the Huon Peninsula and East New Britain was not for the faint of stomach.[68]

A Missing B-17 is Found

At about this time, two of America's previous wars came together in a curious way. For some time the US had been trying to send teams into Vietnam to find and identify the remains of American personnel shot down over Vietnam and listed as missing in action, and teams of MIA (Missing in Action) specialists had been training to do such work. But the Vietnamese Government was not yet ready to allow them to come to Vietnam, so they had little to do. Then someone remembered that there were more aircraft still missing in Papua New Guinea from the US Fifth Air Force alone, about 350 of them, than the entire number missing in Vietnam. So if we knew of a site worthy of investigation, a team would be sent to PNG to do its thing.

Enter Bruce Hoy, an Australian who ran PNG's World War II Museum, which consisted of a big Quonset hut and a large back yard filled with every kind of detritus from vehicles to

---

[68] This trip is well covered in "Barbara letter to Dear Mother and Daddy, May 12, 1987." We also made a diving trip to the Trobriands, by air, to the main island, Kiriwina. It had a tiny unmanned airstrip, where, on the return trip, the young Australian pilot of a small twin-engine plane asked us (including about four other diver/passengers) to leave some of our diving gear behind to be forwarded on a later flight. Since there was no place to leave it except a grass-covered lean-to, no one would volunteer to do so, and the pilot finally said, with a sigh, "Oh, well, it's probably OK," and took us back to Port Moresby over the Owen Stanleys with all our baggage stowed in pods under the wings. Whew for that one!

airplane parts. Bruce even had a pile of WW II beer bottles and he gave us one to replace the one Melata had thrown out, but it isn't as nice, no sea-glass patina.

Hoy was a complete freak on the history of the air war in New Guinea and the possibility of undiscovered crash sites. He had read all the unit histories and was known to villagers all over New Guinea. They would contact him and say, "We have discovered some wreckage, do you want to know about it?" Thus it was that he learned of a crash site high on a mountain slope to our southeast.

Hoy's records showed that a B-17 had gone down at sea not far away, with all crew members lost, but he concluded that they might be wrong, and that the plane in the mountains might be the one in question. The next step was to call in a team from Hawaii, to see if they could determine if the wreck was indeed the missing US aircraft and, if so, identify human remains, usually done by matching tooth fragments with dental records. The team arrived, rented a helicopter, hired villagers to clear a spot where it could land, flew to the site, and went to work. I was invited to witness the operation along with another embassy officer, Todd Greentree.

B-17E 41-2505 had taken off from Port Moresby in pre-dawn darkness on April 17, 1942,[69] for a bombing raid on the Japanese base at Rabaul. It developed serious engine trouble soon after departure but could not return to its base until the sun rose, because a Japanese air raid had knocked out the runway lights a day or two previously. So it circled, waiting, and in the darkness a wing tip clipped New Guinea's mountain spine. The plane broke apart on impact and pieces of it were scattered down the southern slope, where they still were.

At this altitude, around 9,000 feet, thick tropical forest gives way to stunted, spindly tree cover and lots of moss and lichen. The wreckage was quite visible and well preserved, with much of its brown paint intact, the number 2505 in yellow paint still clear on the tail. A machine gun protruded from a waist gunner's position and belts of .50 caliber ammunition were scattered around, each cartridge stamped with the number 41 for 1941, when it was made. One of its

[69] This is exactly Barbara's birthday, not counting the time/date change from the US to New Guinea.

B-17E 41-2505 as it looked when found.

four engines had broken off and rolled downhill and was resting with its propeller buried in the mossy litter.

Most human remains were long decayed, but the twelve-member MIA team formed skirmish lines to search carefully through the surface soil, and they recovered enough tooth fragments to identify most of the crew members.[70] Mr.

---

[70] See Robert M. Pringle, "Embassy in New Guinea Aids Grim Search for World War II Remains," *State Magazine*, August-September 1987. Such discoveries were fairly common. One, a B-24, was written up in the *New Yorker* just before our arrival in Port Moresby. Another, a B-17, which went down in the sea off the north coast, became a prized scuba diving site and was written up in the *National Geographic*. Then, shortly after our departure, a private American group of bomber buffs tried to retrieve a B-17 G which had crash-landed in a huge swamp on the north side of New Guinea. The crew survived, and local villagers led them to safety, but the plane remained. It was a rare model, sufficiently intact and well preserved by the peaty water of the swamp to be deemed restorable to flying condition. With US Air Force help the bomber buffs made elaborate plans to cut the plane in pieces and lift it over the Owen Stanleys to Port Moresby by helicopter. From there it would have been flown home in a giant C-5A cargo plane. But they did not realize that PNG was no longer part of Australia and failed get permission from the PNG government, which, sensing that the plane must be extremely valuable to warrant all this effort, said, "No Way." I don't know where it is now.

Greentree, one of those rarities, a risk-taking Foreign Service Officer, broke off two rounds of machine-gun ammunition, and years later I discovered he was still using them as a paperweight in his State Department inbox.

Paradise and Its Birds, Close to Home

We had been doing a lot of bird watching from the beginning of our tour, usually with groups in areas around Port Moresby which were known to be safe. The avian life was very rich, but most Birds of Paradise were hard to find and to see well. Many are restricted to small areas, others to certain elevation levels. One of the few easy ones is Count Raggiana's Bird of Paradise, known as a Raggi for short.

To see a Raggi near Port Moresby, we went to Varirata National Park, about an hour's drive away. In the parking lot there was a sign reading "This way to the Birds of Paradise." At first we thought it was a hoax! We would end up looking into a cage! But no, after fifteen minutes or so of walking there was another sign saying "This Way to the Bird of Paradise Tree" and then a third with an arrow pointing up a big tree. And sure enough, there would usually be several male Raggis fluffing their gorgeous orange plumes on its higher branches.

You could also hear the Raggianas calling a long way away; indeed we could sometimes hear them from our house. Birds of Paradise, of which there are thirty-nine species, are closely related to crows, and sometimes sound a bit like them. The Raggi's call is "a very loud series of raucous bugles, all on one pitch, but gaining in volume and slowing in tempo at the end: *wau wau wau WAU WAU WAU Wauuu Wauu!*" [71]

We did not realize until we had done a little reading that the Raggis have communal trees where the males go to display, in the hope of attracting females. These are known as *lek* trees, a word from a New Guinea language now used for all birds with similar courting behavior, and that was what we had seen.

The amazing thing is that in spite of rapidly increasing logging in PNG, hence habitat destruction, none of the Birds of

---

[71] Bruce M. Beehler. Thane E. Pratt and Dale Zimmerman, *Birds of New Guinea*, Handbook No. 9 of the Wau [sic] Ecology Institute, Papua New Guinea, Princeton University Press, 1986, p. 232.

Paradise are considered to be seriously endangered—at least not yet. It is relevant that the same people who hunt them for plumes sometimes also like to have them alive, displaying on their *lek* trees, near their villages.[72] In the meantime, if you can't go to PNG, do watch one of David Attenborough's classic television films on Birds of Paradise, and their equally wonderful relatives, the Bower Birds, also found in New Guinea.[73]

Last, Best Diving and a Call from the President

By May, we were getting ready to leave for Washington. I was worried about more travel, because President Reagan always called his ambassadorial nominees personally to congratulate them. The White House switchboard could apparently reach anyone almost anywhere. How about on a live-aboard dive boat off the New Guinea coast? That didn't seem likely. But I learned that I would be safe during a certain two-week period, because the President always called whole groups of nominees serially and these sessions were scheduled well in advance, and as he was off to a state visit to Italy and the Papacy, none would occur during that time.

So off we went on David Halstead's *MV Telita*, based in Alotau at the tip of New Guinea's southeastern tail. Halstead, an Australian married to a Papua New Guinean, had been diving in New Guinea for years, and had been the instructor for our refresher and the kids' certification scuba courses. His wife Dinah came from a village on the coast of Milne Bay, which had a tradition of wooden boat building. So the Halsteads had commissioned a spanking new wooden dive boat, the *MV Telita*, which was going out for a shake-down cruise with local passengers before beginning to show divers from all over the world the seas around PNG, one of the finest diving areas on the planet. One reason for its quality was that the local people were intensely jealous of their adjacent reefs

---

[72] See the example cited in Beehler *et al., Birds of New Guinea*, p. 42.
[73] We have just (November, 2012) returned from the Cornell Ornithological Lab's exhibition on Birds of Paradise, in cooperation with the *National Geographic*. The accompanying book is by Tim Laman and EdwinScholes, *Birds of Paradies: Revealing the World's Most Extraordinary Birds,* Washington, DC, 2012.

and guarded them against poachers and illegal fishermen.

The diving was indeed terrific, so good that we would return seven years later for a longer cruise. This time, however, we had to cut short our cruise by a few days to be back in time for the President's call. We did so by disembarking at Dobura, an Anglican Mission Station on the mainland where Dinah had gone to boarding school, and getting a flight back to Port Moresby via Alotau from there.

A few days later, the phone rang at about three in the morning. A pleasant voice said, "I suppose it must be very late where you are?" "Yes, Mr. President." More pleasantries ensued. Soon we were packing for the trip home and the long business of preparing for Senate confirmation.

Our Melanesian assignment was one of the least important, in conventional geopolitical/foreign policy terms, of any we had. Yet this chapter is one of the longest in this memoir, simply because the subject matter is so loaded with irresistible material of all kinds. Our house caught the gist of it, with its views over rows of forested mountains in one direction, sparkling ocean and miles of coral reefs in another, and, in between, a city in hazardous transition from a spectacularly variegated traditional past to troubled modernity. None of the three countries our embassy covered was pristine. The old religions, often linked with practices like headhunting and cannibalism, were dead and Christianity was ubiquitous. Traditional culture survived only here and there, but where it did, its diversity and sheer beauty was something that we would never forget.

The pace of damaging human encroachment was still quickening. Enormous mining and hydrocarbon projects were becoming commonplace. Coral reefs were increasingly at risk, but in many places villagers were determined to guard against reckless exploitation of them. The hazard of climate change had yet to be recognized.

Today, logging continues apace, but much forest is still left. Especially at high altitudes, a great deal of it is rich in birds and other fauna, but not commercially valuable, or easily accessible. At sea, Melanesia's underwater resources remain largely intact, not yet affected by warming water and coral bleaching nearly as much as other areas threatened by higher levels of human activity and/or less ideal marine environments. There is still hope that much of Melanesia's natural heritage can be saved.

11

Ronald Reagan's Man and Wife in Mali, 1987-1990

After visiting the family in the summer of 1987, we settled into a suites-style hotel in Foggy Bottom, near the State Department, to begin preparing for Senate confirmation. No substantive difficulties were anticipated. Mali was seen as just another African country under military rule. Despite its history of close relations with the Soviets, that alliance was clearly on the wane, as was the Cold War itself. Our relations were cordial, and since the US Mission was largely concerned with promoting economic development, we had a big bilateral aid program. Mali had suffered seriously from the same horrendous drought that we had witnessed in neighboring Burkina Faso in 1983-84, and the US was still placing much emphasis on "food security." That meant promoting more productive agriculture by all possible means and preparing, through grain stockpiling and other measures, for the next really big dry spell, which, more than two-and-a-half decades later, has not yet materialized in Mali.

Getting Confirmed

My only real problem was getting a confirmation hearing scheduled. The Senator who chaired the Africa Subcomittee of the Foreign Relations Committee, which would hold the hearing, was Paul Simon, Democrat of Illinois. A more congenial politician would be hard to imagine, but he was competing to be the Democratic candidate for president in 1988, and was simply never in Washington, leaving a crowd of would-be Africa-bound ambassadors with not much to do.

We didn't mind. Jamie was a sophomore at Dartmouth,

but we saw quite a bit of Annie, a senior boarding student at Madeira. Among her other activities, she was participating in a special weekly seminar program at the Folger Shakespeare Theatre in place of her regular English class. Once, when Washington had a rare November snowstorm, she had come downtown to attend a play with us and then spend the night in our motel room before proceeding on Wednesday morning to her weekly job at the Washington Bureau of the *New York Times*, part of Madeira's "co-curriculum" program.

With snow paralyzing the town the next morning, she contemplated skipping work, because, she reasoned, it would be a snow day at Madeira. But we pointed out that, already being in town, she could walk to her work as easily as Dad could walk to the State Department, and off she went. It turned out to be a gratifying experience; none of the other interns in the office showed up, and she was praised by none other than the Bureau Chief, the legendary Johnny Apple.

Pax was with us, bound for Africa again, and he didn't much mind the confirmation delay either, although when he was left alone in our hotel room he showed his displeasure by clawing and gnawing on the bathroom door. Fortunately the hotel was about to be renovated and its management said it didn't matter. The long-term occupants down the hall from us also had a pet, a very vocal but bored African Grey Parrot, which would answer back through the door if you talked to him. Of course, Bob did.

There is no telling how long we might have remained in limbo, had it not been for a colleague, David Shinn, who was nominated to be ambassador to Burkina Faso. The delay was really serious for him. In anticipation of a foreign assignment, he had rented his house in DC, but because he was not posted abroad when he was nominated, he did not qualify for a temporary living allowance, as we did, and had to pay his own hotel bills. In desperation, he called one of his home state senators, Brock Adams, who was also on the Africa Subcommittee, and asked if he might be able to hold a hearing instead. Senator Simon did not object, and it was duly held in November.

I was one of four nominees, all for little-known countries, at Senator Adams' hearing, and we sailed through the whole thing in about an hour. In my own brief remarks I emphasized the importance of Mali's rich history, its recent transition from radical Marxism to moderation, the devastation caused by the droughts of the late 1970s and early 1980s and our assistance in coping with them. I concluded that our current primary objective was to help the Malians mobilize their considerable resource base to produce more food and lessen the need for outside help in the future. This aim could be achieved partly by implementing economic reform, including the elimination of inefficient state enterprises. I made no mention of democratization, which was not yet a US policy objective. Questions from Senator Adams were sensible and friendly.[1]

The full Senate vote to confirm was almost automatic. The only thing left was to be sworn in. I could choose the

Bob is sworn in as Ambassador to Mali at Dacor Bacon House in Washington, DC.

---

[1] Stenographic transcript of Hearings before the Committee on Foreign Relations, United States Senate, October 28, 1987.

venue, and decided to forego the State Department's formal reception rooms in favor of the Dacor-Bacon House, not far away. It had once been the home of our first Chief Justice, John Marshall, and was now the headquarters of Diplomatic and Consular Officers Retired (DACOR) and available for such purposes. The big event took place on November 10.

During our remaining time in Washington we took a training course for ambassadors-designate, and spouses on certain days. We also selected art to decorate our Residence (for some obscure reason the ambassador's Residence is often capitalized) paid for by the State Department's Art in Embassies Program. To supplement our own antique quilts, we chose American art from local galleries, and from the Torpedo Factory art center in Alexandria.

The course, for both career and political nominees, was about the theory and practical details of ambassadorship. Most interestingly—but also most theoretical—career employees learned that we would forfeit State employment for the duration of our ambassadorships to become employees and personal representatives of the President. Once at post, I could fly the President's flag on the left-hand side of my official car, the US flag on the right. (Whether one did this or not depended on practice at post; it was done in Mali, but not in South Africa.)

Everyone in the US Mission would be subject to my presidential authority, according to a doctrine first formalized by a letter from President Kennedy. There was fine print specifying that US military serving under the authority of a regional CINC (commander-in-chief) were not covered by this rule, although military attachés were. The idea is that ambassadors, aka Chiefs of Mission, should make sure that all the various US agencies represented at an embassy speak and act with one voice.

This theory of ambassadorial supremacy is much beloved by the State Department, but it has always been, truth be told, a worthy fiction. It assumes that an ambassador, just because he is in Bamako, can achieve a greater degree of control over different agencies than the President himself can achieve in Washington. An ambassador does not control the budget of the CIA or AID, or many other agencies now operating abroad, nor does he decide how much money each can spend in his country, although his advice on this subject may be heeded. And the President does not control Congress, as we are being forcibly reminded as I write this more than three decades later. An ambassador can object credibly to what another agency is doing only if he can demonstrate that serious errors are being made.

Everyone knows that the State Department, not the President, issues operating instructions to ambassadors. The ambassador's replies, no matter how important, are addressed to the Secretary of State, not the President, although the National Security Council and other White House addressees get copies, as do up to several thousand other official recipients.

There are other constraints. The ambassador might like to read all the reports generated by his local CIA office (or "Station"), but in fact he cannot see operational messages relating to the more sensitive aspects of the intelligence craft—and he knows this full well. Indeed an ambassador even at a medium-sized post could not, even if he wanted to, read all the messages coming in and out of his Mission, even before the days of classified e-mail. Even then, as today, he has to rely on his staff to tell him what he really needs to read.

So why do many people, including both professional Foreign Service Officers and amateurs with the money and/or political clout, lust after ambassadorships? For the professionals it is a mark of success. It is fun and liberating to have no one in your office who can tell you exactly what to do or when you can travel. People call you "Excellency" or, in French-speaking Africa, "*Son Excellence*," which always amused us. Most people know that being an ambassador is an interesting experience. They also know about Deputy Chiefs of Mission and what they are for. And for many of the wealthier, non-career envoys, the title "Ambassador," valid for life, is worth a new yacht or a mansion in Vail.

The most important part of the ambassador's course covered mundane but invaluable information on issues like managing an ambassadorial residence and coping with the financial aspects of life abroad. On these matters, Barbara took a separate course for spouses, which turned out to be more valuable than the one I took, especially when the man who taught hers, Joe Hilts, was subsequently assigned to be our budget and fiscal officer in Mali.

En route to Mali we had a family Thanksgiving with the children, hosted by sister Kathy at her house in Medford. The oven was in the process of dying and the turkey took all day to roast, so dinner was fashionably late, but we were most grateful for it, because the kids, unlike fluffy dog Pax, were not coming with us to Mali until their summer vacations. Our international flight was the familiar Francophone Africa two-step, first to Paris and then onwards across the Sahara to Mali's capital, Bamako. The connecting flight from Boston to JFK was late, and as a result we had to forfeit our USG-paid for First Class seats to Paris. This was highly annoying because ambassadors got to travel First Class only on their initial arrivals and final departures to and from their posts, and we were looking forward to relishing this rare perk.

But First Class had been filled with standbys by the time we got to the check-in counter, and even Business Class was very crowded, so United gave us separate seats! We couldn't wait for a later flight, because Pax, coming separately from Boston, was already on the plane. That was too much: Barbara was fit to be tied, and she demanded and we got seats together, but they were right next to the smelly, noisy galley. As usual, the subsequent French UTA (*Union Transport Aérienne*) flight to Bamako turned out to be the nicest part of the trip.

We had a special treat in Paris, where we lingered for a day or two so Bob could consult with a range of valuable colleagues at the US Embassy there. We decided to go to the opera, still performing at the Palais Garnier. (The new, much larger, opera house at the Bastille would open a year later.) The performance, which as we recall was Verdi's *Macbeth*, turned out to be a gala. In a panic to be more-or-less suitably dressed, we acquired a starched white shirt and black bow tie (*papillon*) for Bob to wear with the dark suit which we had with us in case of early presentation of credentials in Mali.

However, we discovered that a wide variety of dress was acceptable at galas in Paris, at least in the 1980s; we both remember the gentleman dressed in English tweeds, seemingly all ready for a fox hunt. Though we had seats with a partially obscured view, we enjoyed the performance thoroughly; the lead role was sung by bass-baritone Simon Estes, whom we almost heard again in South Africa. That story comes later.

Arriving in Bamako

Ruffles and flourishes aside, going to Bamako was in many ways more like a homecoming than a new adventure. Mali had been part of the same French West African federation as Burkina Faso, and our new home, which we had already visited three years previously when our friend Parker Borg was ambassador,[2] was only a day's drive from our old one in Ouagadougou. Mali, like Burkina, is a part of the Sahel, an Arabic word meaning "just below the desert." Annual rainfall decreases exponentially as one travels north, from near-tropical in the far south, to lethally dry in the far north.

Unlike Burkina, Mali is largely defined by a really big river, the Niger, the "Strong Brown God" of local folklore. It is 2,600 miles long,[3] the fourteenth longest in the world. It rises in the highlands of Guinea and Sierra Leone, southwest of Mali, flows northeastwards, then pauses in the inland Niger Delta, which floods after every rainy season forming a big seasonal lake at the downstream end (Lake Debo). The river then describes an arc through the desert, the "buckle" of the Niger in French terminology, near the top of which, for good reason, is the city of Timbuktu.

Finally it heads southwards and exits through a more normal coastal delta on the coast of Nigeria. This delta was the first part of the Niger to be discovered by Europeans. Although highly malarial, it was full of palm trees rich in oil, which could be used in making better soap (produced more lather, therefore cleaned better) than anything then used in Europe. However, large-scale trade in oil had to wait until the invention of the steamboat, which could fight the current going upriver, to establish oil-palm plantations in the delta and to explore upriver from it. The French, advancing inland

---

[2] See Chapter Nine.
[3] The classic work on the river is Sanche de Gramont, aka Ted Morgan, *Strong Brown God: The Story of the Niger River*, London, 1975.

from their much older base in Senegal, did not colonize Mali
until late in the nineteenth century.

When the French did arrive, they chose their capital
well. Unlike Ouagadougou, a dusty crossroads on a largely
featureless plateau, Bamako is on the great river, its old
colonial buildings perched on a high escarpment looking out
over what has recently become a sprawling city. It has the
kind of geomantic aesthetic appeal that the Chinese seek for
burial sites. It is within the relatively well-watered southern
third of Mali, and in an average year receives about as much
rainfall as Washington, DC.

When we arrived in 1987, Mali's population was almost
eight million. Today (2017) it is double that and going up at an
annual rate of three percent. Despite recent development of
the gold industry, Mali remains one of the poorest countries in
the world. The population consists primarily of black Africans,
with the Bambara (or Bamana) group the most numerous,
comprising about half the population. Other "black" groups
include the Songhai, Peuhl and Dogon. There are nagging
political as well as racial and linguistic differences between
some of these people and the lighter skinned nomadic groups
of the desert north. These include a small Arab, or Maur
population, most importantly in Timbuktu, and a larger group
of Berber-speaking Tuaregs, or Tamashek. Bambara is almost
but not quite a *lingua franca*; French remains the language of
government and higher education. About 94% of Malians are
Muslims, 2.4% Christians, and the remainder, most famously
the Dogon, still practice traditional animist religions. [4]

Mali is often described as the size of Texas and California
combined. But if you regard the "Texas" half as the desert
segment, you must remember that, impressive as it looks on
a map, less than one percent of the national population lives
there. Only a tiny few are truly in the desert, in widely scattered
oases. More are in towns along the great river, which forms most
of the border between the two halves. This is a geopolitical fact
of great importance, because the real Sahara, north of the river,
is a different world. To exaggerate only slightly, because almost

---

[4] Figures are extrapolated from the CIA World Factbook as of April, 2013,
and Pascal James and Gavin Imperato, *Historical Dictionary of Mali*, 4th
ed., 2008.

no one can live in the waterless interior, no one has ever truly governed it, at least not up to now.

In 1987, the ambassador's Residence was on an unpaved street, almost but not quite bordering the river. There is a story to the effect that the first US Ambassador, appointed after Mali's independence in 1960, personally selected it. He was, it was said, a Foreign Service Officer of the old school, with deep pockets, and he wanted a Residence appropriate for entertaining, so he travelled to Mali to find one before he was formally designated. He spotted a big house near the river, knocked on the door, and asked the owner, a French businessman, if he would be willing to sell it. The owner replied, "Why not, we [the French] are leaving, and this place [Mali] will no doubt go down the drain fast." Our hero proceeded to clinch the deal with his own money, having no doubt that the State Department would in due time pay him back, which it did. To anyone familiar with the extraordinary bureaucratic hassle involved in State Department real estate procurement today, this story seems unbelievable.

We soon settled into our Bamako routine. Marilyn Mattke, my new secretary, arrived in April, 1988. We acquired a Suzuki four-wheel drive; it resembled and had the same comfort quotient as a World War II jeep, but it served Barbara well in negotiating Bamako's rutted streets, especially in the rainy season when many of them turned into mud. When we travelled out of town, we got to use an embassy 4x4— the term "sport utility vehicle" had not yet been invented— driven by Sekou, my driver. This time it was a fully functional Toyota Land Cruiser, rather than a break-down prone (but American made) Ford Bronco, like the one we had suffered with in Ouagadougou.

The Residence was partially a one-storey building, with a second storey over the bedroom wing. There was a lawn in front, useful for Fourth of July ceremonies, and substantial gardens in back where I grew roses, or, more correctly, supervised the gardener who grew them. The rear area also included a large swimming pool, surrounded by a terrace with a bar suitable for big, buffet dinners, and an air-conditioned guest suite separate from the house.

The compound was surrounded by a wall, just beyond

which on two sides were big trees called "*calcedras*," which the French had brought from Indochina. These trees supported a large colony of fruit bats with wing spans of at least three feet, as well as a number of tiny owls, Pearl-spotted Owlets. It took us over a year to see and identify the owls; at first we knew them mainly from their song, a rising, then falling duet sung between the male and female. Although tiny, they are ferocious predators of small birds, as we learned later in southern Africa.

There was a short, graveled driveway where my driver, Sekou, parked my absurd, American-made official car, for urban use only, and Barbara parked the little blue Suzuki. Early on, I learned that every year at the end of the Muslim fasting month, the servants saved money to buy a cow, which they slaughtered in the driveway, dividing the meat for a festive meal. This struck me as a horrid idea. Here I was, the ambassador of a mainly Christian country, allowing this gruesome Islamic(?) spectacle in the driveway of *my* Residence. This objection got me nowhere. Sekou assured me that the deed would be done at dawn, and that no remains whatever, not a drop of blood, would remain by breakfast time. And so it came to pass.

As for the bats, they were quite wonderful, but chronically under-appreciated for several reasons. To begin with, most westerners simply don't like bats. These bats were not only huge, they were noisy and restless. Even during the day when they were supposed to be sleeping, they were always chattering and jostling each other as they hung upside down, having batty dreams.

Then there was the problem of their inefficient digestive system, which caused them to excrete a substance resembling mango pulp, or marmalade, which often landed in our swimming pool. In addition, being large and edible, they attracted small boys with slingshots who tried to shoot them from the street beyond our walls. The boys almost always missed the bats, but the rocks they launched often came down inside the garden wall, breaking the glass tops on our terrace tables, requiring replacements to be ordered from the US at taxpayer expense.

For all their faults, the bats were responsible for a great

Foreign Service story. One of my predecessors, elderly and formal, decided to do something about chronic bat poop in her swimming pool. After much work, the embassy's long-suffering GSO (General Services Office) found a tarp big enough to cover the entire pool and ordered it from a high-end supplier of pool-care paraphernalia in the US (we had to buy this American). The ambassador instructed the servants at length to take the best possible care of it.

All went well for several months until she rose earlier than usual one morning. Looking out of her window she saw the gardener and the houseboy, who were already at work, lift the poop-smeared tarp, flip it over, and carefully rinse it in the pool before folding it up for the day, well cleaned as per instructions. It had disappeared by our time in Bamako.

The bats departed on an annual migration every May. We had no idea where they went. We did not miss them and did not know about their environmental role as seed distributors, helping to regenerate Africa's disappearing savannah forest. (They had not yet been accused of spreading Ebola; that would come much later.) I learned more about them years afterwards when I was working on international environmental issues at the State Department and met Merlin Tuttle, head of Bat Conservation International, based in Texas—that story is in a later chapter.

We settled into our new house as smoothly as could be expected. Our sea freight had arrived, as, finally, did the air freight, which had mistakenly been sent to Durban, South Africa. There it had sat in a warehouse for several months (including December, with all our Christmas decorations inside), until someone asked why several crates for the ambassador in Bamako were thousands of miles south of that city. So the final unpacking took place in April, at which time Barbara observed, "As our houses get more and more completely furnished and our artifact collection gets bigger and bigger, that feat becomes more and more difficult." Further, "besides, here the majority of our living-dining room décor has to be American. And it is hard to put a three-foot mask [from Burkina or New Guinea] in the corner of a closet. Not to mention Annie's grass skirt from the Trobriand

Islands."[5] (Wonder what ever happened to *that*?)

The house had nice downstairs bedrooms for the kids, waiting for their arrival on vacation. The living room furniture, comfortable but somewhat shabby, was slated for reupholstering, and Barbara succeeded in getting permission to purchase colorful fabric locally rather than importing the white or beige material, wildly inappropriate for the dusty environment, proposed by State Department decorators in Washington. Luckily the house had a new model of louvered windows, which let in less dust than the old model, familiar to us from Ouagadougou, although a red film still accumulated on everything once the rainy season stopped.

The electrical wiring was miscellaneous, and no one except an elderly Frenchman who had retired to Bamako with his Malian wife came close to understanding it. Fortunately he lived only a few blocks away and was always available, regardless of the hour, when a power outage occurred.

The embassy itself, more correctly the chancery, was about a ten-minute drive away on Rue Rochester, so named after a sister city relationship between Bamako and Rochester, NY. It was a former bank building with thick walls and labyrinthine layout, and housed only senior staff. Most of our Malian employees and the administrative offices were across a narrow street, making it hard to meet with them. All the surrounding streets were narrow and jammed with traffic.

My office looked down onto the front porch of a Lebanese-owned café. There were some Lebanese Shiite Muslims in Bamako, considered unsafe from a security perspective even then, and we were officially disturbed when a Lebanese Shiite construction company based in Ivory Coast was awarded the contract to build a new West African Central Bank headquarters immediately in front of our Residence. However, we assumed that the proprietor of the café within shouting distance of my office was safe because his daughter, not resident in Bamako, was married to a US Foreign Service Officer, or so I was told.

---

[5] Barbara letter to Dear Mother and Daddy, April 25, 1988. (This is a fairly short hand-written letter the main purpose of which was to ask Mother to send cooling racks for cakes and canning jars from the US, one of many such utilitarian requests that she helpfully fulfilled.)

Embassy Bamako was slightly larger than Embassy Ouagadougou. The State Department staff consisted of myself; my secretary, Marilyn Mattke, who also worked for the DCM, John H. Lewis; two political-economic officers, one of whom was a part-time consular officer, Jane Buchmiller and Patty Culpepper; an information (USIS) officer, Arlene Jaquette, then Linda Buggeln; a doctor, Tom Lucas; a junior officer who rotated through various positions, Carol Stricker; an administrative officer, Stan Jakubowski; a financial officer, Joe Hilts (later), and toward the end of my tour, a security officer who went on to be a hero in Liberia, John Frese.

Mali also had a small CIA station, which Ouaga did not. The AID staff was about the same size as the State Department contingent, headed by a Mission Director, first Gene Chiaverolli and later Dennis Brennan, and their respective deputies. Malian Foreign Service Nationals (FSNs) outnumbered our American staff and were indispensible at every level.

The DCM, John H. Lewis, was a bright bachelor who had preceded me and was replaced toward the end of my tour by John Boardman. Peace Corps had a Director, Hilary Whittaker; a nurse, Shirley Furst, who was the American wife of the World Bank Resident Representative, Michael Furst; and several senior Malian employees, including Mariam Traoré, the wife of senior embassy FSN Gaoussou Traoré, about whom more below. Finally we were served, although not often, by military attachés based in Dakar, who had an airplane we could use if it accorded with their priority job of intelligence gathering. The plane was very small, not like the attaché DC-3s of fragrant memory in Jakarta and Manila. In short, we were a middle-sized African post, typical for the era.

On my commute to the office, I first heard traditional Malian songs and poems, which were daily fare on local radio. My driver, Sekou, was a *griot*, a member of the hereditary entertainer *cum* historian class. He explained to me that the poems were often stories about the history of the Mali Empire, the most famous of three great, multi-ethnic empires which are the pride of the country's long history. It reminded me of the Iban oral history that was popular on Radio Sarawak, and I learned that the Malians were similarly infatuated with their own past. They were especially proud of the multi-ethnicity of the empires which, they believed, had given them an ability, unusual in Africa, to govern across boundaries of language and tribe.

In 1987 this tradition was being invoked to justify a Marxist-style, single party regime. In theory, in former times all the chiefs and elders had assembled to discuss affairs of state with their wise monarch; he would listen to their arguments and then make his decisions, which all would then obey. Later, beginning in 1991, the same theory would be tweaked to legitimize a genuine, multi-party, decentralized democracy. It would succeed for over two decades, but since then has had severe ups and downs owing mainly to worsening unrest in the desert north.

I presented my credentials to President Moussa Traoré on December 15, 1987, eleven days following our arrival, after which I was officially in business as ambassador. My formal diplomatic duties were not onerous. The most annoying was being convoked to the airport when the President or any visiting chief of state arrived or departed. All twenty or so ambassadors had to line up on the often blistering hot tarmac in order of precedence, determined by when one had presented one's credentials, until the dignitary arrived or departed. I had the Soviet on one side and the Mauritanian on the other, both quite charming.

This antique custom did provide an opportunity to meet ministers, who were also convoked, and sometimes to get a little business done, and the drives to and from the airport were abnormally fast because the road was blocked off, creating huge traffic snarls for others. During the hot season, excellencies sported a variety of picturesque hats to prevent sunstroke; I thought of asking my sister Margot to send me a cowboy hat so I could be suitably and practically "American," but never got around to it.

Toward the end of my tour, we were convoked to bid farewell to the President of Guinea-Bissau, a small, ex-Portuguese colony on the coast of the African bulge. This small country is a hot, humid, low-lying place where it is impossible to grow temperate-climate produce. Being on a plateau and nothing if not dry, Mali does not have this problem. So the President and his staff spent the end of their stay up country shopping for vegetables.

The next day the assembled diplomatic corps watched from the tarmac as a Malian Army truck unloaded clay pots, mats, many sacks of fruits and vegetables and one forlorn live sheep. Once all this was on board, the Malian and Guinea-Bissauan national anthems were played, the President and his entourage boarded, doors were closed and the engines started.

And then, nothing. What seemed like hours passed while we sweated. Finally the rear hatch of the plane opened and an enormous sack of potatoes dropped with a splat on the runway, after which the flight took off at last. It had obviously been too tail heavy to get off the ground.[6]

The sheep, no doubt given to the president by some village, stayed on the plane. We knew about this, because we had experienced frequent grief with gift sheep. You couldn't just say, "No, thanks." The best sheep we ever received, a magnificent ram with big horns, we were able to give to a deserving missionary a few villages down the road.

According to State Department regulations at the time, an ambassador could not accept any gift worth more than $60, but had to forward it to the Chief of Protocol in Washington. I always wanted to stuff the next gift sheep in the diplomatic pouch—the really big ones were surely worth more than $60—and imagine the expression on the Chief of Protocol's face when he (or she) opened my present.

Parker Borg had told us that one of the best things about the job would be travel within Mali. I should do as much as I could, he said; the country is charming and interesting, and Washington won't know or care where you are. At first travel would be necessary to get to know Mali. Later, since I was theoretically responsible for everything connected with US policy and presence, I would need to keep my country knowledge honed.

We listened to Parker when he urged us to camp out as much possible in rural areas, since local hotels, when they existed, were often less than comfortable. Alternatively, one could stay with Peace Corps volunteers, about 150 of whom were in villages around the country. We always went

---

[6] Bob letter to Dear Family, April 8, 1989, mostly a description of my daily routine.

well supplied with homemade chocolate chip cookies and sometimes took the village-based volunteers to dinner in town, if there was one near enough. Otherwise, we paid the village women to prepare a dinner to be eaten at our host's modest establishment. Sleeping accommodations were often under a mosquito net on the flat roof of his or her dwelling—much cooler than an inside room.

I continued my habit of writing informal trip reports on what we had learned. They usually did not need classification beyond marking them "For Official Use Only, Not for Publication." It was a label with no official significance, but no one ever published one. Barbara almost always went with me because she is a much more skilled and experienced camper than I am, and such travel was the icing on the cake of her otherwise unpaid employment as spouse of a chief of mission.

I was advised, and good advice it was, to take Gaoussou Traoré (no relation to Mali's President—Traoré is a common name in Mali) along with us on our travels, especially at first. Gaoussou has a degree in animal husbandry from Arizona State University. He had written his doctoral thesis on the seasonal migration of cattle in and out of the Niger's Inner Delta, the huge area which the great river floods every year after the summer rains. He administered the embassy's Special Self-Help small-project program, similar to the one we had in Burkina, the same one I had administered in AF/EPS.

First Visit to Timbuktu

One of our earlier trips, in January 1988, was, of course, to Timbuktu, the only Malian city with universal name recognition, despite the fact that many people think it is probably fictional, much less know where the real city is.[7] To get there, we traveled along a route we would come to know well, northeast from Bamako, paralleling the south bank of the Niger River, then crossing it at Markala, at the upstream end of the Delta.

Here one could still see the remains of heavy equipment

[7] Any letter about this trip has been lost, but there are lots of photos; for the approximate date, see Barbara letter to Dear Family, August 7, 1988.

that we had donated to France after World War II under the Marshall Plan to complete a vast irrigation project. Operated by the Niger Authority (*Office du Niger*), the project had been conceived in the 1920s to liberate France from dependence on British and American cotton. It had envisioned a railroad across the Sahara, which was to have crossed the dam-cum-bridge at Markala. Dreams of cotton self-sufficiency had vanished by the time Mali became independent in 1960, but the Niger Authority survived as a giant project for growing rice. Laborers remained mostly the descendants of workers the French had imported from our old home, Upper Volta/ Burkina Faso, then part of the same French West African federation as Mali.

Beyond Markala, the road to Timbuktu skirted the northwestern edge of the Niger Delta, through a series of river towns: Goundam, Léré, Tonka and others. Our standard conveyance for such trips was a Toyota Land Cruiser with a roof rack for extra fuel and plenty of space behind the passenger seats for carrying water, tents, food coolers and

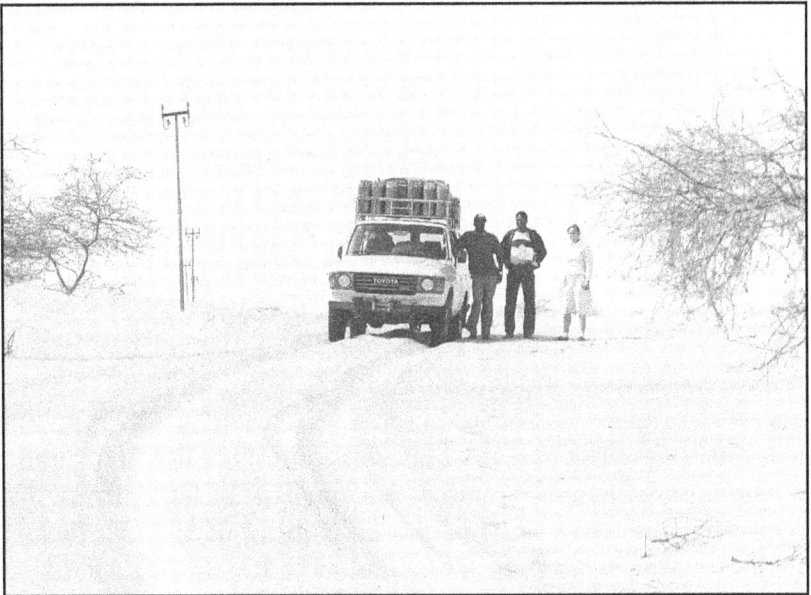

The road to Timbuktu, with, from left, driver Sekou, political and economic adviser to the embassy and friend, Gaoussou Traore, and Barbara. To get to Timubuktu, stay between the old telegraph line and the Niger River.

duffel bags. The road was ungraded dirt or sand, a *piste* or "track" in local parlance. Deep sand can be more treacherous than mud, so we always carried sand ladders to escape from it, the desert equivalent of chains for snow. They were made from strips of perforated steel Marsden matting, which was familiar to us from Papua New Guinea, where it was used for everything from runways to fences.

En route to Timbuktu, to avoid straying into full desert, the rule was to keep the river on your right and a row of rickety telegraph poles on your left. Navigating the river towns was tricky because, on the outskirts of each one, the *piste* fragmented into numerous unmarked tracks and it was impossible to know which one was the real road to Timbuktu, as opposed to one that would trap you in a mud-brick, sand-clogged maze. Of course such unintended exploration was educational up to a point. On this trip we got lost near Tonka and unsuccessfully tried to ask directions from a picturesque, turbaned elder carrying an ornate flintlock rifle. Even Gaoussou didn't speak whatever his language was.

In Timbuktu we visited its mud-brick mosques, which usually underwhelm visitors who have visions of Oriental opulence. (Mali's most spectacular mosque, also mud-brick but rising elegantly on the edge of a market square, is downriver at Djenné, a much older town than Timbuktu.) There was already a passable hotel, a rarity for Mali, frequented by a growing trickle of tourists. There had been no regular air service since a serious crash several years earlier. We witnessed a Songhai wedding by peering over a wall into the compound. We saw the old houses where various explorers had stayed.

Not until later did we learn about the ancient books and manuscripts kept hidden by Timbuktu's inhabitants in very private libraries. They are relics of a time centuries ago when this city was a link in trans-Saharan commerce involving gold, ivory, and kola nuts—and often slaves—arriving from the south by river and finished goods coming across the desert from the Mediterranean. This had been one of Africa's major trade routes until, due to European arrival along the coast, it was eclipsed by the modern sea route.

On the way home, we encountered a file of camels each carrying huge slabs of grey salt strapped to their sides, driven

Arab traders and their donkeys carrying slabs of salt from Taoudenni to the Niger river port of Mopti.

Young women carrying firewood in the Dogon country.

by local Arabs, or "Maurs." At first, because of their blue turbans, we assumed mistakenly that they were Mali's more famous Tuareg people.[8] They were coming from Taoudenni, far to the north on the Algerian border, where the salt was mined from dry lakebeds. The mines were worked under famously hellish conditions by political prisoners and indentured servants, some of them from the tiny settlement of Araouane, about 250 kilometers north of Timbuktu, which

---

[8] The salt train photos were used on our 1988 Christmas card.

had been almost totally recaptured by the desert by our time.

An eccentric Swiss-American, Ernst Aebi, artist-cum-real estate developer cum globetrotter, tried to revive Araouane in the late 1980s, in the process freeing several debt slaves by purchasing their contracts. He thereby proved that slavery still existed in Mali, as we knew it did on a large scale in Mauritania, Mali's neighbor to the West, a fact which we duly reported because it was of interest to human rights specialists in the State Department. [9]

Aebi persuaded Araouane's remaining villagers to dig out the sand-clogged wells and got everyone growing vegetables. He also started a hotel, which he named the Araouane Hilton, hoping that the Hilton chain would attack him and generate useful publicity (as far as I know, it never did). The village was trashed by rebels in the early 1990s, and Aebi left, apparently for good, although it may be once again getting some attention as this written. [10]

Today, the salt itself is taken by caravan and river boat to Mopti, where the slabs are broken into more manageable chunks for sale all over West Africa, and we still have several small hunks in our spice drawer. The dirt that discolors it is supposed to have medicinal properties, but visitors who are startled by its color also have to be aware that this salt is used

---

[9] The French did not officially reach Araouane until 1925; see William Seabrook, *The White Monk of Timbuktoo*, New York, 1934, for the French arrival there; also John Skolle, *Azalai*, New York, 1955, on the awfulness of Taoudenni. There is more on Araouane's history in its surprisingly thorough Wikipedia entry.

[10] Aebi's extraordinary book on his Araouane adventure (*Seasons of Sand: One Man's Quest to Save a Dying Sahara Village*) was published by Simon and Schuster in 1993, after the place was ruined by rebels. Aebi was supported by Lamine Diabaré, an equally zany military officer who was the governor of Timbuktu, whose territory included Araouane. Diabaré told Aebi not to worry about bureaucratic formalities, which were being insisted on by his subordinates, on the theory that anyone mad enough to live in Araouane and to try to help its bone-poor inhabitants deserved his unconditional support. Diabaré was later arrested for coup plotting, although the plot was apparently not serious, if it existed at all, and he had been released by the time we revisited Mali in 2007. He was a graduate of the US Command and General Staff College at Fort Leavenworth and once begged me to get him listed on its list of notable alumni because of his Timbuktu governorship. I tried, but didn't succeed.

in cooking; it is never just shaken on prepared food.

We soon realized why the Niger River was both the backbone and the soul of Mali, its Strong Brown God indeed. Our future trips often took us on a variation of the Timbuktu itinerary described above. Instead of crossing the river at Markala, we would keep going northeast, around the southeastern edge of the Delta, through an increasingly arid landscape. This route followed a good two-lane paved road, the main one ultimately heading east to Gao. In either case, there was a mandatory coffee stop at a Lebanese café in Segou, which was the headquarters of the Niger Authority (*Office du Niger*) and had been an army base since French days.

On one occasion, I had to attend a ceremony there commemorating the birthday of Mali's sole political party, because the President was attending and the diplomatic corps was convoked. I was amazed when, in addition to boat races on the river, big canoes carrying spectacular, much larger-than-life puppets, passed in front of the reviewing stand. One of my pictures of them was published in a book on the subject,[11] but I never saw them again. Barbara, having stayed home since I had told her that the Segou celebration would be thoroughly boring, was most annoyed.[12]

Beyond Segou, the main road crossed the Bani, a major tributary of the Niger coming in from the southeast. Not long after this crossing was a turnoff to the headquarters of *Mali Aqua Viva*, a project run by Father Bernard Vespieren, a cantankerous, charismatic, quasi-retired French priest from the famous missionary order of the White Fathers. Parker Borg had warned us to let him know if we wanted to visit because otherwise, ambassador or no, he would throw us out, and we followed his advice. Père Vespieren turned out to be very hospitable when we called on him early in our stay.

Mali Aqua Viva was making and distributing solar-powered water pumps to villages across Mali, and Vespieren was even training Malian technicians to support them. They cost a lot of money, around $15,000, but one pump could supply water to

---

[11] Mary Jo Arnoldi, *Playing with Time: Art and Performance in Central Mali*, Bloomington, 1995.

[12] This took place early in 1989; see Barbara to Dear Family, January 15, 1989.

Famous but rarely seen river puppets made by the Bozo people, mobilized at Segou to greet the President of Mali.

an entire village. Vespieren knew important people in France who sent him money and new solar technology to experiment with, and he was clearly an expert on his subject. He had more than 500 hectares of land under solar-powered irrigation, plus fishponds, a cattle raising-biogas project, ample guest quarters and an 800-meter airstrip for the French VIPs who flocked to see him. He seemed to be succeeding, but as is so often the case with such projects, this one did not long outlive its founder, and when we visited Mali again twenty years later, he and his solar-powered pumps were gone.[13]

Star Attractions of Central Mali

Five extraordinary attractions (not counting Timbuktu) are located around the big river port of Mopti, about four hours drive northeast of Segou. They include the Dogon Country, Mali's answer to Monument Valley, the home of some rare

---

[13] Vespieren was the subject of the first of my 12 trip reports written in Mali: "A Visit to *Teriya Bugu* [House of Friendship in Bambara]: Solar and Other Development in Southern Mali," December 26, 1987. For more on this remarkable man see http://www.tb-mali.com/e-father-bernard-verspieren.html. He died in 2003.

desert-dwelling elephants, the vast Inner Niger Delta, and the ancient city of Djenné. All these places are within driving distance of Mopti, although to see them adequately takes several days.

Star One: the Dogon Country

Driving east from Mopti, it takes about an hour to reach the land of the Dogon, who are said to have fled there to escape conquest and conversion to Islam. Dogon villages are perched on and around the Falaise of Bandiagara, a spectacular line of cliffs. The Dogon have remained mainly animist, with some conversion to Christianity, and are famous above all for their spectacular art, in the shape of dance masks, granary doors, rock paintings, house posts, and a wide variety of statuary. By the time we arrived in Mali, classic Dogon art was priced way beyond our means, although we did find one piece, an elder riding on a tiger on top of an elephant, which is too weird to be considered classic but is very appealing.

The Dogon cultivate millet, sorghum and onions, the latter grown in small raised beds on hard rock surfaces, fashioned from stones, then filled with soil. They are irrigated by hand from nearby seasonal streams which, after a good rain year, flow in spectacular falls over the cliffs, landing near lines of mud-brick villages. In my trip report I got off a homily on the economics of Dogon onion production:

There is a mystique about Dogon onions. They are supposed to taste absolutely superior, and local chiefs give them away to visiting dignitaries the way chiefs in other parts of Mali give away chickens and sheep. And the onion patches, perpetually being watered by Dogon villagers, who carry the water up from nearby streams in calabashes, are a favorite tourist photo opportunity along the road from Bandiagara to Sangha.

Traditionally, the Dogons pounded the onions into a paste [which was] formed into little round balls, which were and are exported all over neighboring West Africa and beyond. Nowadays a lot of onions are exported fresh as well. There seems to be little doubt that processed onions are a better deal, and [are] a good example of a rural agricultural processing industry with a significant value-added feature. That is to say, raw inions sell on the Sangha market for approximately CFA 120 a kilo, whereas onion balls are currently fetching CFA 500 a kilo.

Inevitably, perhaps, there seems to be an onion glut developing in the Dogon country. This is, however, one problem that we don't have to worry about, since the Germans, who have cleverly staked out the Bandiagara Plateau as their "aid territory," are fully engaged with it. German aid is currently conducting a study of the Dogon onion market, and the Germans are even investigating the possibility of exporting high-grade Dogon onions to Europe by air. Who knows, in a few more years, Dogon onions may show up in Mali's export statistics. When it comes to exports, one thing is certain, every little bit helps.[14]

In the cliff face itself, ancestors of the Dogon, the Tellem, are buried. To the south and east, below the *falaise,* a broad plain with more Dogon villages stretches away toward Burkina. Here we were actually closer to our old home in Ouagadougou than to our new one in Bamako.

Star Two: Mali's Monument Valley.

Driving northeast from Mopti, cutting across the big northward curve of the Niger, the German-built highway to Gao skirts the northern edge of the Dogon Plateau. The high plain gradually trails off into a series of towering rock formations reminiscent of Monument Valley, with names like Napoleon's Hat and Fatima's Hand (which has lost its finger since we lived there). During the rainy season, we once saw some deliriously happy camels wading around in big temporary ponds full of water lilies. Local villagers sometimes grow rice in such places when the water is plentiful enough, evidence that "wet rice" is not new in arid West Africa.

As the paved road begins to curve east at Douenza, a northbound dirt road goes off to the Niger River, where a ferry links it to Timbuktu. This became the preferred route to the fabled city in the 1990s after Governor Diabaré, mentioned

---

[14] Trip report, "Notes on a Trip to Macena, Tennenkou, Jenné and Sangha, January 25-31, 1989."

earlier, used his troops to make it passable. His road, of which he was extremely proud, was used after the 2011 coup by rebel forces trying to get a foothold in the south.

Beyond Douenza, still amid the rock formations mentioned above, there are settlements of Songhai people, including a big village at Hombori,[15] located on a highly defensible cliff adjacent to the road. The Songhai, whose settlements we had seen previously in Burkina, inhabit the whole region, along with Peuhl (Fulani), Tuareg[16] and a few Arabic-speaking nomads, and they are probably the most numerous inhabitants of Timbuktu itself. More important, they were rulers of the last of Mali's three great empires, with its capital at Gao, the ultimate destination of the road through Hombori. The Songhai Empire was overthrown by a Moroccan invasion in 1591, which ended old Mali's period of greatness, leading to a long period of anarchy and domination of the north by feuding Tuareg factions.

Star Three: Desert Elephants

While Hombori had no hotel, it did have what we called the "Hombori Hilton," a modest structure officially used as a warehouse by a World Bank cattle project directed by Noumou Diakité. From him we learned to our astonishment that the area north of the Mopti-Gao highway, known as the Gourma, is home at certain times of year to a herd of several hundred elephants. The northernmost elephants in Africa, they migrate every year in a circular track between the Mali-Burkina Faso border and the Niger River. They are not in any kind of protected area and, and although they are not

---

[15] An indicator of how much this region was affected by the 2011 coup: in November, 2011, a French tourist was kidnapped in Hombori by Islamic extremists invading from the north. They reportedly beheaded him in March, 2013, in retaliation for the French intervention in Mali. *New York Times*, March 20, 2013, p. A6. Since then the situation has steadily worsened.

[16] Including Bella. Although previously "enslaved," most Bella today identify themselves as Tuareg and speak Tamashek. The relationship may have been more feudal than one of slavery in the sense we know it.

*Camels relishing a seasonal swamp in front of Fatima's Hand in Mali's
"Monument Valley."*

unknown to elephant experts,[17] no one in Bamako seemed
to know anything about them. Diakité led us on several

---

[17] The best published account, and a very good one, is "Gourma Elephant
Reserve" in Anthony Hall-Martin, *Elephants of Africa*, Cape Town,
Struikhof Publishers, 1986, pp. 24-29.

Desert elephants south of the Niger River bend, the northernmost herd in Africa. They migrate in a circular path, coexisting with herders and farmers in the area. The Tuareg say that if the elephants thrive, so will they, affording a certain amount of protection for the animals.

memorable expeditions to see these elephants, sometimes using the Hombori Hilton as a base.

These are desert elephants, similar to those in Namibia, which also migrate long distances. They are notable for their large size—among the largest African elephants anywhere—and small, stubby tusks, probably worn down by digging in dry streambeds for water, but surely one reason why they have escaped the attention of ivory hunters. In addition, the Tuareg inhabitants of the Gourma view these elephants as harbingers of good fortune and have not traditionally harmed them; the fierce reputation of the Tuareg has also discouraged other ethnic groups from doing so.

Diakité is a man of many parts. Although a veterinarian, he administered shots to Peace Corps volunteers when they were assigned in the Mopti area, where he lives. As director of the World Bank cattle project, he had become fascinated by the elephants, and during the catastrophic drought of the early 1980s he had used the project's tank truck to haul water

to them. I was confused at first, because I had met another
Noumou Diakité who was Mali's ambassador to the UN. The
veterinarian Noumou explained, "There are four of us. In
Bambara (Bamana) society it is customary to give the first-
born son of each wife the same name. So I have three brothers
with the same name as I do."

On our first expedition, with Annie along, we initially saw
nothing more exciting than "*traces,*" elephant droppings,
some ancient, some moist. I began to think Mali should be
exporting this stuff: "Grow Giant Grey Tomatoes with Our
Special Fertilizer." Finally, near dusk on the second day, we
saw dust, and after some maneuvering, we perceived a file of
elephants, with their trunks held high in the air trying to locate
us by our scent, which by this time must have been powerful.
What a kick! They ran off, but we got a better look at them the
next day.[18] We learned that, quite unlike tourist-acclimated
East African elephants, they were afraid of vehicles, but quite
unafraid of humans on foot! From then on, we would see
them most often as we explored on foot around the seasonal
lakes where they drank, often mixed up with cows and the
small boys herding them. Recently they have received more
attention, but the problem of elephants coexisting with
increasing numbers of herders and gardeners has become
more serious, not withstanding the benign traditional Tuareg
sentiment toward them.

Star Four: The Niger's Inner Delta

Mopti is also one of several jumping-off points for entering
the Niger Delta. During the dry season you can drive, trying to
follow tracks in the sand, into the labyrinthine spaces of the
Delta. Later, after the rains, you can go by boat. In between
these seasons, it is mostly mud and often you can't get into

---

[18] "Discovering" the Gourma elephants warranted, or so I thought, an
official cable: "The Blue and the Grey: Tuaregs and Elephants Coexist
(for the Moment) in Mali," US Embassy cable, Bamako 2676, April 24,
1988. After leaving Mali I wrote an article on the Gourma elephants,
with Noumou Diakité, for a Kenyan wildlife journal: Pringle, Robert M.
and Noumou Diakité, "The Last Sahelian Elephants," *Swara,* Vol. 15 no. 5
(1992), pp. 24-27.

it at all. The true natives of the Delta include the Bozo, river people who live only by and on the river and are mostly fishermen. On higher ground the area is full of ancient towns and the mounds or "tells" marking where they once were. Many have been plundered for their archaeological riches, but others have probably escaped, because the Delta, which includes arms that no longer flood, is just too big and complex.

We first entered the Delta by vehicle to visit Youvarou, site of a project run by the International Union for the Conservation of Nature (IUCN). One of its objectives was to preserve islands of trees, which, during the months of high water, were host to large colonies of migratory birds, but were being cut for wood by a growing population. (We would come back later to see Youvarou at flood season, when many birds stop to breed there, while others use it as a way station on a longer migration to southern Africa.)

On the way, we had to cross shrinking patches of water full of people catching fish, often very big ones, as they were trapped by the receding river. It looked as if most of the fish were being caught, but owing apparently to the fertility of the Niger, they or their descendants would be back again the next year. (The dynamics of this process were being studied by the IUCN.) No one told us that the Niger also has a population of African Manatees, an intriguing fact that we discovered only when we returned to Mali years later.

Not long after our first visit, Prince Philip arrived in his capacity as royal patron of the IUCN. The notoriously cranky Prince was not as easy to host as his daughter, Princess Anne, had been in Ouagadougou, but he met his match in Mopti. He was scheduled to have dinner with the local district head (*commandant de cercle*) at the only hotel, but his host was very late. As he paced up and down, increasingly annoyed, Prince Philip noticed that the hotel walls were liberally decorated with mounted snake skins. When the poor official finally arrived, His Highness pounced. "You realize," he said, "that all these specimens which you have killed are *endangered species*??" "Oh no," replied the official, "They were all found on the highway run over by cars." Things only got worse the next day when the IUCN driver got lost in the tracks through the Delta while taking His Highness to Youvarou.

Star Five: The Great Mosque of Djenné

Everyone has heard of Timbuktu, but only one non-Malian in a thousand has heard of its older downstream partner, Djenné. To get there from our point of reference, Mopti, you drive back toward Bamako for about an hour and turn right, toward the Niger. The road goes along a built-up causeway over much lower land, some of it seasonally flooded, and at this point you are already in the Inner Delta.

While Timbuktu was by tradition founded only about five hundred years ago, Djenné is at least 1,500 years older. Located at the intersection of the Niger and its major Bani tributary, it was both a market center for other Delta towns and a way station for trans-Saharan trade heading to the Mediterranean via Timbuktu. It is famous partly because of the archaeological work done by Susan and Roderick McIntosh in 1977, which established that Djenné, or more correctly its adjacent predecessor, Old Djenné (or Denné Djeno), was a truly urban settlement, meaning that it had had a significant, diversified population of specialized trade and craft groups, well before the arrival of Islam. Prior to the McIntoshs' work, an older generation of scholars had assumed that Black Africans could not possibly have established real cities on their own.

Most modern tourists visit Djenné because of its spectacular mud-brick mosque, the largest mud-brick (aka adobe) building in the world. It was reputed to have been built about the fourteenth century, but it was allowed to disintegrate after a radical Jihadist, Cheickou Amadou, conquered Djenné in 1815, destroyed the old mosque and forced the population to attend a new one.

When the French conquered Djenné in 1893, they reinstated the older, more religiously conservative, and less anti-French leaders of the city and encouraged them to rebuild the old mosque on its fourteeth-century foundations. This led to rumors, no doubt repeated by the opposing faction, that the French had actually built the present mosque from scratch. A classic study of this subject concludes that the French did not design the current mosque or build it from scratch.[19]

The great mosque of Djenné, as well as the old town itself, is a must stop for anyone visiting Mali. When we were there, it was possible to go inside and climb up on the roof, as we did with the children when we first visited it from Ouagadougou. Then an Italian film crew abused its permission to film inside by doing something allegedly pornographic, and the interior has been off limits to foreigners ever since, with occasional exceptions. What we most regret is never having seen the annual "plastering" (*crépissage*), a yearly festival event when the citizens of Djenné swarm over the structure on the timbers that protrude from it, put there for this purpose, not for decoration, and replenish the mud that has been washed away by the rains.

Travel made us painfully aware of Mali's deeply ingrained poverty. As in Burkina, most people were subsistence farmers, living in small villages without electricity or running water and far from the nearest real road, dirt paths being the norm. Women routinely walked long distances for water. Wells were shallow and primitive, one reason why the Peace Corps' well-drilling projects were among its most popular. Schools were primitive, if they existed at all, with thirty or more children crowded on benches in mud-floored, ill-lit classrooms.

During the short growing season, cultivating millet or sorghum in the stony soil was labor-intensive. People kept having children because many died in infancy, and child labor was needed to haul water, herd animals and help with unending chores. In other words, having as many children as possible was still a rational reaction to economic circumstances, even though it made faster economic growth, ultimately the key to ending poverty, extremely difficult. Unfortunately this situation has not changed significantly since we departed more than three decades ago.

US Economic Assistance

At the time I arrived, the United States was already a major

---

[19] Jean Louis Bourgeois, "The History of the Mosques of Djenné," *African Arts* 20, No. 3, May 1987, pp. 54-63 and 90-92.

donor of economic aid to Mali, especially if our financing of multilateral organizations like the World Bank and various UN agencies was taken into account. By 1987 USAID's policy emphasis had swung away from direct assistance to communities and toward attempting to increase economic incentives for farmers. As in Burkina, we did not have to worry about the government manipulating exchange rates to cheat producers and reap profits, because Mali was also part of the French-controlled franc zone and could not print its own money or set exchange rates.

What the Malian government did do that needed changing was typical of the bad policy of which I was well aware from AF/EPS. It was exemplified by the Niger Authority (*Office du Niger*), which kept prices paid to its rice farmers low to guarantee cheap rice to urban consumers, while at the same time employing as many middle-class Malians as possible. This was popular with everyone but the farmers, who had no incentive to produce more rice, and it made the Niger Authority into a money loser. Together with other donors, we pushed the government toward economic reform, meaning "getting prices right," so that farmers would be encouraged to grow more, not taxed into stagnation. These policies, known collectively as "conditionality," were often unpopular with African ruling classes, who regarded them as neo-colonial interference, but they worked in Mali, up to a point.

We and our fellow donors pushed the government to stop controlling food prices in the markets, and then we set up a rural radio system, based on US practice, so that farmers in rural areas would be informed about prices in neighboring towns, and be able to sell in whichever one of them was paying the best price.

When it came to bad policy, however, we did not always practice what we preached. Mali's most important cash crop, often grown by small farmers, was cotton, which thrives in semi-arid conditions. Malian and other western African cotton got a premium on world markets because it was all picked by hand, by black village women, summoning up for some Americans visions of the ante-bellum South. But by heavily subsidizing industrial-scale American cotton farmers, the US Government was lowering cotton prices worldwide, costing the Malians at one time more money than the total value of our aid program.[20]

USAID had lots more in its portfolio. We were still operating under the shadow of the extreme droughts of the early 1980s, and were just winding up a program to enhance "food security" by stockpiling grain in remote rural areas, along with the vehicles needed to distribute it, if and when drought recurred. In fact, as noted earlier, three decades would pass, until this writing, without another period of catastrophic drought, but one will surely happen as soon as the food security system falls into decay. (You can't win, etc.)

We were in the process of completing a regional center for immunizing cattle, a traditional Malian export to neighboring countries where cattle production was extremely difficult due to tsetse fly infestation. In addition, USAID supported a variety of NGOs which had programs of their own, including CARE, Africare and World Vision, whose projects covered forestry (Mali has considerable forested areas in its moister southern section), child nutrition, pump irrigation along the Niger River, and more.

My favorite USAID project, launched toward the end of our stay, was a joint effort with the French and the World Bank to reform education by increasing the number of primary schools in rural areas, where most people lived, and by reducing the proportion of funding allocated to tertiary education, which served almost exclusively the urban upper crust. It was quite an accomplishment to get the French to work with an English-speaking country like the United States on education in a French-speaking country. Interestingly enough, whereas Burkina Faso had a university, there was none in Mali, only an *Ecole Normale* for teachers, in part testimony to the innate conservatism of most Malians.

One thing that USAID no longer did was big bricks-and-mortar projects, and especially not dams. They were out of fashion, at least with us, and, not unrelated, they cost too much. We got involved only minimally with the Senegal River Project, which covered portions of western Mali, Senegal

---

[20] See Roger Thurow and Scot Kilman, "US Subsidies Create Cotton Glut That Hurts Foreign Cotton Farms," *Wall Street Journal*, June 26, 2002.

and Mauritania. There was already debate about the long-term efficacy of dams, and we took a dim view of Mauritania because of the persistence of slavery there (Arab-speaking nobles owning blacks). However, one of the project's biggest dams was, in fact, in Mali, at Manantali, on a major tributary of the Senegal River, and USAID did agree to pay for the resettlement of farmers displaced by the dam. Barbara and I visited the site in 1988 on our first trip to western Mali, and the reservoir was just beginning to fill up, a process that would take several years.

As ambassador, as noted earlier, I had little to say about the development or execution of the USAID program, which was by far our most important activity. Most of it seemed highly worthwhile to me, and I supported it as much as possible. However, soon after my arrival, I did get involved in a nonsensical administrative squabble involving a State Department decision to make other agencies pay their fair share of the costs of the embassy services they used—housing, security, travel services and more. USAID Washington resisted this effort and picked out Mali as a case where it felt that the new program would be especially unfair to them. But I was instructed in no uncertain terms to invoke my presidential authority to support the State Department.

This bothered me, not least because I knew little about the arcane details of embassy accounting, nor did anyone else on my small State Department administrative staff. Our AID Mission Director at that time, Gene Chiaverolli, was a capable professional who didn't trust State Department people generally and thought that ambassadors, in particular, never really appreciated what AID was doing. It was not a happy situation.

Then two things happened. First, Chiaverolli was replaced by Dennis Brennan, a naturalized American citizen of Irish descent, who was an old friend. Brennan felt that he had not come to Mali to argue about administrative trivia with the ambassador. Second, the embassy got a new administrative officer, Joe Hilts, the same expert who had taught the course on this subject at the Foreign Service Institute, to the wives no less. After looking at our books, Joe told me, "You know what? AID is right—the embassy has indeed been overcharging them for our services." Pouf! The biggest single managerial problem of my tour as ambassador suddenly vanished, without a further peep from Washington.

In the summer of 1988, as we neared the end of our first year in Mali, West Africa was hit by swarms of locusts of the Biblical variety.[21] They looked like huge, dust-green grasshoppers, and they came periodically in epic swarms out of the Middle East.[22] They were every bit as destructive as tradition would have it, and during a previous infestation a multi-national West African project, based in Mali, had been created to control them. Unfortunately, since the last such invasion the project had gone out of business, leaving only a collection of deserted buildings near the Niger Delta.

The locust project illustrated the transitory nature of foreign aid generally. Projects were typically established for a set period of time, after which the host country (in this case countries) was supposed to take over. But of course the host country was usually a poor place that could not afford the expenditure, which was the reason they had needed help in the first place. Sometimes the donor would relent and extend the project, sometimes a new donor would pick it up, but sometimes it just collapsed, as it had in this case.

We witnessed another example of why foreign aid is so flight-prone. The year I arrived, the Italians, of all people, were the number one bilateral aid donor to Mali, ahead of the French, the Germans, the US, everyone. They did not even have an embassy in Bamako, only an Italian lady married to a Malian who was a part-time honorary consul. One day someone in the Malian government called her and said, "There is a big column of trucks on the edge of town, which they say is for an Italian project. Do you know what is going on? We don't." The trucks were allowed to proceed, the Malians having learned

---

[21] This was the infestation that figured in the Malian president's state visit to the US; see below.

[22] Much progress has been made since we were in Mali in combating locusts and in understanding how, when stressed by hunger, these normally solitary grasshoppers form enormous migratory swarms. A swarm the size of Manhattan can in one day eat as much food as 42 million people. Rachel Nuwer, "Swarm," *New York Times*, Science Times, April 9, 2013, p. D7.

by this time that when some supposedly advanced country offers you aid, you should just accept it, mysteries and all.

In fact the Italians, as one might have expected, were doing some interesting and useful things. One of them was a center for the study of traditional medicine, located in the Dogon country, in a building constructed in Dogon style. They were also building a hospital in Timbuktu and a modern highway in the often neglected western part of Mali. Then, the year following the one in which they were Mali's leading aid donor, the Italian program vanished completely, victim of a huge scandal in Rome over misappropriation of Italian foreign aid funds.

The Peace Corps in Mali

The United States had a big Peace Corps program, around 125 volunteers, and like Burkina Faso, Mali was an ideal Peace Corps country. The people are charming and hospitable by nature; they love attention from the Great Outside; and they needed moral as well as technical support. The ideal PCV was a farm boy or girl with high technical aptitude, but an English literature PhD with the right personality could do very well. Peace Corps volunteers had changed a lot since we first encountered them in Sarawak two decades previously. In those days, many were ascetics, yearning for a vibrantly other-worldly experience that had nothing to do with government. But by 1987, many were well aware that Peace Corps experience made a powerful line item in a resumé, and they rarely if ever refused to associate with embassy or AID officials who, some assumed, might be working for the CIA.

In Mali, PCVs were teachers, well diggers, small business advisers, and gardeners, among other occupations. One activity that seemed almost perfect was teaching villagers how to do proper bee keeping. Malians are no strangers to bees, wax or honey, but the traditional technology was to find a tree with a hive, perhaps led to it by birds known as Honey Guides—there are four species of them in our West African bird book. These rather drab birds live on grubs and beeswax scattered around by predators, so they specialize in guiding other animals, including people, to these natural hives. Once a hive is located, the villagers climb up to it at night with torches, hoping to smoke the notoriously dangerous bees into flight so they can grab the honey. But this method often results in setting fire to entire forests, sometimes burning down villages in the process. Man-made hives eliminate this pernicious side effect. The honey itself is dark, watery and delicious.

Requirements for a Bush Taxi, and a Visit from Maureen Reagan

Whatever volunteers did, to be a PCV was demanding, often lonely (the cell phone was as yet unheard of), and sometimes as dangerous as a well-paid US military assignment. Because they typically lived long distances from anything resembling a town, volunteers in Mali were at first issued motor scooters, or *mobylettes*. But this led to many accidents on slippery gravel roads, and the practice had to be stopped, leaving them dependent on bush taxis (*taxis brousses*) to get around.

Annie got to know *taxis brousses* well when she went to work for CARE. A *taxi brousse* had to be a battered Peugot 504 station wagon. There were other rules, which she described in her first letter home:

Before the government grants a taxi brousse license, it requires that the taxi:

> *1. Be at least 10 and no more than 50 years old.*
> *2. Have places for six. This way, passengers are assured that they will not suffer from excess space, because:*
> *3. The minimum number of passengers allowed is ten, and up to twelve have been known to fit, plus assorted children, goats and chickens.*
> *4. Have doors that open from the inside, or the outside, but never both.*
> *5. Have only one window handle, the kind that puts windows up or down. You pass the handle around the vehicle as needed. Those by the windows, if they are still capable of moving,*

jiggle the handle around. It works 33% of the
time.
6. A taxi brousse cannot have a schedule. They
just depart from market centers when crammed.
7. Additional requirements: at least two VERY
overweight women in each car, one breakdown
and one flat tire each trip, regular stops to pray,
and a driver who speaks no word of French.[23]

PCVs were by nature irreverent and, as youth tend to be, liberal in their political leanings. In 1990 President Reagan's daughter Maureen paid us a visit. Although reputedly difficult to handle—we got a full briefing on this from her advance Secret Service detail—she was genuinely interested in Africa, and in Peace Corps, and since her visit coincided with the dedication of a new Peace Corps training center, she had to be invited to it. So far so good, but the Malian *commandant de cercle* who attended the event took it upon himself to announce that the center should be named after Maureen.

This did not go over well with the volunteers. To mollify them, the roadside sign for the training center was designed so that "Maureen Reagan" was in much, much smaller letters than "United States Peace Corps Training Center."[24] That was not sufficient. As it happened, one of the first things new volunteers learned in their Bambara language training course was the word for toilet, *nyegen*. And sure enough, within no time the male and female facilities at the camp had sprouted placards labeling them "Nancy Nyegen" and "Ronald Nyegen."

In addition to visiting PCVs on our travels, we always invited new volunteers and their friends to a pool party at the Residence. Such gatherings usually included other members of the younger set, such as the Marine Security Guards, whose Friday evening Open Houses were often attended by PCVs in from their villages *en brousse*. On one occasion a fruit bat, mortally wounded by an urchin with a slingshot outside our compound, fell into the middle of the crowded pool. It was only then that we realized how huge they are. The Marine

---

[23] Annie letter to Varied Family Members Whichever One You Are, n.d., enclosed in Bob letter to Dear Family, July 23, 1988.
[24] Barbara letter to Dear Children and Grandchildren, February 1, 1990.

detachment commander, or "gunny," came to the rescue and took him away beyond the walls. "Semper Fi" indeed!

Beads, Ancient and Otherwise

The Peace Corps Director, Hilary Whittaker, soon became a good friend. Her job, we often thought, was like running a boarding school with students scattered across an area the size of a western American state without any regular means of communicating with them. Partly to decompress from the tension of the day, in her free time she made jewelry from old glass trade beads which she bought in Bamako's central market. We soon discovered that the beads, some of which dated from as early as Roman times, were extremely interesting, and we began to collect them ourselves. We were unaware at first that many of these beads were "by-catch" from illegal excavations in search of the famous terracotta statues found in the Niger Delta and elsewhere. Such artifacts were beginning to fetch enormous prices on the African antiquities market in Europe and the USA.

When Barbara borrowed some beads from the National Museum's collection to display at a meeting of the International Women's Club, she did so only after the museum director, Samuel Sidibé, assured her that it was permissible to buy such beads in the Bamako market. Since they had already been removed from their archaeological context, he said, they were no longer useful sources of information about Mali's past.

However, much later, on a return trip to Mali in the early twenty-first century, we learned that this was not strictly true. In some areas, like Gao, presumably lacking easily datable pottery sherds, beads had become primary chronological evidence. In that area, digging holes in old settlement sites for the purpose of finding beads was becoming widespread and destroying valuable evidence. Therefore, any sale of old beads, no matter where, was likely to be harmful.

At the time that we were resident in Mali, we had bought some beads—even exchanged shells for some—from a Malian church leader in Timbuktu, Pastor Nok. He bought them from local people who said they had found them exposed by the blowing sand, and he sold them to support his parish.

It was a good cause, but we now suspect that it was also archaeologically harmful.

Hilary did not at the time know much more than we did about the beads and their real value. Believing that it would be improper to make a profit, she simply created appealing necklaces or earrings with them and sold the resulting jewelry to friends for whatever the cost of the beads had been in the market. One of the first necklaces that Barbara bought was made of melon-shaped, blue-green beads interspersed with spherical white ones. The latter were clearly ivory, the former were faïence, in an effort to imitate turquoise. Older than the ivory beads, they were most likely from Egypt or the Middle East, where faience beads had been made since ancient times.[25]

Those of us interested in the history of these beads were delighted with the publication of Lois Sherr Dubin's *The History of Beads* in 1987, and we rushed to order copies through the notoriously slow diplomatic pouch. Later, Barbara would join Hilary in her efforts to make a go of the Bead Museum in DC.

Barbara Visits Jamie in Spain, or Why Diplomatic Passports are Overrated

In April, I, Barbara, took a Royal Air Maroc flight to visit Jamie in Spain, where he was just finishing a quarter abroad from Dartmouth. Communication, pre-cell phone and pre-e-mail, was so slow and unreliable as to be non-existent, and the exact date of the end of Jamie's exams was a mystery. So I took an early flight, and rented a car to see a little of Morocco en

---

[25] Ancient and medieval faïence was different from later European faïence (though both have shiny surfaces). The earlier faïence was made in several different ways using glass frit mixed with a soluble salt that rose to the surface and created a shiny glaze when the item was heated; most items decorated this way are small. European faience is a ceramic glaze baked on a porcelain base, and is used mainly for dishes and vases. Although some of the blue-green melon beads that came into the markets in Mali were clearly of ancient origin and often retained little glaze, it is possible that some of the beads on this necklace, most in very good condition, had been made, in imitation of the earlier ones, in Europe much more recently. See Robert K. Liu, *Collectible Beads*, Ornament Inc., 1995, pp. 110-122.

route. Three days in Marrakesh, with a drive into the Atlas Mountains along the high ridge overlooking the desert and a day in the twisted alleys and picturesque shops of the Medina, along with the drive to and from Casablanca, now mainly a center of commerce and no longer picturesque, isn't a bad introduction to the country. My stay was made even more interesting because an AID contractor, a naturalized US citizen originally from Egypt, had also flown up from Mali intent on a little tourism. In return for a ride from Casablanca airport to Marrakesh in my rented car, he helped plan my sightseeing each day, especially in the Medina, and invited me to join him for dinner in a series of local restaurants each evening—a great improvement over staying in the airline hotel and eating there.

After that delightful mini-holiday in Morocco, my welcome to Spain was a rude shock. With four apparently illegal would-be immigrants from North Africa, I got stuck at the Madrid Airport because I did not have a visa. Why a visa? Official guidelines, which I had checked, said that US *tourists* in Spain did not need one. But *diplomats* did!! I had imagined I was a mere tourist, but my passport said I was a diplomat. Never mind that Bob wasn't accredited to Spain. That was when we discovered that some countries, the more paranoid or the more backward the more likely, viewed diplomats as possible spies to be kept under observation as much as possible. Post-Franco Spain obviously hadn't got past the paranoid stage, and it took the arrival of a senior official to obtain a small slip of paper in my passport which allowed me to stay for two weeks, but not to leave and reenter the country, which cooked a day-trip with Jamie to Gibraltar.

Once I had reached Granada and found Jamie, we had a wonderful time. I observed that while "I would not classify him as a great Spanish linguist, . . . he can make himself understood in everyday situations." I continued . . .

As to coping abroad, he has learned plenty, including where the cheapest everything is. Back to my student days—bathroom down the hall, pay for the shower, etc. Actually, many of the little hostals which he found in the famous book Aunt Kathy bought and sent to him (very much used and appreciated) were quite *charming, with courtyards and some history to the buildings. However, most had tile or wood floors with no carpeting, hence every sound echoed throughout, and seldom did the room have windows we could look out. . . . Still, we averaged $30 a night, including four nights at a ritzy establishment (by Jamie's standards) in Madrid that set us back $60 each night and a lovely hotel right on the escarpment looking out over a wide valley in a little hill town called Arcos de la Frontera. . . .[26]*

Through our open window in that one, we enjoyed having our evening glass of wine while gazing out over the plain below, with winter wheat golden in the setting sun spreading as far as we could see. I wonder now whether Jamie's fine book was an original *Europe on $5 a Day.*

After visiting the Alhambra and other sights in Granada, we set off in our Avis rental car and enjoyed dancers in the square in Seville on our way to its famous cathedral, and spent a day in Toledo, which looks just as El Greco painted it. A highlight of the southern swing was a sherry bodega in Jerez through which we were guided by two pretty girls, one Spanish and the other an English exchange student, both of whom gave Jamie far more attention than me. I had to drive anyway, so he enjoyed both the company and the sherry to the fullest.

The only sour note occurred in Cordoba, just after we had visited the fascinating main cathedral, which is built entirely within a Moorish-era mosque. Reputedly the safest of cities, it was there that a couple of n'er-do-wells on a motorcycle attempted to grab my purse. Stout of strap and slung bandolier-style over my chest, it stayed with me and they had to flee because I happened to be walking in front of a sidewalk café with plenty of revelers watching the scene. I suffered only a bleeding elbow and a torn sweater, but I learned that it was most unwise to keep both the keys and the papers for a rental car in the same place.

Later in Madrid, I had to walk behind Jamie always, to keep an eye on his daypack, which contained only sweaters and other daytime necessities, but was a constant target of the

---

[26] Barbara letter to Dear Family, April 10, 1988.

city's gypsy population. Otherwise, we enjoyed visiting the Prado and the Escorial, among many other sights. Like the Madrileños, we switched our daily activity pattern to rising about 9 a.m. and starting to eat supper at the same hour in the evening. Like them, I napped in the afternoon; Jamie didn't.

Soon after my return to Bamako, Bob found that he was about to be not only the ambassador, but also the DCM and political-economic officer, due to normal summer personnel turnover. There were non-stop farewell parties, both our own and those of other embassies. But in August we made our first official visit to the Dogon Country. On our second night out we camped in Mali's "Monument Valley," near Napoleon's Hat.

This mainly touristic stop was meant to give Bob an opportunity to photograph the rock formations in the clear air of the rainy season. . . . So we planned to camp out and have perfect light at dusk and dawn. However, another mistaken assumption: that far north, the winds of the rainy season stir up the sand of the desert. . . . I had just got dinner cooked and cleaned up when we got hit by a sandstorm and all had to crowd into our tent for the rest of the night. We couldn't close the net windows because the tent would have blown away, so we were a sight to behold the next morning. Bob's secretary [Marilyn Mattke], who is not a veteran camper, was along so she could see a bit of the country. . . . She had quite an introduction to travel in Mali.[27]

For the next couple of days we visited CARE projects and Peace Corps volunteers in Douenza and Koro, but our way home, along a road already damaged by heavy rain and truck traffic, was a series of mishaps. First we lost the road and got stuck trying to cross a flooded, normally dry streambed, but were pushed out by villagers. Then we encountered a big truck from the Ivory Coast loaded with kola nuts, an essential ingredient in many Malian ceremonies, which had gone partway off the approach to a bridge, blocking the road.

After cooking another of Barbara's camp suppers, enhanced by a bottle of red wine, we ended up retreating to the top of a nearby hill where we spent the night, with a storm grumbling,

[27] Barbara letter to Dear Family, August 7, 1988.

About to pitch a tent in front of Napoleon's Hat on a trip upcountry where other accommodations are sparse or non-existent. Marilyn Mattke, Sekou and Barbara are surrounded by a welcoming committee from the nearby village.

frogs croaking and lightning flashing in the distance. By this time Marilyn had had enough of tents in storms and slept in our Land Cruiser. We slept in camp beds, occasionally waking to verify that the storm was still in the distance. It was, and gradually wandered off away from us, so that by morning the stream level had dropped enough that we could drive around the offending kola nut truck and ford it, and we were soon back on the paved road to Mopti and home.

Annie Graduates and Works for CARE

Duties in Bamako, however, did not prevent the proud parents from making a quick round-trip to Washington for Annie's graduation from Madeira. She looked lovely in her white gown, made in Bamako and slightly altered to fit by my friend, Martha Myers, the school librarian and also costume mistress for Madeira theatricals. All through her four years at Madeira, Annie had benefited from kind deeds and help freely given by her mother's former colleagues, which made our long-distance parenting a little easier. We were pleased that all three of her living grandparents were able to attend, this being one of Helena's rare sallies out of Woodbine Nursing Home.

Then it was back to Bamako to host our first Fourth of July reception, only slightly marred by the late arrival at our front gate of the official delegation from Mali's sole political party. Although our invitation read 6:30 to 9:30 they had assumed that all national day receptions were from 7 to 9, and when they realized they had missed the ceremonial toasts and flag-raising, they left in embarrassment. The contretemps was probably our fault, but there seemed to be no hard feelings, and due to our unorthodox timing the flag ceremony came just at sunset. It was a lovely sight, with a flock of bats wheeling overhead as they set off from their roosts around our garden in search of nice ripe fruit.[28]

Annie had decided to take a year off in Mali between Madeira and the University of Chicago. She soon got a job working for CARE Mali's office in Bamako, which she found on her own by writing application letters, sent to us by pouch for hand-delivery by Sekou, given the vagaries of international mail from Virginia to Mali. She did forget to sign these letters, but apparently her mother is a good forger.

Once in Bamako, her tasks included running the periodic radio checks with CARE's project offices, scattered around Mali, and coaching her Malian colleagues on how to use computers, which were just being introduced. She was soon eating lunch with them every day, usually *riz au gras*, literally "greasy rice," eaten with one's fingers—a skill her parents never really got the hang of—from a communal bowl. (She was well remembered by the CARE staff when Bob returned to Mali in 2004 to write about its then-flourishing democracy.)

Two of her Madeira friends, Robin Ragsdale and Jennifer Eisenberg, soon arrived for a visit, and they went off together by *taxi brousse* to see some of Mali's rural attractions. (This was the trip that generated her famous rules for the requirements of a *taxi brousse*.) The girls went north, to Mopti and the Pays Dogon, where they also traveled, according to Annie's letter, "*à pied* and by donkey cart. All in all, it was a fun trip, what

---

[28] Barbara letter to Dear Family, July 6, 1988.

Two photos of health workers demonstrating nutrition techniques to rural mothers. Annie took the photo above while working for CARE.

you might call an adventure," she concluded.[29]

Before long Annie had her own Self-Help Project, a garden in Narayan, which she was supposed to visit and encourage (and which we of course visited). In return, she tried to teach us how to use a computer, our first foray into the information age.[30] She took some great photos of Malians who were beneficiaries of CARE projects. Being young and cute, she did not alarm her subjects the way Bob did, even when she got very close to them. The results were used in CARE fund-raising publicity, sometimes without crediting her by name, somewhat to the annoyance of her father.

Her education proceeded non-stop. She got to sit with us in the VIP reviewing stand at Mali's Independence Day parade in September, 1988. Guess who showed up unannounced, only a few feet away from us? Yasser Arafat, as if out of central casting, only it really was the man himself, complete with dishtowel head cloth and a .45 pistol at his waist! The parade itself was non-stop photogenic, beginning with a display of obsolete Soviet military aid, from jeeps to tanks to huge, self-propelled artillery pieces. There was a detachment of Malian *goumiers*, troops especially trained for desert warfare; they were wearing sand-colored uniforms and rubber boots, which gave them their name. MIGs screeched overhead; one had crashed preparing for the parade. A Soviet diplomat told me that there were only a few left, and "when this lot is gone they aren't getting any more."

Even better were the civilian marching groups, composed of everyone from women's organizations to traditional hunters, who actually composed a formal and influential fraternity, armed with ancient muzzle-loaders and spectacular costumes made from mud cloth and decorated with amulets. It was a good thing we got to see this parade, because it had to be cancelled in 1989 due a budgetary crisis.

And then there was the French national day, Bastille Day. The French felt duty bound to invite every French citizen in the country to their celebration, held in the large, dusty courtyard of their chancery. What seemed like thousands of

---

[29] Annie letter to Varied Family Members Whichever One You Are, cited earlier.

[30] Barbara letter to Dear Family, March 19, 1989.

people came each year, ninety-nine percent of them Malians: nuns and priests from remote corners of the country, ex-students, *ancien combatants* (veterans) of the French Army and former colonial civil servants, and who knew who else. It made a picturesque, but a bit rough-and-tumble gathering. When a new French Ambassador, Michel Perrin, arrived, he decided to set up a cordoned-off area for the diplomatic corps and other high level official guests only.

Annie would have none of it, she wanted to mingle with the people, and into the crowd she went, while her parents sipped discreetly with the diplomats. The playing of the *Marseillaise* signaled that the party was on, and everyone rushed for the food and drink set up on makeshift tables. Our daughter was truly astonished to see apparently dignified Malians grabbing bottles of champagne and stuffing them into the folds of their best *boubous* (robes); within a few minutes little food or drink was left.

Her mother was not surprised when told this story, because at her first tea for local ladies, she had discovered that, besides enjoying the cookies and cakes, her guests, high-level and wealthy by local standards, had not too discretely wrapped more sweets in napkins and stowed them away in their ample purses. Barbara had also come to the conclusion that, when serving buffet style, which was most of the time since Malians were not comfortable at long, formal seated dinners, a member of the kitchen staff had to be assigned to serve the meat to each guest in the buffet line, so that it did not all disappear before everyone was fed.

The following year, 1989, Bastille Day was even better. It was the 200th anniversary of the French Revolution, and French embassies all over the world were instructed to do something special. Ambassador Perrin decided to have a fleet of *pirogues* carrying torches process down the Niger, accompanied by fireworks, past a reviewing stand at the Canöe (pronounced "Canooay") Club, a modest boat club on the riverfront not far from our house.

The procession was indeed quite beautiful, but poor Michel, who by this time was a good friend, nearly died of stress making sure that it was properly timed to coincide with the fireworks, the *Marseillaise*, etc. We eventually joined the Canöe Club, having acquired a Klepper Kayak, complete with sail and motor, from the departing World Bank chief, the one whose wife was our Peace Corps nurse. We never used it much, being deterred by the rocks at the edge of the river and the strong current further out. There was also the danger of bilharzia, a snail-born parasite that does bad things to one's liver and is widespread in African streams. (We had the Klepper until recently when we gave it to nephew and niece Chris and Megan.)

Toward the end of our stay Annie caught a very serious case of malaria, probably because she didn't like sleeping under mosquito nets inside a stifling CARE guesthouse somewhere and went outside instead. She still was at the age where kids think they are invulnerable. We were away, traveling in Central Africa in preparation for my next assignment in Washington. Embassy doctor and friend, Dr. Tom Lucas, had left post and his replacement, who had had no experience with tropical medicine, refused to medicate her because when he tested, he found no evidence of malaria parasites.

Of course there wasn't, because, as we all knew, the patient won't test positive at first if she has been taking prophylactic malaria medication. The proper procedure is to treat for malaria if fever rises into the danger zone, which hers had. Fortunately her friends at CARE did agitate for action and he finally did treat her before the fever did lasting damage. When we got back from Central Africa the drama was over, but it scared us anyway, another reminder that fun and interesting as it may be, service in hardship posts does come with real hazards attached.

The State Visit

During the summer of Annie's arrival, we learned, to our great surprise, that Mali's president, Moussa Traoré, was being invited to make a state visit to the United States in early October. President Reagan's second term was drawing to a close, and it dawned on someone that during his entire eight years in office he had invited only one African Chief of State, Felix Houphët-Boigny of the Ivory Coast, on such a visit. Africa was not exactly crawling with allies of the US, so it was decided to ask President Traoré, because he was head of the OAU (Organization of African Unity, known more recently as the AU, or African Union). October, 1988, would be one of our most entertaining months ever, one that, were it typical, would have had young Americans lining up to join the Foreign Service.

A state visit is a big deal, the highest in a tripartite hierarchy of presidential visits, ranging from wholly "unofficial" (no government-to-government business is done), to "working" which means what it says, but without protocolary bells and whistles, and finally to "state." The major distinction of a state visit, from our point of view, was that Barbara and I got to go along as part of the official party, at US Government expense. The main point of having ambassadors and their spouses present is to make sure that there is a familiar face for the guests to talk with—me for the Malian president and Barbara for his wife. The only real problem of this visit was that, leaving aside the details of AID and Peace Corps programs, there was not much for the two presidents to discuss. And neither one of them was into details.

By this time we had figured out the dynamics of the Malian polity. Moussa Traoré had been a rough-cut army officer until 1968 when, as a lieutenant, he led the military coup d'état which overthrew Mali's founding president, Modibo Keita. Traoré was from a rural area near Kayes in western Mali, and he came from a peasant background. He seemed to have no family worth mentioning, and he showed no apparent favoritism to his home region. In contrast, his smart, cultured wife, Mariam Sissoko Traoré, came from a large and powerful clan, and her numerous relatives controlled a significant portion of Mali's admittedly modest economy.

It was widely assumed that Moussa's real job was to keep the country safe for business—more accurately, for Mariam's family's businesses. Collectively the Traorés were often referred to as the "FMI," a pun on the French initials for *Fonds Monétaire Internationale*, the International Monetary Fund (IMF), but in this case meaning "*Famille Moussa et Intimes*," Moussa's family and friends. This made sense in Mali because the IMF, along with the World Bank, played a key role in coordinating foreign aid and determining whether the country was managing its economy properly.

Traoré began with a stop in New York, where the annual United Nations General Assembly (UNGA), which he addressed in his capacity as OAU head, was in progress. He met with our Secretary of State, George Schultz, who was also there for the UNGA, leaving Schultz with one fewer things to do in Washington. Being mainly for UN business, the New York stop was not officially part of the state visit, but we still got to go to New York, hear Moussa address the UN, and then fly with the Traorés to Washington on what Barbara described as "Air Force One" (actually a smaller VIP Air Force plane)." [31]

Fortunately the Malians had stopped in Dakar to refuel their battered rental jet on the way to the US. There the President of Senegal, Abdou Diouf, had asked Traoré if he would ask President Reagan to send a USAID airplane that was spraying for locusts in Mali back to Senegal, which it had previously visited but which was being much harder hit than Mali by the ongoing infestation. At last! Something to talk about.

And so, when various notables, including me, briefed President Reagan in the Oval Office, Colin Powell (National Security Advisor) told him that locusts were on the agenda for his meeting with the President of Mali. Reagan thought about it and then asked if these locusts were not similar to the ones that had almost ended the Mormons' settlement in Salt Lake City, until, in response to their prayers, God sent a flock of seagulls to devour the insects. Should he not mention that to the Malians? Eyeballs rolled toward corners of the room, but Powell, ever the straightforward military man, replied that he did not think that Reagan should invoke God, just stick to the spray plane.

At this point Reagan interjected that throughout his presidency he had never, during state visits, put his hand over his heart for the playing of the visitor's national anthem, only for the Star Spangled Banner. Now, however, he was thinking he should do this for both anthems. Again Powell stepped into the resulting silence and said, "Mr. President, I think that very

---

[31] The details of the visit, as for all state visits, were contained in a specially printed little white book, a copy of which we still have, "The State Visit of his Excellency the President of the Republic of Mali and Mrs. Traore to the United States," US Department of State, Office of Protocol, October, 1988.

special gesture should be reserved for the American anthem; you should just go ahead and stand at attention, as you have always done on such occasions, for the Malian anthem."

The day of the arrival ceremony, Thursday, October 6, 1988, dawned beautiful, cool and sunny. A crowd of suitably cleared government workers was assembled on the South Lawn of the White House for the show. Trumpeters tooted from the balcony, the Army's fife and drummers marched. We were all on tenterhooks to see what would happen when the Malian national anthem was played. Sure enough, Reagan put his hand over his heart, contrary to Powell's advice. Good on you! I thought. And in the official meeting indoors, while our president agreed to send the spray plane back to Senegal, he also told Traoré that he should tell Diouf to think about praying for seagulls. Never a big fan of President Reagan, I concluded that while he might be getting a bit loopy, he certainly had not lost his proverbial charm.

Before leaving Mali for the visit I had been asked to suggest guests for the required state dinner, which was held at the White House later that evening. I had replied with a list of prominent people who knew at least something about Mali or Africa generally. None of them made the cut, but I was able to work most of them into a lunch the same day at the State Department, hosted by the Acting Secretary of State because Schultz was still in New York.

The guests I had suggested included Dr. Pascal James Imperato, a prominent public health expert who had for years worked in Mali with USAID on the smallpox eradication campaign. I had never met him, but knew him from his copious writings on matters Malian, from geography to art history. We have been friends ever since, and he has never forgotten this gesture. The lunch was otherwise notable for the use of finger bowls, which mystified most of the guests, and not just the Malians, as in: Are we supposed to drink this, or what? They were finally cleared after two courses, and only in the third did we have food which might possibly have been eaten with our fingers. They were definitely a conversation starter however.

The black-tie White House dinner that evening began with a small cocktail party for the principals upstairs in the yellow oval room, overlooking the ellipse, before a bigger cocktail reception downstairs in the East Room. Barbara wrote, "Whatever you may think of Reagan's politics, he and Nancy are gracious hosts, and the Traorés had a wonderful time, from minute one."[32]

The dinner was less impressive, because, since it was probably Reagan's last, it was used to repay favors, mainly to domestic political allies most of whom had barely heard of Africa, and the enormous floral centerpieces made it impossible to see, much less talk to, anyone but your immediate neighbor at the table. Bob was fine at the head table, which was not round, but Barbara got stuck with President Traoré's personal physician, who spoke only French, on one side, and the clueless wife of a Congressman, no foreign language fluency even imagined by her, on the other. Another odd touch: the Reagans saw off the Traorés before the dancing, to an Army band, began.

The Traorés and their entourage stayed at Blair House, the first overnight guests to do so since a major expansion and renovation, $14 million worth of antique furniture and restored federal period architecture. The only previous visitors since the renovation had been some staff members of French President Mitterand, who, we were told, during a brief luncheon stop had made off with an unseemly number of Blair House towels.

Members of the Malian delegation, as well as American officials working on the trip, were welcome to eat lunch at Blair House each day. This led to a funny, almost embarrassing glitch on the second day, when the Traorés were scheduled for a relaxed, private lunch in their suite, and most other officials, with time on their hands, were happy to take advantage of the hospitality. However, early in the morning, Barbara had learned from the European-trained Belgian manager, sophisticated but new on the job, that she and the chef had planned and were well into preparing a delicious cold buffet. Malians, like all West Africans, have their main meal at lunch, and it has to include a substantial hot dish. "Not possible," said the manager. "Impossible to have satisfied guests," replied

---

[32] Barbara letter to Dear Family, October 16, 1988.

Barbara. The compromise for that day was to add soup.

As she sat eating a plate from the lovely buffet with several Malians, one remarked that these were certainly wonderful appetizers. She was trying to think of an adequate reply, when into the dining room sailed a delegation from the Association of Embassy of Mali Wives with a huge washtub of special *riz au gras* (the kind that Annie ate with the CARE staff in Bamako, see above) which they had prepared. It had been cooked to honor their President and his wife, but once they had been served, of course it was to be shared with the rest of their delegation. The next day, the Blair House staff prepared a lovely buffet with a variety of hot dishes to choose from. Barbara likes to think that she did a service to more than just this delegation by reminding the manager and chef that the whole world does not eat according to European and American tastes.

It is quite amazing how much can be stuffed into less than three full days in Washington when everything is set up ahead of time and you are whisked through all the traffic in motorcades with flags flying and sirens blaring. For President Traoré there were calls on members of Congress, visits to a think tank (CSIS), a major NGO working in Africa (Africare), and US firms working in Mali, including one (Utah International) that was about to bring in Mali's first modern gold mine.

Mrs. Traoré met with officials at the local universities where three of her children were studying, visited the Smithsonian Museum of African Art, and, at her request, toured a farm breeding beef cattle near Marshall, Virginia. She did not have a police escort with sirens blaring, and was most annoyed when her convoy got held up in rush-hour traffic. She also accompanied her husband to lay a wreath on the Tomb of the Unknown Soldier at Arlington. The Malian Embassy had its own dinner, and a reception for the Malian community. There was, of course, time for shopping.

On Friday evening the Traorés and a few senior members of their party, plus us, sat in the President's Box at the Kennedy Center to hear the National Symphony, again at Mme's request. All went well until the Minister of Education, General Sekou Ly, began to snore loudly. Ly's education qualifications were modest, but as a young soldier he had obtained the key to the arms locker for Moussa Traoré on the night of his 1968 coup d'état, and had subsequently held many different ministerial portfolios. Barbara and I were sitting just above Ly, wondering what to do, when Mme Traoré reached over and poked him awake. We don't remember anything about the music, except that the NSO, alerted to the presence of a foreign president at the very last minute, did play the Malian National Anthem quite credibly.

On Sunday, October 9, we proceeded by motorcade from Blair House to a helipad on the Mall (where the World War II Memorial is today) and a Marine One helicopter took us to Andrews AFB, where we boarded another Air Force VIP jet, a C-9, for Wright Patterson Air Force Base in Ohio. President Traoré received an honorary degree from nearby, historically black Central State University and, after lunch there, toured the National Afro-American Museum. After that the motorcade sped onward to Columbus. The Ohio State Highway Patrol outdid itself, zooming around with lights flashing to block off access ramps to the Interstate so we could pass without slowing down.

For Barbara, who was after all a past Girls' State Governor of Ohio, the final hours of the Traorés' visit were special. She wrote:

Their visit was capped by a splendid dinner given by Ohio Governor Richard Celeste at his residence. His food was truly gourmet, his guest list [in contrast to that of the White House dinner] consisted of people truly interested in his guests. He himself had been to Mali twice, once as Lieutenant Governor of Ohio as part of a trade mission, the other as Director of the Peace Corps under Carter. To make the afternoon even better, just as we arrived at our room at the hotel in Columbus that overlooks the banks of the Scioto River in the middle of downtown, their Columbus Day parade, complete with high school marching bands and vintage cars, began right below our windows. That was unplanned, but perfect.[33]

---

[33] Barbara letter to Dear Family, October 16, 1988.

The presidential couple's chartered aircraft was waiting for them at the Columbus International Airport, and they left for Bamako at 10:30 that evening.

A Week on Mali's Great River

We were back in Bamako a few days later, after a nasty, delay-ridden flight. The rainy season was over, water was gushing down from the Futa Djalon highlands of Sierra Leone, the Niger was, relatively speaking, brimming, and it was the only time of year that it is possible to get to Timbuktu and beyond by river boat. We needed a break after all that hard work in Washington. So on October 18, we departed from Koulikoro, the port downriver from Bamako and the rapids, and the terminus for the railroad from Dakar, on the good ship *Tombouctou,* one of three fairly modern, German-built (and paid for) vessels operated by the state-owned *Compagnie Malienne de Navigation.*

We were accompanied by Annie, Marilyn Mattke, junior embassy officer Carol Stricker, and Georgia Lucas, wife of the embassy doctor Tom Lucas. (Both Lucases were natives of Charleston, SC, where they knew lots of Pringles.) The non-resident British Ambassador, John MacCrae, and his wife, Anne, who had urged us to take this trip, were in town and were among those who came to see us off with onboard cocktails at dusk on October 18. Bob's letter home about the trip continues:

Within a few hours [of departure] at 10 pm the boat ran aground on a sandbar. [There was no such thing as a channel on the Niger; it was like the Missouri in 1840.] It took about twelve hours to get unstuck. Six hours after that we got stuck again, this time for fourteen hours. Getting unstuck consists of the following: (a) don't do anything until the sun comes up and everyone has had breakfast; (b) unload six or eight fourth class passengers with a log to pry feebly at the stern while the diesels are revved up. With luck the propwash blows away enough sand to permit the stern to swing in ever-widening arcs until a channel has been blown out to adequately deep (about five feet) water. However, the second time this didn't work; step

(c) was to wait for a tug [from Mopti] and, amid maximum confusion and some of the clumsiest boat-handling I have ever seen, offload a lot of cargo, after which the Tombouctou came free.

After this very slow start things got better. In the early hours of our fourth day on the river we arrived in Mopti, the capital of the Niger Inner Delta, where the river mushes out into a huge inundated area. The main function of the riverboats is to supply towns in the Delta and on the river below it, where the Niger curves north and then east through the desert and roads are especially lousy. Thanks to good rains the whole Delta region is now emerald green with rice and swamp grass. Villages (mainly of Fulani, aka Peuhl, people) are built on isolated mounds[34], usually the result of centuries of habitation. When the Delta drains later in the year, it is invaded by thousands of cattle [see account of this below] and there is also a major fishing industry; nomadic fishermen follow the retreating flood, and as the fish are concentrated in shallower waters, they catch and smoke and dry them on the spot [as we would see on our way home]. Farmers grow rice in the shallow flooded areas, and millet on the sandy ridges above flood levels. In a good year fish make up to five percent of "landlocked" Mali's exports.[35]

Life turned into a pleasant blur of river sliding by. In the early mornings and evenings we sat on the roof, a magnificent vantage point for watching the passing scene. In the heat of the day we retreated to the side decks. Cocktail hour was on the open stern deck (a tolerant division of the space between bibulous foreigners[36] and Malians saying their evening prayers). The food for the First and Deluxe Class passengers who ate together (us) was great; at one point the chef produced a banana-cream pie with "USA" sculpted on it in my honor. Barbara pronounced it safe, so we ate it with no ill effects. . . .

[Bob left out the most amusing detail: This cake—not pie—was served two nights in a row. The first came out with USA backwards, because the chef had put it at the bottom of the cake pan in the right order, but when he turned the cake

---

[34] "Tels" in archaeology-speak.

[35] I do not know if fish exports are still so important, but I very much doubt it.

[36] There were only the six of us.

out, it was the other way around. The following night's dinner climaxed with an identical cake, except that this time, "USA" read correctly.]

Each stop along the river was a carnival event with crowds at wharfside trying to get on the boat, peddle pottery, mats, dried fish and calabashes brimming with fresh milk, or just gawking. Below Mopti the boat carried its own contingent of market ladies who swarmed off at every stop to sell produce. Local gendarmes tried to maintain order, sometimes taking their belts off to thwack at the crowds. At Macina, a young vegetable wench almost got sucked into the screws by the prop wash, but some people pushed a pirogue to her rescue. Visitors who didn't debark in time ended up jumping off the gangplank into six feet of water. The Tombouctou is supposed to carry about 300 passengers and 140 tons of cargo, but it appeared quite overloaded, which of course was one source of our sandbar problems. Especially between Mopti and Gao the two lower decks were completely packed with freight and passengers—we had everything from 300 lb barrels of cooking oil (dozens of them) to a couple of small tractors. [Added later: A lot of freight has to be moved in the few months when the river is high enough to allow the big boats to travel on it. The year after this trip a final voyage was undertaken too late, and the boat remained marooned in mud until the following high-water season.]

At midnight on Sunday, we arrived at Kabara, the port for Timbuktu. We discovered that being almost two days late (as we were by now) was a tremendous break. It got us to Timbuktu on the night of the Prophet's Birthday, the major religious festival locally and a time when everyone in the colorful Songhai, Tuareg and Arab population (including normally secluded women) is out in the streets showing off new clothing; ancient mud mosques are lighted and decorated and Koran readings are in progress everywhere. The boat company arranged a car for us and we had plenty of time to see the old city celebrating by moonlight. Kabara is connected by a canal several miles long to the river; last year it could not be used at all because the river never got high enough; had it been that way this year, we would not have had enough time to visit the city.

The rest of the trip to Gao took two more days, much of it past isolated Songhai villages and gigantic orange sand dunes that in many places come to the river's edge.[37] Total elapsed time, Koulikoro to Gao, a distance of 813 miles, was six hours short of one week.[38]

With Annie and Georgia Lucas, we returned to Bamako from Gao by road, with a side trip to see Youvarou, the site of the same IUCN project we had previously visited by land. We wanted to see it now, surrounded by water, and check out the thousands of egrets, herons, cormorants and spoonbills

The river steamer, Tomboctou, on which we traveled, at a port along the Niger. Three of our embassy colleagues are barely visible watching the scene from the roof of the vessel.

---

[37] On this stretch we went by Tosaye, just downstream from Bourem, where the Russians, in the middle of the Cold War, had announced they were going to build a high dam, à la Aswan. Ever since then the site has been optimistically marked on maps. Of course they never did, but who knows, maybe the Chinese will.

[38] Bob letter to Dear Family, November 5, 1988, slightly edited.

nesting there. This required a three-hour trip by boat from Sendegé, a small town on the highway, and the IUCN sent a motorized *pinnase* to pick us up.

Youvarou was fascinating, and not quite as blisteringly hot as it had been on our dry season visit. Richard Morehead had described what awaited us in the now flooded delta:

On the day of your arrival, I suggest you go over to Akkagoun, the wood where we saw the pelicans . . . to see it now that it is flooded and the birds have arrived. The best time to go is about 4 pm, and stay until dusk in order to watch the daytime birds come into roost, and the night-feeding birds leaving. Akkagoun is a twenty-four hour dormitory, with two shifts. Take insect repellent with you. [39]

He further recommended Dentaka, where he told us we might see more spoonbills nesting; we went the next day, and we did. Even better, the boatman who took us to see these wondrous sights was Sine Konta, a young fisherman, who spoke French and had worked with Jamie Skinner, the project ornithologist, for two years and knew the birds well. The only difficulty was that the index of our West African bird book was arranged alphabetically by the Latin names of the birds, so we had quite a bit of follow-up searching in it to identify exactly what species we had seen.

On the way back to the main road and our vehicle, the IUCN outboard conked out and a spare motor didn't work either. Our search for viable transport led to a fascinating series of encounters with the nomadic population of Bozo fishermen on sandbars along Lake Debo at the downstream end of the Delta.

The Bozos, smoking their catch, looked mired in poverty, but we discovered that their chief had what appeared to be a brand new forty-horsepower outboard motor, which he was willing to rent to us, stashed under his bed. We teased Georgia Lucas, blonde and pretty and speaking French with a terrific Charleston accent, that we might have to leave her with the

---

[39] The quotation and other information are from Richard Moorehead to Dear Bob and Barbara, October 26, 1988.

Bozo chief as a security deposit; she would have made a great Delta Queen. The Bozo motor worked, and at the small town where we had left the highway from Gao we found a friendly hydrology service Land Rover willing to take us on to Mopti, where we connected with Sekou and our own car, and spent the night at the hotel with snakeskin décor, before the long ride home the next day.

12

Mali (2): Democratic Transition and Desert Rebellion, 1987-1990

Our three years in Mali were studded with anecdotal bits and pieces that don't fit in any narrative sequence. Here are a few:

The Joys and Sorrows of Sahelian Dogdom

Pax continued to enjoy his second African tour, including big stand-up receptions where guests dropped food on the ground. He did not like trips to the vet to deal with skin infections, which flourished on his furry little body in the Sahelian climate. He had gotten older, and less inclined to escape out of an open gate or to go swimming in our pool, which was too deep for him.

Where's my Tux?!

There are things to be said for small-town life. As we began to dress for our second Marine Birthday Ball, always the highlight of any embassy social season, I could not find my tux. We were about to be late for the ceremonial opening. Finally we asked Sekou, our driver, if he could remember taking it to Bamako's only dry cleaner after last year's ball. Answer: Yes. Did he remember ever picking it up? No. Aha: could you please go there and see if they still have it? By now, it was well past small business closing time, but the operators lived over their shop. And there the tux was, nice and clean.

The Most Mysterious Bead

We always visited local markets, if only to check out whether they had any interesting beads. On a trip to Kayes, in far western

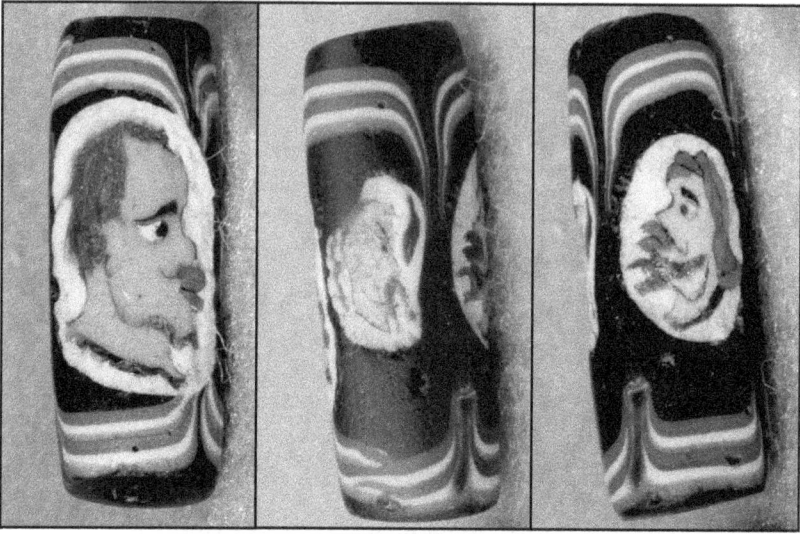

While accompanying Bob on an official trip, which included a stop at Kayes in far western Mali, Barbara took the plane crew to look around the market while he was meeting with local officials. One of them called her attention to this unusual bead.

Mali, the crew of the attaché plane went to the market with Barbara while I had to make official calls, and as Barbara pawed through baskets of beads, one of them spotted an unusual bead and said, "Ma'am, you might be interested in this." It looked like a fascinating, if somewhat battered Venetian glass bead, in *millefiori* style, cylindrical, with three tiny faces embedded on its sides, one exaggeratedly Negroid, one Oriental and one Arab.

Later, at the Second International Bead Conference in DC, we described it to Peter Francis, a most famous bead expert, but an opinionated one; he was sure we must have something made of painted wood. We knew it wasn't, but didn't know what it was, so we took it to the meeting the next day. Peter had to admit that it was glass, and rare. The faces are slices of glass canes, applied when the beads were still hot, and, as we later learned, the bead was probably made to commemorate the 1931 Colonial Exposition in Paris. As to how it wound up in Kayes, that will remain a mystery, but one possibility is that either an African present at the exposition or a colonial civil servant who had attended it brought the bead back to French West Africa. In any case, it is the most unusual bead in our collection. [1]

Protocol and Polygamy

In neither Indonesia nor Burkina Faso, both majority Muslim countries, had we ever dealt with multiple wives at social functions: how to address invitations to them, how to know how many wives would actually show up with their husband, or where to seat them at our occasional seated dinners. However, in Bamako we had a cranky senior official, a Dogon (even though most Dogons are Christians or animists, not Muslims) who did have several wives and was sensitive about the protocols of polygamy. His invitations had to be addressed to *M. le Ministre et Mesdames*. Once when wife number two showed up unexpectedly, we had to transfer my long-suffering DCM, John Lewis, to a hastily inserted extra seat. (DCMs are always long-suffering, as I well knew.)

Bird Watching and Softball

Mali, like most African countries, is full of interesting birds, in addition to the Pearl-spotted Owlets nesting in our bat-laden trees and the migratory water birds we saw at Youvarou. Elsewhere, there are several species of brilliantly colored kingfishers (as opposed to the one kingfisher that lives in North America); bee-eaters, parrots and love birds, hornbills and hawks, and bishops, cute little red or yellow birds which nest along the sides of any watercourse. On the other side of the Niger from our residence was a long irrigation canal, built by the French Army in the 1920s, and along its crumbling banks we occasionally saw spectacular Violet Plantain-eaters (rare) as well as the common grey ones. One of our "everyday birds" was the Long-tailed Starling, familiar indeed, but never boring.

Then a Japanese contractor arrived to rehabilitate the

---

[1] See illustrations of beads # 40-43, 45, 47 and 50 on p. 2 and comments on them on p. 5 in John and Ruth Picard, *Millefiori Beads: Beads from the West African Trade*, Vol. VI, 1991. Also, "Exploring the Mystery of a Three-Faced Venitian Bead," *Bead Bulletin* (of the Bead Society of Greater Washington), Vol. 21, No. 2; April-May, 2003, p. 10. A copy of the latter, which would be very difficult to find, is with our bead.

same canal. Contrary to what everyone assumed was normal Japanese practice, he brought only a dozen or so supervisory officials, and hired Malians for his entire labor force. Everyone predicted that this would not work, given the panoply of cultural and linguistic obstacles involved, but it did. Moreover, the project boss was a softball fanatic, and suddenly our Bamako embassy team had someone to play against, every weekend. It was great until the boss left and his replacement stopped *ordering* his Japanese staff to play softball, whether they wanted to or not. They apparently did not want to, so that was the end of that.

Our Very Own Baobab

The fabled baobab, *Adamsonia digitata*, is actually a giant succulent, an immense, spongy water storage tank. It has about thirty economic uses: fruit and leaves are edible and medicinal, big ones provide shade and shelter from storms in their spooky trunk cavities, rope can be produced from its bark, and more. Then there is the aesthetic value of their extraordinary shapes and the folklore they have inspired— they are "upside down trees," said to get up and walk around at night. And of course the baobab was made literarily famous by Antoine de Saint-Exupéry's *The Little Prince*.

CARE was propagating baobabs in its nurseries for distribution to farmers, along with other valuable plants. The seedlings are about as thick as a pencil, and I decided to plant one on the Residence lawn to see how fast it would grow, a question the local experts couldn't answer. The questions were (a) would it grow on a frequently watered lawn, not in a near-desert, and (b) how would I prevent my successor, who might not like baobabs, from chopping it down, the same way his spouse would replace all our curtains, expel all the fruit bats, etc., etc.?

Baobabs thrive in adversity, which would perhaps answer the first question affirmatively. To try to avoid a negative answer to the second, I decided to dedicate ours to Martin Luther King, an American hero throughout Africa, at the next Martin Luther King Day Ceremony, which was always held on the Residence lawn. I got the embassy GSO (General

Services Office) to procure a large bronze dedicatory plaque, with the tree name in English and Latin, along with the words "Let Freedom Ring," and had it mounted on a heavy concrete block. This ploy worked, sort of; by the time Barbara and I were back in 2005, the tree was way too big to get your arms around and another one, added for good measure near the garage, was even bigger. I had also proved that you can't over-water baobabs. But nothing is forever, and the corner of the memorial plaque's concrete block was already crumbling. Since then, the ambassador's residence has been moved to the new, far-away embassy compound, and the fate of the baobab, as well as the plaque, is unknown to us.

An Ecumenical Bridge

The second modern bridge over the Niger, completed after we left, should have enhanced Mali's reputation for multiculturalism. The design work was done by an American Jewish firm, Nathan Associates; the Saudis paid for it; and a Chinese contractor built it. There is now a third bridge, not counting the antique *Pont Submersible*, which, as it name suggests, can be used only at periods of low water.[2]

Diplomatic Niceties

Back to the main story: By the time we returned from our 800-mile boat trip on the Niger, we were no longer in the lee of the State Visit, and were soon immersed in normal ambassadorial routine. Barbara nicely caught the flavor of it:

The week we got back we attended three dinner parties, one classical piano recital at the German Ambassador's Residence (where else?) and went to a reception full of beer and sausages to inaugurate the new Sabena [Belgian airline] office in town. Week 2, I taught at the International School while the teachers were in Abidjan at the annual conference of international schools in West Africa—a conference I had attended twice in Lomé in my

---

[2] However, word had it, as of 2013, that a *fourth* all-year bridge was being built near the site of the antique submersible one.

Ouagadougou years. The kids survived, and so did I, given the fact that all my social studies lessons were nothing but before, during, and after the US elections. Afternoons and evenings, we attended the Soviet National Day, hosted the first meeting of the season of the International Women's Club of Bamako, an organization which I am enjoying because the Malian ladies run it, contrary to what usually happens in these groups. That means organization is terrible; we plan everything in plenary session instead of having committees, but culturally it is fun, not like the usual pulling teeth to get expatriate ladies to run bazaars.

Veterans Day was the Marine Ball, with the usual flag ceremony, speech by the Ambassador, and birthday cake cutting. It was a pleasant outdoor affair, but the music was too loud. Bob's birthday the next night was swallowed by the arrival of the "Stars of Faith," a black gospel singing group whose tour of various African countries was being sponsored by USIS. The two lead ladies stayed with us; they are remarkable women, the eldest well into her sixties, who are quite famous in the US. Between keeping them nourished, hosting one concert, and seeing to it that they collected adequate souvenirs in the market, we had a busy three days. Although both concerts were small, both audiences were enthusiastic, and we were even able to supply an accompanist, a young AID officer, on their electric piano, their own accompanist having succumbed to alcohol, or something, and fallen off the stage in Zaire. The next week was a mélange of Bead Club meeting here, performance of masks and marionettes of traditional Bambara culture at the French Cultural Center, presenting our retiring Residence cook, Ibrahima, with a long-service medal—he has cooked for American Ambassadors since the year after independence (1961) and got the most applause of anyone at the awards ceremony.[3]

Sometimes, of course, official entertaining turned out to have unanticipated rewards, as I reported in a letter home that didn't get written until January. For Thanksgiving dinner, I noted, we had invited the (still) Soviet ambassador, and his wife and daughter, an invitation he subsequently reciprocated by inviting us, including Annie, to a magnificent Russian meal

[3] Barbara letter to Dear Family, January 15, 1989.

to celebrate Orthodox Christmas on the sixth of January.

That Thanksgiving dinner had been Ibrahima's swan song. My slightly cynical ex-ambassador in Burkina Faso, Leonardo Neher, saw the laudatory article about his retirement ceremony that we had placed in *State Magazine* and sent me a note reading, in its entirety, "I see that you have fired the cook."

Although there was some truth in this—he was getting very elderly, and was no longer keeping the kitchen clean—there was no need to feel sorry for Ibrahima, who came from a socially prominent family and had a daughter living in France. When Barbara encountered him several months later and asked how he was doing, it turned out that the Malian social security office had miscalculated his pension—or maybe he had a friend working there—and he was getting an amount equivalent to his entire former salary.

Barbara's Work with AMALDEME

You would think that with all the duties related directly to Bob's job, I might have subscribed to the old-fashioned Foreign Service conceit that the wife of an FSO, especially an ambassador, should feel completely satisfied if she took care of her children in sometimes difficult, always different, circumstances. Plus, of course, she should support her husband's career brilliantly with entertainment at home and attendance at numerous diplomatic and official functions.

In fact, I always found my own interests at our posts, and I always had sufficient household help so that, while the servants required guidance and supervision, neither entertaining nor housecleaning and laundry required my full-time attention. Besides, what had my Cornell education and subsequent teaching experience been for?

With the possibility of frequent travel to Mali's hard to reach but fascinating corners, I was not interested in being tied down by teaching at the International School of Bamako. However, it didn't take long to find a rewarding substitute—non-remunerative of course, but we had sufficient funds set aside to pay for Jamie and Anne's college, our main financial concern of the day. So when an American friend who was a special education teacher asked if I would be interested in helping a recently founded effort to aid retarded and neurologically handicapped children, I was immediately interested.

Mme. Kadiatou Sanogho, the child of a colonial-era civil servant, was a French as well as a Malian citizen by virtue of her father's previous service to France. As a result, when two of her daughters were born with handicaps while she and her husband were students in France, they would both be cared for by the French social security system for life. One was permanently unable to take care of herself at all, and remained in France; the other, educated as much as possible through her early teen-age years, then came home to live with her family in Mali.

Kady, well off but not wealthy, decided it was her duty to help children in similar situations in Mali, where no assistance for them, government or otherwise, was available. (At the time, blindness and deafness were the only handicaps which the government recognized as needing special help.) So she started Mali's first facility for children severely handicapped by either inherited defects or those resulting from trauma at birth. It was staffed with a physical therapist, an occupational therapist, and several nurses. It opened twice a week, in a tent provided by the army behind a neighborhood clinic in a poorer section of the city. She named it AMALDEME (*Association Malienne de Lutte contre les Déficiences Mentales chez l'Enfant*).[4]

This tent was so far from the center of town that no roads in the area were paved. During the rainy season our Suzuki, which was my car during the week, performed admirably in mud and floodwater. AMALDEME's "waiting room" consisted of mats in one corner of the tent; the various specialists counseled parents and saw the children on other mats in other corners. Educating and advising parents about how to help their children was the main service rendered. But Kady had bigger ideas. They included: first, a real building for AMALDEME, with a greatly enlarged medical staff, which she obtained in 1989, and second, a first-rate school for these

---

[4] Note that "*Déficiences Mentales*," which seems to have a direct cognate in English, really does not. The term, at least as used in AMALDEME, refers to neurologically handicapped children (cerebral palsy, for example) as well as mental retardation.

children, where they would be mainstreamed because local village children would prefer it to the regular village school.

And that is what happened, in the years after we left Mali. The AMALDEME school had to turn away some non-handicapped children for lack of space. Not only that, but Kady also managed to get AMALDEME's school staffed by teachers paid by the national government, an essential step to ensure its continuity, and to add two vocational classes for students who were able to succeed in the basic literacy classes. When Bob and I visited in 2004-2005, we discovered that Kady had even acquired a farm on the main road north of Bamako where the vocational students could do a practical course to equip themselves with money-earning skills for life. Sadly, Kady died not long afterwards, from one of those diseases (we think it was typhoid) that are no longer often fatal in more developed countries but still wreak havoc in places like Mali.[5]

I was immediately valuable to Kady not for any skills I had, but for my connection with the US Embassy. She was a master at fund raising; in particular, she relied on the Knights of Malta (*l'Ordre de Malte*), successors to the Knights Hospitaller of the Crusades, who are still in the business of good works, but today by giving grants of money rather than treating sick or injured pilgrims. I had access to useful items right in Bamako, mainly used embassy and household furnishings which were routinely auctioned off a couple of times a year. Charities known to or sponsored by Americans could buy items before the auctions, at very low prices set by our administrative section.

Soon, AMALDEME had comfortable used carpet underneath the mats in the tent. Later, a portion of the furnishings for the new building came from the embassy warehouse. Khady's office acquired a nice sofa for guests, while treatment rooms and classrooms benefitted from many more rugs over the years, plus more desks and tables

---

[5] The school did outlast Kady's leadership by many years, but by 2017 was suffering severely from lack of funds. It seemed to have lost its status as a government school. *"Cris de détresse de l'association 'AMALDEME.' Le groupe demande urgemment un soutien pour sauver la vie de l"organisation."* See news.abamako.com/h/162456.html. Accessed January, 2018.

for treatment rooms. I was also able to solicit donations from other sources. I remember in particular a desk and chair for the director's office, donated by my sister Jane's book group after her visit to Bamako.

My most interesting involvement, however, derived from my teaching experience. I worked on *"formation,"* or training, of the caregivers for our little patients. Somewhere in my files there is a Xeroxed handbook which I created, illustrated with stick figures, to remind these adults of what they had learned about helping their children: repetition, the use of appropriate utensils—spoons with large handles, thick pencils, Velcro rather than laces, and so on. Above all, both parents and teachers needed to understand the importance of patience, patience, patience.

By our final year in Bamako, two classrooms were being created, with trained Malian teachers to run them, The teachers were receptive to guidance, and so I worked with them, starting with a suggestion that sitting on the floor would be a better idea than trying to make our crippled or palsied pupils sit at desks. I demonstrated and they tried out ideas like making words with cut-out letters, writing on a chalkboard instead of in a notebook, counting and moving objects to learn math sums and and other basic special education techniques. Our two teachers, and later many more, were sent by AMALDEME to France for short training courses.

I joined the Bamako Women's International Club in part to help AMALDEME. It had been founded by some of Bamako's most energetic, and somewhat rebellious, women because Mme. Traoré headed the quasi-official Women's Club and controlled its activities. These interesting and sophisticated women sought challenging programs and charitable activities which they could choose themselves, but their club had to remain under-the-radar. However, they welcomed expatriate members.

This club became a generous supporter of AMALDEME's activities, and although we couldn't advertise our fund-raisers on the radio or in the press, the grapevine worked rather well. The American Ambassador's residence and large garden became a frequent venue for its meetings and social events.

Our masked ball was an International Women's Club fundraiser. It was such a novel idea that many guests were

The famous annual cattle crossing into the Niger inland delta at the end of the rainy season, a great example of effective traditional local government.

flummoxed by what the invitation really meant. The Malians tended to dress up in their best party clothes; the Europeans did too, but they came with dainty face masks on sticks, while the Americans wore costumes, à la Halloween. I don't remember how much money was made, but such fun was had by all that the Russian Embassy hosted at least one more after our departure.

The Cattle Crossing at Diafarabé

By late November 1988, following our boat ride, the Niger was dropping, and we went to see the annual cattle crossing at Diafarabé, a Niger Inner Delta town we had passed through on the boat a month earlier. The local population is largely Peuhl (or Fulani), living in fixed villages, but every year their cattle are herded north across the river to eat the new grass left after the rains. When the dry season begins they head home. This is a tricky business, because the Delta residents include farmers as well as cattle owners.

As per the musical *Oklahoma!*, the farmer and the cowman should be but are not always friends, in this case because the cattle have a way of getting into ripe fields of millet as they seek the tasty river grass exposed by the receding water. Attempting to solve the problem, a famous Peuhl monarch, Cheick Amadou, decreed two centuries ago that herds had to cross the river at specified times and places, beginning at Diafarabé because it is at the upstream (i.e. first to dry out) end of the Delta, and working downstream from there. It was a splendid home-grown example of the kind of "good governance" which our aid programs were eager to encourage elsewhere in Africa.

What we saw, from a reviewing stand set up by the authorities, was a joyous, ceremonial love-in between the local people and their cattle:

Grouped in clusters of 2-300, carefully segregated according to ownership, the cattle swam across the river to be greeted on the other side by delirious villagers. The welcoming crowd included numerous Peuhl ladies wearing their enormous gold earrings. Clusters of cattle, often decorated with blue paint, were surrounded by the crowd, while songs were sung praising their beauty and the courage of the herders who had guided them south on the long trek from Mauritania. No one seems to use horses for herding in Mali; all the cowboys and girls are on foot.[6]

After an hour or so of this, the assembled officialdom retired to another site closer to the mud brick buildings of the town. At this point there were speeches, and awards were presented to the owners of the best (handsomest? fattest?) cattle. The entire town looked on, including elderly veterans (*anciens combattants*) of the French Army. Our host was Alaye Diall, *Commandant de Cercle* of Kati, near Bamako, but from a prosperous Diafarabé family; he fed us a lavish lunch of mutton, not beef. In my report, I noted one of the problems with cattle raising in Mali: it was a matter of passion, not

---

[6] From Bob's trip report, "A Trip to the Cattle Crossing at Diafarabé, Mali," November 26, 1988," slightly edited; but the definitive work on the subject is Pascal James Imperato, "Nomads of the Niger," *Natural History*, Vol. 81, No. 10, 1972, pp. 60-69 and 78-79; it shows the annual migration tracks into the Niger Delta at eighteen points.

profit. Owners hated to sell their animals in good years, when they were in fine fettle, waiting instead until drought struck, the cattle were skin and bones, and their owners were selling into a glutted market for a pittance.

At the end of January, Barbara's sisters Jane and Kathy arrived for a visit. (Very few family members missed visiting us in Mali, but Susie was still teaching and Erin and Ali were still very young.) We took them initially back to the Niger Delta, to more towns which we had seen from the deck of the *Tombouctou* only three months previously. Now the river was back between its dry-season banks, and the "roads," although once again above water, had been churned into mammoth ruts by overloaded trucks, and then baked by the sun into a constant series of speed bumps.

Starting from the CARE guesthouse in Ké Macina, Gaoussou Traoré's hometown, we lurched off to see a series of aid projects and markets, not calculating how slow the going would be. By early afternoon sister Jane, accustomed to regular meals, was almost hysterical with hunger, which we finally could assuage only with some *beignets* (deep-fried African doughnuts) at a local market, before we finally visited the Peace Corps improved cook stove project which Bob had officially come to see. From then on, we saw to it that ample snacks, as well as the gallons of drinking water which we always carried, were aboard when we took off in the morning.

We continued on better roads around the regular tourist circuit to Djenné, Mopti and the Dogon country. In Djenné, a friendly local official gave us permission to go inside the famous mosque and onto its roof, where the sisters took turns posing respectfully (not like that Italian film-maker and his randy crew!) on the stairs inside the minarets. All the sisters had fun looking at the wares of the jewelry peddlers on the ferry coming and going to that town. On to the Dogon country, where we hiked down the *falaise* and our guests posed with some Peuhl ladies carrying their calabashes of milk up the steep trail to market.

On the way home, we stopped in Mopti, did some shopping for beads and textiles, and picked up a local Peace Corps volunteer who was very ill with pneumonia, making for a crowded back seat on the eight-hour trip home. "It is a good thing our family does not run toward obesity," Barbara observed. [7]

Kankan Moussa's Gold: Not a Myth

After that Barbara and I visited what was to become Mali's first successful modern gold mine, thanks to Utah International, an American firm. It was located at Syama, in the southeast corner of the country, a region we had not yet visited. Tradition had it that Mali had once been rich in gold, but the Malians had taken care not to reveal the location of the mines to the Arab traders who bought it for transit across the Sahara. Kankan Moussa, Mali's most famous emperor (reigned 1307-1337),[8] is supposed to have carried enough gold with him when he went on a pilgrimage to Mecca via Cairo to depress the gold market there for some time. There was still quite a bit of artisanal mining going on in Sahelian West Africa, as we had seen in the Lobi country of Burkina Faso, but the prevailing opinion in mining circles had up until shortly before our arrival been that modern Mali didn't have any serious gold.

Two things had changed that assessment. A Utah International geologist became convinced that there had to be industrial-quantity gold in Mali; it was just a matter of finding it. Then the United Nations Development Program (UNDP) did a survey of sites where there was surface evidence of ancient mining. Based on the UNDP report, Utah International did further probing at one such site, Syama, and before long a mine that would yield $40 million in gold in its first year was underway. (File this one mentally if you think that foreign aid, UN aid in particular, is a waste of money and never stimulates economic growth.)

David Huggins, head of the Utah International effort, explained that several centuries ago gold was likely to have been concentrated near the surface, where gold-bearing rock had weathered into a hundred feet or so of loose material. Fragments of wooden mine props and pottery sherds suggested that mining at this depth could have coincided

---

[7] Barbara letter to Dear Family, February 27, 1989.
[8] Pascal James Imperato and Gavin H. Imperato, *Historical Dictionary of Mali*, fourth ed., Lanham, MD, 2008, p. 163.

with the Mali Empire, although if Carbon 14 dating of the prop fragments was ever done the results were apparently mislaid.[9] What made Syama viable as a modern mine was that the gold continued into hard rock, deeper than the ancients could dig and therefore beyond their ability to extract.

On my first visit to Syama it was nothing but forest, a few sheds, bags of ore samples and one very pretty lady American geologist. On our final visit on April 19, 1990, for the mine's dedication, it was already producing gold. Barbara wrote: "We got to watch a gold ingot being poured and hold another (the first was too hot!) weighing 14.6 kg (only the size of an ordinary brick) with an approximate value of $180,000, and representing two days' production. The mine has actually been producing since January."[10]

After my first trip to Syama, we went to a Soviet-operated gold mine at Kalana, not far away. It had been in existence for some years, and I had seen intelligence reports of questionable reliability that the Soviets were stealing all the profits. In any case, the miners, mostly from Siberia, were enjoying Mali's warm climate. They were very hospitable when we visited, and we enjoyed excellent Russian cooking in honor of the New Year (1989).

The mine was astonishingly primitive, consisting of one vertical shaft with a huge metal bucket hung on a cable to raise and/or lower everything—gold ore, machinery, miners, honored guests, the works. A couple of hundred feet down, it intersected a horizontal tunnel with an ankle-deep stream of warm water running out of it, through which one waded up a gentle slope to the mine face. Huggins was convinced that Kalana, as developed by the Soviets, had never been profitable, although a decade later a totally new and much bigger mine was built on the site. By 2013 gold would be

---

[9] There were stories when I was in Mali as ambassador that such tests had been done, yielding dates coinciding approximately with the Mali Empire, but when I looked for the report during my return to Mali in 2004-2005, I could not find one, despite the assistance of the late Dr. Téréba Togola, the government's chief archaeologist.

[10] Barbara letter to Dear Family, April 25, 1990. The price of gold was then about $300 an ounce; it is now (2013) about $1,500, more than double, even accounting for inflation.

alternating with cotton as Mali's most important export, and the country produced 42,000 kilos of it in 2012.[11]

The Malians, like most Africans, are enthusiastic consumers as well as producers of gold. Although traditionally silver was more popular, jewelry has long been a store of wealth as well as a means of self-decoration, and during our time in Bamako a number of Senegalese-origin goldsmiths could replicate anything you showed them in a jewelry catalogue, charging almost solely for the value of the metal. They could also produce traditional and contemporary pieces in intricate filigree. All this was done in tiny, ill-lit shacks, using charcoal to heat the metal, and 22-carat gold. Gold of this purity is soft, which is the reason why the sapphire fell out of Barbara's engagement ring a few years later in South Africa.[12]

The most famous gold jewelry in Mali is the outsize ear pendants worn by the Peuhl women of the Niger Delta. Pure gold earrings work like a bank account: if a family gains wealth, gold is bought and the earrings are enlarged. If financial calamity befalls the family, some of the gold can be sold, and the goldsmith downsizes the earrings. That said, many earrings which one sees today may be gold wash over silver, and poor women wear yellow earrings of the same style, but made of rice straw.

The Peuhl (Fulani) are found throughout West Africa. They are noted for their difficult language and the extraordinary diversity of their social organization. Many are nomads, often wandering through farming villages with their herds of cattle, but they have also had major kingdoms, not least in Mali. Most are Muslims, sometimes fervent, but some are still pagan, most notably the Wodaabé of Niger, whose young men stage all-male beauty contests to attract wives.[13]

The status of Peuhl women is high. To see Peuhl ladies

---

[11] For Mali's 2012 gold production, see http://www.indexmundi.com/minerals/?product=gold&graph=production, accessed at the time of writing. In recent years, South African companies have taken over most gold mining in Mali.

[12] See Chapter 15 (South Africa) for this tale.

[13] See especially Carol Beckwith (photos) and Marion Van Offelin (text), *Nomads of Niger*, New York, 1983, which for my money is the best photo book on Africa ever done.

at rural markets is almost always to see a fashion show. They are invariably friendly and love being photographed. They consider themselves light-skinned, migrants by tribal tradition from the Middle East, and they sometimes explain that this why they have an affinity for Europeans.

Our Daily Routine

Despite all our travel, there was always plenty to do in Bamako, even given the paucity of urgent policy issues. Here is an excerpt from a four-page, single spaced letter home about our daily routine:

Annie's day begins before ours. She is off to CARE by about seven; bikes to the Embassy, parks her bike and continues to her office, still several kilometers away along the Koulikoro Road, by "bachée," one of the mini-pickup trucks that serve as public transportation in Bamako.

We wake up in time for the morning news, five minutes of VOA (Voice of America) summary (The VOA helpfully goes off the air at 7 a.m., but I am not their target audience), followed by half an hour of BBC. The latter, including a section of news on Africa, is excellent, but no amount of radio news substitutes for a good newspaper. We do get the Paris Herald Trib, two or three days late but invaluable nonetheless.

After breakfast I depart for the office in my absurd automobile, underneath the Arch of Bats, flags flying (questions of vanity aside, the flags help get us through traffic). I'm supposed to vary my route for security reasons, and this is making me an expert on lower Bamako geography. Except for a few main arteries all the city streets are either unpaved or full of jagged potholes, and there are a number of picturesque streams (nearly dry at this time of year) cum open sewers. There are many buildings dating back to the French period in various states of repair. The big square has a rather moving monument, a big statue put up by the French in 1924 showing French and Malian troops fighting together in World War I.

Meanwhile back at the house Barb is doing any of the following: negotiating with GSO over the latest construction hassle (at the moment it's installation of a swinging door); doing Bob's financial disclosure statement (an example of government inanity which is right up there with State Department building management); getting ready to go teach handicapped kids (on Tuesday and Friday); or dealing with the latest servant crisis. Lately we have had a series of mobylette (motor scooter) accidents. Malian Embassy employees and our staff are issued these things for home to office transportation. The first accident was a seemingly mild scrape but resulted in what looked like a serious head injury for our elderly cook, Mahamadou. We immediately decreed that all our staff wear helmets (which we bought) while riding their mobylettes, and are getting the Embassy to do likewise for all local employees. Fortunately Mahamadou seems to be getting better after the usual nightmarish progression through the highly deprived local health care system (quote unquote). Now, only a month later, the new cook has had what might have been a much more serious accident: he was hit by a car and thrown head over heels off the cycle; his helmet was badly battered but he seems to have survived with nothing more than some strained muscles. (All of the above is why Peace Corps volunteers who are caught not wearing their helmets are sent home instantly; no appeal.)[14]

As mentioned above, the cook who had worked at the Residence since the first US ambassador's time retired soon after we arrived, and managing the kitchen, with a series of cooks who didn't work out, was a major nuisance for Barbara that first year. Mahamadou, the illiterate but experienced kitchen assistant usually stepped into the breach. By December, he was becoming a trusted asset in the kitchen, but he had previously cooked from memory, and required quite a bit of tutoring at first. As I wrote home:

In preparation for parties at Christmas, he has been baking cookies for weeks; he is desperately trying to learn to read recipes, but every morning we take out the translated recipe, even if it is the tenth time it is being used; I read it aloud, and we line up all the cup and spoon measures necessary, especially those confusing half and quarter ones. We also review which spice bottles to use, whether to use American or local flour, and whether the "levure"

---

[14] Bob and Barbara letter to Dear Family, April 9, 1989.

in the recipe is baking soda or baking powder.

Then in January, Mahamadou had his mobylette accident.

He was making great progress until he was sidelined for several weeks by his mobylette accident. His substitute, literate and eager to please, found a recipe for muffins and decided to surprise us with them for breakfast. Luckily, I came down to check on activity in the kitchen just before he was to mix the dry ingredients with the moist ones: dry—all there and all correct; wet: sucre = sugar, yes; oeufs = eggs, yes; beurre = beer. Oh, no! So we ditched that mixture, and I showed him how to turn the dry ingredients into pancakes.[15]

The end of the tale is that for the second half of our stay in Mali Mahamadou and the substitute mentioned above, who turned out to be very capable and could read recipes (in French, of course), became a kitchen team, sharing all aspects of meal preparation.

Visiting Tessalit and Dakar, and back by Train

At the end of January we availed ourselves of the attachés' C-12 plane to visit Tessalit, a big oasis with a population of about 2,000. It is the last settlement and immigration post south of the Algerian border on the main trans-Saharan road, although still 160 kilometers short of the actual border. This is the real Sahara, with average rainfall of less than three inches a year. At the time we visited, the little town supported itself by selling souvenirs to the trickle of hardy foreign tourists crossing the desert in winter, and there were three *campements* (extremely modest lodgings), stalls selling oasis vegetables (lots of tomatoes), very picturesque saloons and signs, and, its sole industry, a plaster and chalk-making factory created with Belgian aid.

Tessalit had a substantial Tuareg population, clustered here because they had lost all their animals in the drought

---

[15] The first kitchen quotation is from Barbara letter to Dear Family, January 15, 1989, and the second is from the letter quoted in footnote 14 above.

Every inch the ambassador's wife, Barbara poses with a Tuareg welcoming party at Tessalit in Mali's far north, near the Algerian border.

years. But the recent rainy season had been good; the surviving animals were fat and happy. Our hosts mounted camels and they danced for us, resulting in some classic pictures of Barbara, looking every inch the ambassador's wife, surrounded by Blue Men of the Desert on White Camels.

We were impressed by the police (*gendarmerie*) commander, a Tuareg named Henri Mohamadire from nearby Kidal. He took us to see some Tuareg schools, which, he explained, the children attended only long enough to learn sufficient French to be able to travel out of the desert to find work. He also took us into the nearby hills, strewn with black boulders, part of the Adrar des Iforas,[16] to see prehistoric rock art. These were not cave paintings, but drawings of camels, giraffes, horses, and other modern animals, incised on the larger boulders. This art was accompanied by inscriptions in the Tuareg/Tamashek script, but in a language that today's Tuaregs, like Henri, could no longer understand. (For more

[16] The Adrar des Iforas were being mentioned in Western press reports when this was being written as the place where rebels fled to escape the 2012 French military intervention.

on the Tuareg, see the end of this chapter.)

Nearby was a big airstrip built by the French in the 1950s to bomb Algerians fighting for their independence; it was the reason we were able to fly there. When the Algerian Ambassador got wind of our trip, presumably from the Malian government which had given us permission to go, he asked me politely about "rumors" of long standing American interest in Tessalit, and said his government would like to know if we were thinking about establishing a listening post there. I assured him that our interest was purely touristic, which was mainly true at the time, although the attachés no doubt checked out the condition of the airstrip. In fact, he was only about twenty years ahead of time.[17]

After Tessalit, the attachés headed back to their base in Liberia, dropping us off in Dakar to attend WAIST, the West African Invitational Softball Tournament. However, one of our Marine security guards had been needed in our old post, Ouagadougou, where three of its Marines had been sent home for drug abuse, leaving Bamako without enough players to field a team and us with no one to cheer for.

So we decided to go sightseeing in Senegal instead. First we visited Dakar's museum, which had a famous if somewhat moldy collection of West African art. It was created when Dakar was the capital of French West Africa, which included Mali and seven other territories that are now separate countries. We continued to Gorée Island, an old slave trading post, with a famous "door of no return" from which slaves were loaded onto ships for transport across the Atlantic.

Until early in the nineteenth century, it was the colonial settlement, and Dakar did not exist, so the architecture features balconies and wrought iron railings, suggesting a dilapidated (and miniature) New Orleans. However, these houses had first floors with strong walled rooms and tiny windows: they were slave-holding pens. Incredibly, the Europeans lived upstairs, above their businesses, as it were; maybe that fact is explainable by noting that during the slave trading period, all the Europeans were men—traders or military men; their wives or mistresses

---

[17] The Tessalit trip and subsequent visit to Senegal, plus the journey home by rail, is covered in Barbara letter to Dear Family, February 27-28, 1989.

were black or mulatto. From the seventeenth century to 1848, when the French finally abolished slavery, thousands of slaves were exported from Gorée and nearby Saint Louis, the colonial capital.

Then we rented a car and visited Saint Louis, the first French outpost in West Africa. For years, anyone born in Dakar or Saint Louis was automatically a French citizen, creating a very special relationship between Senegal and France, and Saint Louis, like Gorée, is a spectacle of decayed colonial gentility.

From Saint Louis, we visited Djoudj, a nature reserve on the Mauritanian border which, like the Niger Inner Delta, is a major stopover point for migratory birds flying between southern Africa and Europe. The highlight of Djoudj was a huge flock of White Pelicans fishing communally by forming a big wedge to herd quite large fish, and then going after them under water with their massive, pouched bills. They were totally undisturbed by our small boat going into the middle of their hunt, and despite thick, dry-season dust blowing off the desert, I got some memorable photos.

To get home, we took the twice-weekly "express" train from Dakar to Bamako. We knew that the railroad, Mali's only rail link to the Atlantic, had recently been upgraded by the Canadians (new roadbed, powerful new locomotives) so that the journey would take "only" about twenty-four hours.[18] Our embassy travel section in Dakar didn't even know there was a passenger train to Bamako, but, after a protest from Barbara that sitting up the whole time would not do (and, see below, definitely would not have done), they finally got us the best available accommodation, a Spartan European-style sleeping compartment for two.

An hour or so out of Dakar we reached Thiès,[19] the headquarters of the railroad, where its CEO had heard that we were on board. He was upset that no one had told him about our travel; he would have let us use the presidential car, but,

---

[18] In order to make the railroad upgrade successful, the Malians were steadfastly refusing to complete a decent road link between Bamako and the Senegalese border.

[19] Thiès is the setting of a famous African novel, Ousmane Sembène's *God's Bits of Wood* (*Les Bouts de Bois de Dieu*).

to make up for this omission, his staff scurried around making sure there was plenty of "European" food on board. The train cook, working in a tiny cubicle, proceeded to produce the most amazingly good meals for the balance of the trip, and we were served beer with every one, including breakfast.

It was very hot, and there was no air conditioning. The powerful new train roared along, stirring up huge clouds of dust and ashes from the habitual dry-season brush fires, liberal amounts of which poured in the open train windows. To minimize grittyness, we dusted every hour or so with one of my undershirts. After we crossed the Malian border, we discovered that this train was not merely, or perhaps even primarily, a means of transport, but a twice-weekly rolling market:

Some passengers are market women, who sell at one stop and buy down the line; savvy ordinary passengers do the same thing to defray the costs of the trip. We first figured out what was going on in Kita, about four hours out of Bamako, when mobs of people lined up at each door of the train; I knew they couldn't be getting on our car, it was full. Lo and behold, 20-kg. sacks of salt, which everyone had bought somewhere in Senegal, where there is a famously pink salt lake, suddenly began reappearing to be sold. The salt had come on board during the night while we were, believe it or not, sleeping. The same is true of soap that I had seen being loaded in case lots in Dakar. Other than this "international" commerce, there are, at every stop, scores of people selling everything from cups of water to fried chicken to bananas to embroidered cloth and dresses that the traveler might need.... It was a great trip, once.[20]

To top it off, the train was met in Bamako at the picturesque, French-era station, just a block or two from my office, by hordes of would-be porters, liberally mixed with aggressive pickpockets. Fortunately we had been warned about them, and Sekou was there to rescue us.

---

[20] Barbara letter to Dear Family, February 27, 1989, slightly expanded.

Time off in Israel

By May it was too hot to move in Mali, with daily highs over 100 degrees, so we decided to visit Israel, where our friends Phil and Cindy Wilcox were living while Phil was the US Consul General in Jerusalem. We hoped to tour a little of the Holy Land (the first *Intifada* was under way, so we weren't sure where we would be able to go) and do some Scuba diving in the Red Sea. But first we had to get to Israel. We needed visas to travel on our diplomatic passports, and of course there was no Israeli Embassy in Mali. So we asked our embassy to issue us tourist passports. As in the case of Spain, where Barbara had gotten into trouble with her diplomatic passport, Israel didn't require visas from "ordinary," non-diplomatic US citizens.

However, this precaution didn't stop us from getting into trouble in Brussels airport, where we transferred from Sabena (then serving Bamako) to El Al. Everything went wrong. There were two lines to get through security, one English and one French language. We chose the French line because it was shorter. First question: "Who are you?" Answer: "I am the American Ambassador to Mali and these are my wife and daughter." "Why are you in the French language line?" "Because it is shorter." So far, so good, but the young soldier asking the questions was looking dubious. "Why are you going to Israel?" "To visit friends and to go Scuba diving." "Are you taking anything for anyone else?" "Yes." At the request of a friend, Barbara was taking some old beads bought in the Bamako market to a collector in Israel.

By this time we could feel the suspicion thickening, especially because we all had brand-new tourist passports. Why would an ambassador have an ordinary passport? The security agents were young Israelis doing their compulsory military service; they were not empowered to make difficult decisions, and pawing through our luggage provided no helpful answers. Finally, after considerable delay, they passed our case to their boss, who judged us harmless and allowed us to board the plane just in time.

In Israel we learned that Phil's post was not-so-laughingly described as the "US Embassy to the Palestinians," because indeed one of his main jobs was to get to know the large Palestinian community. The Wilcoxes not only met Palestinians professionally, but living in Jerusalem, depended on them to help run and maintain the household—except that during the Intifada, many of their employees did not come to work. Barbara remembers spending one afternoon with Cindy preparing canapés for a previously scheduled reception at their home. We met a number of the Wilcoxes' Palestinian friends, as well as many Jews, and came home much better informed about the complexities of the Israeli-Palestinian interface. The Israeli Government was and still is strongly opposed to our having any representation outside Tel Aviv—unless we agree to move our embassy to Jerusalem—but our Consulate in Jerusalem has survived, so far.[21]

After his retirement from the Foreign Service, Phil ran an organization, the Foundation for Middle East Peace, which lobbied persistently for a two-state solution. He did this without losing his cheerful, can-do assumption that peace based on trading land for security is the only possible solution and will happen, sooner or later. We could not visit contested areas of the West Bank, but we walked around the wall of old Jerusalem, toured and shopped in the old city, visited Galilee and Caesarea, and traveled widely elsewhere with Annie. We discovered that you can't go anywhere in Israel without having a thoroughly interesting time.[22]

We then went to Eilat, at the head of Red Sea, to embark for several days of diving near Sharm el Sheikh from an Israeli live-aboard boat, the *Colona IV*. The diving was top notch, as was the food (this is not supposed to happen on dive boats), and I got excellent underwater photos despite a malfunctioning flashgun. On the way back we stopped off at Masada, the famous Israeli fortress, but we resisted bathing in the hugely salty Dead Sea.

A New Look Soviet Ambassador

Back in Bamako, it was becoming apparent that Alexandre and

---

[21] Just as we were getting ready to go to press with this autobiography, the Trump administration moved the US Embassy to Jerusalem.

[22] Barbara to Dear Family, June 11, 1989; there is much more detail in the letter.

Tatiana Trofimov, the new Soviet ambassadorial couple, were not your stereotypical, glowering, dumpy, Soviet Bloc envoys. He was slight, cheerful and sociable; she was very pretty and stylish, fond of décolletage that soon had *le tout Bamako* on its collective ear. The Trofimovs' arrival coincided roughly with the advent of *Glasnost* and *Perestroika*, and I soon discovered that I could learn more about what was going on in the about-to-vanish Soviet Union by asking its ambassador than by reading State Department cables or the *New York Times*.

In some other respects the Trofimovs were refreshingly naive. They discovered that we enjoyed traveling to interesting parts of Mali, and decided to try this new idea themselves. The first time, they got badly lost because their driver was Russian and spoke no French, much less Bambara; they had no such employee as a trusted local staff member to guide them, and their only ambassadorial vehicle was a low-slung limo with heavily tinted windows, making it hard for them to see the countryside and people they had come to see.

They did, however, following some directions from us, manage to find Peace Corps Baba at his tiny first shop in the Mopti market, where Tatiana bought some souvenirs and ordered several more to be created for her. Barbara soon received two bracelets, with an almost unintelligible note from "Piscod Baba ... pour la femme Ambassadeur de U.R.S.S. [sic]."[23] "Now, when she commissions something while passing through his town, he sends it to me in Bamako for delivery to her," Barbara wrote to Ann Scott as they discussed the first results of the thaw in US-Soviet relations.[24]

As recounted previously, when Barbara organized the masked ball for the International Women's Club, the Trofimovs

---

[23] "Mopti le 15/2/90, Chere Bara Bara." Peace Corps Baba, formally Oumar Cissé, began as a vendor selling handicrafts to Peace Corps volunteers (among others) in the Mopti Market. Infectiously joyful, he proved to be a talented businessman who later built a substantial store-cum-museum in Sevaré and was able to travel to the US and Europe selling his wares and catching up with old friends. He sent a daughter to a university in Canada. When he came down with liver cancer a few years before this was written, his many friends paid for his medical treatment in France, and his cancer is currently (July, 2016) in remission. His business has, however, suffered from recent political unrest in the Niger Delta, as has everything else.

[24] Barbara letter to Ann [Scott], April 30, 1990.

adored it and gave another one on a much grander scale after we left. They have a lovely daughter, Marianna, who they hoped would become a ballerina; she eventually went into the travel business. We kept up with them for several years, but the last time we saw them was in *Ark of Russia*, a Russian film about the last days of the czars, when, in a scene of the final formal ball ever held at the Hermitage, Alexandre and Tatiana come waltzing across the foreground. It was good casting.[25]

Jamie visited in the summer of 1989, and the highlight was helping to "advance" a visit from Ivan Selin, the State Department's new Under Secretary for Management.[26] This allowed him to visit Timbuktu with FSO Jane Buchmiller, riding up on the attaché aircraft and spending a night in a Tuareg encampment. Selin himself was a pleasant person and tireless traveler, but his wife, Nina, wanted to buy everything in sight, always first demanding our opinions on whether the mask (or whatever it was) was worth the outlay, which drove us distracted. Even Peace Corps Baba, who hurriedly rounded up a large pair of real gold Peuhl earrings, which after a lot of discussion she decided not to buy, was put off by her "bargaining." In Africa, the rule of art shopping is, if *you* like it, it's worth it, up to a point. After his visit was over, Selin sent everyone who had been involved a good trip report, accompanied by a T-shirt labeled "I Survived Two Weeks in Africa with Ivan."

Pax Celebrates the Fourth of July

In 1989 we celebrated our second Fourth of July in Bamako. It went well, except for the issue of serving champagne for the ceremonial toast. Our servants, anxious to have it ready on time, would have poured it a half hour in advance, thus ensuring it would be flat and warm by the time it reached our guests. In 1988, Georgia Lucas, the doctor's wife and a good friend, but NOT

---

[25] We corresponded with the Trofimovs for a few years through Christmas cards, at least as late as 1993, when he was Ambassador to Estonia and not enjoying having to deal with a large, unhappy, ethnic Russian community, newly deprived of Estonian citizenship: Trofimov letter to Dear Barbara and Bob, from Talinn, January, 1993.

[26] Barbara letter to Dear Family, August 30, 1989.

an employee of the US government, had volunteered to help, and had organized last-minute filling of the champagne glasses. For 1989, Georgia wanted to attend as a guest, so Barbara asked a junior embassy officer to make sure that things went smoothly. However, the officer in question complained that she was paid to talk to the guests, not to pour champagne.

We felt strongly that since Barbara was not paid at all, and had to be with me for the ceremony, AND since the ceremony/ champagne, etc., had the ultimate aim of advancing US interests, it WAS an officer's job. In the event, Annie, still working for CARE during her gap year between boarding school and college, and so cheerful and friendly that even our elderly, male staff did not object to her supervision, filled in and organized the champagne pouring. For our third and final Fourth of July, 1990, guess who got to order a junior officer to do the job, period. (We were very fond of the now not-so-young lady who hadn't quite understood her representational duties, and remain friends with her.)

Back to our 1989 Fourth: it began badly with rain at noon, aggravating ruts and puddles where our VIP guests would soon be arriving. In a rare fit of initiative, the *Voirie* (Roads and Refuse Department of the city) came dashing over and dumped several truckloads of dirt into the puddles. Then it rained again, turning the dirt piles into something resembling chocolate pudding. In the last act, GSO came to the rescue with several truckloads of crushed rock. This did the trick, but created a misleading rumor in the neighborhood that the US Embassy was paving our road.

We had tons of fried chicken, hamburgers, hot dogs (all beef, flown in from Brussels), California champagne, four bars, a big tent and a big display of photos, supplied by USIS, of President Traoré's state visit to the United States. But it was Pax, our white Peke-Pomeranian mutt, who stole the show. Barbara spotted him eating a chicken bone just as the ceremony began and tried to take it away from him. This resulted in a loud yap from Pax in the middle of the Malian National Anthem. He then escaped and wandered out triumphantly, chicken bone in mouth, right in front of the color guard and the assembled Malian ministers, one of whom later remarked "Lui, il a fêté aussi!" (He's had his own celebration!).[27]

You may be wondering how we could have been so culturally insensitive as to have had a dog running around at a diplomatic ceremony in a Muslim country. We knew that some Muslims consider dogs to be unclean, although this feeling is not nearly as strong as the universal abhorrence of pigs. But Malians never seemed to mind Pax, perhaps because, as in Ouagadougou, they couldn't quite figure out what this small, fluffy creature was, a *cat* maybe? He certainly bore no resemblance to a Saluki, the greyhound-like creatures native to the Sahara and domesticated by the Muslim Tuareg.[28]

Medevac'd to Paris

Soon after July Fourth, I had a sudden and ugly recurrence of my old herpes eye infection, after fifteen years free of it, and when the local eye clinic dismissed it as conjunctivitis, Dr. Lucas lost no time in evacuating me to Paris, possibly avoiding severe damage to my only good eye. Dr. Lucas wanted to send Barbara with me, almost blind with only my bad eye functioning. However, Annie was in Timbuktu, prior to leaving for her freshman year at the University of Chicago in a couple of days, so Mom had to stay behind. I was sentenced to a prudently long stay in France, to avoid complications from Bamako's desert dust (even though by this time what turned out to be an exceptionally moist rainy season was well under way).

Therefore, once Annie was ready to go, Barbara came up to join me and we had ample time to see the new I.M. Pei addition to the Louvre and the famous flea market at Clignancourt. We spent a day at Chartres, which Bob had never visited, attended a Vivaldi concert in the Sainte Chapelle, and explored some of the less famous restaurants and corners of Paris.

Annie spent two days with us in Paris, along with cousins Heather and Jen who were returning from summers abroad. All this was lovely except for shlepping the Theobald nieces' gigantic suitcases to the taxi; how they handled them

---

[27] Bob letter to Dear Family, July 8, 1989.

[28] Parker Borg, my friend and one of my predecessors, had a Saluki running around in the yard of the Residence for a while, along with some kind of desert antelope.

themselves, we weren't quite sure. Then Annie's US-bound flight blew an engine on takeoff and had to circle over the Paris exurbs dumping fuel before returning to the airport. Since there wasn't enough time to rejoin us for dinner with our friends, Professor and Mrs. Jean Capron, she remained at the Charles de Gaulle Holiday Inn, sharing a room and dinner with the older, sympathetic seatmate who had kept her spirits up during the crisis in the air. She certainly had one of the more dramatic starts to college of any of her generation in the family.

The children did seem to attract airline dramas. Later, on the way to Bamako for their final visits in the summer of 1990, Annie's Sabena flight made a hard landing at Conakry, Guinea, an intermediate stop, and the plane was damaged so badly that it couldn't fly, leaving her to spend one night on the aircraft before she could connect with an Air Guinea flight to Bamako. She was hoping to arrive in Bamako in time for the wedding of a good friend, Sally Olsonoski, at our Residence, and with the help of the embassy staff in Conakry, she did.

Two days later Jamie arrived at the same airport and his plane burst its hydraulic system. He was luckier; the airline put him up at a fancy hotel for the night, and he enjoyed both its pool and its food. We were out of town, in Belgium, briefing my designated successor, Dan Gelber, on his new job. At this point Conakry, having taken care of both our kids in succession, cabled Bamako:

> Duty officer understands Ambassador and Mrs. Pringle are in Brussels and will be returning to Mali shortly. Believing that the Pringle family has special effects on airplanes, we will be prepared to assist the Ambassador and his wife. Are there any other brothers or sisters coming through Conakry?[29]

But we made our trip without incident.

---

[29] Conakry 2729, June 16, 1990.

Finding Islam in Mali

Partway through my tour, I began wondering about the political dimension of Islam in Mali. The roughly 90% of Malians who were Muslim were clearly devout and observant, and there was plenty of evidence that Malian Islam had been a political force in the past, when "jihadists" (as the French were calling them even then) sometimes led the resistance to colonization. By the time we arrived, certain foreign powers, especially the Saudis, were subsidizing mosque construction and promoting fundamentalism in Mali. Washington was most concerned about the threat of Shia Islam.

I could find no one willing to speak for Malian Islam generally; a gentleman identified as the Imam of Bamako ended our discussion by asking me for money. I was looking in the wrong places. The most important Islamic authority in Mali, as in neighboring Senegal, lay with the traditional Sufi brotherhoods, located mainly in areas outside Bamako.[30]

The core of Malian Islam is moderate, for the same sort of historical reasons that Indonesian Islam is moderate. Some Malian leaders converted to Islam centuries ago, because it gave them a kind of passport to the outside world, especially important for travelers or those dealing with Arab traders. But the country was still primarily agricultural, and the local spirits of land and water were still needed to make the rains fall and the crops grow. Nor could the ancestors be summarily ignored. And while Islamization has made steady progress against these obstacles, an underlying Malian conservatism and pride in the country's multicultural past has remained strong.

A Closer Look at the Tuareg

Late in 1989 we traveled twice to important Tuareg regions: Kidal, north of Gao, and Menaka, near the Niger River just before

---

[30] Only later did an American anthropologist, Benjamin F. Soares, publish a book which is truly useful for a lay observer trying to understand contemporary Malian Islam: *Islam and the Prayer Economy: History and Authority in a Malian Town*, Edinburgh, 2005.

it crosses the international border between Mali and Niger. [31]
We went to Kidal by attaché aircraft to look at a clinic being
financed by a US military civic action program. This program
marked the modest beginning of a US military involvement
which would grow substantially in the years ahead. Kidal has a
spectacular old fort, built by the French in Beau Geste days, by
this time serving as a jail. The town was and still is the home of
the Kel Adagh Tuareg, who have historically been the primary
drivers of a nationalist agenda to create a Tuareg state, which
they want to call Azawad. In the 1960s, they had launched a
bitter rebellion that was crushed by the Malian army, but we
assumed that it, like so much more about them, was ancient
history. Kidal seemed a stark, unhappy place, but I made no
effort to call on local leaders.

The Tuareg seemed folkloric, fodder for a future tourist
industry, dancing camels and all, but not politically important.
Found primarily in Algeria, Mali and Niger, they speak a
Berber language and often call themselves Tamashek, which
in Algeria is also the word for Berber more generally. They
have a written language and a proud sense of cultural identity,
yet have been endlessly riven by broad divisions based on
kinship, class, and age.

Traditionally they were extremely hierarchical, with
nobles, artisans and slaves, but by the time of our stay in Mali
the power of the traditional leadership had been breaking
down for decades. There was a potent generational division,
linked to diminishing respect on the part of youth for older
traditional leaders. There was also a division between those
who had been abroad to work, frequently as mercenaries in
Libya, and those who had not. It is often noted that the Tuareg,
although Muslim, are matrilineal, but not all of them are. The
men wear turban-like headcloths that cover most of their
faces, primarily to protect them from the harsh desert sun,
but also as a style statement. The most expensive headcloth
material is saturated with indigo, which stains the faces of
those who can afford it, hence the label "Blue men of the
Desert." But Tuareg women do not cover their faces.

---

[31] Both trips are covered in Barbara letter to Dear Family, December 13,
1989.

Tuareg are often seen, and see themselves, as "white," yet they come in all shades of skin color from Arabic light to "black." The "blacks" are, mainly, the descendants of entire villages enslaved by Tuareg warriors and assimilated to the point where they speak, and feel themselves to be, Tuareg; these are the so-called Bella. The Bella are one reason for persistent racial antipathy between Malian blacks and Tuaregs. If blacks see them as slavers, they see blacks as unworthy of governing them, the lords of the desert. Before French rule, imposed on them only after ferocious combat, the Tuareg lived partly by tending their flocks, but they were also raiders and plunderers of cities where they never dwelled. When the Songhai Empire fell after a Moroccan invasion in 1591, feuding Tuareg tribes took over, barbarians to a black Malian Rome.

There are some fine history books about the Tuareg in French, which, it is a safe bet, no one at the embassy, including me, had read.[32] The French continued to have a noble savage crush on them—they had been, to the French army, what the Sioux and Cheyenne were to Custer. My friend the French Ambassador, Michel Perrin, visited a French expert on their culture and history, who was living with them, and wrote a political analysis of Tuareg clans or *kels*, interesting material for cocktail chatter but not much more, or so we thought.

The reason for this obvious (in retrospect) oversight was that the desert north was not yet a subject of official US concern. We were just getting over the anti-communist preoccupation of the Cold War, and barely beginning to be worried about radical Islam, and anyway the Tuareg were anything but Islamic extremists. We were primarily trying to support Mali's economic development. In this bone-dry area, the only important economic asset is the Niger River, and the

---

[32] The best one in English on recent Tuareg history is Jean Sebastian [Baz] Lecocq, " 'That Desert is our Country,': Tuareg Rebellions and Competing Nationalisms in Contemporary Mali (1946-1996)," Academisch Proefschrift, [PhD Thesis], University of Amsterdam, 2002, which I have used, or the published version, *Disputed Desert: Decolonization, Competing Nationalisms and Tuareg Rebellions in Mali*, Leiden: Brill Academic Publishers, Afrika-studiecentrum series, 2012. In French, see Pierre Boilley, *Les Touaregs Kel Adagh. Dépendances et révoltes: du Soudan français au Mali contemporain*. Paris: Éditions Karthala, 1999.

towns along it are populated primarily by Songhai people who are black Africans, solidly in Mali's cultural and political mainstream. As noted earlier, if you subtract the river towns, including Timbuktu, Gao and others, well under one percent of the national population lives north of the Niger.

Adding all this up, and in line with the current policy toward Mali, we saw little point in doing anything other than humanitarian aid in the desert north. This meant trying to mitigate the impact of the mid-1980s drought and preparing for the next one, which, everyone assumed, incorrectly as previously noted, was probably just around the corner.

After the Kidal visit, we went to another Tuareg area by road, beginning at Gao, where our boat trip the previous year had ended. Gao is an important place: a former seat of empire, modern regional headquarters and southern terminus of the more important of Mali's two trans-Saharan routes (the same one we had seen in Tessalit, near the Algerian border). The surrounding region had been hard hit by the 1983-84 drought. As in Tessalit, flocks had been almost totally destroyed and many inhabitants were still severely malnourished. World Vision, a non-governmental organization with Christian roots, was operating a large maternal-and-child health center, which measured the height and weight of children each month and gave basic nutrition lessons and supplementary food to the poorest victims, mainly nomads.

After Gao we continued southwards, paralleling the river, toward Menaka, through a large, purely-on-paper national park, reputed to be the home of Mali's only remaining giraffe. Seasonally flooded valleys, separated by sand dunes, ran from the interior toward the Niger, with a surprising amount of tree cover in the lower areas. Here World Vision was engaged in the multi-faceted Menaka Oasis Project, designed to fit the circumstances of an important Tuareg community.[33]

The Menaka Tuareg, like the Peuhl herders we had seen at Diafarabé, did not spend their whole time wandering in the desert, which was uninhabitable during the hottest weather. Rather, they relied on a seasonal base near the river, at Menaka,

---

[33] The material on our Gao and Menaka visits is drawn mainly from "A Trip Report to the Seventh Region (Gao and Menaka) November 5-11, 1989," also Barbara letter to Dear Family, December 13, 1989.

moving away from it with their flocks in search of grass after the rains came, but returning as vegetation inland vanished in the heat of summer. Recognizing that such nomadism was essential to survival in this environment, World Vision made no attempt to replace it, but rather aimed to supplement it with health, education and seasonal income opportunities around the dry season base. Here they built schools and a maternal-and-child health care facility like the one we had seen in Gao.

To expand income they were introducing a variety of new agricultural techniques: building new "irrigated perimeters" into which water from the Niger could be pumped for rice cultivation and promoting "recessional agriculture" in the seasonally flooded valleys, which meant cultivating fast-maturing millet crops in the muddy areas left behind as the Niger's level dropped.

In swampy areas along the river itself they were planting the nutritious aquatic grass, *bourgou*, for cattle feed, and on higher ground, reseeding with drought-tolerant wild grains (cram-cram and fonio). Fonio is a tiny grain, which is more work to harvest than millet or sorghum and therefore not a staple crop, but it was considered a delicacy by some of our more knowledgeable friends and is today being exported in small quantities. Since wood was in short supply, World Vision was experimenting at all its facilities with "wood free" buildings, using domed and vaulted mud-brick structures.

At the core of the Menaka Oasis Project was an ingenious herd restocking program to help replace the 70% of the animal population lost in the drought years, and thereby put their owners, who had been both pauperized and immobilized, back on their feet. After such disasters, the traditional practice was for relatives and friends to lend animals to those without any, to get started again. But now there were not enough relatively well off "loaner" families to do the job. So World Vision got USAID to provide, at no cost, food which the project bartered for animals. Thus equipped, it selected destitute families and loaned each one a "starter herd" consisting of three sheep, two goats and two donkeys, the latter being the "moving vans" to allow mobility, hence migration. Each family was expected to repay World Vision with four animals to be loaned out to new families, and the first year repayment rate was 100%.

The "moving van" donkeys were supposed to be repaid first.

Chalon Lee, the lady in charge, came equipped with her own horse, acquired locally; riding him, she looked like something out of the Virginia hunt country. The Tuareg had taken to calling her "Queen of the Desert," but she was also a former Peace Corps Volunteer with extensive experience in other parts of Africa.[34] She used her horse to follow the yearly migrations, witnessing scenes of the annual Tuareg-Peuhl festivals described in *Nomads of Niger*.

Chalon told us that arrowheads and other artifacts could be easily picked up along the crests of dunes, like the ones where we would later play golf and have lunch. She collected such things when she spotted them from her horse, and soon little children began finding them too and presenting them to her. She had quite a collection of beads. Some we could identity as very old stone beads, characterized by their large holes. Others were carnelian beads, of Indian origin, or medieval glass beads of the kind known as "Roman" or "Islamic," made in North Africa or the Middle East. There were also more recent glass trade beads of Venetian or other European manufacture.

In addition to its creative developmental activities, World Vision was an important participant in the Mali-wide "food security" program, pre-positioning grain supplies and maintaining half a dozen or so large trucks to distribute it when the next drought came. Far sooner than we had any reason to suspect, this cache of food and vehicles would lead to unanticipated disaster, described below.

We were impressed and inspired by the World Vision program, but then the local Tuareg took over for the fun part of our visit. They were politically poles apart from their glum counterparts in Kidal, and acted as if they had no doubt about their position in the Malian nation, or their role in feting foreign diplomats. Two of their leaders had prominent positions in Mali's government, Bajan ag Hamatou as Menaka's representative in the (admittedly powerless) National Assembly, and Baye ag Mohamed, a much younger man who was a senior party official and reportedly close

[34] Chalon Lee was only at the beginning of an extraordinary career, described years after we met her in the World Vision publication at http://www.worldvision.org, accessed July 24, 2013.

to President Traoré. It was hardly a normal situation for Mali. Compared to these two, both of them politicians and traditional leaders, the local *commandant de cercle*, typically a Malian Army captain, was clearly insignificant.

Our program included, as a starter, hitting golf balls from the top of a local sand dune, aiming at little stone circles on the valley floor below. For multicultural glitz, there is nothing like a blue-robed and beturbaned Tuareg chief whacking a golf ball into the void from an orange dune. Little boys chased the balls and brought them back. Then there was dancing and music, for which we were provided with appropriate Malian dress.

But the big show was the next day, when we had lunch on top of another dune, overlooking one of the tree-covered valleys mentioned earlier. Memorable photos ensued at every step. Our hosts set up a long tents as sun protection during the meal. They explained that we were looking out at Anderamboukane, the site of a famous battle in 1916 in which a Tuareg chief named Firhoun, who had rebelled against the French twice, was finally defeated, because the French had binoculars and the Tuaregs did not. (Bajan ag Hamatou was

Visiting an American World Vision project near Menaka, the Ambassador provided amusement for his Tuareg hosts by riding, somewhat awkwardly, one of their camels.

descended from Firhoun, and remembered his defeat with some bitterness.)

After lunch we rode on camels, in order to amuse the Tuareg audience. With an experienced camel rider behind us on the camel, we galloped away—none of the sedate, camel-roped-together walking found at tourist sites like the Pyramids. But the big amusement of the day was Bob, as he tried and finally, with much help and encouragement, succeeded in getting up on his camel's saddle.

Menaka was a memorable experience, but the ending was not happy, through no fault of World Vision. In June, 1990, roughly six months after our visit, an attempt was made by a UN agency to resettle a group of Tuaregs in nearby Niger. These people, including Malians, some of whom were from the perennially restive Kel Adagh clan of the Kidal area, were returning from employment in Libya. They were allegedly driven to revolt, initially against the Nigerien military, because promises to supply them with housing were not kept. Some of them, led by Iyad ag Ghali of Kidal, crossed the border into Mali with barely a gun among them. They were being chased by the Malian Army when they brilliantly attacked the police post at Menaka.

With the weapons thus procured, they seized all the vehicles and provisions they needed from the World Vision facilities and within weeks a major Tuareg rebellion was under away across the north. By August 1990 an estimated 150 Malian officials had been killed. The World Vision projects in Menaka and Gao were destroyed and have never been resumed, although World Vision has remained active elsewhere in Mali.

This was the second Kel Adagh-led rebellion since Malian independence, and it lasted until 1996. It left the Malian north tortured by chronic insecurity, in the hands of traffickers in drugs and people, and wide open to Islamic extremists from Algeria and elsewhere. It put a quick end to trans-Saharan tourism of the kind some of our friends had experienced. Unrest was soon being exploited by rebels and religious extremists from Algeria, and the US military began to take notice and get involved. The next round of full-scale fighting began in 2011, when it was the main cause of the overthrow of Mali's genuine democracy, by then two decades old.

Obviously we had failed to see the desert crisis coming, and I blame myself partly for this. I accepted too easily the premise that our interests in Mali were primarily economic, and that the desert north deserved little attention because very few people lived there. This short-sighted policy persisted well after the global threat of Islamic extremism became clear. In a study of Mali's new democracy published in 2006, I wrote:

> The Embassy in Bamako should, as a matter of highest priority, master the complexities of the northern political terrain, including historical factors and the dynamics of inter-ethnic relations. Not to do so is to risk missteps similar in character, if less lethal in consequence, to those that characterized the United States' flawed policy in Afghanistan during the rise of the Taliban. This is a critical task that requires a range of analytic skills and that should be undertaken by resident US Foreign Service Officers, not by Foreign Service Nationals or contractors.[35]

At the time this was written, the embassy was wholly reliant for its knowledge of desert affairs on a very bright Tuareg who belonged to the clan (*kel*) that had been the historic driver of desert rebellion.

What would have been our third Christmas in Mali was instead celebrated at home in Cincinnati. This must have been a home leave, but the timing was dictated by a lovely invitation from the Business Council for International Understanding to attend a gala performance of *Aida* at the Metropolitan Opera. This special treat for ambassadors to Africa was followed by more prosaic home leave projects: visiting Helena and doctors and dentists in the DC area, then a pleasant visit with Kate, recently widowed for the second time, in California, and finally a family Christmas in Cincinnati. Then it was back to Mali in a hurry for two important visits.

---

[35] Robert Pringle, *Democracy in Mali: Putting History to Work*, US Institute of Peace, Peaceworks series, 2006, available online at http://www.usip.org/publications/democratization-mali-putting-history-work, p. 65.

Although Mali has very few Roman Catholic citizens, it warmly welcomed Pope John Paul II when he presided over a Mass for his flock in Bamako's football stadium.

Kady Sanogho brought a delegation of handicapped children from AMALDEME and their mothers, all Moslem, to the Mass, on the theory that the more prayers they received, the more they would be helped to overcome their disabilities.

The Pope Visits Mali, as do *Les Mamans*

In January 1990 Pope John Paul II arrived. There were only a hundred thousand or so Catholics in Mali,[36] but the Malians bent over backwards to make his visit a success. A few Muslim clerics objected to all the fuss over a Christian leader, so the government simply locked them up for the duration of the visit. All ambassadors lined up at the airport for the Pope's arrival and departure, as for any other official visitor; so I got to shake his hand twice, later claiming that it had improved my tennis serve no end. However, I decided not to ask him to bless any rosaries for Catholic friends and relatives, lest this be seen as inappropriate. When I mentioned this to one of the Pope's security men (who appeared to be a retired priest) he laughed and said I should have done it!

The highlight of the visit was a Papal mass in Bamako's soccer stadium, which the diplomatic corps attended, as did Catholics from all corners of West Africa. Who should be seated almost in back of us but Kady Sanogho, with her handicapped students from AMALDEME and their mothers. Of course they were mostly, if not all, Muslims, but as Kady explained to Barbara, "These children need all the help they can get."

The visit of His Holiness coincided with that of my stepmother Kate and Barbara's mother Charlotte. Both were planning to visit, so we urged them to travel together, and, although they had never met previously, they hit it off instantly. Both coming and going, they enjoyed the museums and restaurants of Paris thoroughly. In addition to attending the Papal mass, we took them on a four-day foray north to Mopti and the Dogon Country. We overnighted at the CARE guesthouse in Djenné, in a mud brick building, and they loved staying in a "traditional African house" in spite of its squat toilets. In Mopti we went by boat to a Bozo encampment and ate at a newly opened "fancy" restaurant.

The trip to Dogon country was abbreviated in order to avoid very bumpy packed mud roads and to accommodate

---

[36] The current (2013) *CIA World Fact Book* lists the percentage of Christians (all denominations) as 2.4; the population of Mali was roughly seven million in 1989.

Kate's afternoon nap. We first stopped at a prosperous village, well-known for the paintings on the rock wall rising behind the settlement (a substitute for the more well-known, but more distant cliff-hugging villages of the *falaise*). Then we treated them to a picnic lunch next to some of the amazing local onion terraces.

Back in Bamako there were more visits, including to my office, as well as a big reception and a small dinner. Charlotte summed up her impressions with thanks to us for "all your thoughtfulness and care for 'les mamans,' the great four-day trip *en brousse*, the dinner party, the Pope (!), the shopping— Kate and I will long remember our visit to Mali." More extensively, Kate wrote:

It would be hard to say what I remember with most pleasure— the mosque in Djenne, the color of the Mopti market or the pirogue trip across the river there, the Dogon villages and the picnic overlooking the onion fields in company with local women and children, the Dogon credit union members paying their interest—or the artisans of textiles and jewelry—or, finally, simply the people we met, both Malian and American. [37]

It was abundantly evident that the Malians were delighted and moved by this visit of "*les mamans.*" Whether they say so or not, most people in developing countries assume that diplomats are birds of passage; that we are never really comfortable with them. Bringing parents or grandparents to meet them is seen as proof of both trust and genuine affection, and elderly guests are accorded the respect for age still normal in traditional settings worldwide.[38]

A Diplomatic Tour of the North

Not long after *les mamans* departed, I had to go up north on a *tournée* which was reportedly proposed by the Iraqi ambassador (who, in the event, did not show up), although

[37] Mother letter to Dear Barb & Bob, February 7, 1990; Kate letter to Dear B. and B., same date.
[38] Barbara letter to Dear Children and Grandchildren, February 3, 1990, covers both the Pope's Visit and *les mamans.*

officially sponsored by the Malian Foreign Minister. The idea was that foreign diplomats were not seeing enough of the country, and since everyone knew we traveled a lot, I didn't see how I could gracefully wiggle out of this. The government provided its last remaining transport aircraft, a two-engined, Soviet-donated Antonov. Much to our relief Barbara was not invited, assuring that one Pringle parent would survive.

In the dusty pre-dawn of the Bamako airport, we took our places on the long seats lining both sides of the aircraft and soon discovered that there were no seat belts. Baggage had been piled on the floor between the rows of passengers without any restraining mechanism. The engines started with backfirings and bursts of flame. Just as some of us were reconsidering the whole idea the rear ramp clanged shut. I had already asked my good friend the Soviet Ambassador, Alex Trofimov (who was clearly as nervous as the rest of us), whether his military assistance mission was responsible for the maintenance of the aircraft? He assured me that it was not. The good news? With the Iranian, PLO, Cuban, North Korean and Libyan Chiefs of Mission on board, this flight had to be hijack proof.[39]

Once the initial terror of the flight subsided, and we got used to a persistent screeching emitted by one (only one) of the engines, it turned out to be a very interesting outing. Passengers included a number of non-resident Excellencies I had never met, such as the smart and charming female Tunisian Ambassador. Timbuktu was, as always, a hit. Tuareg warriors greeted us at the airport with a simulated sword fight on the runway, after which we all got to make ourselves look silly riding on camels, especially the tubby, dour North Korean. Other events included a tour of the old city:

... with its ancient mosques and the historic houses of various explorers, including Heinrich Barth (German), René Caillé (French) and a certain Mr. Berky, who was allegedly the first American to reach Timbuktu, in the 1920s. Someone quipped that as part of its tourist development plan, the mayor should

---

[39] Trip Report, "The Great Diplomatic Tour of Mali, February 8-11, 1990."

really add the house of the first Japanese to reach Timbuktu,
referring to the Japanese Ambassador who was with us.[40]

It was a big night for the Azalai hotel where we were staying, because the weekly Gambia Air Shuttle flight, which arrived on Thursday and departed on Friday, was also in town. (At this writing, due to the political turmoil there is no commercial service to Timbuktu.)

For dinner [at the Azalai], we were served a Timbuktu mishui
which consisted of a baby camel, or chamalon. Inside the camel,
there was a barbecued sheep, inside the sheep a chicken, inside
the chicken a pigeon, and inside the pigeon an egg, which the
maître d' produced and proudly served to the Foreign Minister.
This is a meal which is normally reserved for visiting chiefs of
state. . . .

After dinner we were ushered back to the center of town
where the population had once again assembled, this time to
indulge in the tacamba, a stately Tuareg dance which, someone
noted, is somewhat camel-like in its slow-flowing rhythms. The
West German Ambassador, Klaus Holderbaum, who is about six
feet four, made a tremendous impression with his magnificent
light blue boubou.[41]

The tour of Timbuktu included a visit to the state-run Achmed Baba Islamic Center, which was beginning the work of discovering, assembling and preserving Timbuktu's ancient manuscripts, and a look at the extensive agricultural project of an American Baptist missionary family, the Marshalls, who had been working in Timbuktu since the 1930's.

As this suggests, all joking aside, the Great Diplomatic Tour did include a number of interesting stops. We had already visited Goundam and Diré before Timbuktu; after that it continued by road and air to Djenné, Koutiala (where I dropped out and returned to Bamako) and Segou.

---

[40] Ibid.
[41] Ibid.

Archaeology in the Niger's Inner Delta

In March Barbara and I traveled to the part of Mali north of Bamako, along the northern edge of the Niger Delta and not far from to the Mauritanian border. The population includes "Rimadi" Peuhl, the former slaves, mostly of southern origin, of the Peuhl aristocracy—another glimpse of Mali's social complexity.

As usual, we visited a number of aid projects, but also some interesting archaeology being conducted by students of the McIntoshes: Kevin Macdonald, Helen Haskill and Téréba Togola, (later Mali's chief archeologist and the National Director of Cultural Heritage). They were surveying Neolithic sites in the Méma, a now dry but once flooded arm of the Niger Delta, hoping eventually to find evidence that iron smelting technology had evolved independently there, rather than having been imported from a non-African source. The team was in a hurry because plans were afoot for the Soviets or others to extend the area irrigated by the Niger Authority (*Office du Niger*) into this place.

McIntosh later wrote a book, based partly on the fieldwork we saw, arguing that the ever-shifting environment of the Inner Delta, which was the cradle of Mali's three great empires, had encouraged the development of multiple political centers, based on farming, hunting, ironworking and fishing, because these different activities tended to flourish or fail at different times under differing conditions. He called this kind of social-political system "heterarchy" as opposed to "hierarchy,"[42] and saw it as the possible ancestor of the kind of urbanism, with dispersed power centers, that he had posited for Old Djenné. He also saw this system as typically African.

In addition, I wrote at the time,

It is obvious that the many-layered evidence of dense settlement north of the river will, if properly researched, yield information about the complicated process of climate change which has occurred there. We know, for example, that there

---

[42] Roderick McIntosh, *The Peoples of the Middle Niger: The Island of Gold,* 1988, esp. pp. 6-10.

were two major "drying out " periods in relatively recent times, in approximately 300 and 1300 AD (virtually all of the Iron Age sites in the region were abandoned around 1300 AD). Systematic archaeology could help greatly in the analysis of more recent climate fluctuations and the probable role of contemporary factors, such as the greenhouse effect.[43]

We spent one night at the "pied à terre" of the *commandant de cercle* of Niafounke, liberally decorated with megaliths from a spectacular nearby archaelogical site at Tondibaru, which had been looted and virtually destroyed for research purposes by a French journalist in the early 1930s.[44]

We went on to see "Lake" Fagubine, one of a series of lakes that were lush and well-watered as recently as the 1930s. Once upon a time, this region was nourished by a complex series of apparently natural watercourses flowing north from the river during the annual flood. But the Niger is no longer flowing the way it used to; blowing sand has blocked some of the canals, and villagers who used to maintain them have been displaced by drought. German and French financed efforts were underway to revitalize the system.[45] Yet the drought-scorched landscape we saw was still rich grazing land for cattle at certain seasons and one of the few places in Mali where one could still encounter wild antelope, although we did not see any. We continued onwards to the village of Bintagoungou, where we promptly got stuck in its famous white sands, and had to put our sand ladders to use.[46]

The trip was another reminder that the Niger River, Mali's most valuable economic asset, was far from being managed in a way that might mitigate the impacts of increasing populations and periodic drought. While there was an organization of the Niger River states (Guinea, Niger and Nigeria, in addition to Mali), it did nothing beyond research; there was no regulation of who took water out of the river for what, or when. This

---

[43] Robert Pringle, "A Trip to the Fourth and Sixth Regions, March 7-13," 1990.

[44] McIntosh, *The Peoples of the Middle Niger*, p. 221.

[45] Niger Basin Charta [sic] and Investment Plan, in Wikipedia, http://en.wikipedia.org/wiki/Niger_River, accessed April, 2013.

[46] Pringle, "A Trip to the Fourth and Sixth Regions."

might have been partially corrected by agreement on a Niger River Charter in 2008, authorizing a number of new dams, but prevailing political unrest since then has no doubt kept those intentions on paper.

During all our adventures that last year, we were sure that all was going well for the Junior Pringles at their respective universities in the US. Internet and e-mail were still in the future, but they were only a domestic phone call away from family members in case of real emergency. Thus, Kathy informed us:

The enclosed pictures were taken at the Harvard-Dartmouth game last fall. I thought we needed to have some lasting record of Jamie's days in the marching band. It's too bad you never saw them ... they are pretty funny .... They are intentionally quite disorganized, although they sound just fine.

Then she went on to add, in a more serious vein, "Have heard nothing from Jamie, but will track him down over the weekend to see if he has a firm offer from Mississippi." He did, and the physical oceanography lab at Stennis gave him his first real job. A little later, Kathy added this about the new job: "I think it sounds like lots of fun; and since he is used to living in tropical climates, the location shouldn't be a problem!"[47] Of course, from Jamie's point of view, living a short drive away from New Orleans would never be a problem.

Diplomacy, Cultural Artifacts, and Democratization

1990 brought two bouts of interesting diplomacy. The first was asking Moussa Traoré to sign a bilateral treaty with the US that would help reduce the illegal export of cultural artifacts. Looters were digging into ancient village mounds all over the country, but especially in the Niger Delta, in search of gold and, especially, beautiful terra cotta statues, the most famous being figures on horseback, which were commanding prices of a million US dollars and more from wealthy collectors and museums.

---

[47] Kathy letters to Dear Barbara and Bob, April 18, 1990, and May 15, 1990.

Once an archaeological site is dug up in search of such treasures, its value for scholarly excavation is often ruined, and on our travel the previous March we had learned about the damage being done to such sites in Mali. The treaty would give the US authority to forbid importation of any object which the Malians certified to be an illegally procured antiquity. A special envoy from USIS, Phillip Pillsbury, visited Bamako, where he had served in the USIS office in the 1960s, to explain why, under the terms of a UNESCO convention signed in 1970,[48] we were promoting such treaties, an idea which was supported by archaeologists and hotly opposed by art dealers.

When I called on the normally unexpressive president to seek his support for such an agreement, he came to a life in a manner I had never experienced before. He answered my official *démarche* of March 6 on April 13, telling us to work out the details with the appropriate ministry.[49] It is possible that his wife, Mariam, who had worked in the USIS office in Bamako before her husband staged his coup d'état, had urged him to be cooperative. Pillsbury had, it turned out, taken pictures of the Traorés' wedding, which they still treasured.[50] The agreement was not actually signed until after Traoré's overthrow and replacement by an elected government in 1991, but Mali was the first country anywhere to sign such an agreement.

---

[48] *The Convention on the Means of Prohibiting and Preventing the Illicit Import, Export and Transfer of Ownership of Cultural Property.* As this is written, the issue is in the headlines again due to the looting of Egyptian artifacts since the 2011 overthrow of the Mubarak regime and subsequent disorder: Tom Mashberg, "Egypt Asks the US to Impose Sharp Curbs on Importing of Antiquities," *New York Times*, March 15, 2014, p. C1.

[49] President Traoré sent me a signed copy of his official response, one of several that we received, and it is in the final of ten scrapbooks that we kept on Mali. When I mentioned it to Rod McIntosh, he was surprised, assuming that the negotiations had been initiated with Traoré's far better educated and democratically elected successor, Alpha Oumar Konaré.

[50] Mariam Traoré had to leave USIS employ "on account of her husband's military career." Barbara Pringle, "Call on Mme. Mariam Traoré," notes on Conversation, July 18, 1990. Pillsbury had been PNG'd from Mali, then under the radical regime of Modibo Keita, for taking unauthorized photos in a village, and for recording our friends the fruit bats around the Embassy Residence—how suspicious!

By the time we revisited Mali in 2004-2005, the amount of illegal excavation had apparently diminished. Maybe this had something to do with our agreement, although similar accords were not signed with many—if any—European countries, and Europe, not the US, was the biggest market for African antiquities. Maybe rich, unpillaged sites were running low, although that seems unlikely, especially in the Delta.

Or maybe it was the difficulty of detecting forgeries. The age of fired clay, not subject to radio-carbon dating unless it is clearly associated with remnants of the fuel used in firing it, can be dated by another technique called thermoluminescence dating.[51] However, the forgers have discovered that if they grind up ancient potsherds and mingle this material into their new "antiquity," it fools the test. Several prestigious museums did not understand this at first and reportedly paid large sums for forged products.

By this time, the demise of communism in Europe was stirring restlessness across Africa, and my only attempt to influence Malian political behavior resulted from that. Countries such as Mali that had one-party systems modeled roughly on communist systems had always responded to western criticism by citing the socialist model. "Democratic centralism," they said, had as much claim to legitimacy as the western model, and was more in line with chiefly traditions. Now communist governments were falling right and left, and their validity as models was increasingly challenged.

By 1990 a pro-democracy movement was underway in Mali. It was headed by Alpha Omar Konaré, a former Minister of Culture, and his smart historian wife, Adama Ba Konaré, and tacitly supported by the Catholic Church. We had known the Konarés for some time, thanks to an enthusiastic introduction from John MacCrae, the non-resident British Ambassador, but I have to say that at that point I never dreamed that Konaré might become Mali's first elected president. Before long, there was a new pro-democracy newspaper, *Les Echos*, edited by Alpha, and even the super-stodgy official *L'Essor* was livening up. An increasingly noisy

[51] For the basics see http://en.wikipedia.org/wiki/Thermoluminescence_dating.

debate was joined over whether democracy should be allowed only within the single political party, which clearly would be meaningless, or whether a multi-party system was necessary.

The US had not yet arrived at a policy of supporting democratization in general, but we did frown on human rights violations, which we feared would result if the debate got out of hand. We knew that Mrs. Traoré and her family would put pressure on Moussa to take a tough line, as he did. I expressed our concern, albeit very gently, in a farewell speech and press conference on US-Malian relations, noting that:

> In countries where there are strong monarchical or authoritarian traditions, and Mali is one, rural people often equate good government with harmony, unity and consensus. As a general rule, however, the more people become educated, the more they want and expect a more active role in the political process. As this process continues, existing institutions are faced with a demand for change.[52]

I added that, at a time when aid funds were increasingly scarce, our Congress would inevitably cut aid to countries with serious human rights violations. (It was always handy to invoke the threat of an uncontrollable Congress in situations like this.)

But I also noted that our own democracy had many undemocratic features, especially as originally created by our founders, and we realized that other countries would have to adjust their own systems to the needs of the time, as we had done. I concluded approvingly that the Malian government had already espoused a policy of decentralization, which ultimately became a major and perhaps the most valuable feature of its future democracy.

Our last Fourth of July went without a hitch. Both children

---

[52] Official Text, "The United States and Mali – a 1990 Perspective," c. August 28, 1990.

were on hand, as were two of their friends, Jamie's college buddy Roth Herlinger, a talented musician and entrepreneur who played the piano for us at the official reception, and Annie's pal Mary Kroner. Afterwards, for the last time, Jamie and Annie took off up country with their friends to see Djenné, Mopti and the Dogon country. Jamie and Roth got splendid Malian robes to celebrate the Islamic feast of Tabaski with Gaoussou Traoré, our travel manager and by now a close friend.

By this time I had accepted a position as Director of the Office of Central African Affairs in Washington, so Barbara and I took off on a trip to some of the countries I would be working with: Congo B (for Brazzaville, the old French Congo), Congo Kinshasa (the huge former Belgian Congo), Cameroon and Chad. In the next two years I would see more of all these places, not to mention Burundi, Rwanda, Gabon, Equatorial Guinea, São Tomé and Principe, and the Central African Republic.

We apparently kept no record of this trip, but we remember especially the international ferry ride from Brazzaville to Kinshasa, with its incredible chaos—nothing had changed much since my visit of 1979 (see Chapter 8). In Kinshasa, where we stayed with Ambassador Bill Harrop, Barbara was able to visit a rich collection of art acquired for a projected national museum, which was to replace one that had been destroyed in a previous period of political unrest. Sadly, the new museum was never built.

Brazzaville had far fewer tall buildings and felt less crowded than Kinshasa. However, the view from the DCM's home, where we stayed, was of a garbage dump and a slum.

In Cameroon we traveled by road to Douala and looked across from the base of Mt. Cameroon to its twin volcano, a few miles out to sea in Equatorial Guinea, which we did not visit. Then it was on to Yaoundé, Cameroon's capital, where we stayed with Ambassador Frances Cooke, an old friend, and traveled north with her by rail as far as we could. The VIP railroad car we were on flooded, due to some kind of plumbing malfunction, so our special car was actually a rolling puddle. The next day our guide got lost on the way to call on one of the picturesque local potentates and we were hours late, much to both his and Frances's annoyance. But the pomp and panoply in the round chiefly hut where we were finally received made our prolonged search for it worthwhile.[53]

We continued north by ourselves towards Chad through increasingly arid country, a transition similar to what one experiences in Mali, and the reason why Cameroon, with a tropical south and a near-desert north, tries to attract tourists by claiming to be "Africa in One Country." We did go through the well-known Waza Game Park, which has beautiful rocky scenery, although we saw only a few giraffes.

Then we crossed the Chari River into Chad for the last few miles to Ndjamena, its capital, which had lots of picturesque mud-brick buildings liberally pock-marked with bullet holes— it had once been, after all, Fort Lamy. I was about to find out in my new job that these scars of combat were not just signs of the bad old days, but also an artifact of modern Chadian politics. In addition to consultations with the embassy, we had a good time shopping in the market for old glass beads, and found one real prize—a small, seven-layer, red, white and blue Venetian chevron, the seven layers proving that it probably dated from the seventeenth century. Such beads are rare and small ones particularly so.

Then we returned to Bamako for an intense round of farewell speeches and parties, a medal from the Malian government, a portrait of me executed in chicken feathers,[54] and more. We departed Bamako on September 20 and invited everyone to the Residence to say goodbye, to avoid the chaos and inconvenience of friends thinking they had to trek to the airport to see us off.

The Malian political pot continued to bubble, but did not

---

[53] It was on a later trip to Cameroon on AF/C business that I bought a beaded stool and small bird being sold along the road. These exquisite artifacts were evidence of an unexploited craft industry; such things were not at the time available in Yaoundé, Cameroon's capital city. The Grasslands area, near the border with Nigeria, has more recently been troubled by Islamic extremism.

[54] The chicken feather portrait was given to me by the artist, who obviously expected to be compensated. I thought it was awful, but somehow it got home with us and is now with my daughter, who loves it. It does look better as time passes and I feel guilty about not having paid the artist.

really explode until the spring of 1991, six months after our departure. Increasingly assertive demonstrations finally provoked President Moussa Traoré, very likely goaded by Mariam, to order the Army to fire on demonstrators, which they did on March 22, killing up to 200 people.[55] Indiscriminate looting and burning followed, leading to a military takeover headed by Lt. Colonel Amadou Toumani Touré. ATT, as he is better known, promised to turn the government over to a democratically chosen government and return to the barracks.

To surprise of many, he did just that in 1992, when Alpha Konaré, our journalist friend and critic of Traoré's regime, was elected president. The story does not end there; ATT retired from the Army and was himself elected President in 2002. Mali's democracy seemed to be working well in 2004-2005, when I wrote a paper for the US Institute of Peace explaining its apparent success.[56] But in 2011, ATT was overthrown by a military coup, the result of his own sagging performance, resurgent problems in the desert north, and the return home of well-armed Tuareg rebels from Libya following the US-led overthrow of Muamar Qadafi.

Mali's democracy, successful or not, owed little to US policy, as I hope I have made clear. We were officially focused on development, on the assumption that Mali would succeed politically only if it could provide a better standard of living for its people, and that therefore economic development should be the highest priority. I think we succeeded in beginning to meet that objective, without being under any illusion that it would happen in less than decades.

A Postscript on Mali

After 1990, when we left the country, Mali became a major gold producer, although not sufficiently to make the country rich. Despite global warming, there has still not yet been

---

[55] For the history of these six months, see Andrew F. Clark, "From Dictatorship to Democracy: The Democratization Process in Mali," in R. James Ningen *et al.* (eds.), *Democracy and Development in Mali*, Michigan State University Press, 2000, pp. 251-264.

[56] Robert Pringle, *Democratization in Mali: Putting History to Work*.

any recurrence of catastrophic drought comparable to what happened in 1983-84. But Mali's progress, both economic and political, has not been enough to offset increasing population, from roughly seven million in 1990 to over fourteen million. One result has been an increase of unemployed youths in Bamako, creating an urban underclass which provided critical support for the overthrow of Mali's democracy in 2011.

In the intervening period aid donors, delighted by the unusual phenomenon of a real democracy in an impoverished African country, continued to shower money on Mali without paying enough attention to how it was used. For all too many Malians, and without much evidence to judge the truth of the matter, all this money seemed mainly to be fueling more corruption. While it may be true that Mali was even more corrupt under single party (or single family) rule, democratized corruption seems to have become been just as controversial, if only because it has been more visible. So the ideal of a "just king" remains alive, although the decentralization achieved by Mali's democratization was genuinely popular and has apparently remained so.

It is worth remembering that the democracy would not have been overthrown without the spark provided by a new influx of Tuareg rebels, the direct result of US intervention in Libya and the overthrow of Qadafi. New elections were scheduled at the time, and they might have worked well enough to provide rejuvenated leadership had the 2011 coup not occurred. The new elections actually held in 2013 were not sufficient to overcome increasing insecurity in the north; indeed it continued to spread southwards, threatening the very important area of the Inner Delta centered around the town of Mopti, which we had visited so often.

One thing is certain: most Malians will not willingly accept an independent desert state for the Tuaregs that encroaches on Mali's established borders, nor would such a state be remotely viable given the economic conditions of the desert. Decentralization was once working well in the habitable areas of northern Mali, and it could again, but not unless the drivers of desert lawlessness can be brought under control. These forces include, in addition to Tuareg nationalists, Islamic fanatics, malcontents from Algeria, uprooted military from

Libya, traffickers waxing fat on drugs, and—now especially—refugees from sub-Saharan Africa fleeing poverty and war-driven turmoil, and desperate to reach Europe.

The current situation is best compared to rampant piracy on the equally stateless high seas. To eliminate it we need specialists in desert warfare located in each Saharan country, expert on the local terrain and its peoples, and working across borders with each other and with international support. As far as I can tell, no one is seriously considering such a solution, nor will they as long as massive unrest continues to grab headlines in better-known portions of Africa and the Middle East. Meanwhile the French have resumed a quasi-colonial military presence in Mali and other Sahelian countries, which, welcome though it is, cannot be permanent.

13

Career and Family in the United States, 1990-1996

Our second long stay in Washington would be different from the first. We were, for the first time, empty nesters. Daughter Anne was at the University of Chicago, and son Jamie was already headed for a scientific career, beginning with a relevant job at an oceanography lab at Stennis Air Force Base in Mississippi. Barbara, once again, had to begin a prolonged and trying job hunt, the perennial and costly fate of Foreign Service spouses. Bob adapted to being, once again, no longer an *excellence,* but a mere office director. For the moment that meant being partially responsible for an unruly collection of crisis-prone countries ranging from tiny archipelago states like Equatorial Guinea to continental giants like Zaire. Taken together, this assemblage illustrated dramatically both the failures of colonialism in Africa and the equally negative results of the Cold War rivalry that followed it.

We unwound from our last hectic days overseas and rested up before tackling the job of settling back into Washington by spending two weeks at Pine Knoll Shores with Char and Clay. This was probably the time that Barbara made grape jelly from the wild grapes that used to grow at the edges of undeveloped lots. Then we prolonged the easy part of re-entry by attending an International Bead Conference, the first of two organized by the Bead Society of Greater Washington (BSGW), at the Mayflower Hotel. We paid our lodging and food bills with the *per diem* allowed before we were able to move into our house. Happily our furniture, which was not coming from abroad, but from storage in Washington, arrived the day after the end of the conference.

At the conference, we received a magnificent introduction

to the world of bead artists, scholars, and collectors in the United States, finding out more than we had ever learned by perusing Lois Sherr Dubin's seminal *The History of Beads* in Mali. We also met many of the members of the BSGW, of which we became active members. This was the occasion when Peter Francis misidentified our face bead from Kayes. Much later, Howard and Marie-José Opper, BSGW friends who had lived for a long period in Senegal, moved to France and studied bead records there. They identified its origin, citing several other examples of beads decorated with faces that must have come from the same glass canes.[1]

We settled in fairly quickly at 216 Wolfe Street. As we had returned well after the school year started, there were no immediate job openings for Barbara. So,

I have been supervising some minor construction projects at the house, getting everything organized (our nice, little, colonial townhouse is littler than all the art we acquired while abroad, not to mention our books), and substitute teaching at the local public schools."[2]

The "art," mainly in the form of wood carvings and clay pots, which we acquired in Africa and Papua New Guinea, was the largest we ever collected.

Barbara Hunts for a Job, Again

There were no relevant jobs available at Madeira, where I had been teaching before we left for Ouagadougou. So the great job search began again; it took most of the year and finally resulted in a position teaching World History, Russian History, and AP Modern European History at the Potomac School, which had recently expanded to include a high school. For the rest of my teaching career I would remain in independent, rather than public schools. Meanwhile, however, the remainder of the 1999-2000 year was less than idyllic. As I wrote to several friends:

---

[1] See Chapter 12, Footnote 1.

[2] For this quotation and following ones concerning schools, see Barbara letter to Chuan Pit and Jean-René, May 5, 1991. See also letter written on the same day to Barbara Brennan.

I have been substituting in the Alexandria City School system, which pays miserably, but has made me an expert on the problems of education in America today. It really is discouraging; I don't know how I would reform schools to reach the huge, and increasing, number of students who do not accept the consensus values of American society.

I then went on to make clear that I saw two sources of these problems, the inadequate resources for language teaching to the Spanish-speaking children from Central America, who were just beginning to pour into Alexandria, and the deteriorating behavior of many economically disadvantaged students, the same ones whom I had taught successfully in 1976-77: "How do you teach children who have no view of the long-run and no consideration for anyone but 'me'? I have had more than one pupil in a class I was teaching say, 'Why should you tell me what to do'?"

I concluded,

Anyway, next year I will be teaching European history at the high school level at Potomac, the private school in McLean. That was not a policy decision; they were just first to offer me employment, and I like the school, which Jamie once attended, but I do look forward to peaceful, calm classrooms after this year's experience.

This from a teacher who had thirteen years previously successfully and happily taught difficult classes of unenthusiastic, low performing juniors American History.

My mother had asked that we resume our family letters, and what follows is drawn from a short-lived effort to comply. (Somehow our lives at home just didn't seem quite as interesting as our adventures during our time in Burkina Faso, New Guinea, and Mali.) While I job hunted, we patched up wear and tear on our house from eight years of tenancy and upgraded it slightly, putting in new kitchen cabinets and a dormer window on the third floor. Underscoring the exasperations that can come with living in an historic district, the latter required clearance from Alexandria's Board of

Architectural Review, or BAR.[3] Bob resurrected the garden (often the first victim of tenancy), and we bought a new car. Remembering the dependable performance of our Subaru in Port Moresby, we purchased a fire-engine red Subaru station wagon.

We flew out for Parents' Weekend with Annie at the University of Chicago, and joined a very earnest seminar group, with the students seated on the floor so the parents could sit in the chairs, to hear a discussion of the Greek philosophers. We got a kick out of the historical markers for the world's first nuclear chain reaction—under Stagg Field, previously the university's football stadium:

In addition to brass plaques there is a Henry Moore sculpture called "Atomic Energy" which is a superb example of how to editorialize in bronze; it looks a bit like a skull, a bit like a mushroom cloud, and might have served as the inspiration for Darth Vader.[4]

While there, we all went to lunch at Marshall Fields, where Barbara's grandmother had always taken the Cade girls as a special treat.

We tried to keep up with Mali through numerous visitors and social occasions with other Old Mali Hands, and, in cooperation with Noumou Diakité, Bob wrote the article on the Gourma Elephants for a Kenya-based wildlife magazine.[5] Every weekday morning, Barbara took me to the Metro

---

[3] The BAR staff initially attempted to tell us we could not add the new dormer on the front of the house, because it would disturb the historic roofline of the block. We prevailed over this argument by pointing out that old houses, in Alexandria as elsewhere, were often built in stages, piece by piece, as the owners had sufficient money; therefore our action was totally historical. Charles Hulfish, the BAR chair, from an old Alexandria family, stopped Bob, who had come dressed in a pin-striped suit straight from some official function, right in the middle of his presentation, saying, "Why are we even discussing this dormer?"

[4] Bob letter to Dear Family, November 10, 1990 (two days before Bob's 54th birthday).

[5] Robert M. Pringle and Noumou Diakité, "The Last Sahelian Elephants," *Swara* (Journal of the East African Wildlife Society), Vol. 15, No. 5, September/October, 1992, pp. 24-6.

station. Evenings, I walked home from the Metro, about fifteen blocks away, to get some badly needed exercise. I was entitled to a parking pass at the State Department, but this would have meant a second car, which we decided was a bad way to spend money. Including the commute, my work day began at 7:15 and rarely ended before 7:30 in the evening, relatively short hours compared to many State Department jobs.

Life in a Regional Office: Central Africa (AF/C)

Regional offices like AF/C, manned by desk officers for each country, serve as first points of contact between our embassies and Washington. We maintained contact with "our" countries primarily by cable, e-mail being still in its infancy, and unclassified telephone. All of them had problems, sometimes lethal. I had visited several of them at the end of my tour as ambassador to Mali, but I still had a lot to learn.

My job as head of AF/C began on October 15, 1990, just in time for the onset of one of modern Africa's most notorious conflicts. It began in Rwanda, a former Belgian colony, with the invasion of a rebel force from neighboring Uganda. The rebels were led by Paul Kagamé, an officer of Rwandan origin serving in the Ugandan Army. He was a Tutsi, an aristocratic ruling class which been ousted by the more numerous Hutus in 1959. Like many Tutsis he had fled to Uganda, where he had served in the Ugandan Army and attended the US Army Command and General Staff College. It was in the United States that Kagamé founded the Rwandan Patriotic Front, dedicated to a Tutsi restoration.

Kagame's invasion succeeded all too well. It led eventually to modern Africa's most famous genocide, in 1994, and then ignited an even more costly war for control of the region, including eastern Zaire (now Congo), which still smolders at this writing. I would spend much time in the months ahead trying to understand the deep-rooted causes of the Hutu-Tutsi antipathy, which was equally virulent in nearby Burundi, Rwanda's virtual twin—indeed the two of them had been one colony under the Belgians, who had succeeded the Germans as the colonial rulers after World War I.

Referring to the six-week old Rwandan civil war, I wrote:

The Rwandans assume that the Ugandan President, Museveni [still in office as this is written] who happens to be Chairman of the OAU (Organization of African Unity), is in back of it. We aren't sure, but the suspicion is certainly reasonable. In any event there is great danger of another ethnic bloodbath. We have been running around ever since worrying about everything from security of missionaries and Peace Corps Volunteers, to how we can provoke or encourage a peace process without taking the lead away from the Belgians, who sent troops to maintain order, then got nervous when this set off a domestic political uproar. At the moment the Rwandans seem to have won the war because the exile army leader was killed, and there hasn't been any bloodbath, but we aren't sure it's over. . . . [6]

It certainly wasn't over. And the real exile leader, Kagamé, had certainly not been killed and is still President of Rwanda as this is written (2017).

To deal with these places we had an office director (me), a deputy office director, several country desk officers, one economic specialist, and two secretaries. One of the secretaries, Thelma DeVaugn, was an AF/C institution, with a razor sharp memory and great interpersonal skills. With her IBM Selectric typewriter, she could convert anyone's sloppiest draft into a flawless final within minutes, proofreading it in the process, and of course she took dictation. AF/C was supervised by one of four Deputy Assistant Secretaries (or DAS's), the one theoretically responsible for Central African Affairs.

My Washington routine included alternating with my deputy to cover the office every other Saturday morning,. The idea was to be there in case there was a crisis. If a crisis came on Saturday afternoon or Sunday, it was the job of the Operations Center, which is staffed 24/7, to call whoever needed to know about it. It is not clear why this system could not be applied on Saturday mornings as well. Saturday duty was usually eventless, a good time to bond with one's colleagues and to write letters such this one:

---

[6] Bob letter to Dear Family, November 10, 1990.

PS: I was just upstairs to the front office where, it being Saturday, things are informal. A NIACT cable ["Night Action," meaning it had to be read and reacted to right away] has just arrived from Ndjamena [Chad] with the news that Chadian rebels have just attacked a government outpost on the Sudan border. Said my acting boss, "This is a dagger pointed straight at the heart of the Central African Republic [which borders Chad on the West]; go wake up the Joint Chiefs!" With any luck you may not read about this in the New York Times, but there does always seem to be too much going on.[7]

My boss had no idea what was going on in Chad, or he might not have been so flip, and I was no wiser. I had no idea of how Chadian politics were played, and would not until I talked to a Yale professor, William Foltz, the only American I ever met who came even close to understanding the place. "Government" in Chad, he explained, was a game of musical chairs played out by a few warlike ethnic groups (often called "tribes" or "clans") in the north of the country.[8] The protagonists in this case were Zaghawas, under the leadership of Idriss Deby, who would become Chad's president in short order. The Libyans, under Muamar Qadafi, were helping Deby up the ladder of power, and he is still (2018) the President of Chad. The part of Sudan he was charging out of in 1990 was the province of Darfur, which would be the site of another round of conflict, often considered a genocide, two decades later. The Zaghawas live in both Sudan and Chad.

Deby's invasion soon gave us a typical AF/C headache. He was not really in the thrall of the Libyans, he was just using them, although Qadafi no doubt thought it was the other way round. The man Deby finally ousted from the presidency was Hissène Habré, who had fought a long war with the Libyans in the 1980s over some disputed territory on the border between the two countries, the Aouzou Strip. The Chadians were liberally assisted by France, including air support and

---

[7] Ibid.

[8] Based on conversations with Foltz, but see also his book, *From French West Africa to the Mali Federation*, New Haven, Yale University Press, 1965.

its Foreign Legion, and the United States, or more exactly the CIA. The Chadians eventually won, and the Aouzou Strip was formally awarded to them in 1994 by a decision of the International Court of Justice.

During the struggle for power, there had been plenty of fighting, including a famous battle at Wadi Doum, where the Chadian forces captured hundreds of tanks, self-propelled guns and other late-model Soviet military hardware. The CIA was so proud of this accomplishment that it published a brochure called "The Battle of Ouadi Doum."[9] Toward the end of the battle, an entire regiment of the Libyan army, made up of unhappy "students," had defected to the Chadians. They couldn't go home, so several hundred of them had remained in Ndjamena, still armed and being supported by the CIA, on the theory that they might be useful if Qadafi invaded again.[10]

That was all very well until Deby invaded. It was assumed that since Deby was supported by Qadafi, he would massacre them in short order. To avoid this, the US Air Force mounted an emergency evacuation, and they were all spirited out of Chad in a few days. One flight is supposed to have set a Guinness world record for the number of passengers who could be crammed into one USAF C-141.

What to do next? We (the State Department) wanted to bring the hapless Libyans into the US as political refugees. Other branches of the US Government did not agree. Our old friend President Mobutu Sese Seko of Zaire (another of "my" countries) agreed to take them off our hands temporarily, while we dithered. Then they were in Kenya for a time. There was a third temporary destination, which I can't remember. Finally the inevitable happened and they were "paroled into" the US as refugees, as the State Department had wanted to do all along. They were scattered around the country, and if you have ever had a Libyan taxi driver, you may have met one of them.

Their commander, one Colonel Haftar, went into exile with them. Fast forward two decades to the US intervention in

---

[9] There was a dusty copy of this publication languishing on my bookshelf in AF/C; "La Bataille de Ouadi-Doum (Bir-Koran)," 22 Mars 1987, *Service de la Presse Presidentielle*, Avril 1987, with an introduction by Hissène Habré as well as a statement by then Colonel Haftar (see note 10 below).

[10] They were being referred to as the "Libyan National Army," or LNA.

Libya in 2011 and the demise of Qadafi. Colonel Haftar (or Hiftar—see footnote 11) suddenly surfaces in news reports as one of many Libyan exiles hoping to go home and get a prestigious new job. He no doubt had friends in high places in the US intelligence community. Whether or not they helped him, by 2013 he was a Lieutenant General and the third-ranking officer in the post-Quadafi Libyan Army. [11]

Africa is like that. It seems unstable, but things that go around come around. And there is continuity. Of the ten countries which were in AF/C when I worked there, five had the same leaders two decades later: Biya of Cameroon, Obiang of Equatorial Guinea, Deby of Chad, and Kagamé of Rwanda (although he was technically only well on his way up in 1991) and of course, right next door to Rwanda, Museveni of Uganda. And in Gabon the son of the 1990 ruler is still in power. So, half of these much maligned countries are actually politically quite stable, right?

But there were always encouraging things to be seen. I began to think that Chad, for all its cowboy past and all the odds against it, could be a country of the future, as I wrote in my travel diary during a trip there:

The arid Tibesty area in the north, including mountains up to 10,000 feet, is sprinkled with well-watered and potentially productive oases. There is a game park in the southeast (the Zakouma Reserve), which is reported to have a fauna concentration comparable to East African parks. (CARE and the European Community are working together to develop a management regime for Zakouma, and the Embassy has requested additional help under the biodiversity program.) . . .

---

[11] But Haftar's story continues to evolve. As of May 20, 2014, he had reportedly gone back to Libya and was attempting to overthrow the new government, with or without the help of Old Friends: Abigail Hausloner and Sharif Abdel Kouddous, "Leader of Libyan revolt spent years in N. VA," *Washington Post*, May 20, 2014. The story gives his surname as *Hiftar*, not Haftar, but there is no question that it's the same person. For more on him, see https://en.wikipedia.org/wiki/Khalifa_Haftar. Also, Jon Lee Anderson, "The Unravelling," *New Yorker*, February 23-March 2, 2015, pp. 108ff, a detailed but patchy account of Haftar's career. Currently, he is back in Libya, heavily involved in politics, and more important than ever (2018).

Lake Chad, still shrinking despite good rains, is populated by divers rebel groups but also by a population of AID-assisted vegetable farmers whose thriving cooperative at Karala we visited. There is clearly room for considerable agricultural development in the Lake region, which could lead eventually (as in other Sahelian countries) to counter-season exports to Europe. [12]

By 1992 a major new oil field was being developed in the south by EXXON and a French partner, Elf. As for Chad's capital,

Ndjamena looks neat and the rag-tag military presence is much less obvious than in the last days of the Habré regime. The town is beginning to regain a little of its Fort Lamy charm. The Chari Hotel, renovated and reopened, once again offers its famous terrace, overlooking the river, setting for the classic opening scene in Romain Gary's The Roots of Heaven.

In April, 1991, I made my first trip as AF/C Office Director to four of our key countries: Burundi, Rwanda, Congo (Brazzaville), Zaire, plus one not-so-key, the Central African Republic. It started with a flight to Burundi, Rwanda's neighbor and ethnographic twin: hours flying over the yellow-brown expanses of the Sahara, then above an increasingly green landscape. At first this lush verdure looked like untamed tropical forest, but as we descended into Burundi's capital, Bujumbura, I could see what looked like tiny specks of shredded tinfoil scattered across the hilly landscape.

Lower, I could make out that these were reflections from tin roofs, not some curious mineral encrustation. These were typical Burundian or Rwandan settlements, dispersed across the countryside, and known quite logically as *collines*, or "hillsides," rather than "villages." The soil is rich due to its volcanic origin, and the population density was very high. Just like Java, I thought, thinking of Indonesia in 1965-66; maybe this cheek-by-jowl existence explained, at least partially, the recurrent tendency to self-slaughter.

In the course of consultations with our embassies in both

---

[12] This quotation and the following one, reordered, are from diary entries about travel in February, 1993.

Rosamond (Roz) Carr, who was famous for her friendship with Diane Fossey, as related in the film Gorillas in the Mist, *in her garden with Ambassador to Rwanda Robert Flaten and DCM Joyce Leader.*

Rwanda and Burundi, I admired the magnificent views of Lake Kivu, failed to see Rwanda's mountain gorillas, but did meet Roz Carr, who had recently played herself in the film *Gorillas in the Mist*, about Diane Fossey, which made the Rwandan gorillas famous. I called on the (Hutu) President of Rwanda, Habyarimana, to discuss efforts to end hostilities with the Uganda-based invaders led by Paul Kagamé (Tutsi). We still had no more than an inkling of how bad things might get in Rwanda.

Then I took an Air Zaire plane from Goma, just across the border in Zaire, to Kinshasa. Goma was littered with ruins from the latest volcanic eruption—as in Java, the price often paid for fertile soils in the tropics. My departure was interesting because it was the end of university holidays, and students were demonstrating all over Zaire by sitting down on airport runways to protest the suspension of free transportation back to campus. Miraculously, the embassy expediter—typically an extraordinarily valuable employee—got me through the crowds and onto the plane.

My main objective was to see a bit of Katanga (known as Shaba under Mobutu), famous for its mineral wealth, and to visit our consulate at Lubumbashi (Elizabethville under the Belgians). Under colonial rule, Katanga had been a state-within-a-state, governed by the enormously wealthy *Union Minière du Haute Katanga*, the Belgian mining conglomerate. It had produced mostly copper and gold, but at that time it was also the site of the world's only significant uranium mine.

In 1940, with Belgium threatened by German invasion, Edouard Sengier, a high official of the *Union Minière* who was well aware of the weapons potential of this material, sent 1,000 tons of top grade pitchblende (uranium ore) to the *Union Minière* warehouse in New York harbor. He did this on his own initiative and informed the US government in such secrecy that the staff of the Manhattan Project didn't know about it until they began to wonder where to find the uranium for the first atomic weapons. When a Project representative went to the New York office of the *Union Minière* for help in getting uranium ore from the Congo, the only known source, he was told not to worry.[13] And the pitchblende in question was indeed used in the first atomic bomb.

At the time of Congo's independence in 1960, with the supposedly pro-communist Patrice Lumumba in office, a Katangan, Moise Tshombé, attempted secession with help from Belgian mining interests. The CIA handed Lumumba over to the future Zairian president, Mobutu, then an ambitious army officer, for assassination, but Tshombé continued to rule Shaba as a breakaway state, supported by European and South African mercenaries paid with ample funds from mineral revenues. However, most independent African countries were not amused. Eventually the United Nations was drawn in, and by 1963 Shaba had been reintegrated into Zaire. Its minerals were by this time seen by the US as strategically important, since alternative sources for cobalt and others were mainly in either South Africa, still a pariah state, or the USSR. This, of course, was one reason for US support of Mobutu.

When I visited, Lubumbashi was a special place, still, like

---

[13] This story was told for the first time in John Gunther's *Inside Africa*, London, 1955, pp. 663-65. By the time of my visit in 1991, the Shinkolobwe mine that produced the fuel for the first atomic weapons had long since closed. Sengier was appropriately recognized and honored by President Truman in 1946.

many mining towns, reflecting its heritage of mineral wealth and the varied population it had attracted. This included a substantial Spanish-speaking Jewish population. We had a big consulate, recently enlarged as part of a very secret global communications project, which was soon to be closed due to political turmoil,[14] and a large contingent of Peace Corps volunteers scattered around the province. While visiting several modest USAID projects, I passed through huge areas of fertile farmland, only a small fraction of which was being cultivated.

Katanga is at the upstream end of the Congo River drainage, cooler due to higher elevation than the tropical areas downstream, and with better soils. There are enough such areas in Sub-Saharan Africa to make clear that the continent could easily grow much more than enough to feed itself, were it not for endemic warfare, political turmoil and, as a result, lack of infrastructure and primitive farming technology. (Maybe the Chinese will fix that!)

I toured the site for a new copper mine, reputedly extremely rich. Facilities for a new town had already been constructed when the Japanese investors abandoned the project. The recently finished roads were littered with hunks of green, copper-bearing malachite, the attractive stone used to make the familiar green stone beads sold at airports and mineral shops throughout Africa.

My last stop was the Central African Republic, already famous for the antics of "Emperor" Bokassa, an army colonel who had staged a coup and ruled from 1965 to 1979. Landlocked between Sudan, Chad and Congo, the CAR, known under French rule as Ubangi-Shari for its two main rivers, was and has remained a sad stereotype of Africa's problems. I did not get far beyond the capital, Bangui, but had some interesting conversations with a young official who was hoping to protect the CAR's extensive natural treasures, including a large population of forest elephants. The objective was probably hopeless, and destruction of these resources has accelerated in recent years. However, there is always hope in such situations, and the only sensible strategy is to support

---

[14] US Consulate Lubumbashi has never been reopened, despite somewhat improved conditions in recent years.

Bob (on far left) meeting with local officials on a visit to the Central African Republic. Ambassador and Mrs. Dan Simpson are at center.

the good people who exist everywhere, trying to accomplish something against the odds, by giving them training and as much funding as possible, and introducing them to other sources of help.

I stayed with our ambassador, Dan Simpson,[15] a friend from my days in AF/EPS. Some Peace Corps volunteers showed me a place littered with quartz crystals too big to carry, and there was a missionary who made and sold interesting souvenir paperweights consisting of beetles, snakes, tarantulas and more, enclosed in Lucite blocks, just the thing for your non-squeamish friends at Christmas.[16]

After my return to the US, Barbara and I made an expedition to New Orleans and across Lake Pontchartrain to Jamie's new workplace at Stennis Air Force Base, also home to a large oceanographic lab. There he was honing his computer skills by helping to break in a new Cray computer. The hit of that

---

[15] Simpson went on to a distinguished diplomatic career, including ambassador to Congo (Kinshasa). He retired to head the editorial board of the Pittsburgh *Post Gazette.*

[16] Based on Bob letter to Dear Family, April 14, 1991.

trip was to discover that in New Orleans there is not only one major Mardi Gras parade, but also several very lively pre-parades, one of which we watched for several hours. We finally understood that the city is built lower than the Mississippi River, and downtown sits alarmingly under the level of the huge ships sailing by behind massive levies that hold the water back.

We acquired our first home computer, a desktop Macintosh and a fancy laser printer to go with it. We have a series of thank-you notes for Christmas presents from various family members, each written in a different typeface which, I carefully explained, was a way of finding out which style we liked best. And, as Barbara wrote to Jane, Jamie didn't know it, but he was starting on a new career: computer adviser to parents:

Jamie put lots of his useful programs in our hard drive, but there are no instruction manuals to go with them. I spent the better part of New Year's Eve being tutored by him, but you can't think of everything that is going to happen—so if it happens there are bound to be bizarre effects. So far, the only hitch has been the ten minutes it took me to get rid of the parents' letter and start yours; I should have pressed "quit."[17]

Midwinter also saw the first of two visits by Barbara's good friend from Bamako, Kady Sanogho, the founder of AMALDEME, the association to help handicapped children in Mali (see Chapter 12). She came on a USIS grant, and in Washington had appointments with various institutions which help such children, including the Lab School which Jamie once attended for a summer session. Despite snow, she also managed to visit the National Gallery, the Museum of African Art, and the Air and Space Museum on the Mall, as well as several monuments and the National Cathedral, reminding us of her attendance at the Pope's visit to Bamako despite being a Muslim. We also hosted a reception for her, which I noted occurred on a wet, snowy evening, and "Daddy's fire was a big hit."[18]

---

[17] Barbara letter to Dear Jane and Ron, January, 1991.
[18] Barbara letter to Dear Annie, January, 1991,

Just before leaving us, she was spooked by the change-of-regime riots in Bamako, and wanted to rush right home. She was afraid to fly out to Montana where Peggy Phelps, a trained preschool teacher and the other American who had worked diligently at AMALDEME, had arranged a huge program for her. We finally persuaded her that going by train would be safe, and so she had a lovely cross-country trip on the way to the second part of her program.

A Southern African Interlude

In the summer of 1991 we returned to Africa, this time southern Africa, for an unadulterated vacation. This might seem like the ultimate busman's holiday, given the time we had already spent in Africa. But we knew South Africa was a world apart, and Barbara had just read a fascinating article on the Okavango swamp and its wildlife in a current issue of the *National Geographic*. Assuming that our Africa assignments were probably finished forever, we decided to expand our acquaintance with a part of the continent in which we had never lived or traveled.

It was a good time to go there. Nelson Mandela had been released from prison in 1990, and would not be president until 1994, but change was very much in the air. We flew first to Johannesburg, and stayed with Ambassador Bill Swing at his residence in Pretoria. He took us to see an exhibition by a black South African artist, George Pemba. Bill had known him during an assignment to our Consulate in Port Elizabeth (which then had a factory making American cars). Pemba had been drawing scenes of life in South Africa's black "townships" for years without the white upper crust, or much of it, paying him any attention, but now, in the euphoria of the dawning New South Africa, his work was suddenly in great demand to hang in corporate boardrooms.

Our tourism began at Victoria Falls, where we spent a couple of days exploring on our own. The most memorable moment of our Vic Falls sojourn occurred on a sunrise foray to an island above the falls on the Zambezi. As we happily sat down to a picnic breakfast, an aggressive monkey bounded onto our table and stole most of Barbara's eggs and sausages;

we got a photo of him eating them.

Then we joined a local tour for the Botswana part of the trip. There were seven of us including our South African guide, Patrick Bodham-Swettam (!) who had grown up on a farm, spoke Setswana (the language of Botswana), knew all the animals and birds, and was great on the organizational details. Our group included a New Zealand veterinarian and a delightful South African family from Cape Town, Rosalind and Tony Bush, with two children. Rosalind was interesting because she was a member of the famous anti-apartheid women's organization called the Black Sash and, although reluctant to talk at length, did discuss some of its activities with us.

We spent eight nights tenting in Botswana's game parks. The first three, Chobe, Savuti and Moremi, were near the southern edge of the Caprivi Strip, a curious tongue of land between what were once Portuguese (Angola) and British (Botswana and Zimbabwe) territories. The Germans managed to grab it for a railroad that was to connect what was then German Southwest Africa (now Namibia) to German East Africa (now Tanzania). The railroad was never built and the Strip was unsafe to enter at the time of our visit due to the remnants of an insurgency relating to war in Angola.

These were classic African game parks, with lots of elephants, lions, giraffes, antelopes and birds. Our tour was somewhat unusual in that it was "participatory," meaning that we stayed in designated campgrounds, pitched our own tents, and took turns assisting with the cooking, although there was a Botswanan to do the dishes and handle heavy work. Once a day everyone helped gather firewood, at least once with elephants watching us from the shade of a large tree not far away. Our vehicle was a converted South African army affair on a Land Rover base, well arranged for photography and including everything from an icebox to a small nature library.

Although the campsites were fenced, they were quite exciting:

Savuti is the site of an old river channel which periodically goes dry and comes back to life, apparently because of tectonic plate shifts; it has now been dry for about ten years but still has lots of animals. The campsite wasn't quite as nice as the others, but we got invaded at night by hyenas and elephants, which kind of made up for it. The hyena was after left-overs in our camp trailer, where they shouldn't have been; he had to satisfy himself by grinding a wine bottle practically to powder to get at the dregs. The noise and uproar was spectacular. There was a flimsy electric fence to keep out the elephants but they were after acacia trees with seedpods and ignored it. They shake the big trees to get the pods to fall down; it is quite something. They have also been known to dig up the water pipes serving the campsite but didn't this time. At Moremi, the Bush children's tent was invaded by baboons looking for candy, etc.; they chewed up flashlight batteries and peed on their sleeping bags (they may have left their tent flap open). Another night at Chobe we had lions roaring and a related highly audible buffalo stampede. And constantly a symphony of other animal and bird noises. All in all it's a bit like a zoo with the people on the inside and no bars.[19]

Our next stop, the Okavango Delta, was different. Flowing southwest out of Angola and Namibia, the Okavango gets lost in the Kalahari Desert, where it ends in a huge wetland. Of course we thought it might be like the Inner Niger Delta, although that has an exit as well as an entrance, but in fact it is much more spread out and, for some reason, crystal clear rather than muddy, and quite chilly. Being a national park, there are no cattle. There are lots of birds and animals, but they are scattered, partly because hunting is allowed in some areas. The animals include two distinctive varieties of antelopes, lechwe and sitatunga, with hooves modified for living in (or on) swamps (think snowshoes), so uncommon elsewhere that they don't have English names.

One gets around by being poled in dugout canoes by Botswanans employed by the safari company, Okavango Wilderness Safaris. There are lots of hippos, notoriously the most dangerous animals in Africa. You hear them constantly and, through the reeds and water lilies, see their broad trails, which the boatmen religiously avoid. As our guide Patrick remarked, to a hippo a dugout full of tourists can look like shishkebab. Unfortunately

---

[19] Bob and Barbara letter to Dear Family, July 22, 1991.

this situation precludes snorkeling, which would otherwise be a great way to see underwater scenery reminiscent of a coral reef, if quieter.[20]

From Maun, the airstrip that serves the camps in the swamp, we flew back to Pretoria, where we stayed with Patty Baron, who had been my secretary in Port Moresby. Then we took the Blue Train to Cape Town. It is no speedster, 900 miles in twenty-four hours, but justly famous for its luxury accommodation and food: ostrich filet and fine South African wines, including a split of champagne to welcome us to our private compartment. Until the 1960s it was powered by big steam locomotives equipped with condensers to convert exhaust steam back to water, useful in crossing the Kalahari Desert. This is a technology that was used on steamships from the early twentieth century, but only in South Africa on steam railroads, because the rougher ride on land makes for expensive maintenance. We were later glad we had taken the Blue Train when we did, because by the time we returned to South Africa in 2006 it had new equipment and was at least four times as expensive.

Bill Swing had invited us to stay in his ambassadorial residence in Cape Town's toniest neighborhood, just down the slope from the DCM residence where we would later live, and we gladly accepted. We had as good a time as we could exploring Cape Town's many attractions, given that during most of our few days' stay it never stopped raining, nothing unusual during the Cape winter.

We wrote home about lunch at the famous Mt. Nelson Hotel—a five-course meal with two wines for the equivalent of $12 per person. However, apparently for fear of alarming the parents, we did not mention being mugged on the way to the Mt. Nelson by two drunken colored men.

We had no idea whether they were armed—maybe knives? One of them grabbed my camera bag and tried to pull it away. I was not about to let that happen—it had all the film from our safari in it—but thus preoccupied I never saw the other one come around in back of me and get my wallet. Of course we

---

[20] Ibid, slightly edited.

were both yelling, and the multi-ethnic local citizenry chased the inebriated bandits. Because they did, the thief with my wallet, having relieved it of the small amount of cash I was carrying, threw it on the ground with the important items like credit cards still in it. The South African police wanted to interview us, but it took a lot of persuasion to get them to come into the ambassador's residence, because they feared that they be might be accused of violating US diplomatic immunity. All in all, we were very lucky, because even in 1991, South African crime, including in Cape Town, was not typically so harmless.

Travel notes: We flew to Europe and returned on Pan Am, which was in the process of being swallowed by Delta. On the return trip, waiting for our departure from Zurich, Barbara commiserated with the airline employee at check-in about the possibility of losing her job as a result of the merger. Just before boarding, she summoned us back to the counter and offered to upgrade us to business class for the trans-Atlantic flight. It always pays to be nice to people. On the Africa links we flew on South African Airways, which was clearly trying harder in order to free itself from the opprobrium of apartheid, and the service was terrific.

The Potomac School

During our long absence, the Potomac School had added a high school to its classes. I knew several of its administrators from my work with freshmen at Madeira, and I benefited from some growing pains in personnel to land my job there. Madeira, by this time, had the one European history teacher it needed, and it was in the middle of a very awkward transition to a new headmistress. My former colleagues advised me to steer clear of any administrative position. Ultimately, both Bill Brown and Ann Scott from Madeira wound up teaching at Potomac too, as did music teacher Katherine Nevius.

To get ahead of the story, I finally taught for ten years at Potomac, in two stints. When Bob was assigned to South Africa for a three-year tour in September, 1995, I faced the choice of staying home or leaving my Potomac job and possibly losing it forever. I did not want to do that, but I also wanted to share his time in a fascinating and important country.

As it happened my friend Ann Scott, who had gotten me my job at Madeira, was just returning from five years in China, where she had accompanied her husband Doug, who had headed the IMF mission there. She was interested in teaching another few years. Voila! Bill Brown and I, along with Katherine, ganged up on the Upper School principal, Andy Watson, and persuaded him that only Ann could fit seamlessly into the History Department, as she certainly did. So I left for Pretoria and Cape Town in July, 1997, and Ann stepped into my place. Andy was astonished when, two years later in spring, 1999, I wrote telling him I was ready to come back to my former job, and Ann said she was retiring, an arrangement which the two of us had agreed upon before I left.

My years at Potomac were pleasant and professionally satisfying. Teachers at Potomac enjoyed strong support from administrators, but were left to create their own courses in consultation with other members of their department. In contrast to my recent experience as a substitute in the Alexandria junior and senior high schools, my students at Potomac were generally cheerful, interested, and as diligent as their age allowed. Their opinion of my classes tended to be that "history is hard; memorizing dates and names and getting facts straight is not always interesting; but—I learned a lot."

And they did. I always got strong results in my AP class, whether it was composed of seniors during my first years or the top sophomore students in their second year of World History in later years. Russian History was finally dropped because the version I chose to teach was apparently too intense for the students who selected it. The previous teacher had included more cultural topics, like cooking Russian dishes, learning the Russian alphabet, and so on. Perhaps that was my mistake, but it was a senior elective, supposed to be college prep, and a part of me thinks that any such course should have been as challenging as my version based on political and economic history, with a little art and literature thrown in.

In my final year at Potomac I was pleased to teach a seminar course on African History, requested by seniors I had taught earlier in freshman and sophomore World History. Since it was an extra course for me, I put the burden of conducting many discussions on the class members. I was gratified when the student responsible for the day's lesson having not prepared it, the other students were disappointed that I canceled the class. We never had another episode of a discussion leader being unprepared. I like to think that I taught a good pre-college lesson, as well as some African history in that course. For a long time, I heard from the two students most interested in African studies.

The high school was fairly new when I arrived, so I was expected to help round out the extracurricular offerings that were being developed. School officials were thinking in terms of a debate team, but, influenced by Stuart Davis' success with Model UN and Model OAS (Organization of American States) at Madeira (in which Annie had been enthusiastically involved well after my teaching stint there), I suggested Model UN and Model Congress. To get going, I took interested students to visit all three possibilities. Debate was ruled out after we visited a very boring meet in which debaters over-prepared on a specific topic talked as fast as they could, mostly unintelligibly, to make as many points as they could. I did not know it then, but there are many other types of debate that might have been more appealing. In the event, we went on to visit Model Congress and Model UN, and decided to participate in both the following year.

Interestingly, the students who had investigated possibilities with me and then participated during the first couple of years were mostly inner city black students. The first small delegations they composed were enthusiastic and performed well, although it took a few years before they won any gavels, the top awards given in each "Senate" or "House" committee in Model Congress. After that, Potomac's ever-expanding delegation regularly took home one or two, and lots of runner-up certificates.

However, perhaps because team athletics were required two seasons out of three each year and the athletes always practiced after school, coupled with the fact that Potomac is a day school with students living all over the metropolitan area, our Model UN delegations were never as successful. They just could not find time to prepare together beforehand and never got the hang of working as a team at the actual event.

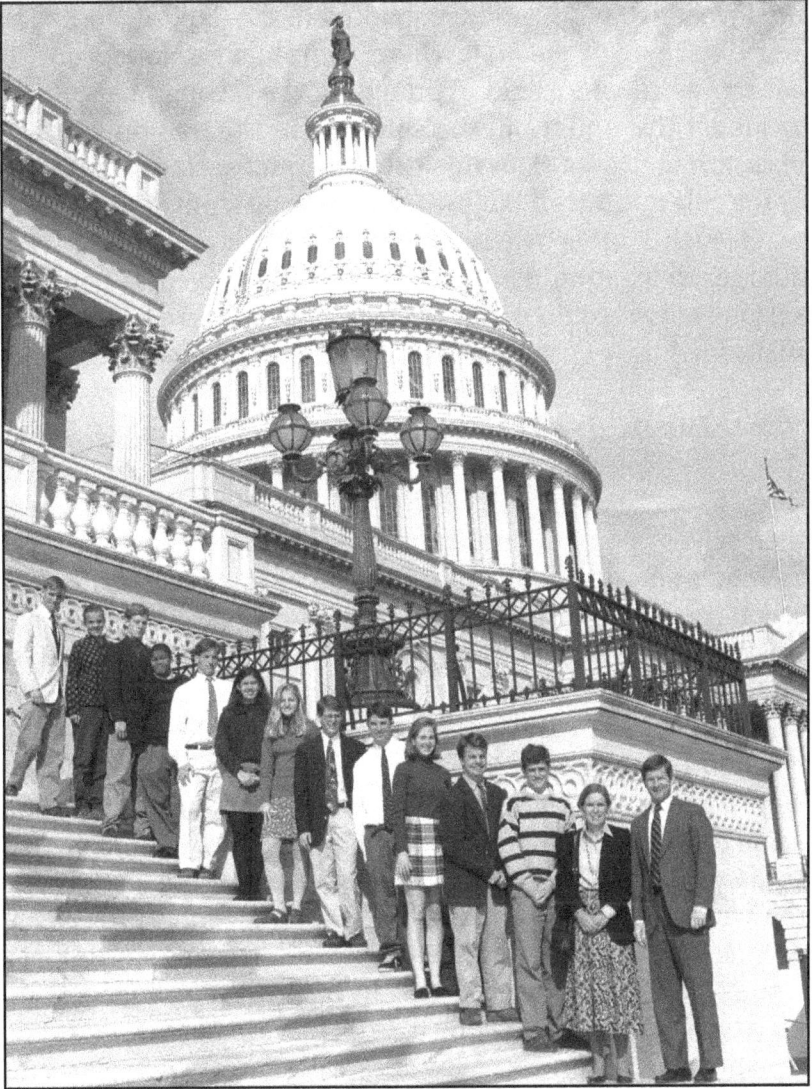

On the steps of the US Capitol, a Model Congress delegation from Potomac School, with their host Representative Lamar Smith of Texas.

I advised and chaperoned both events each year until we left for South Africa, and then again after we returned. At first, I took the groups by myself for the three-night events. Most of the time, my "trust but verify" policy worked fine; I could check that each student was in the meeting he or she was supposed to attend, and then rest or explore for the remainder of any given session. This is the reason I have seen the lovely painted Brumidi corridors in the Capitol.

I did have an episode where some boys skipped out to eat on the town instead of attending the boring final dinner at Model UN, and a puerile skirmish in the hall on another occasion at Model Congress. But the only serious infraction of the rules occurred later, after I returned from South Africa, when Rick Waples was with me as a second chaperone for a larger delegation. That one involved smuggled-in beer; no serious harm resulted, but the participants were sanctioned. All in all, these two activities were fun, but exhausting, to lead.

The Heart of Central Africa: Congo Kinshasa

After a year on the job, Bob's ten countries had arranged themselves along a spectrum of difficulty, defined usually as potential for political crisis, often meaning civil war accompanied by massive suffering. Zaire (Congo Kinshasa), was by far the largest in terms of size, population, perceived importance and—viewed as a problem—insolubility. The ongoing civil war in Rwanda seemed to be localized, except for neighboring Burundi, but events would prove how wrong we were about that. Cameroon was an average African dictatorship, analogous to a B-minus student. Oil-rich Gabon and Congo (Brazzaville) were both still nestled more or less calmly under the wing of Mother France. With its Libyan exiles now safely driving taxis in Chicago and Washington, Chad was more or less settling down under its latest strong man, or so we hoped. Then there were three that no one but AF/C ever heard of except as questions on geography quizzes—two small archipelagos and one landlocked nominal state: Equatorial Guinea, São Tomé and Principé, and the Central African Republic.

However, during this first year, the policy context was changing. A major alteration in US policy toward Africa had occurred since my time in Mali, when I had been able to tell its president that it was up to him to decide how to respond to popular protest, and that the US would be concerned only if he committed major violations of human rights in the process. Now we were beginning to press African leaders to enact specifically democratic reforms. Congo (Kinshasa) was to be a major testing ground for this policy. It is worth noting that this liberal-leaning policy shift took place under a Republican president, Herbert Walker Bush. One operative factor was no doubt the fact that, with the disintegration of the USSR, we no longer felt constrained to compete for the favor of dictators, no matter how obnoxious.

The overriding issue in Congo was what to do about Mobutu. He was our creation (with a little help from our allies). We had always assumed that he was an essential safeguard against chaos which might lead to some kind of pro-communist takeover. Every time we were about to be totally fed up with him, he would do us some new little or big favor. Accepting (if only temporarily) those homeless Libyans from Chad (see above) was a good example of his statecraft.

But as time went by, it became increasingly clear that his plundering and police-state tactics were aiding, not controlling, chaos. The once well-oiled infrastructure of colonial Congo had already disintegrated, symbolized by the long lines of inoperable river steamers rusted and sinking at their moorings in Kinshasa. As I had seen, even the mineral industry of Katanga was in ruins, with potential investors fleeing.

Meanwhile, Mobutu's excesses kept generating noxious publicity: he was said to have stolen at least $5 billion[21] for his various mansions on the French Riviera, and other luxuries. In fact, he channeled much if not most of his money to local leaders to insure their loyalty, much as machine politicians in the USA once did. Another irksome factor was the collapse of the Inga-Shaba project, a scheme to tap the enormous hydroelectric potential of the Congo River falls, downstream from Kinshasa, and transmit the power thus generated 1,100 miles to the only possible consumer, the mining industry of Katanga. The US had guaranteed approximately one billion dollars in private sector loans to help finance Inga-Shaba, and then had to assume the debt as the Zairian economy crumbled and the government defaulted. This too was blamed, not unreasonably, on Mobutu.

Meanwhile villagers along the lengthy transmission line, the most expensive part of the project, were stealing the

---

[21] How anyone arrived at this tidy figure was never clear to me, but it was the one most often cited by Mobutu's critics.

insulators and copper wire, so it wasn't all bad for them. Most of Inga-Shaba's electric power potential has never, to this day, been successfully developed—again, the Chinese may eventually change that.

By this time Mobutu's foes in the US had generated a small but effective lobbying operation, consisting mainly of academics and former missionaries. They were led by Dr. Bill Close (father of movie star Glenn Close),[22] who had once served as Mobutu's personal physician after having been a missionary doctor in Zaire, then had had an extreme case of guilt mingled with remorse and returned to the US.

From his home in Big Piney, Wyoming, Dr. Close launched a crusade against his old employer. He had many friends in Zaire who fed him information by telephone about Mobutu's latest excesses, and often he knew what was happening in Kinshasa before Washington did. What drove me nuts was that he would then immediately call my boss, Deputy Assistant Secretary Robert Houdek, who would then call me and ask why our embassy in Kinshasa hadn't reported the latest mishap. The answer usually was that they were still writing the cable and being careful to get the facts as right as possible, a nicety that didn't concern Dr. Close.

Houdek had that most valuable of diplomatic assets, a sense of humor, and he didn't want simply to agree with what Dr. Close was telling him, especially on a probably insecure phone. Instead he would pick up an antique auto horn that someone had given him, and honk it at the receiver to signify that he had heard what Close said, before calling me. The anti-Mobutu lobby generated strong congressional support from Congressman Steve Solarz, chair of the House Subcommittee on Africa, and his energetic staff. Their activity taught me how little it can sometimes take to change policy in Washington, especially when the issue at hand is of little or no interest to the broader American public, most of which would have had trouble finding Zaire on the map, despite its enormous size.

The result of all this was years of diplomatic warfare aimed at replacing the strong man with a democracy,

---

[22] According to some accounts, Mobutu paid for Glenn Close's wedding ceremony: see http://www.newafricanmagazine.com/how-the-father-of-glenn-close-became-mobutus-personal-doctor.

however imperfect. As early as March, 1990, Secretary of State James Baker visited Kinshasa and warned Mobutu to heed the forces of democratization or risk being swept aside by them. The following April, the Zairian leader announced the end of single party rule but continued to repress student demonstrations against it, meaning himself. By the end of the year, major donors, including Belgium and the US, were halting or restricting military aid to Zaire.

In April, 1991, after months of procrastination. Mobutu signed an order convoking a "national conference," the normal step under French-style systems toward eventual elections. Our extremely capable ambassador, Bill Harrop, wrote an analysis before leaving post concluding that no real progress would be possible as long as Mobutu was president. But despite Harrop's advice, and after much inter-agency deliberation, Washington opted for "power sharing" between Mobutu and his opponents. The best-known among them was Etienne Tshisekedi, a dogged enemy of the president but one who lacked broad appeal and was hopelessly unsubtle (who could blame him?). In July, 1991, Mobutu offered him the post of Prime Minister, and he rejected it.

On September 23, a major military mutiny began, leading over the next few months to the evacuation of Embassy Kinshasa (down to a level of 35 employees from more than 200), the closing of our consulate in Lubumbashi, and the repatriation of all Peace Corps volunteers, ending what had been, despite all odds, a highly successful program. Also closed: a USAID facility in Kinshasa doing research on HIV/AIDS, the first of its kind anywhere in the world. Research on the origin of what would become a global pandemic was suspended, and the facility did not reopen until after Mobutu's fall.

By 1992 we were debating whether or not to abandon our advocacy of "power sharing" and call for Mobutu to stand aside. Proponents of power sharing won, and I wrote a "dissent memo" arguing for a high-level envoy to pressure Mobutu into leaving. Unlike most dissent memos, this one did not require any courage since I knew my immediate superiors in State's Africa Bureau were on my side; indeed Assistant Secretary Hank Cohen, its head, cleared the memo.

The situation in Zaire did not change. We did alter our

policy, calling ever more loudly for Mobutu to step down. President Bush signed at least three letters to the stubborn Zairian ruler in 1992 alone, but none of them did any good. Mobutu continued to manipulate the situation, and there was continuing violent unrest. In the end he succumbed to armed opposition combined with his own failing health; he left the country in 1997 and died of prostate cancer shortly thereafter.

By far the most attractive of the Congolese opposition figures during my time in AF/C was the Roman Catholic bishop of Kisangani Province, Laurent Monsengwo Pasiya. We all dreamed that he might end up as President of Zaire, but realistically we never knew how far he could go, given the Vatican's disapproval of priests getting too deeply involved in politics. Monsengwo became the Archbishop of Kinshasa, but apparently dropped from political prominence once Mobutu was gone. However, his church obviously did not forget him: in writing this chapter I was delighted to discover that in 2013 he was named by Pope Francis as one of his "Group of Eight" advisors drawn from outside the Vatican.[23]

An English Vacation

In the summer of 1992, as a relief from all this Africa exposure, plus from the rigors of being a teacher again for Barbara, we chose a brief vacation in England, organized by British Airways. It offered a package deal that included the flight, a few days in a hotel in London and then a week's car rental combined with call-ahead-the-night-before B & B stays to anywhere in England that we wanted to go. Perfect: little advance planning and the ability to choose what we wanted to do once we were already on vacation—all at a bargain price. Visits to the Churchill's Cabinet War Rooms underneath 10 Downing Street and a return to the Percival David Museum with its fabulous collection of Chinese ceramics highlighted our London stay.

Then we picked up our little VW Golf and headed to visit old friends from Sarawak days and a few from more recent

---

[23] http://incaelo.wordpress.com/tag/laurent-cardinal-monsengwo-pasinya/. According to the same blog site, he had become a member of the "Ordinary Council" of the Vatican by September, 2014.

overseas posts, in the process visiting several magnificent cathedrals—Canterbury, Winchester, Salisbury, and Exeter. Our first stop was Brighton, where we reconnected with a friend who had worked on conservation in the Niger Delta, and then visited the famous Victorian-era seaside pavilion, originally built for the royal family, a wedding-cake anachronism still enjoyed by beachgoers.

A special side trip took us to Sheepstor (Sheep's Tower) village church, where the three Brooke Rajahs of Sarawak and their family members are buried. Despite all Bob's historical research about the Brookes, we had never seen it. En route, we stopped at the summer cottage of Stephen Morris, Bob's mentor in preparing for Sarawak. We just made it to Stonehenge the day before the summer solstice when it would have been impossible to get near that famous prehistoric site because, despite the best efforts of the constabulary, counter-culture worshippers flock there to enact what they believe are ancient rites of summer. Finally, we paid a visit to one of Bob's Charleston cousins, Mary Pringle Anderson, and her English professor husband in their adorable cottage with a meticulously tended garden, not far from Cambridge. We had visited them once before, when the children were small, on one of our trips back and forth to Southeast Asia.

Since our return from Mali, Jamie and Anne had not been wasting their summers, even though they no longer got free trips to see their parents in exotic postings. In 1990, having just graduated from Dartmouth, Jamie spent the summer moving to Mississippi and settling into his first real job at a physical oceanography lab near New Orleans. Annie was at the end of her first year at the University of Chicago, and was heading out west to wait tables at Eaton's Ranch near Sheridan, Wyoming, where dude ranching was invented, an area well known to Bob's family.[24] Ever since, she has had strong feelings about tipping servers adequately. But she did have some good times, especially when Aunt Margot, living nearby, lent her a car to drive around.

1992 was a year for Jamie to move, from Mississippi back to

---

[24] Domo Anderson, subject of Bob's mother's book *A Bride Goes West*, was a member of the family that had founded and was still running Eaton's.

Boston to start graduate studies in physical oceanography at MIT/Woods Hole. We will never forget his arrival at 216 Wolfe, en route north, with his car packed, more or less like a suitcase, or maybe a laundry bag, with nothing folded, but everything essential jammed in. As we recall, the only item valuable enough to be brought into the house overnight was his computer.

Annie also had an academically focused summer; she had to study organic chemistry at Northwestern in order to proceed with transferring her major at Chicago from religion to botany. The required commute occasioned the purchase of her first car, with the help of Uncle Ron.

The Rwandan Genocide

Meanwhile I remained preoccupied with Rwanda's ethnically charged civil war. I kept trying to get a handle on why the Hutus (85% of the population, including President Habyarimana of Rwanda), loathed and feared the Tutsis (13% of the population, including future President Kagamé), and why the two had fought each other with such sporadic persistence. I am leaving out the Twa, plus or minus ten percent of the population, jungle nomad pygmies scorned and ignored by almost everyone else.

Aside: Once I was at the Washington, DC, airport meeting the President of Burundi, whose country has approximately the same ethnic makeup (with similar tensions) as Rwanda. While waiting for his plane, which was late, to arrive, the Burundian ambassador and I were killing time. As we twiddled our thumbs and looked out the window, he observed several aircraft with "TWA" painted on their tails in big red letters. Having a sense of humor, he observed to me, "Goodness! This really is a great country! You even have an airline for the Twa!" (He was a Tutsi himself.)

By then I already knew that the Tutsi and Hutu live mingled with each other in their scattered, hillside settlements. They speak the same African language, Kinyarwanda, and the great majority are Christians. I also knew that the Tutsis (also *Batutsi*, or *Watussi*) are the traditional ruling class, and that they have genealogies which seem to prove that the Rwandan royal family is as old as many European monarchies.

According to local tradition they arrived from Egypt, or

Ethiopia, centuries ago. Tall and elegant, famous for their high-jumping ability (clearing eight feet is ordinary), they were traditionally warriors and herders, with spectacular long-horned cattle. They did no work aside from tending their herds. They had subordinated the pre-existing population, much shorter and more typically African in appearance, the Hutu.

I found a few more clues in an extraordinary book, *In Deepest Africa*, about the German colonization, published with German Foreign Ministry support in 1990. The first Europeans did not see this place until the 1890s, and then only because they were looking for the sources of the Nile. They found a stark distinction between the two main groups:

> The great mass of the rural population have been in the country from time immemorial and live by agriculture—the Wahutu—Bantus identified by different tribal names based on the territories they occupy. . . . [But] the Watussi hold all the power, while the Wahutu have practically no rights and possess nothing of their own.[25]

The pictures they took revealed a Tutsi culture of almost pharaonic elegance and style. The cover photo on the book shows two Germans officials with a high-jumping Tutsi warrior soaring over their heads.

The book also makes clear that the Germans did not hesitate to use brute force against people with no firearms. One photo shows the Rwandan monarch, King Yuhi V, with Captain Werner von Grawert, "who was named Bwana (Mister) Tikitiki because of his frequent resort to the machine gun."[26]

The book's magnificent photos reveal a countryside of wide open spaces, very different from today's densely settled

---

[25] Gudrun Honke, *Au plus profond de l'Afrique: le Rwanda et la colonisation allemande, 1885-1919*, Wuppertal, Peter Hammer Verlag, 1990, published with the support of the Cultural Development Department of the German Ministry of Foreign Affairs, p. 101. Author's translation, slightly paraphrased, of comments by two colonial officials.

[26] Ibid. The photo is on p. 55 and the caption is on p. 54, in French. The Germans assigned Roman numerals to keep track of successive Rwandan monarchs with the same name.

Rwanda and Burundi. But after I visited Rwanda, I was confused: not all the Tutsis I met were tall, and not all of them had the distinctive physiognomy shown in the old photos. Had there been a lot of intermarriage? If so, why had there been such a pattern of recurrent killing, dating back to the earliest days of independence and possibly well before that? Some scholars blamed the Belgians for ruling through the Tutsi aristocracy and strengthening its power. But looking at those old photographs and accounts of Tutsi dominance even before colonial rule I found this difficult to believe. Many if not most colonialists elsewhere practiced similar forms of "indirect rule," because it was cheap and convenient, without such horrendous consequences.

I thought maybe the ambassadors of the two countries in Washington might be able to help. The Rwandan, apparently a military intelligence official, was preoccupied with tracking down rebel Tutsi (RPF) plotting. He was certain it must be taking place somewhere in Washington and was interested in little else. However, I hit pay dirt with the Burundian, the one I mentioned in earlier in connection with his Twa joke. He was from the Ministry of Education, not a career diplomat, which was perhaps why he was so forthcoming.

He explained that many people in both countries were in constant fear of a new outbreak of reciprocal mass killing, similar to those of 1959, 1972, and 1993 (in Burundi), and of course the Tutsi invasion of Rwanda, ongoing since 1990, had fanned this paranoia.[27] While it was true that Hutus and Tutsis lived in the same *collines*, and equally clear that there had been significant intermarriage, everyone knew who was what, and if killing should recur, they knew whom to fear, or to kill before being killed. It was, in other words, a situation of aggravated paranoia based not on ethnic tension *per se*, common enough in Africa, but on hereditary consciousness of virulent *class* distinctions and awareness of past history.

We remained convinced that the civil war could be stopped by a negotiated peace, and that underlying tensions and violence could be overcome by an inclusive government based

---

[27] It is likely that research into pre-colonial history could extend the record of Hutu-Tutsi killing back into the pre-colonial period, but so far as I know no one has made such an effort.

on elections.[28] Negotiations were duly launched at Arusha in Tanzania in September, 1992, and an agreement was signed on August 4, 1993, just after I had left AF/C. But on April 6, 1994, a plane carrying President Habyarimana was shot down approaching the Rwandan capital, presumably by the same Rwandan Hutu extremists who immediately launched the infamous genocide against resident Tutsis. This is the time described in the film, *Hotel Rwanda*.

The extended uproar over the Rwandan genocide has focused mainly on why the United States, among others, did not respond faster and more robustly to the crisis. Part of the answer is that we were hobbled by the bitter experience of the "Black Hawk Down" episode, and were determined to avoid "another Somalia." An equally valid but neglected question is why did we not respond to the recommendations of our ambassador to Rwanda, Robert Flaten, who insisted that a stronger peacekeeping force be sent to the Rwandan capital *before* the peace agreement was signed. We knew that the projected arrival of Kagamé's Tutsi representatives and troops in the Rwandan capital *after* the agreement was signed would be intensely provocative.

The answer, of course, was that we had hoped that the ill-fated Rwandan president, Habyarimana, would be alive and able to control "his" Hutu fanatics. The hard fact was and still is that neither we nor the UN nor any one else had—or has—the rapid-response capability or the political will necessary to prevent such crises, which have continued to flourish in Africa and elsewhere. Indeed, what happened next illustrates that preventing the immediate genocide in Rwanda would not have halted the broader conflict.

In due course Kagamé became the supreme leader of Rwanda, expelling and wreaking extended vengeance on the "genocidists." The US decided that the restoration of Tutsi hegemony was not so bad and pundits were soon talking of him, along with his friend and supporter, President Museveni

---

[28] For this sentence, see Joyce E. Leader, *Rwanda's Struggle for Democracy and Peace, 1991-1994* (Washington: The Fund for Peace, 2001, p. xi). The author, who had been my colleague in Burkina Faso a decade previously, was DCM in Rwanda from 1991 to 1994, and our principal representative at the Arusha peace talks. She witnessed the genocide and wrote a vivid account of her experience in the book cited.

of Uganda, as one of Africa's new generation of leaders, not perhaps democratic but competent; they would make the trains run on time, if there were any, and it was pointless to worry about democracy.[29]

Before very long, however, Kagamé's pursuit of genocidists began to involve the large populations of Tutsis and Hutus in the eastern Congo—those sloppy colonial boundaries again—and the resulting vicious, never-ending struggle required the dispatch of what grew into the largest UN peace-keeping force in the world. What has been called Africa's World War[30] continued, with total casualties eventually far exceeding those of the 1994 genocide.[31]

Gabon, Equatorial Guinea, and São Tomé-Principe

When we were not worrying about Zaire, we often had unexpected new crises in Central Africa. The one I am least likely to forget occurred in Equatorial Guinea, one of our two archipelago countries, an impoverished (at that time) former Spanish colony. In February, 1993, I was on a routine visit to several other countries when the Africa Bureau asked me to drop everything and head straight for Equatorial Guinea. Our ambassador there, John Bennett, had done consular work throughout his long career, and this assignment was supposed to be his reward.

The problem was that someone was harassing our Peace

---

[29] For a good example of such thinking see Marina Ottaway, *Africa's New Leaders: Democracy or State Reconstruction?* Washington, Carnegie Endowment for International Peace, 1999.

[30] Gérard Prunier, *Africa's World War: Congo, the Rwandan Genocide, and the Making of a Continental Catastrophe*, Oxford, 2009. Prunier was one of the first scholars to see Kagamé as something other than the hero of the anti-genocide.

[31] Nicholas Kulish, "A Reason for Hope in Congo's Perpetual War," *New York Times*, October 27, 2013. The story notes in part, "The fighting in eastern Congo is one of the world's most intractable, prolonged and deadly conflicts, claiming millions of lives over a decade and a half.... The majority of the rebel commanders come from the same Tutsi ethnic group as the leadership of Rwanda [still Paul Kagamé], which Congo and the United Nations accuse of backing the rebels. Rwanda denies involvement. ... It remains to be seen whether the Obama administration's increasing pressure on Rwanda will have any effect on the fighting here."

Corps volunteers and sending death threats to Bennett, and it was clear that only the president of the country could have authorized them. His likely reason was our increasing advice, conveyed by the ambassador, to stop oppressing his people. My instructions were to seek an appointment with the president and tell him to cease his threats immediately.

"EG" had been the site of one of the more macabre incidents in diplomatic history, fit for an opera plot. Sometime prior to 1970, we had opened a small consulate in Malabo, the capital. The country was then ruled by Francisco Macias, who called himself the "Unique Miracle" and made Idi Amin look like a pussycat. Under the Spanish, the economy had been based entirely on cocoa, and labor was imported from Nigeria, but Macias sent them all home and used forced labor instead, sinking all the boats on the island so the residents couldn't escape.

The rusting hulks were still visible in 1991.

Macias was a member of the Fang tribe (85% of the population); the rest were mainly Bubis (6%), who were the native inhabitants of Fernando Po Island, where Malabo is located. In 1979, suspecting the Bubis of who knows what, Macias had embarked on a program of mass murder against them, killing thousands. The violence reached a climax with Bubi victims being burned to death in the soccer stadium.

It was at this moment that our tiny consulate went off the air, simply vanishing into the ether. The State Department sent an experienced FSO, Lannon Walker, to Malabo to find out what had become of our two American employees, the consul and a communicator. The story, which I do not think grew much in the telling, was that they had been competing for the affections of an Equatorial Guinean houseboy, and one murdered the other with a pair of scissors just as the soccer stadium mass burnings were taking place. To fully appreciate what might have happened you have to realize that the stadium was well within earshot of the consular residence, Malabo being a tiny place.[32] Not too long thereafter President Macias's nephew, Teodoro Obiang, who was also his chief of

[32] For an account of this episode see http://articles.latimes.com/1993-10-10/news/mn-44238_1_equatorial-guinea. Accessed January, 2018.

security, overthrew and replaced him.

We had had enough, and closed our consulate. But the foreign minister of the post-Franco government in Spain, the overwhelming source of aid to EG, begged his US counterpart, Secretary of State Cyrus Vance, to reopen as an embassy, because although the new president was not a homicidal maniac like his uncle, the situation was still deplorable. We did so in due course.

Despite its execrable politics and sinister culture— witchcraft was still a major force in the lives of the dominant Fang group, and was punishable, along with other crimes like advocating democracy, by prison sentences—EG has many interesting and attractive features. Malabo perches on the flanks of a big volcano, looking across a patch of ocean at its twin, Mt. Cameroon, and the city of Douala, the major port city of Cameroon. Its roughly seven hundred thousand people[33] are divided between the island where Malabo is situated, and a rectangular enclave on the mainland. A few more live on several of a long string of islands extending southwestwards into the Atlantic. Geologically they include Tristan da Cunha as well as the separate country of São Tomé and Principe, located between other islands on the same chain that belong to Equatorial Guinea. Like other islands and old fortresses along Africa's west coast, both Equatorial Guinea and São Tomé and Principe were once colonies (Portuguese, Spanish, French and English) established to facilitate the slave trade.

Malabo's tiny harbor is a small volcanic crater open to the sea on one side, a geological pimple on the side of the big volcano, which you can drive to the top of, something that is not possible on its twin across the water. In 1993, the little capital had elegant Spanish architecture, and the government had given our embassy two large stone houses originally built by the Spanish for official residences and office space. In a letter home I wrote:

EG is not all bad. It is quite something to encounter Africans speaking Spanish and with names like Don Faustino. Due probably to growing French interest in possible oil development

---

[33] 2013 population rounded; it was about half that in 1991.

EG is now in the CFA [French] franc zone, which has helped somewhat. The island of Fernando Po, where the capital is located, is gorgeous and very fertile and the standard of living is relatively high. There is some real wilderness in the forested mountain heights where there are some endangered species of monkeys with a project from the Atlanta Zoo looking after them. An American company has just brought in a small oil development (6,000 barrels a day).

The Embassy has a small boat and a mountain retreat. There is a very lively and effective Peace Corps program. The Spanish still have a big hand in education and much else. Cocoa production, for which conditions are perfect, . . . is now down to one-tenth of colonial levels but there are still a couple of old Spanish firms in business. People known as "Fernandinos" are descendants of freed slaves who came back from the New World, like the Americans to Liberia, ex-French slaves to Libreville (Congo Brazzaville); ex-British to Freetown (Sierra Leone), etc. We met one, who is the mayor of a small port city. Her name is Jones, pronounced HO-ness. Her grandfather came to Fernando Po in the eighteen-fifties, prospered as a cocoa planter, and ended up very wealthy indeed.[34]

I inspected Equatorial Guinea's sole oil producer, an American firm named Walters. It was operating out of a couple of shipping containers on Malabo's black sand beach, with a small drilling rig visible in the distance offshore. The production, displayed in a glass jug, was a clear yellow green liquid which the project director assured me was "distillate" from crude petroleum, and not the effluent from his outhouse. He was convinced that much bigger strikes were in the offing. We, including our ambassador, were skeptical (previous exploration efforts by the Spanish had failed), but he proved to be correct.

The French ambassador, whom I interviewed a year later, must have been better informed, because he seemed to be making a determined effort to have France, already the dominant oil power in the Gulf of Guinea, supplant Spain

---

[34] Bob letter to Dear Family, February 1, 1992, about my first of two visits to EG, slightly edited.

as the leading aid donor in Equatorial Guinea. As for the US diplomatic representation, we were thinking of pulling out once again, but when it turned out that that predictions of an a oil boom were accurate, we stayed, although we did shut down the Peace Corps program.

As for the major business at hand, I did see President Obiang in his palace, under the watchful eye of a security guard force provided by the King of Morocco. Obiang listened politely and denied the allegation. That was not quite the end of that, but the death threats did cease. I departed, leaving Ambassador Bennett to his thankless job. I wrote, perhaps too optimistically:

Why doesn't the US close its embassy and pull out of this sinister mess? We have already stopped virtually all aid and the Peace Corps has been terminated. But the arguments against hanging in there apply with equal force to many other small African countries. None matters much individually, yet Africa (arguably more important than the sum of its parts) is made of such material. In the case of EG, thanks to its geographic and linguistic isolation, it is unlikely that a non-resident mission will have any influence. If we pull out the break will be total, a victory for one of Africa's last tyrants .... Our presence can keep other donors (especially the French) relatively honest by making sure they are informed about human rights abuse. Obiang's attempts to intimidate Ambassador Bennett are certain evidence that our influence is being felt.[35]

Almost three decades later President Obiang is still in power and President Obama has received him—a picture of them together with spouses is available on the Internet—although his political habits have improved only marginally. But we are a tolerant or at least forgetting people, especially when oil is involved, and today Equatorial Guinea is the third largest producer in Africa.

On my initial trip to Equatorial Guinea, I visited two other countries in the neighborhood, Gabon and São Tomé and Principe (STP). Gabon was quite dull. Because of its oil wealth,

---

[35] Diary entry, February, 1993.

it was securely in the pocket of French interests and so wealthy it hardly needed anyone's economic aid. The ruler, El Haj Omar Bongo, was not a very solid Muslim, having apparently converted to Islam to please his Arab friends, but he also liked us and possessed none of the knee-jerk anti-Americanism fairly common elsewhere. Our only real difficulty with him during my time in AF/C came when he received a check for five million dollars from President Qadafi of Libya. We had no idea what it was for; Qadafi, among his other quirks, had a habit of showering cash on his friends and acquaintances simply when the mood struck him.

The problem was that Bongo had just switched all his international banking activity to Citibank, and when Bongo deposited the check there, the US Treasury, which was already monitoring all US international bank activities, immediately impounded it, the Libyan leader being near the top of our Bad Guy List for his terrorist activities. Bongo was not amused; he wanted his check credited to his account pronto or, he promised, it would be the end of his relationship with Citibank, which, of course, chimed in loudly on Bongo's side. What to do?

There ensued an interesting episode of State Department decision-making. Opinion among State's bureaus was fairly evenly divided. AF wanted to let Bongo have his money. If we enraged him, it would simply punish Citibank. The Economic Bureau agreed with us; Bongo would tell every African country to avoid banking with us, and US business generally would suffer. On the other side, practically all the bureaus involved with security, anti-terrorism and/or human rights were convinced that it would set a bad example if we let the Gabonese go unpunished for accepting payment (however mysterious the reason) from the toxic Libyan leader.

In such a situation the State Department would typically engage in lengthy internal negotiations, with opposing bureaus rewriting each other's memos until a compromise intended to please everyone was produced. In this case, however, the Secretary, Lawrence Eagleburger, was a career diplomat who disliked cutting babies in half. He told all involved to send him a so-called "split memo," with the opposing arguments clearly stated by bureaus. It was, he said, his job as Secretary of State to review the evidence and make the decision as to whether to release the check to Citibank, and hence to Bongo, or not. It came back to us with the "release check" box checked. Wow, I thought, it's a shame we don't have more top bureaucrats like this![36]

My Citibank contacts invited me up to New York to have a thank-you lunch with them. I would have found that amusing, especially in light of Uncle Max's experience with Citibank (not yet called that) and its ill-fated St. Petersburg branch back in 1917,[37] but I did not accept the invitation because I wasn't sure I was supposed to be wined and dined for doing my job.

Eagleburger, a career Foreign Service Officer, was famous for his extraordinary work in Yugoslavia, as well as for his conservative politics and rough-hewn style. He liked to eat lunch in the crowded State Department cafeteria, and he was there once when a sudden, progressive ripple ran across the crowded room, causing people to jump up from their tables. It was only a rat that had ventured out from the kitchen, perhaps hoping to meet the Secretary.[38]

Check problems aside, our ambassador to Gabon, Keith Wauchope, spent most of his time struggling to get the Gabonese to give US oil companies a fair shake vis-à-vis the big French company, ELF, a hopeless task if ever there was one. There were plenty of pricey French restaurants in the capital, Libreville, and warm champagne seemed to be the national drink.

Elsewhere there was still lots of tropical forest in Gabon because its wealth from oil and manganese had made it unnecessary to log it much, at least not yet. The people had never been farmers, but hunter-gatherers, and so they had not destroyed it for cultivation. Because of this, Gabon has one of the highest populations of forest elephants in Africa, or so they say. It's not clear how anyone knows since forest

---

[36] Eagleburger became acting Secretary of State in August, 1992; for more on him see his obituary in the *New York Times*, http://www.nytimes.com/2011/06/05/us/politics/05eagleburger.html?pagewanted=all&_r=0. Accessed January, 2018. The check episode would have been late in 1992. I have a Xerox copy of the check stub, dated December 23, 1992, in the 1991-92 photo album.

[37] See Chapter 2 for Uncle Maxwell's adventures in Russia and beyond.

[38] I was in the cafeteria at the time.

elephants, smaller than ordinary African elephants, are notoriously hard to find and count.

There is one place where the elephants come out on the beach and wade in the surf, but I didn't get there, nor did I get to Lambaréné, where Albert Schweitzer had his famous unsanitary hospital. Although a great organist, philospher and generator of publicity (especially, one suspects, the latter), Schweitzer did not believe in hygiene for Africans, and when he died, the hospital was so bad that the Gabonese president immediately ordered it modernized.

I went to Port Gentil, the oil center, and spent the morning visiting Amoco offshore oil rigs and a storage facility (a converted supertanker). The skilled rig operators were all Filipinos; they spent their spare time fishing off the rigs, drying the fish (big ones) on the metal catwalks, and taking large quantities of dried fish back to Manila when they went home on leave (the tour was four months on, two months off). They were paid $900 a month, less than our ambassador's cook in Libreville.[39]

On the same trip I paid a short visit to São Tomé and Principe. Although it was part of the same island chain as Equatorial Guinea, it was a far calmer, less paranoid place. There were only about 125,000 people living there. Like all the former Portuguese colonies, STP had become independent in 1978, in the hands of communists or near-communists who had backed the overthrow of the Salazar dictatorship in Portugal. But by 1992, both its Maoist party and a Stalinist rival had dropped Marxism and converted to democracy. Moreover, one of them had defeated the other in a free election, perhaps the only one up to that time among AF/C's ten countries.

However, STP, like EG, had the what-to-do-except-cocoa problem. One solution being discussed was to grow vegetables and ship them to Libreville in Gabon, where produce was very expensive. Another was tourism to take advantage of the largely

---

[39] Bob letter to Dear Family, February 1, 1992.

undiscovered, hence unspoiled, local beaches.[40] But the biggest thing actually going was an air freight service run by a raffish German named Chris Hellinger, who had once ferried supplies to the Biafran rebels in Nigeria and now serviced South African-owned gold mines in Angola from his STP base. Four of his C-130s were parked at the tiny airport when we arrived.

He also owned a reportedly luxurious deep-sea fishing resort, and managed the government–owned hotel where I stayed. It was no prize, having only feeble air conditioning and the worst mildew I experienced in thirty years of frequenting the mildew-ridden tropics, as well as attack mosquitoes, no doubt highly malarial, that emerged at four a.m. The currency was the *dobra*, selling for about 700 to the dollar.

During my visit with Ambassador Wauchope, he turned over a "patrol boat" to the STP "navy." Lest you think we were leading the natives into an arms race, this craft was a stubby little fiberglass cabin cruiser made in Little Rock, Arkansas, and small enough to trail behind a Volkswagen, but we hoped it would allow them to patrol their Extended Economic Zone (at least in good weather). STP's territorial waters in the Gulf of Guinea are rich in fish as well as oil, although unlike EG and Gabon they had not yet produced any oil.[41]

Despite the fact that we had no embassy or other resident representatives in STP, the Voice of America was about to install a large, medium-wave transmitter there to replace one that it had lost in Liberia. The location was ideal because the tiny country is almost exactly in the middle of the Gulf of Guinea, and President Trovoada was delighted to have anything that would help his economy.[42]

---

[40] As of 2013, according to a *Lonely Planet* blurb, only about twenty tourists a week were visiting STP: "On these shores, the only way to raise your heart rate is to participate in the astoundingly sensual pelvis-mashing moves danced nightly in bars across the islands. São Tomé is the kind of place you may never have heard about, but once you visit, you just might never leave." Read more: http://www.lonelyplanet.com/sao-tome-and-principe#ixzz2joi0iCBx. Accessed January, 2018.

[41] Bob letter to Dear Family, February 1, 1992.

[42] In 2015, Alan Heil, former Deputy Director of the VOA, informed me that more than twenty years later, the STP transmitter is still invaluable, covering as it does a wide swath of Africa's mid-section, including all of Nigeria.

By this time the promotion of democratization had become one of the most important US policy goals in Africa, along with economic development. We recognized the connection between the two, while well aware of a third and complicating imperative, dealing with endemic crisis and its aftermath. A meeting of US ambassadors to Africa in June 1993 was largely devoted to democratization, and I wrote a country-by-country assessment of my ten countries.

No surprise, none of them were doing very well, but there were signs of hope and progress in several, including Burundi, Chad and tiny STP. The overwhelming problems were long-term and cultural, but in only one country, Rwanda, did we have a long-term strategy. It was about to be demolished by the catastrophic failure of our efforts to end Rwanda's civil war, culminating in genocide, in 1994.

When it came to nurturing democratization, we as a government often let our determination to punish human rights violators get in the way of helping high-risk, non-performing countries, who were of course the ones that needed help the most. Focusing our aid on low-risk, high-performing countries would have put us out of business in the AF/C area, because there weren't any. I think that since 1993 we have gradually learned that democratization is a long-term goal which foreigners can help achieve, but only at the margins and not without constant attention to the latest short-term policy preoccupation (such as terrorism after 9/11).

A Family Crisis Intervenes

Besides a new assignment for Bob in the State Department, the year 1993 was notable for family events. June proved to be a bittersweet month—a milestone for Annie, who graduated from the University of Chicago, but sad news for Barbara's mother, who was unexpectedly diagnosed with kidney cancer when a large tumor in her lung began to interfere with her digestion. She had just returned from a memory-lane trip which repeated a much earlier tour of Rome and other sites in classical Italy that she had taken on her own, but was now sharing with Clay. Once back in Cincinnati, she checked in with her doctor expecting a prescription of extra-strength

Tums and found out that the cause was much more serious than anyone had expected.

Clay always remembered how energetic she had been in examining every painting, ruin, and palace on the itinerary, and he couldn't believe at first how ill she was. I have always been happy that Mother finished up in style, but after the diagnosis, she declined rapidly, enduring only palliative radiation treatments to keep the pain manageable. She remained interested in life until very late in the summer. She and Daddy had, sadly, not been able to attend Annie's graduation from Chicago, which was also Daddy's *alma mater*, and which had occurred right after the cancer diagnosis, so Annie made a special visit to Mariemont shortly thereafter. Mother was fascinated when her granddaughter, setting off to visit England for the first time, showed her the new feminine backpack she had bought to be her sole piece of luggage and explained all its woman-appropriate features. Mother, I am sure, had never carried anything larger than a daypack, if that, in her life.

I spent the summer at 6508 Park Lane running the household and helping with transportation to and from the hospital for treatments. The family came and went from their far-flung residences and, notably, so did Ruth Rach, the German AFS student whose year in America Mother had salvaged long ago, and her daughter Jessica.

Mother died just before Christmas, and we all gathered in Montgomery, Ohio, near Jane's house for her memorial service. With a small musical ensemble from the Cincinnati Conservatory of Music and remembrances and literary contributions by children and grandchildren, we paid tribute to her life before we all returned to work in the new year.

Mother had became semi-conscious and unable to perform any bodily functions about two weeks before her death, so she spent her final days in a welcoming and kind hospice on the west side of Cincinnati. I had made the very hard decision to say my good-byes shortly after she went there and to go with Bob, Annie (now teaching at St. Ann's School in Brooklyn) and Jamie (in graduate school at MIT/Woods Hole), on a long-planned dive trip to Bonaire. I did so partly because I thought it would be the last such trip we would take together as a family, as it proved to be.

Located in the Netherlands Antilles, Bonaire has no rivers to muddy its pristine surrounding waters, and it regulates dive boats, where they go and where they anchor (or don't) very carefully, so we all enjoyed lots of time underwater as well as our pleasant accommodations overlooking the ocean. But on Christmas Eve, a phone call came telling us of Mother's death, and we returned to the US on Christmas Day. That must be the only day of the year that a traveler can clear customs and immigration and catch a domestic flight in Atlanta in 45 minutes, all the while lugging along diving gear. We made it to Cincinnati for the memorial service in time to practice our parts as well as to participate fully.

Then it was back to work for all of us, including Bob.

Diplomacy and the Environment (OES/ETC)

My AF/C directorship was a two-year assignment, and by mid-1993 I had started a new job, heading the Office of Ecology and Terrestrial Conservation (or ETC) in the Bureau of Oceans and International Environmental and Scientific Affairs (OES). I had always been interested in environmental issues, and the OES portfolio was fascinating, including as it did issues ranging from climate change, already a big issue, to the management of oceans and fisheries and the international legal aspects of science and technology. These were not subjects that diplomats were normally trained to handle, but, for better or worse, the Constitution gives the State Department a lead role in the negotiation of *all* treaties, and if we didn't know a thing about global warming (for example) we simply had to work with other agencies that did. Indeed, State was often the *de facto* lead player in a complex process.

I was aware that an OES posting would probably not be "good for my career." Had I really wanted another, more important, ambassadorship it would have behooved me to stick to the Africa Bureau, because it was the regional bureaus which had the most clout on such matters, and AF was the only one that owed me for anything I had done within bureaucratic memory.

But I did not want just another African country less

important and/or less interesting than Mali. Nor did it seem like a good idea, given my heart condition (discussed below), to spend two or three more years in a place with inadequate medical facilities, although the State Department did try to send me to one, Nigeria. The other alternative would have been at least two years and maybe more of staff work in Washington with late hours and weekend work, in the thin hope of currying enough favor to get a non-hardship ambassadorship, either in Africa or somewhere else. Besides, OES wanted me, on short notice, to lead a team to create an international treaty (or convention, which means the same thing) dedicated to combating desertification.

My new office covered all non-nautical, hence *terrestrial*, conservation issues. This was a mystifying distinction to most people, and once before giving a talk I was introduced as head of the State Department's Office of *Extra*terrestrial Conservation, which at least sounded familiar, if mysterious. The reason for the "terrestrial" office is that there is a separate office for "oceanic affairs" in the State Department; indeed it is the oldest entity in State, having been created even before we were a nation to resolve fisheries disputes with the British and Canadians.

In addition to deserts, OES/ETC covered forests, wildlife (including the Convention on International Trade in Endangered Species, CITES), liaison with the International Union for the Conservation of Nature (IUCN), and, I liked to think, anything else relating to All Things Bright and Beautiful.

The idea of a treaty for deserts arose during the negotiation of the Convention on Biodiversity (aka the Rio Earth Summit) signed in Rio de Janeiro in June, 1992. It was proposed by African countries who let us know that they would not support a separate treaty on forest issues, which we badly wanted, unless we gave them one of their own, focused on a problem of enormous interest to Africa, namely desertification. (These particular Africans were apparently not aware that Africa does indeed have a major interest in forests, especially in Central Africa and the Congo Basin.)

Apparently no one in the relevant US agencies favored a desertification treaty, feeling that it would duplicate ongoing efforts and create nothing new. However, during negotiations in Rio one of the leaders of our delegation, White House Chief Counsel, C. Boyden Grey, capitulated without consulting anyone else, and the US was henceforth on the hook to help make a desertification treaty happen. The deserts and forests agreements were envisioned as part of a family of treaties, the most important of which was to be a treaty on climate change. All of them would nestle like happy puppies at the

Bob at the Desertification Treaty negotiations in Paris.

flank of Mother Rio. [43]

My first problem was anything but bright and beautiful. My predecessor had been a chain smoker, and although smoking was already forbidden in all government offices, he had simply closed his door and smoked anyway, and no one had stopped

[43] The full title of the convention is "The United Nations Convention to Combat Desertification in Those Countries Experiencing Serious Drought and/or Desertification, Particularly in Africa" or UNCCD. A forest treaty was signed in 1994 and revised in 2006; a climate treaty has famously been signed but not been ratified by the US Senate at this writing, although Barack Obama approved it by an executive order which Donald Trump has promised to revoke.

him. I demanded that my windows be unsealed (all State Department windows were sealed, heaven knows why) and the office scoured until it no longer reeked of tobacco smoke. No one was impressed with the incongruity of such a situation in an office promoting environmental enlightenment, but after much prodding the requisite detoxification finally took place, or anyway I hoped it had, and the room no longer smelled.

Fortunately, perhaps, the creation of the desertification convention involved much time away from the office, mainly at UN headquarters in New York, but also in Geneva and Paris. A senior diplomat from Sweden headed the process. All UN members were eligible to participate, and most of them did.

As in any major UN negotiation, decisions were made by consensus, meaning any one country could block the process. Many countries had no real interest in desertification *per se*, but their UN delegations, comfortably housed in New York, never missed a chance to engage in politicking on more general issues of north-south contention, such as the percentage of their GDP that rich countries were (or not) obligated to devote to helping poor ones. A more tedious and inefficient process can hardly be imagined, and for those of us who had long admired the UN from afar, without knowing much about it, the experience was a shock.

Our particular *bête noire* was the head of the Malaysian Delegation, Madame Ting.[44] (Why she alone among the female delegates was always referred to as "Madame" was a mystery.) Her specialty was attacking the United States for its manifold sins on behalf of the wealthy, and no one cared that there were no deserts in Malaysia, a highly moist place (as we knew from personal experience). What mattered was that it was now ruled by a nasty dictator, Mahathir bin Mohamad, to whom Madame Ting was close.

The good news was that the Cold War had disappeared and was no longer a pervasive, distracting force. The bad news was that especially on issues not of headline-grabbing importance, including desertification, one never knew who one's friends might be. The Chinese, for example, were often

---

[44] I can't remember Mme Ting's full name and much Googling has not helped.

surprisingly helpful. The French were solidly on our side, to be expected given their broader interests in Africa.

The biggest single issue was, as usual, money. The Africans, supported by many developing nations, wanted a new, dedicated budget for the new convention. The US and other big foreign aid donors saw the convention primarily as means of rallying attention to desert issues. We felt that enough was already being spent on relevant issues, including irrigation (large- and small-scale), the development of drought-resistant crops, pest control—I recalled those Biblical locusts in Mali—in sum, what USAID called "integrated dry-land resource management."

Some of the travel was interesting. In Geneva, I found time to visit my old school, Le Rosey, which I had not seen since I was there in 1947-48 and which was now one of the most expensive schools in the world. I asked to be added to their alumni rolls, and in due course began to receive invitations to $2,000 per day annual gatherings at very high-end locations, none of which we could remotely afford to accept. Le Rosey had added many more buildings, some named after my old teachers, including my nemesis, Mme Stickel.

Right in the middle of all this negotiating, starting during the holidays in 1993, I began noticing a peculiar although mild tightness in my chest, once when when pulling a scuba tank out of the water on our family trip to Bonaire and again when dragging luggage to the train after some kind of work at our UN Mission in New York. When I consulted my GP, Dr. Alan Stone, he told me in his usual understated way that while I didn't seem to have any obvious risk signs, I should get a stress test. It ended with the cardiologist stopping the test and offering me a nitroglycerin pill, meaning possible imminent danger. Within a week or so, on March 3, I had coronary bypass surgery.

The operation coincided with a foul, wet snowstorm (my heart problems always do), but I was out of the hospital in four days. I lost over twenty pounds, most of which I have managed to keep off. And since my heart was not damaged—I did not have a heart attack—the surgery combined with exercise, medications, and diet changes that followed, with constant help from Barbara, almost certainly added years, if not decades, to my life. I was back at work after about six weeks, but it took longer to get fully back to speed.

The desertification negotiations took about a year to conclude, ending in Paris at the UNESCO headquarters, by coincidence on the fiftieth anniversary of the June 1944 Normandy landings. France dissolved into an extraordinary orgy of pro-Allied, especially pro-American, gratitude. Several Paris newspapers printed their entire front pages in English. One of my colleagues, arriving late, had never been in France before. Forewarned that the Parisians didn't care much for us, he was walking to the convention site when it began to rain. To his astonishment a woman ran up and thrust her umbrella into his hand exclaiming "Here! Take this! You are an American!"

Near the end of the negotiations, Mme Anne de Lattre, the head of the French delegation, invited us to her ancestral home an hour or so by rail from Paris. She came from a noble and still prominent family which included Marshall Jean de Lattre de Tassigny (I think he was her uncle; she herself did not use "Tassigny"), a distinguished soldier best known for his command of the French Army in Vietnam. She had attended Barnard, then the women's affiliate of Columbia University, where she had roomed with Jean Kirkpatrick, ardent conservative and later Ronald Reagan's ambassador to the UN. They had became good friends, and de Lattre had learned bilingual English. She lived in an old house, once one of the outbuildings of a great family estate, in Ognon.

She told us the Germans had occupied it during World War II, then the Americans. Between them, they had had made such a mess of the place that the de Tassignys had never been able to afford fixing it up. The vast park surrounding the main house was full of classical statuary and formal gardens now overgrown with forest. She was a charming, smart, sensible woman who made working with the French delegation a pleasure.

The final session, on June 18, was not so cordial, ending in all-night dickering, commonplace when decisions required consensus. I had the flu and the brunt of this ordeal fell to my deputy, Bill Milam (later US ambassador to Bangladesh), who was our financial expert, fortunately so because the main disagreement was still over money. We won and no special funding was voted for the new treaty. Instead the emphasis was to be on mobilizing community participation, quote unquote, and USAID identified $500 million in existing or planned projects that addressed desertification issues.

I wrote in an optimistic diary entry:

The treaty does not envision a centralized, "global" effort. Indeed its strongest point—one the US worked hard to achieve—is its focus on a "bottom-up" approach featuring community participation, a strong role for NGOs, implementable planning, and better coordinating and planning among the donors. The Convention and the African Annex recognize that this effort, articulated through "new partnership" arrangements between donors (including multilaterals and NGOs) and individual governments, must be flexible and tailored to local conditions. It must be initiated by national governments and centered in their capitals, not Geneva or New York. The key institution in each case will be a national committee linked with a parallel donor coordination mechanism.[45]

We were also pleased that although it was theoretically global in scope, we had been able to avoid any obligations on the United States to do something about our own deserts, which would have been a red flag to Congress and thereby imperiled US ratification. Of such chicanery are treaties too often made.

Like all such treaties, this one set up a permanent mechanism, known as the Conference of the Parties, to monitor implementation and keep track of ratifications, fifty countries being required to ratify before it entered into force. The US did ratify it, along with virtually every other country on earth. I heard little more about the treaty until 1998, when, in the course of preparing for President Clinton's trip to South Africa the White House discovered it, and we suddenly began to publicize it as one of our major contributions to development in Africa.

---

[45] Diary entry, June 1, 1994.

On the Rivers of Russia

The busy season at the office concluded, Barbara and I took off on a personal trip to Russia, which we had postponed from the previous summer because of Charlotte's illness. When we had to cancel at the last minute in 1993, we had been able to get reimbursement for both international airfare and boat travel within Russia simply by explaining to the relevant carriers the unexpected family situation and the need for Barbara to care for her mother—no travel insurance or other hoops to jump through.

Though we were unable to reschedule stops in the Baltic nations and in Poland to visit the Sienkiewiczes (our UNDP friends from Manila days)[46], we revived our plans to take the river/canal trip from Moscow to St. Petersburg and to spend several days at each end exploring the two most important cities in Russia. We left early enough that Bob could fit in several days of environmental policy consultations (about exactly what is lost in the mists of time) in Moscow, and the State Department paid the cost of a decent hotel room during that period.

These were clearly post-Soviet times, but old habits were dying slowly. Clerks and wait staff in the state-run hotels still considered themselves the bosses of the guests, and stories of their butting into occupied rooms abounded. Restaurant food was often dull and tasteless, long on overcooked meat and starch, although it was fine on our boat trip where it mattered most.

We stayed in a newly opened Radisson Hotel. We had a slight but telling kafluffle there when we overstayed the checkout time for our room by ten minutes, and had to appeal to the manager to avoid paying for a whole extra night. Luckily he was a new hire, a Russian trained in capitalist ways by Radisson to oversee the new venture. After instantly overruling the desk clerk who had refused to budge on the issue, he confided, "We just hired her from a government hotel, and she doesn't understand the new rules of hospitality

---

[46] We finally visited them at their home in Warsaw in 2017, and were given an extensive tour of the city by Jamie's childhood friend Peter, now a very successful IT engineer and businessman.

yet."

We had great fun in Moscow before the boat tour started. Barbara had brushed up the Russian language she had studied at Cornell and recouped enough to read menus, ask questions (to which she often, nevertheless, could not follow the answer until a kindly soul who spoke some English happened by), and most importantly, to navigate the Metro. The stations in the famous system are stunning, decorated with Socialist Realism tile murals and huge stone or bronze statues, but the routes are complex, consisting of three concentric circles, intersected with straight lines, like spokes of a wheel. Trains stop only for seconds; riders boarding or getting off need to be nimble, and there is a lot of pushing.

Tourist information warned us about thieves in the Metro. We had no trouble, and one reason may have been that Barbara was carrying miscellaneous stuff, or purchases, or extra sweaters, in a net bag (*bilum*) from Papua New Guinea; wearing a bandana in the Moscow chill, she must have resembled Russian babushkas with their Russian-made net bags.

Red Square had not yet changed much—St. Basil's Cathedral at one end and Lenin's Tomb below the walls of the Kremlin on one side, facing the old GUM Department Store on the other. Nor had the Kremlin, where mere tourists like us could now see the Tsarist museum in the Arsenal, featuring royal crowns, swords, jewelry, and much more. Our favorite tourist destinations, though, were the Tretyakov Gallery, with its old icons and other Russian fine and folk art, and the Ismailovsky Park flea market on the edge of the city (a real Metro route challenge), where poor women still sat by the side of the entrance road selling half a dozen eggs, or used kitchenware, or handmade items one or two at a time in an attempt to make ends meet in the new Russia.

However, the larger merchants, displaying their wares outdoors, from quilts to tractors and even to old glass beads, created one of the largest and most interesting places to browse and shop that we have ever encountered. We still have a wonderful string of highly various old beads bought there, probably excavated illegally, most likely in the Crimea. They had been coated with something like Vaseline or motor oil to make them shine, and Barbara had a terrible time washing it off at the hotel, so that she could wear them as we left Russia. She thought—we'll never know whether justifiably or not— that officials at the airport might object to such old beads being taken out of the country if they found them in her luggage.

Vibrant as the market was, Moscow was still full of signs of economic distress for ordinary Russians, not only at Ismailovsky. On our above-ground trips around the city, we passed long lines outside various financial institutions; upon inquiring, we found out that all citizens were receiving shares in former state enterprises, which were being privatized by being "distributed to the people." What was really going on, however, was that these promises of gain in the future were being sold for kopeks on the ruble to big investors, some of whom would ultimately become the oligarchs of today.

After Bob had finished his consultations and we had explored a bit of Moscow, we boarded the *Andropov*, a riverboat formerly used to reward faithful Communist Party members with vacations similar to the one we were about to take. This one had been upgraded to handle English-speaking tourists, complete with tasty American/English meals, including fabulous dark bread, fresh vegetables purchased along the way, and beer to make capitalism cringe in shame (this was before micro-brews in the US). Other boats handled French and German speakers, complete with gastronomic specialties from their countries, one aspect of the new tourist industry doing its best to attract foreign guests.

Before we sailed from Moscow, our tour included a day trip to Zagorsk to see the famous Holy Trinity Monastery, with its lovely blue-and-white domed Cathedral of the Assumption and stand-alone baroque bell tower. Outside the entrance was a row of vendors where Barbara bought her especially well-crafted set of nesting dolls, which tells the story of a peasant mother, her growing daughter and finally a granddaughter.

The boat trip, via canals, the Volga River, two large lakes, and finally the Neva River, was non-stop interesting and scenic. As we cruised along slowly, we could sit on the deck and watch the villages and farms go by. Signs of the new Russia were frequent. Every village we passed had the steeple of its church surrounded by scaffolding now that Soviet repression of the Orthodox Church was over. However, we also sailed by two steeples poking up through the waters of newly created reservoirs, so progress cut two ways. Smaller towns and villages in which we stopped, at least once a day, seemed lively and agriculturally prosperous, even if the lovely June weather helped to create that impression.

The trip finished in St. Petersburg, "Leningrad" having gone out with the Soviet Union. The tour included both an opera, *Evgenie Onegin*, and a ballet at the Mariinsky Theater, and we have a photograph of our group standing in the twilight at 11:15 when one of the performances finished—just in case you are wondering how far north St. Petersburg really is. It was June, the month of the summer solstice.

At this time (1994), Barbara was still teaching Russian History and that made a home stay seem attractive during our post-cruise days in the city. In any case we had no choice because the Goodwill Games were absorbing all hotel space. The experience was certainly educational. Our hostess, a PhD scientist and her son (who had to vacate his sliver of the apartment to make room for us), lived in a one-tiny-bedroom walkup apartment in a dirty and crumbling apartment building, with stairwells that stank of urine. Two locking doors guarded her apartment, which consisted of a small living/dining/guest room, the bedroom, a Pullman kitchen, a toilet cubicle and a separate bathtub, plus a connecting hall lined with cupboards and wardrobes. The whole thing was the size of one floor, or slightly less, of 216 Wolfe Street.

St. Petersburg was in the middle of a heat wave, and the apartment had no screens, but plenty of huge mosquitoes, one discomfort that we had never associated with Russia. We were given the only fan, to cool our sleeping couch. Barbara certainly learned what she was talking about when she taught about the hardships of the lives of citizens of Soviet Russia; she has often wondered how long it took for the life of someone like our hostess to change, if it did. All in all, the Russia trip was a memorable summer vacation.

Annie took a special memory lane trip that summer too. She went to Indonesia with her friend, Lynn Davidson, to explore her roots; including a stop in Kuala Lumpur, her birthplace. Among other special experiences, they particularly remembered climbing to the top of Bromo Volcano in East Java to witness the sun rise over its boiling cauldron, something we parents never did in all our years living in and traveling around Indonesia. Also in East Java, they visited Moertini, who had traveled back with us across the Pacific on our first home leave from Indonesia; there had always been a special bond between her and our family because of that.

Back home, Bob had discovered that the Office of Terrestrial Conservation was markedly different from the Office of Central African Affairs in culture and composition. It had fewer Foreign Service Officers and more civil servants who were not obligated to serve abroad, a distinction broadly typical of regional versus functional bureaus and one that has steadily increased since then. Due to the legal nature of treaties, we also worked far more closely with "L," the State Department's Legal Bureau, which had an entire office dedicated to OES support.

"Our" lawyers always worked with us on treaty formulation, and were almost always dedicated to helping us. By contrast, it seemed to me, in a regional bureau the lawyers involved, even though they also worked for the State Department, seemed to concentrate more often on telling us what we couldn't do, rather than helping to achieve our goals. Among my favorite OES lawyers was a very bright young lady who came from a Jewish family in Elizabethville, Zaire, now Lubumbashi, many of whom were still living there.

Beyond the building we worked as much with non-governmental organizations (NGOs) as with other agencies. My immediate supervisor, Rafe Pomerance, was a political appointee who had come from the NGO world and later returned to it. This confluence of backgrounds and experience was interesting and productive. I was able to recruit my old friend Peter Kaestner, master bird watcher as well as FSO, to be my Deputy Office Director, just as a pair of very important migratory bird treaties with Canada and Mexico dating to 1916 were being rewritten. This was in part because Canadian law had evolved to exempt Native Americans from provisions protecting nesting grounds of waterfowl in northern latitudes, traditionally a major source of protein for them.

Other negotiators were astonished to be working with a diplomat who knew at least as much about birds as they did, and Kaestner regards this experience as one of the most valuable of his career. Moreover, thanks to him, we were able to hire Bruce Beehler, a prominent ornithologist and expert on New Guinea, giving us a real expert on one of the world's biodiversity hotspots. He stayed for only a few years and then went back to his work for Conservation International in Indonesia, in the course of which he received a lot of publicity for discovering a new species of bird on the Indonesian side.

There was no shortage of interesting characters in this realm. I got to travel to Spain to lecture with Thomas Lovejoy, a biologist with the Smithsonian, who is credited with inventing the term "biodiversity" and is one of the leading public intellectuals in the field. One of my other favorite naturalists was Merlin Tuttle, founding director of Bat Conservation International.

I met Tuttle when he asked us for help in saving the Free-tailed Bat, a species which cruises at high altitudes, eating tons of crop-destroying pests, in the American Southwest. But they migrate every winter to Mexico, and there ranchers were mistaking them for vampire bats and destroying them so efficiently that the population was going into decline. Tuttle wanted our embassy in Mexico City to help him enlist the Mexican authorities in support of his campaign to stop killing the wrong bats. In return, he would tell them how to control the vampires. (You put some poisoned blood on a cow, which the vampires consume and take back to their colonies, with lethal effect.)

Despite this story, Tuttle loved all bats regardless of size or eating habits. I was assigned to be note-taker when he met with Under Secretary of State Tim Wirth. Tuttle arrived at the State Department carrying an elegant slim-line briefcase, and after we sat down to talk he opened it, revealing a baby fruit bat hanging upside down, gazing at us with big brown eyes through her long eyelashes. Fortunately, security guards at the building's entrance had neglected to inspect his briefcase when he arrived for his appointment. I later established that this bat was quite probably the same kind we had hosted in Mali around our swimming pool. Of course, Wirth agreed to help Tuttle, whose rich Texas accent made him irresistible regardless of how you felt about bats.

My second year as OES Office Director was very enjoyable. I did some speech-writing for our Assistant Secretary, Elinor Constable, as well as for Tim Wirth, and some testifying on Capitol Hill. With Wirth's strong support the office kept expanding. I lobbied to have its name changed to the Office of Biodiversity, but other offices in OES saw that as a power grab and the proposal went nowhere. However when it came to action that would actually help to preserve biodiversity, as opposed to exhortation, we were challenged:

In many ways our treaty obligations (and negotiations) are OES's raison d'être: they are what State must do (in the environmental area) that no other USG agency can do. At the same time, the connection between the treaties and what sovereign governments do on the ground remains maddeningly vague. This poses a dilemma: in the long run the treaties represent a system of international commitments, but if you want save Suriname's forests [which were under immediate threat from rapacious Malaysian loggers, no less] you can't wait on the Biodiversity Convention. Hence the need to balance multilateral with bilateral and regional efforts, hopefully in such a manner that the two categories will reinforce each other.[47]

The International Coral Reef Initiative (ICRI), which my office staffed, was a good example of this bilateral-multilateral approach. It proved that if you stimulated enough NGOs in enough countries to assemble enough roomfuls of people and make a fuss, you could attract the support of multilateral organizations, in this case the World Bank. It could then pledge seed money to develop projects that would get results on the ground, such as outlawing practices that destroy reefs (e.g., fishing with dynamite and poison chemicals) and educating villagers on the long-term benefits of healthy reefs (e.g., attracting tourism and serving as nurseries for little fish

---

[47] "Pringle's Transition Report on Leaving OES/ETC," August 22, 1995. I got the idea of doing a comprehensive report on my two years in OES from the old Dutch colonial practice of end-of-tour reports. I did it because State's functional offices tended to be fragmented and specialized, and an incoming office director had a hard time catching up with even the most recent developments.

so they could grow up to be big, valuable ones).

State's role went beyond treaties; through its embassies it could identify, encourage and assist local environmental NGOs and sympathetic officials. State could also persuade USAID, which had serious money, to join the effort, which was often essential.

The best example of AID's importance was CARPE, the Central African Regional Program for the Environment. It was painfully apparent that although forest conservation was a critical factor in safeguarding biodiversity, no progress was being made toward a new international forest treaty as envisioned by the Rio Earth Summit. Environmental treaties had lost their appeal, particularly in the US. So we decided to take a regional approach, focusing on a large area, mostly in the Congo basin, containing the world's second largest aggregation of tropical forests after the Amazon, building on the work of American NGOs and supporting them with AID funds. I had a number of friends in AID's Africa Bureau who were immediately supportive, and State Department help was instrumental in bringing AID's senior leaders on board. They were used to State being preoccupied with getting money for political goals and when we proposed a development objective they were pleasantly shocked.

It was often more difficult persuading State's regional offices to believe that the environment should be an important foreign policy concern (I called it the "Real Men Don't Eat Quiche" syndrome), but they could be brought around by internal diplomacy. CARPE finally got off the ground with only $19 million in AID money over a ten-year period, but it also provided staff, including consultants, to help in coordinating with other donors. We launched similar but smaller forest initiatives with Brazil (buying into a larger, $150 million German project), Papua New Guinea, and Suriname, the latter being the emergency operation alluded to earlier, needed after the Suriname government decided to sell most of its magnificent forests to loggers—a decision we persuaded them to reverse.

A Seaborne Conference on Forest Issues

Leaving aside negotiating sessions in humdrum places like Paris and Geneva, travel opportunities were scarce, but the ones that came along were often fascinating. Despite lack of progress towards a treaty, there were endless meetings on international forestry issues. I told our forestry expert, Stephanie Caswell, who was the mother of small children and complained about too much travel, that I would be happy to relieve her at a meeting in Indonesia. I thought this made sense given my Indonesian background, and so did she. It gave me a chance to call on the Indonesian sponsoring organization[48] and to attend the subsequent conference, followed by visits to several theoretically sustainable logging sites elsewhere in Indonesia. To this end, our hosts hired a small P&O cruise ship based in Bali. From there we were going to sail to the logging sites, which were located along the southern coast of Borneo.

All began well, with a sunset departure from Bali and smooth steaming until, after a few hours, we turned north into the Lombok Strait and suddenly encountered heavy seas. Most of our delegates were from developing countries and many had never experienced ocean travel. Our little steamer bucked and plunged all night. The plenary session of the meeting was supposed to be the next morning on board the ship, but only a handful of participants could stagger out of their bunks.

Our first site visit went well and we traipsed up hill and down through a property where the "valuable" old growth timber—trees of the *dipterocarp* family— had been selectively cut, leaving behind immature trees that would hopefully keep growing and enable future logging after a decade or two. All species that were deemed not marketable had been clear-cut. As we walked along, the experts among us pointed out the probable fallacy of this approach: healthy tropical forests depend on a tremendous diversity of species of all kinds which interact with each other. If you strip out all the "weed trees" you might get something like a plantation of several "valuable" species only, for a short time. But, our experts thought, the experiment would probably fail to produce valuable trees for long. I am not sure whether anyone has been able to harvest

---

[48] The meeting was hosted by the Government of Indonesia and the International Tropical Timber Organization (ITTO), located in Bandung, a newly established member of the research group that includes the International Rice Research Institute (IRRI) and others. It was entitled "Science, Forests and Sustainability" and an introductory session had been held in Bandung on December 9, 1994.

tropical forests sustainably, except on Java, where the Dutch did successfully establish plantations of non-native teak trees.[49]

That was our only site visit, because it turned out that our ship, however small, drew too much water to get into our next destination, Banjermassin. What to do? Well, *faute de mieux*, we sailed on to the island of Komodo and saw its famous Komodo Dragons (huge, carrion-eating lizards) and lovely coral reefs, as well as a group of sperm whales frolicking near the ship on the way.

This account does not exhaust the interesting aspects of my OES job, but I will mention only two others. Somehow during my tenure we inherited Man and the Biosphere (MAB), a UNESCO program that sponsors "biosphere reserves." The assumption behind this program is that human developmental and conservation requirements need to be integrated. Thus, a biosphere reserve has a relatively pristine core area dedicated solely to conservation, surrounded by one or more transitional areas where human activity is allowed but limited, the idea being to encourage a sustainable relationship between man and nature through activities like eco-tourism. The program got off to a slow start in the US, partly due to suspicion of any kind of UN activity, linked with phobias involving black helicopters, but by 2013 there were more than thirty-five MAB reserves in the US, and the global network of over 500 is impressive.

The one-man MAB office, affiliated with my office, was located on the old Naval Observatory grounds across from the State Department, which included a low-slung brick structure to which Abraham Lincoln's body had been taken after his assassination. I used to wander over to make sure that MAB's sole employee, to whom we provided administrative support, was still alive and to chat about his programs.

Another interesting responsibility was the problem of Farmer's Rights. It was a backlash from developing countries, which were forever being harassed by us about violating our patent rights, including patents on items like seeds and other agricultural products which poor farmers needed. They

---

[49] I briefly searched the web in January 2014 and found reference to an article that sustainable harvesting of *dipterocarp* forest in Borneo might be possible on a forty-year harvest cycle, so the idea is not yet dead. See http://www.afs-journal.org/articles/forest/abs/2003/08/F3807/F3807.html.

came up with the idea, not wholly unjustified, that it was the developed world, the "north," that owed *them* compensation for appropriating *their* native plants (such as corn) in the first place, and developing them commercially. I noted at the time:

More realistically, the "south" sees the issue of Farmers' Rights as a handy club to beat us with in retaliation for our constant nattering at them about intellectual property rights; indeed they want to equate the two. Needless to say, and as intended, this gives us fits.[50]

Malaysia and India were among the most vocal, and the subject threatened to dominate and politicize international discussions of biodiversity. I thought we were too often put in the position of being against "Farmers' Rights," when in fact we were already working to help conserve traditional crop strains, which were all too often being allowed to die out under the onslaught of modern varieties. I recommended that we publicize what we were doing more effectively lest the affronted southern countries pass laws excluding us from their genetic resources, as India and others were threatening to do. I suspect this is still a live issue.

Our Old House Gets a Fix

Meanwhile, on the domestic scene, both in our house and in Cincinnati, change was afoot. We had decided to do a major renovation, to make the Wolfe Street house larger by extending the attic out over the ell and more liveable by redoing the kitchen and bathrooms. The law that had required all bathrooms to have an exterior window had been repealed thanks to stronger exhaust fans. Now, by moving the powder room from the rear of the kitchen to the interior and adding French doors, we gained a full view of and improved access to the garden. At about the same time we improved the safety and performance of our three eighteenth-century fireplaces by adding tubular steel linings.

---

[50] "Pringle's Transition Report," pp. 9-10.

Our chief contractor for the kitchen and attic was Steve Lord, a model of competence in construction and reliability in work habits. When he pointed out that one large room in the attic would be far more attractive than the two small ones that our rather useless architect had planned, Steve worked out the details of the construction on his own. The big drama of his effort occurred early on, when he began to dismantle the roof. He intended to brace the front (street) half by propping up the roof ridge beam against the top of the back wall. But there wasn't any roof ridge beam; the rafters just met each other in a mortise-and-tenon arrangement, meaning they were held together with wooden pegs.

You never saw anyone work so fast. A new beam was ordered from Smoot's, Alexandria's heritage lumber company, then still located at the north end of Royal Street; plastic sheeting was stretched over the exposed back half of the attic, and fortunately it didn't rain that night. By the next evening, we had a new roof beam and a temporary plywood roof. The attic turned into a lovely library, clothes and textile storage area, and guest bedroom, with a trundle bed that all grandchildren love.

After Charlotte's death, the sisters came to Cincinnati together more than once to clean out the attic and help Clay to revise the house for himself. But his heart was no longer in Cincinnati, and he spent longer and longer periods at Pine Knoll Shores, our family place in North Carolina. There a recent widow, Newell Haller, who with her husband Ken had been a friend of Clay and Charlotte, pursued him persistently. She was a very different person from Charlotte, but intelligent and still vivacious, and Clay was lonely. They were married, and Clay sold the house in Mariemont to Barbara's niece Heather and her husband Lamont; it was easier for him to part with it that way, and Heather and Lamont undoubtedly got a really good deal from Grandfather.

The Senior Seminar

I continued to enjoy my work in OES thoroughly and wanted to extend there for a third year. The mix of conservation issues and methodology—lobbying, PR and diplomacy, both internal and international—was intriguing, and I was just getting up to speed on how this game was played. I received as much recognition for my work on the central African forestry project, CARPE, mainly from AID colleagues, as for anything else I ever did in the Foreign Service.

For reasons already stated, we were reluctant to go abroad again. But we were up against a new rule which limited Foreign Service Officers to five years in the US, after which a foreign assignment was mandatory. By this time Foreign Service families, like others, were increasingly dependent on two incomes, and a multi-year posting abroad, once preferred, was imposing an increasingly serious financial burden. The result is a growing, potentially mortal threat to the future of the Foreign Service, a problem discussed in the closing chapter. I was saved when I managed somehow—I cannot remember how—to land a one-year job as Dean of the Senior Seminar, which gave me time to keep looking for a solution.

The Seminar was located at the Foreign Service Institute in Arlington and would run from August 1995 to June 1996. Its objective was to train a small group of FSO's for ambassadorial and other high-level assignments. Although it included representatives of other national security agencies,[51] the content was designed primarily with State Department and USIA needs in mind. The assumption behind it was that while senior diplomats may be assumed to have proficiency in the conduct of foreign relations, they are often out of touch with their own country beyond the Beltway. The Seminar was designed to correct this deficiency by carefully planned domestic trips, organized to introduce regions of the country and selected domestic policy issues important to each region, supplemented by activities in Washington.

For example, the first big trip of the year was to Alaska, where we studied:

---

[51] The Seminar Class of 1995/96, of which I was dean, included 31 participants, not counting me, of whom 16 were State Department, 2 USIA (which was not yet integrated with State), 2 CIA, and one each Army, Navy, Marine Corps, Air Force, Air Force National Guard, Coast Guard, National Security Agency, FBI, Environmental Protection Agency, USAID, and Department of Agriculture (Foreign Agricultural Service).

- The role of individual states in foreign affairs (Alaska had been fast off the block to develop trade and travel relations with post-Soviet Russia);

- The place of Native Americans in the US polity (there are more of them in Alaska than anywhere else, and the agreement leading to Alaskan statehood had to feature a widely underappreciated new deal for them, or they would have rejected it); and

- Environmental policy (no state has a greater stake in it than Alaska).

Another trip, to the Midwest, was designed to get diplomats up to speed on agriculture and industry. Major events included an overnight visit for each seminar member to a working farm, a lecture by a professor of agricultural economics at Purdue University—who turned out to be our old friend Otto Doering—and a visit to a very successful Ford factory making Taurus station wagons in Indiana.

Two trips were solely devoted to acquainting civilian seminarians with the military: Army, Navy, Marines, Air Force and Coast Guard. Seminar participants were themselves a mix of civilian and military, partly to educate the civilians about the US military and vice versa, and thanks to our uniformed members we were often able to use military aircraft. That saved money and could get us to places like Point Barrow, Alaska, where we saw stacks of whale meat drying and ate at Pepe's North of the Border Mexican Restaurant. At a North Slope oil terminal we saw both the famous pipeline and the visible increase in air pollution concentrating in the Arctic North.

In Washington, visits to domestic agencies and the Congress alternated with local travel and relevant speakers. We were able to attract an astonishing array of high-quality speakers from all fields, such as the future head of the AFL-CIO, Richard Trumpka.

Hit trips locally included Baltimore, where we rode with police on patrol into the seamier areas of the city and toured a medium-security prison, where we met both prisoners and the warden. The warden expressed eloquent frustration about what he saw as the sheer stupidity of the Maryland State Legislature, which, fearful of appearing to coddle criminals, was constantly cutting funds for prisoner education. As he explained, this was a program which was not just morally desirable; by reducing recidivism it saved the Maryland taxpayer money.

Not far away, thanks to a student who in real life was a senior staffer at the NSA, we were privileged to watch a huge screen reflecting in real time the minutiae of air traffic and related communications over the Balkans, where hostilities were in progress. And courtesy of the FBI, we all got to practice pistol tactics on both real and electronic ranges.

A few other exceptional experiences:

> - Flying, all of us, out to a modern aircraft carrier, the USS *Carl Vinson* on a nasty little transport plane known as a CoD, whose barely beyond teen age crew delighted in making extremely tight, probably unnecessary turns on final approach to the carrier to test the stomachs of tenderfoot non-aviators. (Several of our stomachs flunked.)

> - For me, riding in the cockpit of our Air Force plane as we took off from Juneau, Alaska, up the middle of a big glacier at dawn.

> - Curtailing the Northeast trip due to the government shutdown in November, 1995. We had just met with George Soros at his Manhattan office to hear his views on finance, a major focus of this trip. We had three more days of meetings scheduled, some that same day, with senior faculty members at Yale, when we were suddenly instructed to drop everything and come back to Washington. Some of our more rambunctious State Department members strenuously favored continuing anyway, although it was clear

that our orders meant what they said and all
activities at FSI were being suspended, and they
were understandably annoyed when I insisted
on doing what we were told.

This was the only remotely unpleasant moment of my
nine months as Dean of the Senior Seminar. The student
participants planned the trips, scheduled the appointments,
and wrote the theme papers and evaluations of each trip or
outreach event, leaving me with little to do except tag along
and write personnel evaluations at the very end.

We all agreed that the Seminar's concept was well founded,
indeed brilliant. American diplomats were constantly
expected to explain the United States to foreigners anxious
for enlightenment on what makes us tick. Of course we had
to understand them, but they also expected us to understand
ourselves. They were especially interested in knowing how the
US was dealing with issues similar to those they were facing.

Major issues, like our federal system and the division
of powers, were a mystery to many, but small things were
often just as important. To cite one example, one Seminar
graduate, Greg Engle, went on to become our Consul General
in Johannesburg, South Africa, at a time when a debate was
underway about a museum to memorialize the apartheid-era
uprisings in Soweto. Because the Seminar had visited the Civil
Rights Museum in Memphis, Tennessee, on the site where
Martin Luther King was assassinated, he was able offer much
appreciated advice to Johannesburg leaders and to arrange
travel to the US for them to see relevant sites in person.

Unfortunately the Senior Seminar was not so popular
beyond the ranks of its participants. Others often saw it as
elitist because only a few senior officers could participate. The
training bureaucracy at the Foreign Service Institute felt it
was unprofessional, because it did not sufficiently emphasize
courses on "leadership" of the kind then in vogue in business
schools and elsewhere in government. All that travel was
widely seen as frivolous, and it became more expensive as
wartime needs made it more difficult to get free military air
support.

So the Seminar was replaced in 2004 by a shorter senior

tradecraft course that more officers could take. The idea behind the Seminar—that prospective senior diplomats needed more than anything else a total immersion course on their own country—was perhaps a little too good, and certainly too unconventional, to survive.

Sometime in the spring of 1996 I learned that Jim Joseph, a political appointee with long experience in South Africa, had been nominated as our next ambassador to that country. He

The family in front of our second Alexandria house, at 216 Wolfe Street: Barbara, Annie, Pax (the only dog we ever had, but he lived to be eighteen and accompanied us to Africa twice), Jamie and Bob, sometime during Bob's second long Washington assignment.

was reportedly looking for a career FSO to serve as his DCM, someone who could help him navigate the State Department bureaucracy but was sympathetic to his personal outlook on South Africa. I interviewed for the job and he chose me.

We were excited by the prospect—Nelson Mandela had just become President of South Africa—but there were issues. Barbara had already committed to another year at Potomac, which meant that she would not be able to accompany me for my first year. Moreover, neither of us wanted to move all the furniture out of 216 Wolfe Street, inflicting further blemishes on its already battered, elderly walls and floors. Finally Barbara was not happy at the prospect of leaving her job at Potomac School without a reasonable chance of getting it back after two years (three for me) abroad.

All these problems were solved in due course, with a lot of help from our friends. As already recounted, Ann Scott agreed to replace Barbara at Potomac for two years before retiring permanently. In the course of the first year in Pretoria, Bob found a colleague, Ken Thomas, who would be on his way home in summer, 1996, and by chance was itching to find a furnished rental home in Old Town. He was then a bachelor (though he married while in our house), and we have never had a better tenant. And we agreed we could tough out a nine-month separation, with Barbara coming out to visit over Christmas holidays.

14

South Africa (1): Present at a Creation, 1996-1999

By September, 1996, when Bob arrived in South Africa, Nelson Mandela was president. The struggle against apartheid was over; the longer battle for racial equity was just getting under way. But South Africa was not yet just another African country, not by a long shot.

It was for one thing not underdeveloped, like the rest of sub-Saharan Africa, notwithstanding massive poverty in places. Beginning in the late nineteenth century the exploitation of great mineral resources, first diamonds and then gold, had led to the creation of modern infrastructure, from banks to railroads to universities. Demand for labor, plus coercion, pulled Africans off the land and into the mines. By the First World War it already mattered whose side South Africa was on in any given global struggle, especially to the British. It was not as big as Congo or as populous as Nigeria, but was more important than either. It seemed certain, and still does, that its importance will endure.

Bob's Role as DCM—Again

People often asked me how I could accept an assignment as a mere deputy chief of mission—my third such assignment— when I had been an ambassador. The answer was that it was like comparing the captain of a tugboat with the first mate of an aircraft carrier. In addition, my understanding with Ambassador James Joseph was critical. He had made it clear that I would have broad responsibilities, including but not restricted to the management of an embassy with three subsidiary consulates (in Johannesburg, Durban and Cape

Town) and additional support responsibilities for our much smaller embassies in a clutch of neighboring countries from Namibia to Mozambique.

More important, what Ambassador Joseph and I had agreed on was not the stereotypical relationship between a career DCM and a political ambassador. His concept was sound. He would deal with the South African leadership: he knew most of them from Mandela on down and had been working with many of them for years. I would deal with the intricacies of Washington's foreign affairs bureaucracy, and he would respect my advice on other matters. Since he was a generous and forgiving person, the latter point was never in doubt.

One big question was whether I should pay more attention to being his adviser-in-chief versus being manager-in-chief of a big mission. Being adviser-in-chief, for instance, meant accompanying him to Cape Town where parliament met, and where he went when it was in session because Mandela and all his ministers would be there. Being manager-in-chief meant spending more time in Pretoria. When I raised the question to Jim, he usually said, "Use your own judgment," knowing full well how much everyone, including me, enjoyed Cape Town. So I did, perhaps presuming too much on his kindness at times.

The DCM's management role was expanding along with the size of the US Mission. Now that our relationship with South Africa had been normalized, it seemed that every agency in Washington wanted a regional office in South Africa, and most of them soon had one. The law-and-order agencies were among the most eager to move in. They included the FBI, Secret Service, Customs and Immigration, and Drug Enforcement Agency (DEA), not counting State's own security officers. You wonder why all these folks needed a regional base in Africa? So did we. Well, the Secret Service is not just in charge of protecting the President; it is also, for example, responsible for stopping the counterfeiting of US dollars. The South Africans have good printing presses and know how to use them. Every agency had a similar rationale.

True, South Africa was not exactly centrally located for an office with Africa-wide responsibilities, but it had excellent airline connections plus a glorious climate, world-class golf courses, famous game parks, good (and cheap) food and wine, adequate to excellent medical and educational facilities, even good opera, and a dizzying assortment of pretty girls of all races (think movie actress Charlize Theron).

In the bad old days, the US Embassy had been in downtown Pretoria, in a slightly grimy neighborhood. It was on the top floors of a multi-story building next door to the apartheid regime's secret police headquarters, which meant that it was an obvious target for anti-regime bombs. So a new embassy had just been constructed in a prettier area outside the city center, a tall glass tower with lots of "set-back" (empty surrounding land) to minimize the bombing risk.

Many South Africans thought that big as it was, the building must be a missile base. But it wasn't as roomy as it looked, and no one had anticipated the change in relations and the resulting influx of US officials. So we soon ran out of space, and within a year of my arrival we were frantically leasing new offices on all sides of the new embassy, most of them with no set-back at all, just in time for a new spate of concern about bombing, this time linked with radical Islam.

US Relations with the New South Africa

It could be argued that, by 1996 the headline-grabbing days of a South African posting were gone. We were no longer supporting the epochal fight against apartheid,[1] or encouraging the Afrikaner regime to mend its ways, with a surprising degree of success. We were rarely on front pages back home. But we were trying in every possible way to help Mandela succeed in building his new Rainbow Nation on a more equal economic base. This involved much technical assistance, some of it in the form of financial aid, more through expanded cooperation in multiple areas. We had just established a new Binational Commission headed by our respective Vice Presidents to energize and implement this cooperation, and this project took a lot of embassy

---

[1] For what the previous era in US-South African relations was like, see the book by my former boss in AF/ETC, later our ambassador to South Africa: Princeton Lyman, *Partner to History: The US Role in South Africa's Transition to Democracy,* United States Institute of Peace, 2002.

preparation and follow-up.

The new relationship had unexpected problems, large and small. Many of the former freedom fighters of the African National Congress (ANC), now cabinet ministers or other government officials, were still on our list of terrorists and/or were members of the South African Communist Party, and therefore couldn't enter the US. The old South African arms manufacturer, ARMSCOR, was still under US indictment for apartheid-era misbehavior. Indeed it was still doing things of which we didn't approve, like selling arms to Syria—*plus ça change!* So reaching a settlement with them took several years. This was true notwithstanding that the company was on good terms with the Mandela regime, Afrikaner staff and all, and that before long we ourselves were buying military technology from South Africa, especially anti-mine technology and vehicles, such as the "m-raps"[2] we later employed in Afghanistan and Iraq.

We, of course, were eager to have Mandela's government as a friend and potential ally. But the South Africans did not want be seen as American allies on our terms, especially on issues where we thought we were running the show, such as the long-drawn negotiations over Libya's role in the Lockerbie shoot-down (more on that later). We really didn't want these rank amateurs meddling in our big-time diplomacy, unless they were directly concerned. Trouble loomed in this department. Meanwhile, every member of the US Congress and Cabinet member who came to South Africa assumed a right to meet the world-famous South African president. This got tiresome after a while.

Nevertheless, to be serving in South Africa at this time was a rare and enthralling opportunity. Among my earlier memorable experiences, before Barbara arrived, was representing the United States at a ceremony commemorating Enoch Sontonga, the author of *Nkosa Sikelel'i Afrika* (God Bless Africa), the African National Congress hymn and today part of the new national anthem. His modest grave in the "Native Christian" section of an old cemetery in Braamfontein,

---

[2] In South Africa they were known as "rhinos," often shown in photos of the apartheid police quashing riots.

The Minister of Arts, Culture, Science and Technology
has the honour to invite

*the Ambassador of the United States of America and
Mrs J. A. Joseph*

to the unveiling of the memorial to Enoch Sontonga,
the composer of Nkosi Sikelel' iAfrika,

at the Braamfontein Cemetery, Johannesburg
on Tuesday, 24 September 1996 at 10:00

RSVP Debbie at 012 - 348 2133 before 12 September 1996

DEPARTMENT OF ARTS,
CULTURE, SCIENCE   UMNYANGO WEZ
                                    AMASIKO, ISA

President Mandela spoke at a ceremony honoring the composer of the African National Congress hymn.

a suburb of Johannesburg, had been neglected for decades; now the leaders of the new South Africa were gathered to dedicate an appropriate monument at the site.

I realized that I was not only going to be present at the creation of what was in many ways a new nation, I was also going to meet its founding fathers. In my first letter home from Pretoria I wrote:

Mandela and his entire cabinet were there. It went well except that "Madiba" [Mandela's clan name, widely used as an affectionate nickname] *insisted on shaking hands with the entire orchestra and chorus at the end—about 400 of them— which tangled things up a bit. . . . One of the fun things . . . was Archbishop [Desmond] Tutu, who was all over the place meeting and greeting like a little, all smiles, purple banty rooster. What a character! They had a four-way ecumenical prayer, Tutu, the Jo'burg chief rabbi, a Muslim "Malay" cleric from Cape Town and a Hindu (Indian) priest.* [3]

A Bit of History, for Perspective

At this point you need to know just enough South African history, simplified, to understand what follows.

Pretoria was originally the capital of the Transvaal Republic, one of two Boer, or Afrikaner, states which were gradually established in the early 1850s, before the big diamond and even bigger gold rushes. The second was the Orange Free State. The founders of both were descendents of the Dutch who had established a settlement at the Cape of Good Hope in 1652 to supply water and provisions to ships of the Dutch East India Company en route to what is now Indonesia. I should explain that the term "Boer," which sounds pejorative in English, is not seen that way by South Africans; it is simply the Dutch/Afrikaans word for "farmer," and can be used interchangeably with "Afrikaner."

In 1814 during the Napoleonic Wars the British took control of the Cape, and before long England abolished slavery. This caused many slave-owning Boers to head north on the Great Trek, slaughtering hostile Zulus along the way and miraculously avoiding being slaughtered themselves as they gradually began to establish farms far north of the coast. But in 1866 diamonds were discovered at Kimberly, followed twenty years later by the world's biggest-ever gold strike at what is now Johannesburg. Until then the British had not cared much where the Boers went. However, the minerals boom changed everything, and they decided that South Africa

---

[3] Bob letter to Dear Barbara, September 24, 1996, handwritten.

had to be under their control, for the sake of orderly business and imperial profit. The Boers, having trekked north to escape British rule, were not happy. One thing led to another, ending in the Anglo-Boer War (1899-1902).

It was supposed to be a short, easy war, but the British discovered that the Boers, like most frontiersmen, were born fighters, and it dragged on and on. Finally both sides, but especially the British, who had gained grudging respect for their tough opponents, realized that the war, like so many wars, made no sense. The antagonists shared an interest in ending it, allowing the Boers to be partners in joint rule, and being sure that the natives were sufficiently oppressed and relocated to provide a safe and reliable source of labor for the mines. At the same time, this resolution of the Boer-British conflict made room for white farmers employing black labor.

As a symbol of power sharing, the new Union of South Africa which emerged from the war had three capitals: a parliamentary capital located in Cape Town, British territory for almost a century; an executive capital in Pretoria, capital of the former Transvaal Republic; and a third, judicial capital, in Bloemfontein, once the capital of the Orange Free State.

Over time the Boers emerged as the dominant voice in domestic policy, most notably an increasingly radical form of racial segregation, or *apartheid*, meaning "apartness." From about 1917 onwards, blacks were systematically deprived of their land and shunted onto "native reserves," some of which were later redesignated as "homelands." These "Bantustans" were given phony nationhood, which fooled no one and enraged an emerging anti-apartheid movement led by the African National Congress, or ANC. Guerilla war against the government and international opprobrium followed.

Among many other agitators, a young lawyer and ANC leader named Nelson Mandela was jailed in 1962; he spent twenty-seven years as a prisoner, mainly on Robben Island, offshore from Cape Town. The Boers, assailed internationally and increasingly nagged by their own Christian consciences, finally began to waver. Mandela was released from jail in 1990 and was elected president in 1994. You may have seen the film *"Invictus"* about that period. A minority of hard-core Afrikaner extremists did not rebel, as many had expected they would. F.W. de Klerk, the last Boer President of South Africa, was awarded the Nobel Peace Prize jointly with Nelson Mandela for his contributions to achieving a settlement.[4]

The tripartite capital arrangement bequeathed by the Boer War has, amazingly, remained in place. Before Mandela was president, much of the US Embassy moved to Cape Town whenever the South African Parliament was in session. We had little business to conduct with the South African executive branch in Pretoria when all the ministers were in Cape Town. But with the election of Mandela, sessions of Parliament in Cape Town became longer, while from our perspective the Pretoria civil servants became more important, as did the US presence there. I arrived on the cusp of this transition.

At first we were not even sure if the extravagantly wasteful triple capital system would continue. The new black-dominated government did not initially share the enthusiasm of most whites and foreigners for Cape Town, where the majority of the natives were not even "black," but Afrikaans-speaking "colored," people descended largely from the original, pre-Dutch native inhabitants (Bushmen and Hottentots). The hearts of most blacks (sometimes lumped under the term "Bantu") were in the big, gritty city of Johannesburg, the second largest city in the southern hemisphere after São Paulo. It was there that Mandela and most of his colleagues had lived and worked, many of them in the famous black suburb of Soweto.

It was widely assumed that the parliament would move to Pretoria, and rumors flew around town about exactly where its new building would be located. But after a year or two, black parliamentarians began to like Cape Town, and the rumors faded away. The ANC leaders were also aware that relocating parliament would deeply offend the colored and white population of the Western Cape Province, where Cape Town is located, and that it might even provoke them to secede. So Cape Town remained the DCM's second home during my tenure.

---

[4] Anyone interested in understanding South Africa should begin with Alister [sic] Sparks, *The Mind of South Africa*, New York, 1990, a book modeled partly on W. J. Cash's *The Mind of the South,* on US History.

Getting Settled in Pretoria *and* Cape Town

I had an overlap of several days with my predecessor as DCM, Priscilla Clapp, which was informative. Overlaps make sense, but most Foreign Service Officers don't like them for reasons I never comprehended. I met the servants, and Priscilla gave me lots of advice on really important things like where to go shopping. The house itself had once been the ambassador's Residence, but when it became the done thing for chiefs of mission to live in Waterkloof, a more fashionable neighborhood just up the hill from us, with a better view, our ambassador did likewise, and the DCM inherited the ambassador's former home. That was not wholly an improvement for the ambassador, because the new Residence did not have nearly as much, or as good, space for entertaining.

Many upper-crust South African houses had names, and ours was "Eloff House;" it was located at 270 Mackenzie Street. It had been the house for a farm that covered much of what was later subdivided and renamed Brooklyn. It had a very large garden, a swimming pool, a tennis court and small, but separate servants' quarters, equipped with its own kitchen and bath. There the cook, housemaid, and sometimes the houseboy (or "butler" in South African usage), lived during their workweek.

The house came with a gardener, which was just as well because the soil was extremely heavy clay. This not withstanding, roses loved it, and we had about 200 of them all over the yard, as well as masses of agapanthus lining the front of the property facing Mackenzie Street, and many other types of plants and shrubs. The house had two fireplaces, one of which, in a relatively new addition, did not draw, but we used the other, in the living room, all the time during Pretoria's chilly winters, and the embassy even provided us with wood free of charge.

The house also had a thatch roof, as did an antique shed used for swimming pool maintenance. We learned that thatch roofs in South Africa are no cheaper than ordinary roofs, but, as in England, they are considered more stylish and prestigious, especially on boutique farms, game parks and golf courses. People who live in grass houses shouldn't have fireplaces, you ask? I was aware of that and made sure we had hoses at each corner of the building, with enough pressure to reach the top of the roof. Of course the roof was full of bugs, but we had an inner ceiling, which kept them from falling into our soup at dinner. We had no trouble with water; there was a good supply from a local dam.

Pretoria is less than two hours' drive from Johannesburg, along a heavily trafficked multiple-lane highway through an increasingly industrialized strip. But the surrounding countryside is still mainly farmland. The rainfall is actually less than it is in Bamako, but the farming technology is modern, and the farms look a lot more like Kansas than Mali. It is not for nothing that the Afrikaners are also called Boers (farmers), and we would see much more of their agricultural proficiency, as well as the land tenure issues which accompany it.

Pretoria's elevation is a little over 5,000 feet, typical for the South African "High Veld," which means "high prairie." As a result it is malaria free. It is hot with some rain during South Africa's southern hemisphere summer, coinciding with winter in the US. Winters are cooler, and completely dry. At that time of year we were comfortable outdoors as long as we were in the sunshine, but in shade or in the evening we wore sweaters. We had seventeen immediate neighbors, fronting (or backing) on our property, all of them Afrikaners. The best security always involves knowing your neighbors, so after Barbara arrived, we decided to invite them all to a party. It turned out that we were the first American occupants of Eloff House in memory to have done so, and the gesture was greatly appreciated.

Pretoria was considered safe by South African standards, especially in comparison to Johannesburg, but there was a violent crime problem. All embassy employees had a "panic button" which would summon a car-full of "armed response" security guards, all burly Afrikaners. On arrival they would jump over the fence or wall and immediately fan out into the garden to make sure there were no bad guys lurking there, before even knocking on the door. We had a couple of false alarms during our stay, but never a serious intrusion.

I gradually settled into bachelorhood, and since Barbara would be coming for a Christmas visit it was bearable. The embassy was getting ready for two major visits, by Secretary of State Warren Christopher and First Lady Hillary Clinton, plus a few CODELS (congressional visits). We were also serving as home base for a team from Washington hoping to help negotiate an end to the nasty war in progress between Zaire and Rwanda plus its ally, Uganda.[5]

In October I had another illuminating glimpse of Mandela, when he agreed to meet the children of US diplomatic personnel, in batches of twenty so it wouldn't be too impersonal. One of them, Sarah Wharton, age eight, recorded her impressions for the *Jacaranda Journal*, the embassy newsletter:

> Mr. Mandela is a strong, calm, patient person. He didn't goof around about what he was saying. He was very interesting to listen to. I think the reason he wanted to meet with all us children was that he is always listening to grown-ups' problems and has to solve them. And he wanted to get to know our problems.[6]

The resulting pictures were priceless. Everyone knew that Mandela was a sucker for children. Not having any of them around was one of things he had hated most about being on Robben Island.

By contrast, we had a flap when Secretary of State Warren Christopher couldn't get an appointment with him. Christopher, or maybe one of his staff—he seemed like a genial sort— threatened to cancel his entire trip to Africa, including several other countries, if he couldn't meet Mandela. I wrote home:

The logic is, no Mandela, no South Africa. The rest isn't worth it!! And we lecture them about their adolescent failings! Anyway, M et al. may be disorganized but they are blissfully unruffled by this kind if thing and not about to be pushed around by anyone.[7]

---

[5] See Chapter 13.
[6] *Jacaranda Journal*, October 3, 1996, by Sarah Wharton, daughter of Bruce Wharton, a USIS officer who later became US Ambassador to Zimbabwe.
[7] Bob letter to Dear Barbara, September 24, 1996.

Children of US Embassy staff meet President Mandela.

Christopher finally got the appointment.

I settled into my big office at the embassy, separated from Ambassador Joseph by lots of space for two secretaries (by then called "office managers"). We were among the few in this glass tower-cum-bunker to have windows! More seriously, the only access to this executive area was by elevator, which greatly inhibited walk-in visits by embassy staff and easily led to an impression of haughty isolation from the worker bees. This led to a morale problem, discussed at greater length below.

On weekends, I explored the countryside by car with Political Counselor Reed Fendrick, a friend from other assignments. The driving was hair-raising at first, but easy once you got the hang of it. Except for the big thruway to Johannesburg, traffic was usually light beyond Pretoria. One soon became accustomed to driving on the left, but the speed at which most South Africans drove was another matter. The roads were mainly two lanes, with a narrower lane on each shoulder. You were supposed to pull into it without prompting when someone approached you fast from behind, so it was mandatory to be constantly looking in the rear-view mirror.

Larger towns followed a pattern, with a prosperous-looking white area on one side, and a crowded black "settlement" on the other. The countryside is mainly grassland, with undulating hills, and you could often see for a mile or more with nary another car in sight. In other areas there was hideously dirty industry burning locally mined coal. In winter the black "settlements," which burned the same stuff for heating and cooking, were enveloped in clouds of toxic smoke.

Heading toward the Indian Ocean coast on the national highway (Route 4), the elevation drops sharply toward the scenic escarpment, canyons, and waterfalls of Mpumalanga, the home of the Ndebele people whose colorful house decoration, beadwork, and weaving are world famous. Further east, Kruger National Park occupies the malarial Lowveld to the north of the road. To the south, the independent enclave country of Swaziland, the Drakensberg Mountains with their sheer cliffs, and finally the lower grasslands of KwaZulu/ Natal offered excellent bird watching, trout fishing, exploring the battlefields of the Anglo-Zulu and Boer Wars, and many other interesting things to do and places to visit. One of our favorite discoveries was the famous Ardmore Pottery, source of the imaginative, and imaginary, animal tea set which we display in the dining room breakfront.

In mid-October I went to Cape Town for the first time and checked into "our" house there, "Fiesole," named for a scenic height above Florence, Italy. It is located at 24 Upper Bebington Street in the highly desirable neighborhood of Bishopscourt,[8] under the southeast wall of Table Mountain. I wrote home that it was "really quite gorgeous without being pretentious, we must spend some time here."[9] Within walking distance, on land donated by Cecil Rhodes, is the world renowned Kirstenbosch Botanical Garden. From there you can climb the mountain in a couple of strenuous hours, through the heart of the Cape Floral Kingdom amid some of the most interesting botanical surroundings anywhere, and gaze down on Cape Town, or descend to it by cable car, or

---

[8] Indeed, the residence of the Archbishop of the South African Anglican Church, then and still Archbishop Desmond Tutu, is located in this neighborhood.

[9] Bob e-mail to Dear Family, October 11, 1996.

Houses in the gentle hills somewhere in Kwa-Zulu Natal.

Another rural house style, perhaps Ndebele, east of Pretoria.

even slide downhill (almost) on another, even steeper trail.

Fortunately, we had been prepped by Annie about the Cape Floral Kingdom, one of only seven in the world, and certainly the smallest. Its special nature is not easily visible to the untrained eye. I first saw Table Mountain[10] from an airplane, and it looked like an arid gray mass of rock surrounded by city, which it is, up to a point. It is hard to imagine that this place is among the most biodiverse in the world; new species of flowering plants are still being discovered in its nooks and crannies. A closer view reveals shrubby, heather-like vegetation, known as *fynbos* ("fine bush"), which is the main but not sole source of the biodiversity. Thanks to energetic early collectors, many of our common garden plants come from this area, including some species of gladiolus and geranium.

The key is partly climate, very different from Pretoria: drenching rain in the winter, and warm, dry summers, favoring ample vegetation but few big trees. This rainfall pattern also makes for frequent brush fires, as a result of which many local species are "fire endemics," meaning that seeds need to be heated by fire to germinate. When human development eliminates most fires, such species go extinct; this has happened most seriously all over the Cape Flats in back of Table Mountain. But beyond urban areas, if you see a patch of roadside or pasture that has been burned, remember to come back in the spring, after the rains, and you will probably see a profusion of flowers. "Flower peepers" have become almost as common and enthusiastic among South Africans as bird watchers, which is saying a lot, and in the spring there are flower jams on the roads leading north from Cape Town.

A few blocks from Fiesole, near the entrance to Kirstenbosch, there is a remnant of Van Riebeck's Fence, made of living thorn. It was planted by the most successful of the early Dutch governors to keep his European and Asian subjects from wandering off into the vast interior and getting into trouble

---

[10] Mandela declared a Cape Peninsula National Park in 1998, his "Gift to the Earth," including Table Mountain and portions of the land between it and the Cape of Good Hope. There has been talk of extending this park to adjacent marine areas, which would make it one of the world's few major land-sea parks.

with the native Hottentots, when they were supposed to be raising vegetables to feed the crews of passing VOC (Dutch East India Company) ships. In his essential book, *The Mind of South Africa*, cited above, Alister Sparks uses Van Riebeck's Fence as the symbol of South Africa's historic obsession with fences and keeping races apart. It didn't work even then; Van Riebeck's Dutch subjects later ignored it, headed out with their flocks and Bibles, and over time became Afrikaners.

Fiesole itself is country cottage in style, with another big garden and lovely grounds frequented by wild guinea fowl. It has a magnificent view of Table Mountain's back side, and from the porch off the master bedroom, if you crane your neck, you can see both Table Bay, which is today the main port and the center of Cape Town, and False Bay, now popular for seaside vacations and whale watching and formerly a trap for VOC ships who thought they had already reached the Indian Ocean.

On the same lot, but downhill from Fiesole and separated by the world's most beautifully located tennis court, is the ambassador's Residence, where we had stayed briefly and been interrogated by the police after being robbed in 1991. The Josephs did not play tennis, but we did, and reveled in the view as we played as much as we could on that court. One of our Christmas cards from South Africa shows us there, with the mountain in the background.[11] The interior of the house was appropriately furnished with flowery drapes and slipcovered furniture, which we augmented with art that we purchased in Africa or, in some cases, sent out when Barbara came the next August.

There was a small, attached apartment for a maid who was to keep the establishment neat and attend to small details when the DCM was not in residence. A complete staff came with him or her (or us) from Pretoria if the stay involved entertaining. Unfortunately, the longtime maid, a pleasant elderly woman named Elphine, was very ill with poorly treated high blood pressure by the time Barbara arrived. On her first visit to Cape Town, she was shocked to hear Elphine reply to the routine greeting "How are you?" with "I think I am

---

[11] As of 2017, the Residence has been retained, and Fiesole is now the residence of the US Consul General.

dying." It turned out she had been skimping on blood pressure medicine, which we immediately bought for her. But by then, it was too late, and she died a few months later.

There ensued, for the rest of our tour in South Africa, a futile search for the right person to replace her. Just before leaving, we found that person, a young Khoi (or Hottentot)[12] woman who liked living alone and whose earnings were supporting the extended family she came from up north. However, a devout Christian whose main outside activities centered around her church, she was killed in a car accident coming home from a church-sponsored field trip just after we left. The takeaway from all this, and from the experience of hiring a new houseboy (Donald) in Pretoria and being sure that he was totally recovered from communicable disease, was that, even in the New South Africa, life was still nasty, brutish, and short for many of its non-white citizens.

To get to work I had to drive around Table Mountain on the often jammed M5 highway, to the US Consulate, then located downtown on the eighth floor of a dowdy office building.[13] The commute was not a great hardship, because on long visits my official car and driver migrated with us to Cape Town. All I had to do was sit back and enjoy the constantly changing views of Table Bay, including the famous Robben Island ex-prison and any ships that might be arriving or departing, or Table Mountain, with its cable car and profusion of flowers and greenery above the suburbs clinging to its side.

I soon learned that for all its sometimes California weather, Cape Town, especially in the winter, has unpredictable bouts of gale-force winds, which shrieked and howled around the Consulate, rattling the windows to the point where it was hard to concentrate.[14] During my first few days working there, a pedestrian below us on the street was killed by a flying hunk of construction debris. But the locals do not mind

---

[12] One of the Cape area's indigenous groups, briefly defined later in this chapter.

[13] Due to security concerns, the consulate was eventually moved to a new location near Muizenberg, well away from downtown Cape Town.

[14] The Cape Town weather is hard to predict because the city is far into the South Atlantic and there are no weather stations between it and Antarctica.

the wind, which they call "the Cape Doctor" on the dubious premise that it blows away all the germs. This goes along with the story about Table Mountain's "tablecloth," which appears when, under just the right conditions, clouds form on top of it and then dribble over the edge. That is supposed to be caused by the Devil, sitting up there smoking his pipe.

There was talk of closing down the Cape Town consulate, but we never did because of Cape Town's parliamentary role and, one suspects at least equally important, the fact that all VIP visitors had been told how beautiful Cape Town is and would not hear of passing it up. So, we could argue, we just had to have an official presence there, the better to tend to their myriad needs.

The first business at hand was preparing for Secretary of State Warren Christopher's visit, which went well once the irksome matter of an appointment with Mandela had been resolved. Christopher also made routine calls on the various politicians and officials who were in town for the parliamentary session. His personal aircraft was a Boeing 707 with tail number 26000, the former Air Force One on which Lyndon Johnson had been sworn in at the Dallas airport immediately following President Kennedy's assassination.[15] I later taught at the National War College with its jovial pilot, who by that time (1999-2000) had become an expert on the dangers of biological warfare and was constantly on television.

Cape Town is indeed entrancing, with its old parliamentary buildings dating to British times, near the "Company Garden," where the VOC grew vegetables for its transiting ship crews. Not far away is the main reason for Cape Town; a year-round water supply fed by a stream coming off Table Mountain, now preserved under a downtown intersection. The harbor itself is not good, and given the frequent high winds must have been terrible in the days of sail.

Starting in this area, I often explored the center of the city on my lunchtime walks from the Consulate. Nearby is District Six, site of a picturesque, multi-racial slum razed by the old regime because it was a nest of anti-apartheid sentiment; a few old buildings remain and an excellent museum displays

---

[15] The plane is now in the National Air Force Museum in Dayton, Ohio.

mementoes of the former neighborhood.[16]

An extended walk up Long Street took me past the Space Theater where the famous Jewish-Afrikaner-Gay comedian Pieter-Dirk Uys had started his memorable career of political satire-in-drag as a preposterous Boer matron named Evita Bezeidenhout. Beyond that, Long Street led up to the base of the mountain, passing Signal Hill, with its startlingly loud noon gun, and the pastel houses of the "Cape Malay" quarter, residences of "Cape Colored" people, many of whom are Muslim, giving the city one more ethnic twist. In addition to a wonderful bookstore, the Episcopal Church where Desmond Tutu preached was just around the corner. I could cover this whole itinerary, albeit quickly, in a long lunch hour, and it never got boring.

In contrast, around the back of Table Mountain, between the vineyards of Constantia on its slopes and the shores of False Bay, are the Cape Flats. This large area was mainly farmland until after World War II. The entire Western Cape Province was a "Colored Preference Area" under apartheid, meaning that "blacks" (or Bantu) were not allowed to live there. It had special schools and even a university for coloreds. The nearest "blacks" were originally hundreds of miles away in the Eastern Cape and there were none anywhere near Cape Town when the Dutch arrived. The British tried to keep them out militarily, resulting in the so-called "Kaffir Wars," from 1818-1852, but it didn't work.

Today black immigration, mainly of Khosa people, has filled up the Cape Flats, creating vast, slum-ridden "settlements" like Gugulethu, hard by the modern airport. This is by way of saying that you cannot escape the harsh realities of modern South Africa even in beautiful Cape Town, including a crime problem which is not much less serious than that in Pretoria or even Johannesburg, albeit less notorious.

There were so many attractions outside Cape Town that I, and later we, never had time to visit more than a few of them. Driving north from the house into town, one passes the world-class University of Cape Town and the government hospital

---

[16] For a beautiful view of what District Six once looked like, see the small watercolor which hangs in our kitchen.

where Christiaan Barnard performed the world's first heart transplant in 1967. Continuing north out of town up the West Coast, one comes quickly into beautiful farm country. Fields of magnificent wild flowers bloom in the spring, which starts here in August. The West Coast also offers great birding, scenic drives in the Cedarburg Mountains, and flower festivals in every town as one travels farther up the coast during the season. Heading to the interior, northeast of Cape Town, there are the famous wineries around Franschhoek, Paarl and Stellenbosch, with a mountain backdrop everywhere, Kipling's "Ramparts of slaughter and peril."[17]

Poking straight south into the Atlantic, there is the long, lovely extension of Table Mountain ending at Cape Point, which is *not* the southernmost point in Africa. En route one passes the navy base at Simon's Town and an upper-crust neighborhood, Boulders, named for its boulder-covered

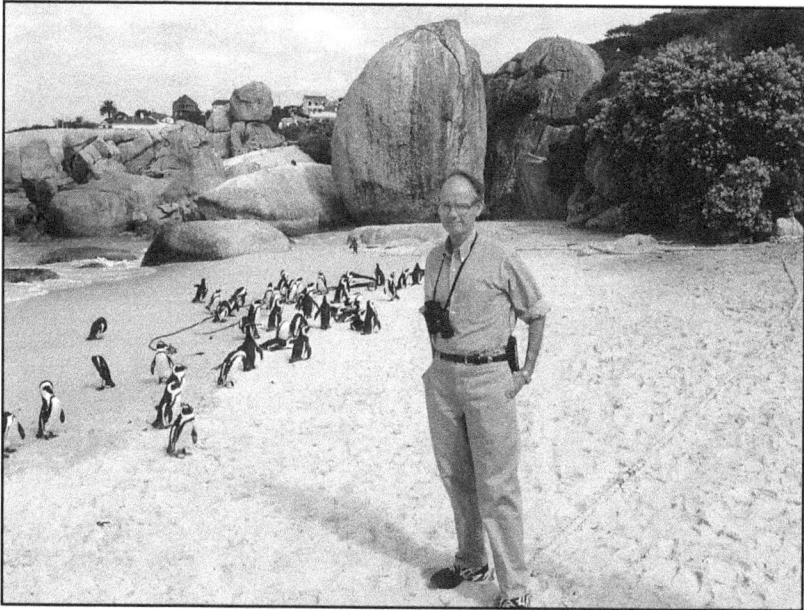

Bob at Boulders, enjoying being able to walk among the penguins. Later we even snorkeled among them there, but now there is a boardwalk above the beach and visitors must stay on it.

---

[17] From his poem "Bridge-Guard in the Karoo," http://www. poetryloverspage.com/poets/kipling/bridge_guard_in_karroo.html.

beach. The beach became a breeding ground for jackass (more correctly, African) penguins, a major tourist attraction, after some of them were caught in an oil spill, rescued and cleaned up at the nearby navy base and released. They decided to come settle down and have children right in front of the fancy vacation homes along the shore. In the late 1990s, you could still swim among the penguins and wander close to their nests on the sand beach, but now visitors must stay on a boardwalk and view them from there.

Head eastward around False Bay and you come to Pringle Bay, a tidy beach resort named after a British Admiral, not one of the South African Pringles (about whom more anon), mile after mile of almost empty beaches, and, eventually, Cape Argulhas, which *is* the southernmost point of the continent. On the way, you pass Hermanus, where, from May to December, you can see Southern Right Whales, including females with calves, lolling around just off the rocky shore within easy sight of tourist-filled restaurants.

At Arniston, further along the coast, there are extraordinary middens of shells left by prehistoric visitors, amid the bones of a sail-era shipwreck (of the *Arniston*, after which the little town is named) and the whitewashed, thatch-roofed houses of colored fisher folk. South Africa has done a good job of regulating its fishing industry, and local fish were readily available and cheap. All these places we visited on day or weekend expeditions out of the city. The interesting stuff goes on and on along the attraction-laden "Garden Route," before the main highway bends north up the east coast along the Indian Ocean.

We were frequently reminded that South Africa's oceans are not very friendly waters, not a California ocean, appearances to the contrary notwithstanding. During our stay, a surf fisherman was killed by a Great White Shark at Pringle Bay; there are many in the area thanks to a large population of seals. I had thought of scuba diving in Cape Town, having read that many South Africans did so, and not quite realizing how crazy they can be. The fact is, the water is far too cold for comfort, even with a wet suit. Once, however, we rented equipment and went for two dives in the Indian Ocean north of Durban (read: a little warmer than off Cape Town's west coast, which is affected by deep ocean currents coming up from the Antarctic). The dives were interesting, but because of the cool waters even there, not nearly as beautiful or as full of coral and small fish as our Southeast Asian and Pacific dive sites had been.

The Colored Conundrum

A word more about South Africa's "colored" inhabitants, mainly of the Cape: they are descended primarily from slaves who intermarried with their Afrikaner owners. Today most have lost their native tongues, although there is some effort to revive them, and all speak Afrikaans (descended from Dutch) from birth, much as American blacks all speak English, not African languages. Most of the slaves were indigenous people: "Bushmen" (San) hunter-gatherer nomads, or "Hottentot" (Khoi) herders.[18] But some came from other parts of Africa, especially Madagascar, and from Indonesia—the Dutch used to exile Indonesian political prisoners to the Cape, creating the present population of Muslim "Cape Malays" mentioned earlier.

Well aware that over the centuries their ancestors were enslaved and/or displaced elsewhere in South Africa and that they are a vulnerable minority today, most coloreds have, since independence, allied politically with the white population against the majority African National Congress. That is why the Western Cape is the only province in South Africa not controlled by the ANC, meaning that without its large colored population South Africa would have something approaching single-party rule.

---

[18] These terms are imprecise, concealing social and linguistic differences. Just to complicate matters further, there has been an effort to create a pan-colored "Khoisan" movement, modeled mainly on American pan-Indian but also American black prototypes. Its most famous leader, Benny Alexander, now deceased, renamed himself "Khoisan X." Meanwhile, across the border in Namibia, there are populations who still speak some of the enormously diverse Khoi and San languages, with all their clicks. Listening to them on the radio, it sounds like someone talking with a mouthful of glass. The question of who was and is "colored" is a fascinating, ultra-complex topic recently clarified somewhat by DNA studies, but you can learn a lot from an excellent Wikipedia entry at http://en.wikipedia.org/wiki/Coloured.

There is, moreover, the extraordinary story of *Hier Kom* (or *Daar Kom*) *die Alabama.* The Confederate raider *Alabama* stopped in Cape Town to reprovision in 1863 on its deadly path around the globe destroying Union commerce. From this fact somehow emerged the practice of Cape Colored minstrel groups parading through the city at New Year's, dressed as American-style minstrels in blackface, strumming banjos and singing *Hier Kom die Alabama.* The celebration used to be called, with a straight face, the "Coon Carnival," until the South Africans realized how pejorative the term "coon" sounded to certain foreigners and, officially at least, changed the name. There is an exhibit about the song and the parade, complete with photographs of the *Alabama,* at the Cape Town Museum, and plenty of recordings of the music are on sale. One story about the origin of the song is that the money the Alabama's crew spent while in port was so much that the ship's visit was remembered with hope it might happen again. Alas, the *Alabama* was sunk before the end of the Civil War, and we were never in Cape Town at New Year's, so we never saw the parade.

By December, 1996, I had returned to Pretoria to meet Barbara on her Christmas break from teaching at Potomac.

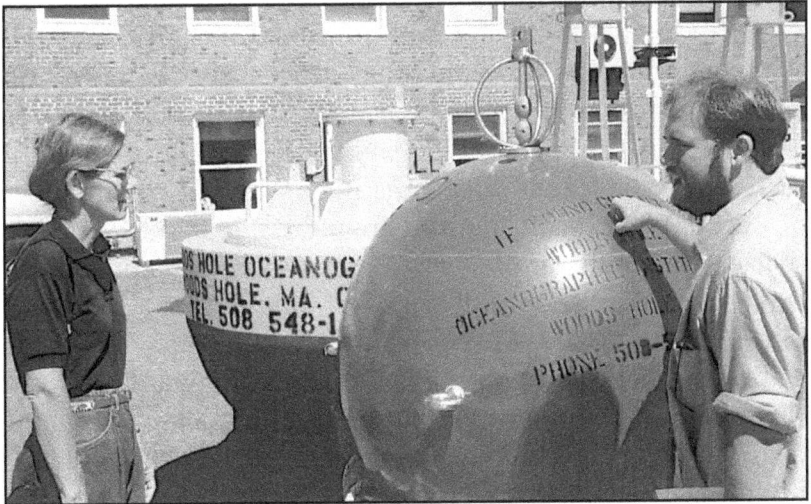

Although Jamie's research concerned studying long-term trends from extant records and study of alongshore wave patterns, he enjoyed showing us the hardware which Woods Hole engineers were producing for deep water research.

This was to be Christmas *à deux*. Jamie was finishing up his graduate studies at MIT/Woods Hole and Annie had just started hers at Duke University. They would spend the holidays with family in the US.

For us, there was plenty to do together around Pretoria: visiting the Voortrekker Monument, with its murals celebrating Afrikaner expansion, the Great Trek, and warfare against the natives; the truly elegant Union Buildings, home of South Africa's executive branch; the redoubtable Paul Kruger's home and private railroad car, with exhibits showing the initial outpouring of international support for the Boers at the beginning of the Boer War (the British, being Top Nation, had plenty of enemies, including many Americans); and Melrose House, where the treaty that formally ended the war was signed in 1902—it is now the site of a great Saturday morning antique and book market. Finally, there was the school-cum-makeshift prison from which young Winston Churchill, then a Boer War newspaper correspondent, escaped after having been captured from a British armored train that the Boers had ambushed, in no small part due to Churchill's own recklessness.

We also visited Soweto, including its nascent museum featuring moments of the anti-apartheid struggle, and the homes of Mandela, Tutu and other heroes. Between Pretoria and Jo'burg was Irene (pronounced EE-ri-nay), once the rustic country retreat of General Jan Smuts. He was a brilliant anti-British guerilla leader during the Boer War and the architect of Boer-British reconciliation afterwards, and subsequently twice prime minister of South Africa. His former home there had become a museum, full of memorabilia, which also hosted interesting cultural events.

I remember one in particular, a talk on Rudyard Kipling's role as unofficial poet laureate of the Boer War. It is hard to believe that this Rhodes-loving sycophant was the same Kipling who later wrote "Recessional," but his work at the time also included "Bridge-Guard in the Karoo,"[19] one of the best poems he ever wrote. Irene was also the site of a great weekend market.

---

[19] Cited earlier.

We had no time for long distance outings, but did make it to the De Wildt Cheetah Research center, not far from town, and Pilanesberg, a smallish game park three hours drive north of Johannesburg. It had been created only in the 1960s from farmland, precisely for people who didn't have time to visit more famous but also more distant parks. Today Pilanesberg has just about everything in the way of animals, including all the Big Five (elephant, lion, buffalo, rhinoceros and leopard) and 360 bird species. For some time it experienced interesting trouble with its introduced population of young elephants, who misbehaved badly until a few older females were imported to provide some hierarchy (matriarchy?) and parental supervision. From this trip we have a saucy photo of Barbara bathing in the altogether in our room at Pilanesburg's very pleasant lodge, with a water hole for game visible in the background through the window.

Barbara's trip ended with one of those little episodes that restore one's faith in human kindness. She had parked the car at Dulles airport, and it had snowed, a lot, while she was away. When she arrived on the shuttle bus in the middle of that vast economy parking lot, late at night, the bus driver waited at her stop as she turned on the motor and defroster, scraped the windows clean, and then gingerly backed out through what was left of the ice and snow. He followed her until she drove safely through the exit from the parking lot. A nice end to a really nice trip, even though the drive to Alexandria took about an hour and a half, leaving her only a few hours' rest before she had to be in front of a classroom full of students again.

Two Big Visits

By late January of 1997 Bob was back in Cape Town preparing for two big events. First was the arrival of Vice President Al Gore for the US-South Africa Binational Commission (BNC) meeting, which he chaired with Mandela's deputy, Thabo Mbeki. Then came the visit of Hilary Clinton, or FLOTUS, First Lady of the United States, married to POTUS (who would visit later), and accompanied by Chelsea (FIDUS). I accompanied members of the advance team (there were twelve of them) to various possible visit sites: Cape Town's excellent children's hospital, a school in its most famous black "settlement," Gugulethu; the District Six Museum, the Simon's Town penguins, and more. I also found time to hear Mandela speak at the opening of Parliament:

The opening of Parliament was fun although Mandela's speech was long and tedious except for a fascinating bit at the end where he ad-libbed about his political philosophy, etc., and told the cabinet he was going to reshuffle everyone who had slept during his speech but couldn't because they were all equally guilty![20]

The goal of the BNC was to build high-level bridges between our two governments. It would last only another two or three years, but by then the bridge-building objective was pretty well accomplished. It did not generate major policy changes, nor was it expected to; they were not needed, but it did help to make up for the decades of non-communication between us. The Americans probably learned the most, because while all of us appreciated Mandela and had at least a nodding acquaintance with the challenges facing South Africa in building a new, more racially equal society, we were not fully aware of the country's assets—what it was already doing right, from which even the mighty Americans could learn a thing a two.

One example was South Africa's national parks, originally inspired by US precedent, but by then even better that ours in certain respects, as I heard Interior Secretary Bruce Babbitt acknowledge. He was particularly envious of the South Africans' ability to make commercial concessionaires working in the parks contribute substantially to park revenue.

One of the more interesting BNC events was a site visit to "Working for Water," a BNC Project. For many years the South Africans had promoted tree farms, eventually to excess. By the 1990s they covered vast areas of the country with plantations of pine and especially eucalyptus. Together with invasive species like Australian wattle they were, in

---

[20] Bob e-mail to Dear Barbara, February 8, 1997.

some areas, sucking the already arid land dry and driving out valuable indigenous flora, including the rare *fynbos* cover. This made South Africa a place where it was actually good for the environment to destroy trees, at least some of them.

The project created jobs by hiring young, un- or underemployed youth to pull out the alien species, then process the wood so it could be sold for barbecue (*braai*) fuel, *braai*-ing being a South African national passion. Then the land was left alone, because it had been discovered that *fynbos* seeds that were still in the soil had stayed dormant, hence much of the original vegetation would regenerate over time. Gore, Mbeki, Babbitt and Babbitt's counterpart, Kadar Asmal, Minister of Water Affairs and Forestry, trooped up to the site for a briefing. They were each presented with a potted Strelitzia (Bird of Paradise flower) plant, another famous South African botanical export, this variety developed at the Kirstenbosch Botanical Garden and named "Mandela's Gold." For the photo the dignitaries all wore floppy yellow "Working for Water" hats, leading to much hilarity.

There was time for more fun while preparing for these two visits. One evening Reed Fendrick and I attended a party at the Cape Town Marine House, only a few blocks from Fiesole. Our Consulate had the usual complement of four Marine Corps "watch standers," in this case one of them female, and a detachment commander, or "gunny," who lived separately from the others with his wife. (According to Marine rules only he was allowed to be married.) A South African friend of one of the watch standers had asked and received permission from him to celebrate his girl friend's birthday at the Marine House, with the theme of "funky." It got completely out of hand because the friend asked other friends and before long a large, all-white contingent of young Cape Town glitterati had arrived with their often gorgeous, stylishly but scantily clad girl friends.

Reed and I left fairly early—we really did—but as the night wore on more drink was consumed and one of the friends of friends decided to pick a fight with a real, live US Marine and had to be subdued, as it turned out, by our lady Marine—at least that was the story we heard the next morning. I am not sure whether any police or other authorities were called, or any reports written. We were concerned for the gunny, who was off in Kenya for the weekend climbing Mt. Kilimanjaro, and we hoped he would not get into trouble. Both he and his wife, who was the Consulate CLO (Community Liaison Officer), were smart, nice people.[21]

The next story, about "kloofing," also has a Marine angle. Thanks to Ambassador David Newsom, a friend from Indonesia days, I had met an American astronomer, Don Kurtz, who was living in Cape Town with his South African wife and teaching at the University of Cape Town. He wanted to take me kloofing.

A kloof is a canyon or gorge, and one might assume that "kloofing" is nothing more than hiking downstream through one. But due to the geology and winter rainfall pattern at the Cape, streams cut deep and often extremely narrow channels through rocky plateaus. Kloof walls are nearly vertical, in deep places they are dark, and the streams running through them have considerable waterfalls, with no paths around them. You have to jump off the ledge, trusting that the falling water has hollowed out a pool deep enough so that you land below without fatal results.

It was quite fun, except that although I had my Nikonos underwater camera with me, I had brought the wrong lens, the one that works only under water, so most of the more interesting above water pictures were out of focus. Also, I nearly froze to death. Although I got up enough nerve to jump where jumping was required, one of our Marines who had come along was seriously and visibly unhappy about one requisite leap, whereas his South African girl friend, who was with him, thought nothing of it. In the end, with her watching, he got his nerve up and jumped.

There are places in the Cape where you can kloof for days on end, so long and interconnected are the streams. Fanatic kloofers are said to do it stark naked, except for flip-flops and a hat.

Kloofing may sound frivolous, if not hare-brained, but thanks to our friendship with Kurtz, Barbara and I were later able to visit the site of a big new telescope, which South Africa

---

[21] Bob letter to Dear Family, March 9, 1997.

had just decided to build in the Karoo. It was to be called SALT, for "Southern Africa Large Telescope." The site, Sutherland, was already an observatory, but its equipment was hardly modern enough to take full advantage of its Southern Hemisphere location. (When a comet slammed into Jupiter in1994, it could be seen only from Sutherland; a telescope in Chile, which was SALT's sole competition, was clouded over at the time.) Meanwhile, even getting there was educational:

Go straight up the main road from Cape Town, cross the Border Range, thread the scenic Hex River Valley, and look for the Boer War-era hotel next to the railroad station at Matjiesfontein. Turn left and proceed straight north for 110 kilometres. You won't see anything but scattered farmsteads, sheep, arid shrubbery and increasingly spectacular scenery until you reach Sutherland.

Sutherland is your classic dorp, *a sleepy old Karoo farm town of 1500 people, with its big Dutch Reformed church, a filling station and a general store or two. The town center is where the Afrikaners live. One side of town, only recently connected to the town center by a direct road, is the inevitable "settlement," in this case not black but colored, dominated by an ancient, decrepit housing project.[22]*

The South Africans opted for SALT in part because they believed it would help promote popular interest in math and science, especially among disadvantaged blacks. It would thereby help the country achieve its long-term goals of both scientific excellence and scientific equity. It would include a visitors' center and a strong outreach program to schools. SALT's twin, a telescope in an equally remote area of West Texas, was attracting 100,000 visitors a year. Already the observatory had put out a poster portraying the stars in African (as opposed to Greek) mythology.

Back to the visit of our own star, FLOTUS, in Cape Town. As the big day approached, I gave a house warming for Fiesole which doubled as a thank-you party for about seventy-five people who had been helping with visit preparation, including

---

[22] "South Africa Opts for SALT," Pretoria 7983, July 2, 1998.

White House advance staff,[23] employees of hotels and the airport, friends and neighbors, and Consulate personnel. For the latter, it was potluck, but for the others, Susan, our cook, prepared a couple of turkeys and a ham. This was not standard practice, but I thought it was a great use for our representational (official entertainment) budget.

The Clintons, mother and daughter, finally arrived on March 18, having already been to Pretoria and Johannesburg. Our colleagues Greg Engle and Ann Berry, supervising her visit in those cities, told us she had been a model visitor. I wrote, "To her great credit, she likes to do long, in-depth stops with lots of interaction and discussion, and since she is very well informed and articulate on the social issues this works well." About this time Barbara replied to one of my e-mails: "What is FLOTUS? Remember this method of communication is not secure and don't put in opinions you might not want others besides me to see."[24] She had a point, but I assured her that the term FLOTUS itself had long ago ceased being secret, if it ever was.

But in Cape Town, things began with a bump. Only just before Hillary's arrival on March 18 did we discover that the South Africans were having a big event the next day on Robben Island to raise money for a museum and a former prisoner welfare fund. Mandela and many other ANC notables and other prominent guests were attending, including comedian Bill Cosby, who was a friend of Hillary.[25] Of course it would have been unthinkable NOT to have Hillary there, and, in the end, after some hard work by Ambassador Joseph, she was included.

Meanwhile, the press van needed for the ANC event was being carried out to Robben Island by helicopter, dangling

---

[23] White Houses advance teams were headed by volunteers, often people who had worked on presidential campaigns. David van Note headed this one, and was superb to work with.

[24] Barbara e-mail to me, n.d. At this point our incoming e-mails were not recording dates. Reading the last sentence in 2016, during Hillary's election-year tribulations with her State Department e-mails, evokes *plus-ça-change* twinges, the difference being that our rudimentary e-mail of 1997 was not remotely official.

[25] The episode recounted here took place long before Cosby was charged with sex crimes, and I personally admired him greatly.

from a long cable, when it fell into profoundly deep water offshore. This gave rise to an urban legend that the "bus" had been laid on at Hillary's request, which wasn't true, but was still being repeated by tour guides when we revisited Cape Town in 2011.

I was able to be there for most of the Robben Island events, including a visit to the stone quarry where Mandela had labored, but not the fancy dinner that night. When Mandela led a guided tour of his old cell, Cosby couldn't resist pretending to escape.[26] Mandela probably loved it. It was utterly weird to think that only seven years previously he had still been a prisoner here. It had only stopped being a jail in 1993, and indeed nothing had changed physically. I went back to Cape Town on Hillary's press boat, on a gorgeous evening, with Table Mountain rising to meet us. Famous portrait photographer Annie Leibovitz was among the passengers, and I remember finding out from another photographer on board that it was now possible to send photos by e-mail.

On the first evening of the visit, before the Robben Island fund raiser, Ambassador Joseph had given an informal dinner for Hillary, Cosby, Bishop Tutu and Mamphela Ramphele, the widow of martyred journalist Steve Biko and at this time Vice Chancellor, meaning chief executive, of the University of Cape Town. It is testimony to Joseph's generosity that he also invited me, instead of someone of higher rank, to this informal but priceless event.

It was quite an evening. Cosby apparently never goes out of character and never stopped teasing Tutu, who is no slouch at repartee in his own right. Sample: Ambassador asks Tutu to say grace. Cosby: "And keep it short!" Tutu: rattles off something in Khosa – brrrrp! – in about fifteen seconds. Mostly it was Cosby teasing Tutu about being too much of a comedian for a man of the cloth. Hillary delivered an off-the-cuff blockbuster about both Bills (Cosby and Clinton) having married above themselves.[27]

At one point Hillary and Ramphele discussed whether it made sense to maintain the full panoply of prestigious,

---

[26] Bob e-mail to Dear Family, n.d. but shortly after March 19, 1997. Chelsea was following her own program and was not at the dinner.
[27] Ibid.

formerly all-white universities like the University of Cape Town, gradually admitting all eligible South African students to them, while underfunding the old, segregated, black and colored ones. Hillary suggested this policy was questionable, citing US experience with historically black universities, many of which, with increased government support, have improved and are attracting students of all races now. Ramphele disagreed, because, she said, the old, segregated all-black schools in South Africa were created wholly to serve the needs of apartheid, unlike historically black universities in the US. I commented in a letter home:

It's one big part of a bigger and wrenching debate over whether/how SA can keep up its first-world institutions while at the same time channeling the resources needed (almost endless) to bring up the previously disadvantaged. Hillary's response, interestingly enough, was to cite our community college-type focus on needed job skills as what appears to be relevant to SA. In fact, as I told her (no one from USAID being present), building such an approach is a major objective of our large USAID educational program here. (Whether or how well they are going to do it is another issue; the relevant ministry is very weak, and our help, although large by current American aid standards, is a drop in the bucket.)[28]

Hillary's last big event was a speech at the University of Cape Town before a largely white and no doubt somewhat skeptical audience. She began with routine if nonetheless welcome praise of South Africa for setting an example of reconciliation and democracy, but reserved half her time for a much more effective Q and A period:

They were bowled over by her combination of good looks, cool articulate delivery, and obvious mastery of issues such as welfare (in the US) and whether a woman could ever become president of the US, both of which she got questions on. Her response to the latter—gist of which was that it was easier for women to win political acceptance in a parliamentary system

---

[28] Ibid.

than in a presidential system—was really very interesting and funny and drew crashes of appreciative laughter. At the end of her answer she said that when it does happen, she'll be interested to see how the public treats her spouse, clearly a reference to her own rough handling [for taking a leading role] on health care reform. It was the only time I sensed even a hint of bitterness or rancor, although you had to read it in. [29]

So much for FLOTUS. As for FIDUS, she had her own low-key program, avoided publicity, and impressed everyone she did meet, which did not include me. All in all, the mother-daughter visit was a great success, we thought. Except that mother left promising to come back *soon* with POTUS in tow. Groan! We knew what *that* meant for us!

Durban

I was back in Pretoria by late March, and one of the first things I did was to visit Durban, the site of our smallest consulate, but also in some ways the most interesting. Durban is the biggest city in Kwa-Zulu Natal, once simply Natal. Ethnically it is about half black, mainly Zulu; a quarter Indian; and a quarter white, a mix of British and Afrikaners. It is a modern, go-go kind of place, with a long beachfront on one side and some poverty-ridden black settlements on the other. It is the biggest port in the country, has a highly energetic business community, and is the only city where a noticeable number of whites speak an African language, Zulu.

It is also the only city in South Africa with such a large Indian population. They came originally to work in the sugar cane fields, which still stretch for miles north of town. Gandhi, then a young lawyer, spent two decades in South Africa, mainly in Durban. As you may know if you have seen the great Richard Attenborough movie, it was in Durban where, on June 7, 1893, Gandhi boarded the train from which he was physically thrown off at the next stop, Pietermaritzburg, for sitting in first class (for whites only) and refusing to leave.

This episode set him on the road to his career of nonviolent

---

[29] Ibid.

social protest and is commemorated by a bronze plaque on
the wall of the former Durban railroad station, which now
houses the best craft shop in town. It was reenacted when we
were there, period steam locomotive and all, and we rather
hoped that the Indian Ambassador would play Gandhi and be
thrown off the train—it would certainly have generated some
publicity—but he demurred. Almost none of modern Durban's
Indian population still speaks an Indian language. Just under
half are Hindu, with the other half divided between Christians
and Muslims, one of whom was my favorite minister, Kadar
Asmal, the Minister of Forestry and Water Affairs mentioned
earlier.

Durban's blacks are also different. They are ethnically
Nguni people. The term "Zulu" derives from the clan name of
their famous leader, Shaka Zulu, the upstart "Black Napoleon"
whose military campaigns in the early nineteenth century
wreaked havoc on his neighbors. To simplify, those *Nguni*
who were related to and/or supported Shaka became "Zulu."
But many did not, including the Ndebele people who fled to
what is now the country of Zimbabwe and to Mpumalanga
in South Africa, the Swazis who now live in Swaziland under
their own king, and others who were massacred or scattered
over a wide area. [30]

After fighting first the Boers and then the British, the Zulus
were eventually defeated and relegated to reserves much as
other blacks were. But they preserved their monarchy and
claimed never to have lost their independence. Under Chief
Mangosutu Buthalezi and his Inkhata Freedom Party, still in
power when we were there, they initially resisted cooperation
with Mandela's ANC, and even at one time collaborated with
the apartheid regime, to the horror of ANC supporters in the
US and elsewhere. But for better or worse, they were not
beaten down, the way too many other blacks in South Africa
were. On a personal level, the idea that anyone might ever
have considered them inferior never seems to have dawned
on them.

No surprise, then, that one of the main jobs of our Durban

---

[30] For a good discussion of Shaka Zulu and his impact, a story without
close parallel in European history, see Stephen Taylor, *Shaka's Children: A
History of the Zulu People*, London, 1995.

consulate was to keep us up to speed on what Buthalezi and the Zulus were up to politically. And we had the right man for that job. Fred Hassani is Jewish and half Iranian, with a Jewish wife and two children; he is an information technology virtuoso, and the kind of polymath we will always need more of in the Foreign Service. He quickly became friends with Buthalezi and wrote highly readable analytic reports on this idiosyncratic Peck's Bad Boy of South African politics, but it did not end there.

Somewhat to the annoyance of Ambassador Joseph, who gave serious speeches that the press seldom covered, Hassani was perpetually in the Durban newspapers. He had a talent for attracting publicity by doing things like dropping into downtown pool halls to play with whoever was there.

During one of my visits, Hassani had planned a big reception in Durban for an African-American opera star, Simon Estes, who was well known in South Africa for his support of good causes. But Estes caught a cold which threatened his vocal chords and had to cancel his trip from the US. It was too late to call the reception off, so Fred ordered a life-sized cardboard cut-out of Estes with which each guest could be photographed, and managed, at the last minute, to engage the world-famous local singing group, Ladysmith Black Mambazo, to perform instead.

Each year he came up with a new idea for an end-of-year gift to send to Consulate friends and employees. One year it was a mug with a decoration celebrating US-South African friendship, selected by a competition among local schoolchildren. When the winning design was printed on the cups the group of smiling children waving US and South African flags seemed, on close inspection, all to be white. Fred was uncharacteristically non-plussed and called me to ask what he should do. I said not to worry. However, he decided to send a letter with the mugs explaining that small children are naturally innocent about such matters. "I'd like to think they represent the color-blind future of South Africa," he wrote.[31]

I was fond of telling people that the US Foreign Service had no educational requirements: as long as one passed the

---

[31] Hassani, Consulate end-of-year letter, December, 1998.

oral and written exams, one could become an FSO even if he had never been to kindergarten. I had not actually met such a person until I mentioned the subject to Fred, and it turned out that, having gone through a drop-out phase, he had neither a college degree nor even a high school diploma, although, he explained somewhat indignantly, he did have the equivalent of an MA from a State Department training course at Yale.

In writing his performance reports I did everything I could think of to get him promoted, but Hassani, although he did get promoted, was, in fact, too bright to last in a big bureaucracy. He did not conceal his intention to retire as soon as he reached the twenty years of service required for a pension, and then to make more money exercising his IT skills on the outside. That is what he did, among other occupations working as a contractor for the State Department. One of his early accomplishments on the outside was to help develop a classified version of Wikipedia for the intelligence community. The idea was that analysts with the necessary clearances could compete to produce the best version of a text open to scrutiny and correction by all.

On another visit to Durban, I went to see the huge warehouse on the waterfront where sugar was stockpiled for export, a matter of interest because the US had, post apartheid, started giving a South Africa a sugar quota. This meant the country could export a designated amount of the sugar it produced to the US at our inflated domestic price, rather than at the much lower world market price.

When I was there, the quota was worth about $10 million a year to South Africa, but something else was going on that I didn't realize at first. We were out to protect our sugar refiners as well as our inefficient sugar growers, and US law said that sugar exported to us under the quota program had to be raw, unrefined sugar so that US companies could profit by refining it. The problem was that the South African industry was set up to produce only partially refined sugar. Partial or not, it was too clean to meet our requirement, and that was why, as I was gleefully shown, there was a huge pile of sugar in the Durban warehouse with a machine mixing molasses into it, so it would be dirty enough for the finicky Americans. (Department of things most US taxpayers never dream of!)

On a drive up the coast with the Hassanis, I visited a sugar industry research laboratory seeking to develop improved varieties of cane. Daughter Anne was by this time beginning her mycology graduate research, specializing in mycorrhizal fungi, a symbiotic type needed for many plants to flourish. When I mentioned this to our guide at the lab, she told me only half jokingly that Anne could get a job there any time.

Not much further up the coast the sugar cane fields ended, and the road led to a variety of other attractions, including pristine beaches that are prime sea turtle breeding areas, and a number of wonderful game parks that are operated by the Kwa-Zulu Natal Parks Board. We would see them later.

David and Anne get Engaged

Almost as soon as Barbara left, my attention was turned back to the family in the US. On January 25, 1997, David wrote me formally asking for Anne's hand in marriage, by e-mail; his message was prefaced by the words: "Although this medium lacks a bit of the personal touch I would prefer, I am writing to ask your permission to marry your daughter." I felt a twinge of guilt because I was reminded that I had never formally asked Clay for his permission to marry Barbara. The e-mail continued,

I have purchased a lovely engagement ring in New York on my recent trip, complete with an antique setting similar to Barbara's as that is Anne's favorite [ring, the one Barbara inherited, via Clay, from his Grandmother Riesch—it had been destined for her oldest granddaughter, but Clay and his brother Art were the only grandchildren], and I plan to pop the question the weekend of Feb. 8. Your daughter and I have a truly wonderful relationship—built on trust, respect, love, communication, and compromise. The transition to cohabitation, while still a bit socially unacceptable, has been easy and enjoyable. Annie cooks and cleans; I wash dishes, fix the car, noodle around the house, and keep us on the financially straight and narrow. We have virtually decided to postpone the wedding until after Annie's exams in September, which will put the date sometime early '98.[32]

My reply to David was "Of course, it is a resounding YES."
Annie's version of events soon followed:

*"Hi Dad! I think you must know by now, but I want you to hear
the news from me too, so, we're engaged! Officially. I'm very
happy. We took a long hike in the woods on Saturday and at our
favorite vista, surrounded by acres of woods and under a light
drizzle (well, can't have everything—besides—you know what
they say, rainy engagement means a sunny wedding). . . ."*[33]

And so the wedding date was set for June, 1998, after Annie
had finished her PhD exams, and that day did turn out to be
sunny. We knew that Annie was on the right track when the
following arrived from Kate: ". . . attended Annie's engagement
party [during Kate's annual trip east, which always included
visiting friends in Chapel Hill], which was delightful; met
David at last—I approve. . . ."[34]

Meanwhile David was settling in teaching economics
at Duke. His first reviews, he reported, had been ". . . quite
complimentary to say the least. It always amazes me how
starved undergraduates are for good teaching." He was going
to get a raise, and thinking about accepting a different job at a
new private high school nearby.[35]

Barbara and I began planning for a family gathering in
Kruger Park around Christmas, 1997, and we would get to work
on that as soon as she came back to South Africa. Jamie, by now
working on his PhD at the MIT-Woods Hole Joint Program, kept
us advised about the sub-surface world to our east:

*Saw an interesting talk on ocean currents off Durban, where
the deep water (1500 to 3000 feet down) flows to the north,
despite its having the chemical signature of Red Sea water.
A rather large puzzle, that, since everyone expected Red Sea*

---

[32] David W. Johnson, "Good News," email to Dear Bob, January 25, 1997.
[33] Anne Pringle e-mail to Bob Pringle, nd, but clearly late January, 1997.
[34] K[ate] Massel e-mail to Bob, May 4, 1997.
[35] David e-mail to Bob, January 25, 1997.

water to flow away from the Red Sea....[36]

Later, when he came out at Christmas, we would enjoy getting him together with members of the University of Cape Town oceanography faculty. At the same event, Anne decided that since the guests were scientists, they would understand if she asked for a mouth swab from each of them for a project that a graduate student friend of hers was doing on global distribution and variation in *Candida* yeasts, which cause thrush infections in humans. The Pringles may not have been the swankiest diplomatic entertainers in town, but our parties *were* different. However, that is getting ahead of the story.

Barbara came to South Africa to stay after the school year ended at Potomac in June, 1997, and remained until we went home together two years later. I took R&R, partly to help her get the house ready to be rented, furnished, to Ken Thomas, and then to accompany her back to Pretoria. The trip also gave me a chance to visit Helena at the Woodbine nursing home in Alexandria. The quality of service at Woodbine had become much more flexible and compassionate than it had been at the beginning of her stay, and I think she actually enjoyed much of her time there near the end of her life.

Barbara soon got used to the peculiarities of our extended household. In some ways it resembled "Upstairs, Downstairs," except there was no "upstairs" above our thatched roof. When I had arrived, we had three household servants: Susan, cook and senior team member; Afia, wash and cleaning person; and Albert, "Butler," which included serving drinks and managing the alcohol supply. There was also a gardener, Jonathan, a good one, too. He never entered our lives in quite the same way as the others, but he was a good tennis player and often participated in embassy tournaments. My indispensable driver, Johannes, technically worked for the embassy, not for us.

Susan was rock solid and a very good manager. Afia had a lively streak; it was she who christened one of our bedrooms "the photo room" because Barbara put together our photo albums there—we would really miss that room post-South

---

[36] Jamie e-mail to Bob, [also] January 25, 1997.

Africa. Albert, who was Mozambican,[37] had a big red sash that he wore at fancy parties, which I gave few of, but I never really got to know him, and Barbara never met him. One Sunday evening in 1996, after a foray into the countryside with Reed Fendrick, I returned to find the Administrative Counselor, Mike Hinton, standing in front of our house looking very agitated. "Your butler has been murdered," he told me. Fortunately it did not happen at Eloff House, and there was no question about who did it: his wife, reportedly enraged beyond limit by his frequent womanizing.

There ensued a long search to find a new butler. The first candidate, Willie, was a part-time minister who finally decided he didn't have time for a second job. The second, Donald, came highly recommended from a previous job at the Swiss Embassy. He was so elderly as to be of limited assistance except at large parties, and Barbara had to send him for repeated medical exams for some contagious malady he had when he first applied for the job, but we hired him anyway. He was honest, got along with the ladies, and loved to polish silver. I am ashamed to confess that we never learned any of our servants' last names. Chalk it up to laziness, not prejudice, plus the fact that we simply never used their surnames, not to mention prefixes like Mr. and Mrs. to indicate family status.

On one memorable occasion we (Susan, Afia and Johannes, plus Barbara and I) were all flying down to Cape Town together on the airline that had been the flag carrier of Bophuthatswana, one of the most advanced and wealthy of South Africa's notorious homelands; it once sent a trade mission to Israel. "Air Bop," as we called it, somehow survived into the post-apartheid era and was well known to have better service on the roughly two-hour flight from Johannesburg to Cape Town than the alternative, South African Airways. This time we all got upgraded to Business Class, which had big, soft, leather seats, and came with a fancy lunch. The servants thought the trip was fantastic and probably never forgot the experience. When we flew, my official car was sent down by train, and Johannes knew exactly how to arrange the transfer. You couldn't do that in the US, and the South African railroad is a narrow gauge railroad!

---

[37] I was never able to figure out why, but quite a few domestic servants working for foreigners in Pretoria came from Mozambique.

The Embassy's Morale Problem

In Pretoria my daily work was about managing the US mission, including our three consulates, as well serving as point person on the embassy's relationship with the State Department, as called for in my original understanding with Ambassador Joseph. In practice, it was the small, day-to-day things that became most troublesome, including questions of morale.

Having served at a number of real hardship posts where almost everyone was happy, I was amazed to realize, however slowly, that in this land of good roads, cheap wines, and multiple entertainments, we had a morale problem. Part of it was a severely split constituency. Some of us were old Africa hands, used to the Ougadougous of the world, with a culture and a standard of living vastly different from the United States. More adventurous embassy personnel ventured out to explore the local arts, crafts and music scenes and to try out local restaurants, such as they were. In these small, tightly-knit embassy communities, we all knew each other (as well as the other Americans in town), often sent our kids to the same school, and socialized at the Marine House every Friday. In South Africa, this cohort missed "the real" Africa, with its village charm.

Pretoria was more like Washington. Few embassy employees hung out together after office hours. We all went our separate ways in the evening and especially on weekends. Official Americans played golf, went to the opera, traveled to game parks, or frequented the shopping malls, as glossy as any in the US. *Chacun à son gout,* one might have thought. We had a Community Liaison Officer (CLO) who was supposed to help find us all things to do. But in Pretoria it almost seemed as if there were *too many things* to do, and the CLO couldn't help much with that.

However, many in the official community were not particularly interested in Africa, *per se.* Some would have preferred not to serve abroad at all, especially if it meant losing the income provided by working spouses, but they were being required to do so by new regulations limiting how long Foreign Service Officers could remain in Washington. This cohort was bothered primarily by the crime problem and, in several families, by unrealistic expectations with regard to special education for their children, a problem Barbara would be hired to help correct.

We were aware that some of our American staff felt that there was a shortage of American community events, such as a Christmas Party. Barbara and I were happy to have such parties, and offered to do so after she arrived. At first, our offer only exacerbated the divide within Americans at the embassy, when a certain segment asked to limit the invitees to American employees only, on the grounds that that was the way it was "always" done. Exercising our prerogative as hosts, we sent invitations to all embassy employees, American and South African, and almost everyone accepted.

Admin Counselor Mike Hinton worked hard on other community events: a beefed-up, non-official Fourth of July celebration, for example, at a large recreation area adjacent to the ambassador's Residence, and a "Fall Into Spring" community picnic at a small but interesting urban game park (Rietvlei) in Pretoria. Barbara and I hosted the awards ceremony for the annual "Boston Tea Pot" Tennis Tournament between the Americans and the British. And we found that there were many ways to include embassy personnel in official diplomatic events, such as parties for those working on major visits, like the pre-FLOTUS one mentioned earlier. All these events required a lot of work, especially on the part of the (unpaid) spouse.

Of course, no amount of local attractions, American community activities, adequate schools for children, or equal employment opportunities for dependents would suffice if morale in the workplace was not also high. As DCM, I drafted most of the annual performance reports for other State Department senior staff, subject to review by the ambassador. This meant I had to know what they were doing, which meant visiting them in their workplaces and not just relying on their "brag sheets."

These reports needed to be exaggerated to be competitive in the struggle for promotion. They required creative writing skills and a cooperative effort between the writer and recipient. One hurdle was to concoct genuine "areas for improvement," without seriously damaging the recipient. As I would discover, the system was so degraded that *any* criticism would jeopardize the subject's prospects for promotion. Nonetheless, I had about thirty of them to write or review every spring, and I usually worked at home for a few days to get them done.

Whenever possible I attended staff meetings of the Economic and Political Sections, as well as USAID. I thought the latter was particularly important for several reasons: the usual tension between State and USAID, which always needed attention; the large number of USAID employees and contractors; my genuine interest in what our assistance was accomplishing, and finally the fact that they were separately located in downtown Pretoria, hence easily neglected. Ironically they were in a modern office building which had been staked out by *white*, mainly Afrikaner panhandlers, as if to remind our aid givers that not all the poor people in South Africa were black.

I had already had a good reputation with USAID from previous experience in other parts of Africa, but the South African staff greatly appreciated my interest in what they were doing. I did not call on Peace Corps headquarters often, but Barbara and I continued our normal and always fruitful practice of visiting volunteers in the field.

"Walking around" and "dropping by" were, as always, essential management tools, as was an open-door policy. In fact, I had no door, but as mentioned earlier, in order to reach the DCM/Ambassador suite you had to make a special trip by elevator, and our South African employees were not cleared to do so. I was the first point of contact for senior staff with a problem to discuss, unless it was very serious, and even then they would usually come to me before going to the Ambassador, whose preference for focusing on the most important policy issues was well known. So I spoke especially frequently with senior staff from the State Department and the growing number of other agencies. Our "bunker" did have a cafeteria and that was a good place for opportunistic conversations with any embassy employee.

By far our greatest and least expected management problem involved the growing number of US law enforcement agencies with offices in the embassy. Four of them had set up shop in South Africa since Mandela came to office in 1994, and they were increasingly active in working with their South African counterparts, at first with very limited embassy awareness of what they were doing. Any US government agency operating in a foreign country, except for active duty military under the authority of a regional military commander (or CINC), is subject to the authority of the ambassador. Ambassador Joseph authorized me to set up and chair an embassy law enforcement working group, to meet periodically and keep track of what was going on.

Most of these men were police officers, accustomed to carrying arms. They soon found that their South African counterparts, almost all Afrikaners, were eager to have them participate in pursuing criminal suspects. However, a problem arose when our officers wanted permission to carry weapons in such cases. I told them they could not, because we had no agreement with the South African government permitting them to do so. If one of them wounded or killed a South African, almost inevitably black, and the local press found out, we would have a problem. We began to negotiate an agreement with the South African government immediately, and in fact it was completed within six months.

I thought this was no more than common sense: surely, at home, we would take exception to foreign police using lethal weapons on our streets without full approval by higher authority. The Ambassador backed me up on this, but several of the officers involved were very unhappy. They thought I didn't understand their work, and was simply trying to obstruct it. I felt justified when the most adamant of this group, the DEA officer, went on leave. His house was burgled and when the South African police investigated, they found a stash of weapons and ammunition that he had brought into the country illegally. He got off with a friendly reprimand from the South Africans, but there would be serious ramifications for my career, as explained in Chapter 16.

In retrospect, I was witnessing the beginning of a trend in which US embassies would become unable to manage or control increasingly numerous law enforcement agencies and contractors, the ambassador's vaunted Chief of Mission authority to the contrary notwithstanding. Nothing illustrates this better than the behavior of Blackwater in Iraq in 2007, in which Blackwater's top manager threatened to kill a State Department investigator who was looking into the contractor's behavior. The threat worked. State Department officials in Washington supported Blackwater, and the investigation was suspended. However, weeks later Blackwater guards shot and killed seventeen Iraqi civilians. The broader problem seems still, at this writing, to be unresolved.[38]

Meeting the South African Pringles

In the second half of 1997 I went back to Durban and Kwa-Zulu Natal with Barbara. We visited the heavily touristed Drakensberg Mountains and the Zulu War battlefields, then set off to find, if we could, the South African Pringles. We knew about them because, when I was in high school, a pair of them had showed up at 3319 N Steet, my father's house in Washington, to seek his help on finding out more about the American Pringles.

My father knew little about South Africa—and what he did know, he didn't much like—but he listened politely and told them to consult the Charleston Pringles, who were the real experts on this subject. They apparently did so and eventually sent him an autographed copy of the book they had published, entitled *Pringles of the Valleys: Their History and Genealogy*,[39] which I inherited and brought with me to South Africa. Judging by photos on the dust jacket, the authors were clearly not young when the book was published, but perhaps if they were no longer living we could locate some of their children.

The South African Pringles were among the "1820 Settlers," the first English-speaking whites to arrive in the Cape area. Without revealing their real motive, British colonial officials cynically located them to provide a buffer between the hostile Khosa tribes of the Eastern Cape and the Cape Colony.

[38] James Risen, "Before Shooting in Iraq, Warning on Backwater, Alert to State Department, Investigator Reported a Threat to his Life Documents Show," *New York Times*, June 30, 2014, lead front-page article; "Guards Guilty in '07 Killings in Iraq Square, *New York Times*, October 23, 2014. At this writing, the conviction is under appeal.
[39] Eric Pringle, Mark E. Pringle and John A. Pringle, published by Eric Pringle of Glen Thorn, Adelaide, Cape Province, 1957.

Promised fertile farmland, what the settlers got was semi-arid bush exposed to constant attack during the "Kaffir Wars" and good for little but sheep grazing, if that.

But many persevered, and I was told that their descendants were especially numerous around the town of Cradock. The most famous Pringle, Thomas, moved to Cape Town, started a newspaper, wrote poetry, annoyed the Governor, successfully protested being censored, and became, as South African friends told us, "The John Peter Zenger" of South Africa.[40] Thomas Pringle awards for journalistic excellence, somewhat similar to our Pulitzer prizes, are still awarded every year.

While most South African Pringles are English-speaking, usually with some Afrikaans as a second language, we heard about one who was clearly an Afrikaner in everything but name, with extremely right-wing views.

We knew that John, one of the three authors of *Pringles of the Valleys,* had been head of the Natal Museum in Pietermaritzburg (where Gandhi was thrown off the train). Pietermaritzburg was on our way home from Durban so we, assuming he had probably passed away, decided to stop there and see if the museum knew the whereabouts of any of his family members. A friendly museum employee set us straight: "He was in yesterday; would you like his address?"

And so we met John, quite alive, and his wife Ingrid, in a retirement settlement in the nearby suburb of Howick. We learned that he was one of the pioneers of the conservation movement in South Africa and author of the first book written on its history.[41] He was in the middle of a project exploring the use of smoke to propagate seeds in fire-prone-areas. We were able to keep up with him and his wife until recently.

---

[40] At the bookstore on Long Street in Cape Town I discovered a very battered copy of *The Poetical Works of Thomas Pringle*, London, Edward Moxon, Dover Street, 1838, which includes a sketch of his life as well as his poetry. Its original incised paper binding was meticulously restored for us by Marie van Eyndhoven, a Dutch friend we met in South Africa.

[41] John Pringle, *The Conservationists and the Killers; The Story of Game Protection and the Wildlife Society of Southern Africa*, Bulpin, 1982 (called to my attention by Ken Thomas).

The Kwa-Zulu Natal Battlefields:
Isandlwana and Rorke's Drift

The area is saturated with history. Pietermaritzburg itself was founded by Voortrekkers, but they were expelled by the British in 1843, a precursor to the later Boer War. Cecil Rhodes emigrated from Britain to farm in this area in 1870, but dropped his plough within a short time and headed for the diamond mines, where he became the founding genius of South African capitalism.

Battlefields from the Anglo-Zulu and Boer Wars are numerous. At Isandlwana in 1879 the British, out to punish the Zulus, made all the mistakes Custer had made before his Last Stand and were similarly massacred, 1,400 of them. But that evening, at Rorke's Drift ("Drift" means ford), a tiny British rear guard, having survived the daytime battle, recouped honor for the Empire against fresh waves of Zulu warriors.[42]

The main battlefield at Isandlwana is supremely dramatic: a towering pinnacle (or *kopje*) at the foot of which half the British forces with all their supplies waited as their commanding general, Lord Chelmsford, took the other half off on a chase in the wrong direction, leaving them fatally exposed to massive enemy attack. The surrounding grasslands, still dotted with Zulu dwellings, have not been manicured or developed. I wrote:

It was four months before the British dared to go back to Isandlwana to bury the dead; the graves are marked by rough piles of stones and there are only three individual grave markers or monuments, all to white colonial troops, none to the British, suggesting that the defeat was regarded as a terrible disgrace in England. [As in the case of the Little Bighorn, although the Zulus won the battle they had of course no chance of winning the war.]

No medals were given for Islandwana; in contrast, seven Victoria Crosses were awarded for the British who fought and

---

[42] Rorke's Drift is the subject of the 1963 film "Zulu," although the setting was moved to a supposedly more dramatic location in the Drakensburg Mountains.

won at Rorke's Drift, an all-time record. [43]

The resident guru and tour guide par excellence was David Rattray, whose family-owned farm included portions of the battlefield. His tours attracted VIP visitors, like Prince Charles, and you had to book them months ahead of time. He was well aware of the similarities between Isandlwana and the Little Bighorn, and toward the end of our stay we arranged for my sister Margot to visit him, but the trip fell apart when she had a severe emotional breakdown. Rattray himself was killed on his farm in 2007 in an armed robbery attempt by six men.[44]

Wakkerstroom: Birds, Schools, and Tourism

We also visited Wakkerstroom, an old Boer settlement not far from the Zulu battlefields, which was fast becoming an internationally known bird-watching hot spot. It boasts some nice wetlands, plus a lot of prairie farmland. I had gone there with Reed Fendrick soon after my arrival, at the invitation of Peter Sullivan, editor of the *Johannesburg Star*, a major newspaper. Sullivan was an avid birder in the South African manner, which included roaring around in a car on slippery farm roads, then slamming on the breaks in a shower of gravel whenever someone spotted a rarity. Often these were larks such as Botha's (pronounced *Berta's*) Lark, a stripey brown job similar to the other South African larks, which were camouflaged in the meadows.

When Barbara and I revisited Wakkerstroom a year later our pace was slower, and we probably didn't see as many birds. The big sighting occurred after I noticed something, stopped, then pulled ahead to get off the road after letting Barbara out. When she returned, there was a big spitting cobra coiled up next to the car on the passenger side, which she spotted just at the last minute. Spitting cobras can be dangerous because the venom they spit, projecting it several feet, can blind a person if it gets in the eyes. Although she was

---

[43] Bob letter to Dear Family, January 25, 1997.

[44] Rattray made a recording of his tour, entitled *The Day of the Dead Moon.*

wearing glasses, Barbara felt lucky to have missed provoking it. The snake retreated, but not before I got a picture of it. We never saw another one.

Wakkerstroom provided some insights into the very important question of how South Africa was managing the key question of its still largely white-owned farmlands. I wrote home:

Wakkerstroom is an old town about three hours' drive southeast of here [Pretoria] where the High Veld drops off toward the Indian Ocean. It is the biggest expanse of relatively pristine high altitude grass country left in South Africa, so it has quite a few endemic species (found in SA only) as well as a great variety of [other] birds. We met a group of interesting people who are working both with the local farming/ranching population and with local Zulu school children to generate interest in conservation. We saw a field full of Blue Cranes (South Africa's national bird, but endangered) as well as the commoner but still spectacular Crowned Cranes.

The farmers (average holding about 2500 hectares) are still entirely white Afrikaners with black tenant farmers who are allowed to grow patches of corn and run cattle in return for labor. Nothing has changed, you think, and you are partially correct, except that the blacks are now free to get educated and move into the New South Africa. Except that the black schools, crippled by the appalling legacy of "Bantu Education," similar to but even worse than the segregated system in the old US South, remain very under-resourced, and the blacks who are not living as tenant farmers in the countryside are in "settlements" of shacks and modest small houses in small towns. Indeed the latter are a considerable majority, nationwide, which explains why there isn't major pressure for expropriation of all white farms; the majority of blacks here (in contrast to the rest of Africa) no longer aspire to be peasant farmers.

In the case of Wakkerstroom, the formerly all-white primary and secondary schools [in the town] are now all black. The white kids (children of local farmers) have fled to a larger town thirty kilometers away, which blossomed after the Wakkerstroomers refused to allow the Durban-Jo'burg railroad to come through in the 1890's, beginning a long period of stagnation for their town. But now it is also beginning to attract white retirees from Johannesburg who enjoy the bird watching, the gorgeous scenery, the old houses they are busily restoring, and the peace and quiet (at least compared to Jo'burg). They run B&B operations and a small hotel, "The Weaver's Nest," for birding groups, now increasing in numbers (and to include Kathy and Fred with us when they come). And the local, all-black high school has an energetic environmental club, run by a couple of teachers who are former ANC activists, nurtured by a (white) representative of the provincial parks board, John McAllister, who is himself a dropout from the private sector.

It does make your head spin sometimes.[45]

A major part of the conservation challenge at Wakkerstroom was getting the local farmers to understand what was going on and cooperate, for example, by not using toxic chemicals where possible. One farmer whose land was a frequent haunt of the Blue Cranes was a leader of the local "commando"[46] (self-defense group) and of the militantly right-wing AWB (*Afrikaner Weerstandbeweging*, or Afrikaner Resistance Movement). I wrote in my official report:

Although [the farmer] was initially hostile, John McAllister persuaded him to apply for (largely honorific) South Africa National Heritage Site status, and in due course he received a certificate signed by President Mandela. The result was amazing. The erstwhile hard liner was overcome with emotion ('Look! Look! The old man has actually signed it!') and now has the certificate proudly displayed in his home.[47]

---

[45] Bob letter to Dear Family, n.d., but end of October, 1997. I would later write an official report on the rural school situation and the role of Peace Corps volunteers working in these schools, which began after this trip; see Chapter 15.

[46] "Commando" was originally an Afrikaans term, made famous during the Boer War.

[47] "Can Biodiversity and Social Change Prosper Together in South Africa's Threatened Grasslands?" Pretoria 10811, October 21, 1997.

I recommended that Wakkerstroom be included in the United Nations' Man and the Biosphere program, which I had previously helped manage during my time in OES, since it is specifically designed to support conservation in areas that are heavily impacted by human presence, as Wakkerstroom was. Apparently nothing ever came of this suggestion, but South Africa has designated it a National Freshwater Ecosystem Priority Area. Twenty-one years later, in 2018, Wakkerstoom's birding-based tourism is flourishing, along with more recently established annual music and garden shows, with more than fifteen B&B's and small hotels advertising on the Internet.

In September, Barbara and I represented the embassy at the dedication of a statue of Steve Biko, a famous martyr of the anti-apartheid struggle killed by the South African police in 1977. The event was held in East London, an industrial center east of Cape Town. It was a major occasion for the ruling ANC, and President Mandela was the featured speaker. But the huge crowd gathered to hear him was unruly, partly due to the presence of relatively radical, anti-ANC black activists from minor parties we had probably never heard of, including AZAPO. They were upset because they saw Biko—who indeed had been the pioneer of a black consciousness movement in South Africa—as being one of them, in contrast to Mandela's ANC, which had been multi-racial in its philosophy from its inception.

As the official US representative, I was seated in the grandstand facing the crowd, while Barbara had been relegated to a row of chairs on the edge of the crowd facing me, and I remember being distinctly worried that the police would not be able to hold back the crowd, welling up from the center of the city, and she would be caught in a stampede, friendly or otherwise. Mandela finally scolded everyone into silence with a call for unity among black political organizations. Luminaries present included British pop singer Peter Gabriel, who sang his hit song about "Biko" without benefit of a sound system—it didn't work—and film producer Richard Attenborough, director of *Cry Freedom*, also about Biko, both of whom had helped pay for the statue. It was an enthralling experience, and Barbara, seated almost underneath the speaker's podium, got a nice picture of the great man speaking, but we were both relieved when it was over.[48]

[48] Our invitation and press reports with headlines like "Mandela in Call for Black Unity as Biko Statue unveiled," *Saturday Star*, September 12, 1997, are in SA scrapbook 3.

15

Finale in South Africa

As was the case in Mali, there were aspects of our South African experience that don't fit smoothly in any narrative. Here are five of them:

Ancient pre-Humans and their Study

Early in 1999 we were lucky to meet Little Foot, a very old hominid (*Australopithecus africanus*) in Sterkfontein cave, not far from Johannesburg. Our guide was Dr. Ron Clarke, then a researcher in archaeology at the University of the Witwatersrand.[1] He emphasized that it was his black assistant who had spotted the critical foot fragment protruding from a hard rock deposit secreted by water dribbling into the cave centuries (or millennia) ago. Clarke had then been able to match that bone with a known *Australopithecus* fragment in the university collection of material from the same cave. That was a major discovery, because it signified that an entire skeleton might be preserved in the hard rock. Previous *Australopithecus* finds in Kenya and elsewhere had been recovered from looser material in which the bones had been scattered. However, the hard rock matrix also meant that extracting the bones would be slow, painstaking work. Indeed, they had not yet been completely removed as of fifteen years later.

Thanks to Clarke, whom we came to know socially, we got to crawl around in the cave and see what was visible of Little Foot. Since he or she is already three to four million years old, there is arguably no great rush about getting him or her released from

---
[1] Often abbreviated "Wits."

stony interment.[2]

It used to be said that every other Israeli is an amateur archaeologist, and maybe someday every other South African will be a paleoanthropologist, given the amount of interesting material available. Ron McMullen, who was our Deputy Consul General in Cape Town, was a talented finder of old stones and bones, and he discovered that wineries in places like Stellenbosch and Franschhoek are a great place to find hand axes from the Acheulean period. All you have to do is look underneath the vines after they have been cultivated. The axes are common in this setting, if you have an eye for such things. The oldest ones date to about one and one-half million years ago, and they are found from Africa to Europe, where they were first discovered.

The fact that South Africa, largely because of Wits and other universities, can do the kind of work needed to explore its own ancient past is indicative of its scientific assets, important if not vital for long-term national growth and welfare. We encountered such evidence constantly: at Kirstenbosch Botanical Garden (unstinting research on the Cape Floral Kingdom), at the University of Cape Town (*inter alia*, its fine Oceanography department), at the sugar industry research station north of Durban, at the site of the new telescope in the Karoo (SALT), and of course in South Africa's controversial if productive arms industry, which enabled it to develop its own nuclear weapons capability, later wisely relinquished.

Opera, Classic and Home-grown

Opera was one of the least expected joys of South Africa. For the equivalent of US$40 apiece we could enjoy both a good dinner and a bottle of wine at the Opera Cafe in Pretoria, followed by the performance. The first one I saw, before Barbara's arrival, was Verdi's *Nabucco*, and I was amazed at how good it was. Casts were mostly, if not entirely, white South African. The State Opera was being heavily subsidized

---

[2] Clarke is currently Professor and Reader of Paleoanthropology and Director of the Sterkfontein Research Unit at Wits. See http://www.wits.ac.za/academic/research/ihe/staff/7134/ronclarke. html.

by the central government, and, as was the case with many mostly white perks and passions, one could only wonder how long it would last. There were also occasional operas in Cape Town, but not as many and not as good.

All in all we saw about twenty of them. Some were superb, particularly a performance of Puccini's *Manon Lescault* not long before we left. Most were grand opera, but white South Africans adored American musicals, so we were also treated to performances of *Oklahoma!*, *Porgy and Bess*, *Fiddler on the Roof*, and *The Buddy Holly Story*.

Of those that we saw, only two were set in South Africa. One was *Ipi N'tombi*, meaning *Where is the Girl?* in coarse Zulu. It is the story of a chief's son who goes off to work in the mines and falls in love with a city girl, neglecting his duty to return home and succeed his father. That is bad enough, but in addition he is Zulu and she is Khosa, or something along those lines, leading to no end of drama. It was originally made under apartheid in 1974 and criticized by both blacks and white liberals for being Uncle Tom-ish, and what we saw was supposedly a new, more politically correct version. It was staged in Johannesburg at the Market Theatre, and I remember being nervous about going there after dark—even though Johannes was right there with the car. The theater was small, far from full, and we sat in the second row. Right in front of us were two young black men who, we surmised, must have been given tickets by cast members.

In any case, it was clearly a new experience for them. In Act Two of the opera a witch doctor emerges and dances wildly with a (stuffed) snake, right up to the edge of the stage directly in front of us. That was too much, and one of the men levitated up and over the back of his seat, never taking his eyes off the snake, and almost landed in my lap. Never before or since have we seen a play with such energetic dancing and singing, or with such audience impact. *Ipi N'tombi* later came to Cape Town, where Anne and David, and later Jamie, were able to see it during their visits.

In 1998 we saw *Buchuland*, a new South African opera about the descendants of Khoi inhabitants who were able, under post-apartheid law, to reclaim land they had lost forty years previously when a Dutch Reformed Church mission sold it from under them. All this was set in a valley near Citrusdal, a town we would come to know.[3] We thought the opera itself, by a contemporary South African composer, was excellent.

One thing is for sure: there is enough vocal talent in South Africa to feed an operatic tradition. We recall going to hear a well-known Danish student choir not long before we left. They sang at the University of Pretoria, which had invited local choral groups to attend. The guests were sitting quietly in the back rows when the Danish young people very correctly offered a version of *Shosholosa*, sometimes referred to as South Africa's informal national anthem. Originally an Ndebele folk song, it became popular among migrant miners in Johannesburg as a call-and-response work chanty, which imitates the sound of a locomotive and becomes a soaring, melodic struggle song. The visiting singers did their best with it, but the local audience could not help reacting to their muted, piping version by rising to their feet and roaring it out the way it ought to sound. You have to have heard *Shosholoza* sung like this to appreciate the story.

I can't leave the subject of opera and song without mentioning *The Three Tenors*, Placido Domingo, Jose Carreras and Luciano Pavarotti, who sang in Pretoria in 1999 on their first trip to South Africa. The venue was the lawn of the Union Buildings, which tower over a semi-circular amphitheater covered with elevated terraces. That night, bleachers set up on them looked down on a temporary stage. The weather was perfect, which in South Africa means exquisite, and all went well until, just before intermission, a big section of the bleachers slowly collapsed under its load of music lovers. No one got excited, most people, including us, found new and better places to sit on the flowered terraces, and the show went on.

Two Houses

Many foreigners associate Groote Schoor, meaning "Big Barn," with the hospital in Cape Town where Christiaan Barnard did

---

[3] *Inter alia*, we had a famous flat tire on the main highway near Citrusdal in 2011, not long after we had visited a mission settlement in the hinterland, although apparently not the same mission as the one featured in the opera.

the first heart transplant in 1967. But it is also the name of the Cape Dutch-style mansion of Cecil Rhodes, who bequeathed it to the state to be used to be as a prime ministerial/visiting chief-of-state residence, as it was until Mandela chose to live in the nearby VIP guest house instead. Foreign diplomats could tour it during very limited hours, which required advance registration with a fussy curatorial staff, but was worth the effort.

Mandela, the most tolerant of great leaders, was of course correct in wanting nothing to do with Rhodes or with most of the apartheid-era South African prime ministers who later lived in the house. To read a biography of Rhodes,[4] especially the part about his "creation," with Maxim guns, of what became Southern Rhodesia and is now Zimbabwe, is to wonder why anyone would be willing to be associated with him, scholarships or not. This High God of imperialism wanted his house "large and simple, barbaric if you wish."[5] It has a lot of conventionally gorgeous furniture, made with rare local woods, as well as numerous Flemish tapestries, Persian rugs and Chinese porcelains. Two aspects of its decor speak more clearly to the man's character: several hundred volumes of English translations of classical works specially reprinted and bound to order, and a vast granite stone bathtub from Zimbabwe in his private quarters.

The altogether estimable Jan Smuts did live in this house twice, as Prime Minister. But a greater contrast with Smuts' own home and rural retreat at Irene, basically a long bungalow with no pretension whatsoever, can hardly be imagined.

The Outenequa Tjoe-Choo

Here's a clue as to what this is about: "Tjoe" is Afrikaans for "Choo," as in sneeze. No, not quite. Rendered bilingually it is a train that runs along the southern coast of South Africa between George and Knysna. Indeed it is (or was) a whole division of the state railway (Spoornet) and operated until recently only with

---

[4] See Anthony Thomas, *Rhodes: The Race for Africa*, Johannesburg, Jonathan Hall, 1996, especially Chapter 7, for a critical view.
[5] "Groote Schuur: A Valuable Heritage," n.d., a guide to the house being used at the time of our visit.

steam locomotives.

After the Boer War, the colonial government embarked on a many-faceted kind of "New Deal" to improve the lot of the Boers, who had never shared in the English-dominated industrialization of the country and of course had been knocked flat by the war. (No similar effort was made for blacks.) A certain amount of this effort was make-work, plus outright subsidization. Spoornet played a key role, and the countryside was eventually laced with branch lines to every rural town on the map. Spoornet was an Afrikaner preserve, and only as late as 1996 was the first black train driver (engineer) at work.

Understandably the Boers have a sentimental attachment to railroads. There are railroad clubs and preserved locomotives all over the place. Today there are also luxury trains (including the famous Blue Train between Johannesburg and Cape Town) and very modern, high capacity freight lines carrying miles-long ore trains to new industrial ports on both coasts.

But the Outeniqua Tjoe-Choo was always a toy, built only in 1928 to see how many bridges, tunnels and spiraling grades could be fitted into thirty miles of narrow gauge track looping around along the rugged, scenic coast. It uses mainly 2-8-2 (Mikado) coal-burning locomotives with Vanderbilt tenders which are reminiscent of those once used by our Southern Pacific and Baltimore and Ohio Railroads. Although a successful tourist attraction, it was knocked out by floods in 2006, but the "Friends of the Tjoe-Choo" are raising money to get it going again, and I am betting that they will succeed.

The Lady of Nieu-Bethesda

On a trip back to Pretoria from Cape Town we stopped to see Nieu-Bethesda, a village in the dry hills of the Eastern Cape, not far from the Valley of Desolation. It is the setting for *The Road to Mecca*, a play by Athol Fugard based on the life of Helen Martins, a reclusive widow and artist who filled her garden with strange, but strangely attractive, statuary and ceramics. As she grew older and weaker, she resisted efforts to be transferred from her dusty house to a nursing home because that would separate her from her art. She won in the end.

No theater set could do justice to the isolated, arid setting of the real Nieu-Bethesda, and although Fugard fans do come to see her Owl House, they don't seem to have injected any cash into the local economy. Nieu-Bethesda is still a tiny, poor, place with a few artists living in scattered houses and nary a paved road for miles. Helen Martins' "Mecca," was her garden crammed with statues, mainly of owls, and it is still there. One expects to see her colored servant, with whom she may or may not have had a relationship, come in the door. Read or see the play and you will want to go there first, and save the Big Five for later.

Madiba Stomps on Uncle Sam

On October 17, 1997, Barbara and I had another memorable experience filling in for Ambassador Joseph and his wife. The event was a dinner for Julius Nyerere, former President of Tanzania, held at the Carlton Hotel in Johannesburg, once the flagship hotel of the city, but increasingly disused due to the crime problem in the neighborhood.[6] Nyerere had been an unswerving supporter of the anti-apartheid cause, and the purpose of the black-tie dinner was to launch a fundraiser for one of his favorite causes, the Mwalimu Nyerere Foundation. The leaders of South Africa's business community were there in droves. As ranking representatives of the US, we were seated at a table in the front row.

It happened that the State Department had just publicly, and against the embassy's advice, chastised President Mandela for announcing that he was going to Libya to help us negotiate with Qadafi about the Libyan destruction of a Pan American airliner over Locherbie, Scotland. The State Department's message to Mandela was clear: We adore you, old man, as long as you stay in your place and do not interfere with the work of us professionals.

President Mandela reacted furiously in his opening remarks at the dinner. He angrily blasted our arrogance in trying to tell him that he should not visit old friends who had stood by him and

---

[6] The Carlton was closed and mothballed in 1997. As of 2014 downtown Jo'burg seems to be recovering, and there is talk of restoring it.

the ANC at a time when the western powers were ambivalent at best, and at worst regarded those struggling for freedom as terrorists. This was partly a dig at Margaret Thatcher, who was supposed to have said in 1987 that "Anyone who believes the ANC could govern SA is living in cloud cuckoo land."[7] But I was quite sure that everyone in the room was staring at me, and studied my napkin. Barbara wrote home:

However the end of the story of last night is rather amusing. Having sat through two courses and an hour of speeches, I decided to visit the ladies room while Mandela was exiting before the main course could be served. (He often does not stay for the whole of a ceremonial function, and in this case . . . had just come back from a flying trip to Mozambique to wish Graca Machel happy birthday, so he had had a long day.) However, he is a consummate politician in the get-out-of-your-car, drive-the-security-people-nuts-while-mixing-with-the-crowd school, and he never goes fast through a group of people. The result was that just as I was passing by the elevators on the way back into the ballroom, Mandela arrived at the elevator bank. Seeing me, another potential constituent in his eyes, he proffered his

[7] This famous quotation may have been based on something said by her spokesperson, according to Internet sources, but it certainly reflected her thinking.

hand and shook mine. The kind of person he is, he wouldn't have refused even if he had realized that I was the American chargé d'affaires' wife, but it was an ironic twist to the evening for me. [8]

Press coverage of this event included a contribution from South Africa's foremost political cartoonist, the irrepressible Zapiro. It showed Mandela, labeled "world's moral leader," striding away from Bill Clinton, who is dressed as Uncle Sam and labeled "world's policeman, self-appointed," lying on the ground, flattened by Mandela's giant footstep.[9]

The Joys of Kruger National Park

In November 1997 we made our first trip to Kruger National Park, only about five hours' drive from Pretoria. It was in part a reconnaissance trip for the planned post-Christmas visit of family and friends. We had acquired a small four-door Nissan sedan[10] for private trips, and this was one of its first major outings.

It had been a dry spring, there had been lots of fires in Kruger, and everything not burned was parched and

---

[8] Barbara letter to Dear Family, n.d., but presumably late October, 1997, shortly after the dinner.

[9] The cartoon, drawn for *The Sowetan*, dated 21 October, 1997, also appears in *Zapiro, End of Part One: Cartoons from Sowetan, Mail and Guardian and Sunday Times*, David Phillip, Cape Town and Johannesburg, 1998. Zapiro is Jonathan Zapiro, but he never uses his first name. A typical headline from the *Sunday Independent* of October 19: "Mandela Tells United States Where to Get Off."

[10] South Africans drive on the left, and we decided to buy a right-hand drive car for safety reasons: it is hazardous to pass if you are sitting where you cannot see what is coming at you, especially in a country with mainly narrow, two lane roads, where most people drive way too fast. The best way to purchase such a car, according to experienced friends at the embassy, was second-hand, from a dealer in Japan, also a country where one drives on the left. At this time many Japanese sold their cars after two or three years, often in very good condition, because there was no market for used ones, and reportedly a tax penalty for keeping one too long. It was bit nerve-wracking, because you had to buy sight-unseen, from a mimeographed list of what was available, and odometers were always reset to zero! In the event, we had to put in a stronger air conditioner, but otherwise the car was fine.

dusty. During our first hour or so in the park we saw only a scattering of impala, the default antelope in this part of Africa, and a warthog or two. Our first excitement was an irritable old bull elephant, walking slowly along in the middle of the road just ahead of us. He would not get out of our way and we were nervous about trying to pass him; since his knees were higher than the roof of our car, one grumpy step in the wrong direction could have been dangerous. Finally he swerved off the road into a streambed, and only then did we see that he was following a whole "breeding herd" of females and young ones.

The first of rule of all big game parks seems to be that every trip into a park is different. The second rule is that there are usually long periods in which you don't see much of anything, especially if your eyes are not the greatest, followed by unpredictable bursts of drama, like the time we witnessed five young lions ambush and kill a wildebeest at a waterhole, and, on the same trip, a duo of rare sable antelopes mating.[11]

Kruger is especially varied because of its long, narrow shape, about 220 miles from north to south, and an average of 50 or so from west to east. Like many national parks it exists in no small part because historically the area was remote and, due to malaria and poor soils, not of much value for farming or ranching. Today, its narrowness means that for better and worse, Kruger is often not far from "civilization," including access to airports, incongruous glimpses of distant shopping malls and superhighways in the south, and proximity of poachers.

Given its problematic location and dimensions, the South Africans have done a splendid job of managing Kruger. The park operates many and varied camps, designed primarily for South African visitors. They are not the Ritz, but they are more than adequate if the object of your stay is primarily to see natural attractions, and you don't require champagne breakfasts and swimming pools.

The camps are connected by hundreds of miles of roads, the main ones paved, the others well-graded gravel. You must be back in your camp at sunset, and you cannot go out again

---

[11] Bob letter to extended family, May 26, 1998.

until dawn. You are not allowed to get out of your car except inside the camps and in a few other fenced areas. Not following these rules is dangerous. Not long after we left, a ranger (who should have known better) walked away from his clients on an evening game drive and went a few yards across a small bridge for a cigarette break. A leopard emerged from the trees lining the stream and killed him. Lions fairly regularly ate illegal immigrants from Mozambique trying to cross the park and had to be put down; autopsies revealed stomach contents consisting of shredded tennis shoes, *etcetera*.[12]

Barbara and I soon worked out a system for seeing Kruger from the endless back roads. One of us would drive, and cover the right-hand side of the car, while the other was in back, covering the left side, but able to scoot across the seat if the main attraction was on the right. It must have looked a bit like "Driving Miss Daisy" when I was at the wheel. Things we never experienced included a really good sighting of a leopard, although they are common. Rare animals that we did encounter: wild dogs, although not until 1999, then seen on consecutive visits. And there were many living creatures we saw a lot but never tired of, mainly elephants, giraffes, buffalo, lions and an infinity of birds. Our best, and most numerous cheetah sightings came on the other side of the country, in what was then Kalahari-Gemsbok National Park (now Kgalagadi Transfrontier Park).

For those who don't know how good Kruger's public facilities are, there are private lodges that are more than happy to take their money. Several of the most expensive are very cleverly located adjacent to Kruger's western border, so that game can circulate between private and public land. If you go to one of them, Sabi Sands or Timbavati for example, the staff will meet your private airplane and reportedly *guarantee* that you will see the Big Five within the limited time available to busy you. The area where the most famous of these luxury lodges are located happens also to be near the north-south escarpment, along which, in much higher, non-malarial territory, there are a host of other tourist attractions, as well as a great deal of densely-settled black-owned farmland.

---

[12] The last tidbit is from B&B e-mail to Dear Family, October 17, 1998.

The old farmhouse, our residence in Pretoria, was dressed up to welcome our family visitors for the Christmas holidays.

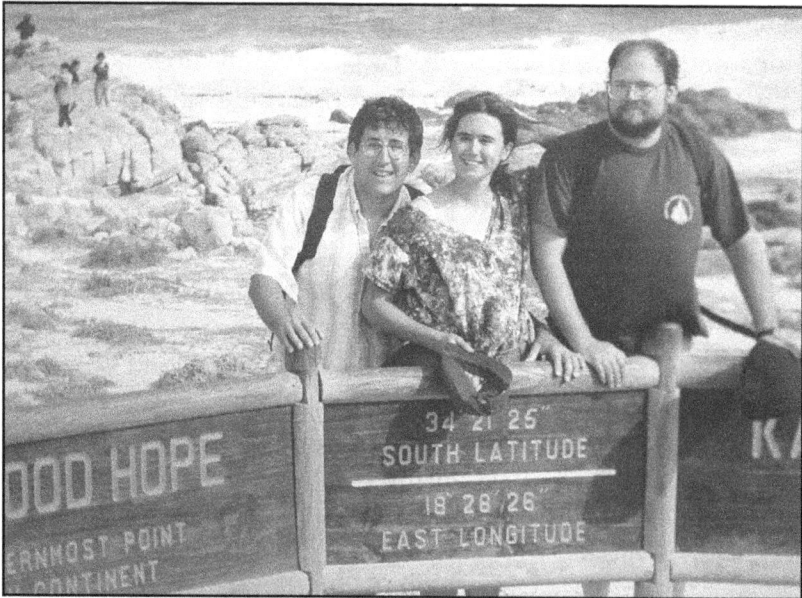

During their stay at the Cape Town house, David, Annie, and Jamie explored Cape Point.

Also not far away and next to Kruger: a training school for future national park rangers that draws students from all over southern Africa and beyond. All South Africans are aware that tourism is one of the fastest growing economic sectors in the world, and nowhere is the problem of black employment more important than in their own country. When we were living there from 1996 to 1999, almost all Kruger's rangers were white, usually the offspring of Afrikaner farmers. On a return visit in 2011, those proportions seemed to have been reversed, and the same was true for other non-management jobs. (For senior management jobs, the speed of transition has been understandably slower.) The old fear that that once apartheid ended, the parks would be abolished and turned into farmland for blacks is looking less and less justified. It is well recognized that these infertile lands are not much good for growing "mealies," the local term for corn; what they are good for is growing jobs and money.

Almost Everyone Visits South Africa

Based on our reconnaissance trip, we decided that we wanted to concentrate our post-Christmas visit with family in the central portion of Kruger, the best place to see elephants, and also take a camping/walking tour in the south of the park, where rhinos are most plentiful, on the Wolhuter Wilderness Trail.[13] Our party included the next generation in (or about to be in) our family, plus David's brother Rich and his wife Sherry, and Megan Waples, the daughter of Barbara's Potomac School colleague Rick Waples, who was working in South Africa.

Kruger's wilderness trails—there are several of them—are very popular, and use of them must be booked months ahead of time. Our visit began with a drive to a fenced camp, with basic thatched, A-frame cabins where we slept and ate, very hot, no air conditioning, followed by two days of walking through the countryside, a mix of forest and savannah, with park rangers carrying rifles fore and aft.

---

[13] The trail is named after a famous pioneer game ranger, Harry Wolhuter, who once single handedly killed a lion with his hunting knife while patrolling on horseback, but not before the lion almost killed him.

We saw plenty of white rhinos. They are bigger than black rhinos and are grazers, much more easily seen since they feed in open country. Their mouths are wide, shaped for cutting grass, hence the name ("White" = "wide" or "*wyd*" in Afrikaans), whereas a black rhino's mouth is pointed, so it acts like a pruning shear, because they live and eat in dense shrubbery. You can also identify the latter from their poop, often full of neatly cut twigs. Color-wise, no rhinos are ever really black or white, they are various shades of grey or brown or even red, depending on what kind of mud or dust they have been rolling in recently. Is there a moral here?

Anyway, we got quite close to several white rhinos, enough to more than make up for hours of walking:

> We learned that the standard technique, when the rhino is upwind, not quite seeing or hearing the walkers, but approaching inquisitively, is for the rangers to pick up branches, which in due course they throw in the general direction of the approaching rhino. Meanwhile the walkers have been advised to stand still in a group or in a clump of trees. This technique usually causes the rhino to wake up in the presence of *Homo sapiens*, that most deadly of all predators, and then to rumble off rapidly.[14]

One female ran away from us, herding her calf in front of her. "That's another way you can tell white from black rhinos," one of our rangers explained. "A white rhino mom goes with her baby in front, like a white woman pushing her baby in a pram. A black rhino goes with her baby behind, like a black woman carrying her baby on her back."

As to seeing elephants, we saw plenty. Before our rustic trail experience, we had spent several nights in a large house, probably once used to entertain important officials, perched right on the edge of a cliff overlooking the riverine plain at Olifants Camp. As well as exploring the central park grasslands

---

[14] Bob and Barbara Pringle, "A Walk on the Wilderness Side," from the embassy newsletter, the *Jacaranda Journal*, January 22, 1998.

during the day, we could sip our evening refreshments while watching the elephants and other animals come in to drink and play in the river below.

Since it takes a while to drive out of the park, given the low speed limits on its roads, we made a two-day trip out of the return to Pretoria. We stopped overnight near Pilgrim's Rest in the High Veld, after exploring the views from the top of the escarpment and, notably, shopping for souvenirs at a craft market where Anne and David acquired the giraffe which still stands tall in their house.

Just a note on the rest of the Christmas visit: Since Anne and Jamie were now grown, they did not get free visits to their diplomatic parents any more, and this was the only visit for Anne and David, and only one of two for Jamie. We had had a jolly family Christmas in Cape Town, enlivened by the arrival of Anne and David in the Jo'burg airport with Santa hats on their heads, and the reception for scientists mentioned elsewhere. After a traditional Christmas Day, we decided to spend Boxing Day, still a huge holiday in many ex-British colonies, on Table Mountain. Along with a young friend of friends, we climbed the trail up a rocky ravine from Kirstenbosch and then walked the length of the mountain tabletop, whence Bob, David and Anne retraced their steps to retrieve the car.

Barbara was to go down in the aerial tram that goes up the mountain from the center city while Jamie and friend hiked quickly down the steep mountain face under the tram. All this so Barbara could help them hail a taxi to get home quickly and take off to see *Ipi N'tombi*, which only they had not yet done. However, the line for the tram was at least half a kilometer long, so Barbara returned to that trail and practically ran down it, knees wobbly at the end. The young people got to the theater on time.

After everyone else had left, Jamie and Barbara went on a short trip to Rorke's Drift and the Isandlwana battlefield, and then drove over to Giants' Castle National Park in the Drakensburg to do some hiking. Jamie would get one more visit, which we made special by scheduling our trip to Madagascar so that he could accompany us, a sort of recompense for having already been away at college and having missed the Israel/Red Sea trip that Annie took with us from Mali.

Before this Christmas visit, however, we had welcomed several personal friends as tourists. At last we were staying in a place they had at least heard of! Even before Barbara had really settled in, they started coming, the first two families for the good reason that they were both constrained by the US school year. My former colleague from Madeira days and his wife, Stuart and Pam Davis, arrived in Pretoria barely two weeks after my arrival and just after Bob had taken off to return to Washington for a meeting of the Binational Commission. About ten days later, Bob's *Harvard Crimson* buddy Phil Boffey and his wife Ronda, with their two young daughters, arrived in Cape Town the first time I did. So I got acquainted with the lay of the land in Pretoria by driving around with Stuart reading a map and telling me which roads to take. In this fashion I was introduced, *inter alia*, to Soweto, and also saw *Ipi N'tombi* for the second time.

Later, after the Davises had rented a car, roles were reversed while Stuart practiced driving on the left in preparation for the their trip through Kwa-Zulu Natal and its game parks and then down the Garden Route along the south coast to Cape Town, where they again stayed with us. Meanwhile, the Boffeys had arrived in that city too. Luckily, Fiesole had four bedrooms, and everyone had a great time discovering the joys of Cape Town and Cape Point together.

After this first spate of visitors, it being mid-August, Bob and I managed to make two short trips up the West Coast to see the flowers carpeting the fields everywhere we looked. The only other time I have seen such a spectacle was in the Big Horns above Sheridan when we took a camping trip in the western United States with Anne and Jamie before we left for Ouagadougou in 1983.

The first family visitor, independent as ever, was Kate, who visited in November. With Bob tied up during the workweek, I, who was still exploring many areas for the first time, enjoyed showing her around. Early in her stay, I returned with her to Pilanesburg Nature Reserve, where she loved the views from the modest cabins on the hill, and saw plenty of animals without the strain of driving all the way to Kruger. We took advantage of the Thanksgiving holiday to go *en famille* to the Drakensburg and the nearer parts of Kwa-Zulu/Natal and then, by special request, Kate and I rode the overnight train from Pretoria to Cape Town. The Blue Train by this time cost a fortune, so we took a first-class compartment on the Trans-Karoo, the regular express train, and Kate sat transfixed during daylight hours by the scenery rolling by. This was just as well, because her traveling companion, me, was recovering from a terrible bout of food-poisoning and spent the day in the upper bunk asleep. By November, the fields-of-flowers season was over, but Kirstenbosch was as wonderful as ever and Kate was able to see many of the other glories of the Cape Floral Kingdom—and its birds.

A duo of important official visitors was waiting in the wings: first the Secretary of State, Madeleine Albright, in December 1997, then President Clinton himself the following March, just a year after Hillary had promised to produce him. The Albright visit turned out to be a grind, mainly because her staff was difficult and sometimes downright rude. It was by far the most unpleasant official visit of our State Department years.

Two defining moments are worth mentioning. The Secretary had agreed to meet with embassy staff and families in the courtyard of the chancery, and according to plan, all hands were gathered there well ahead of time. She kept everyone waiting and then spent about five minutes delivering a few platitudes for the children, but not shaking hands or exchanging a word with any of the parents or embassy employees who had been assembled to meet her. The other low point came when, at Ambassador Joseph's request, Bob was sitting with him at a meeting, which was already in progress, only to be pulled from it because one of her senior staff members, James Rubin, decided he should be there instead. Had I known why I was being summoned with such apparent urgency, I would have refused and stayed in the room. This kind of behavior persisted throughout the visit, and we were all rubbed raw by it.

Fortunately, before the challenge of preparing for the most demanding of all visits, that of the President of the United States, we looked forward to guests whom we knew would be appreciative and would be enchanted by whatever we chose to show them: Daddy (aka "Grandfather") Clay and Newell. They arrived in mid-February to be greeted that evening by a reception for participants in the embassy's Self-Help program at the Pretoria house. Of course, they had had all day to sleep and recover from the long flight in one of the five bedrooms in the old farmhouse.

The next evening, we whisked them to a ballet at the State Theater, probably with dinner in the Opera Cafe beforehand. Then it was off to one of the country's smallest game parks, Tau, on the Botswana border, where they were enchanted by their own little cottage, with a view out over a marsh frequented by colorful birds and the occasional antelope. The game drives were a huge hit, as was just wandering around among the other cottages; they spent an hour or so watching laborers re-thatch one of them. Cheetahs don't live in that environment, so upon our return we visited the DeWildt Cheetah Research Center and saw and learned about them at the breeding area there.

Then it was off to Cape Town, with most of the household staff accompanying us because we would stay through the presidential visit, and there was still no experienced staff (except, happily, the gardening crew) at Fiesole. Oh that Barbara's Mother had still been alive to participate in that one! The hit of their stay was a two-night visit to a new, private game reserve called Bushman's Kloof, a classy operation that had been bought by a foreign operator (and had become much more expensive) by the time we returned to the area in 2011.

There was plenty of game, mostly of the herbivorous kind, like antelopes and giraffes, but the reserve also had numerous pre-European rock paintings in good condition. Getting to them was a bit of a hike, but both Daddy and Newell gamely followed wherever the guide suggested that there was an interesting archaeological feature to be seen. And the evening game drives featured "sundowners," usually consumed from a high point with an excellent view.

Right on the heels of their visit, and coinciding with the presidential visit, came Susie and Jane. They had planned their trip to coincide with spring vacation at whatever school Susie was then teaching, and there was no possibility of changing the dates when the Clintons announced their plans. So with fair warning, the sisters arrived three days before POTUS and FLOTUS. I got them oriented and we saw a few sights together while Bob was totally occupied with planning for the official visit, including seeing to it that all the Cade sisters would be on the guest list for the presidential reception at the ambassador's Residence, of which more later. Cape Town proved the perfect place to leave Jane and Susie on their own—all those arts and crafts and shops!

The next week, the second of the sisters' visit, we three flew back to Pretoria, rented a car, and drove to Honeyguide, a modest private tented lodge on the edge of Kruger, one of several that share animals with the National Park. There Jane and Susie saw the Big Five, at least most of them, and many, many more animals. This natural history expedition was the perfect complement to the diplomatic and urban first week.

Another set of personal visitors proved once again that Foreign Service families abroad, like Peace Corps volunteers, help to broaden the horizons of Americans as well as of friends they meet overseas. These guests were Fred Tilton, one of Barbara's high school beaus, and his wife. They are a couple who has lived in Mariemont all their lives and whose prior idea of a big trip was to drive to Florida. In thanking us, Fred wrote, "We never would have even thought about going to South Africa if it had not been for you guys." Except for a brief visit with us in Pretoria, they traveled by themselves in South Africa and Zimbabwe, and had a wonderful time. *Inter alia*, they reported that "We did just about wear out the windshield wipers every time we had to make a turn, but for the most part we did all right driving on the wrong side of the road. . . . A baboon stole my submarine sandwich right out from under my nose at Cape Point. . . ." The letter finished by reporting that on their last evening, they had a picnic at a famous winery "alongside a picturesque stream while the African sunset reflected off the Cape Mountains in the background."[15]

A more experienced traveler, who was on the whole unfamiliar with Africa but wanted to see the Cape Floral Kingdom, was Ruth McVey, a scholar of Indonesia who had retired to a farm in Tuscany. We had a delightful time showing her Cape Town and arranged for her to join a tour, which she

---

[15] [F]rederic Tilton e-mail to bbpringle, 6/24/98.

very much enjoyed, up Cape Province's West Coast.

FLOTUS and POTUS at Last

The Big Visit finally happened in March, 1998. The Clintons ended up spending four days in South Africa on a trip which included five other African countries (Ghana, Uganda, Rwanda, Botswana and Senegal). The fact that Hillary had preceded the President, and no doubt had some sensible ideas about what he should do, was a big help for us. Once again, we gave a pre-event dinner at Fiesole, this time chili and cornbread, for those, especially the South Africans, who were helping us with the details.[16]

The most important event was, of course, Clinton's

President Clinton and three of the Cade sisters—Susan, Barbara and Jane—plus Bob, at the end of the big reception.

[16] It is funny how little things can live on. In 2011, when we revisited Cape Town, we were dying to stay at the Cape Grace Hotel, but could not afford its by-now astronomical rates. However, their staff remembered us from the Clinton visit, and gave us the diplomatic rate—to which, being retired, we were no longer automatically entitled—a big saving. (On a visit there in 2003 with a National War College visit the group had also gotten a big discount, but that had nothing to do with me.)

meeting with Mandela, and once again, the Libya-Locherbie issue raised its head. We knew well ahead of time that something funny might be going on, because our Consul in Cape Town, April Glaspie, had reported that the private four-engine aircraft of the Saudi Foreign Minister, Prince Bandar, had been parked at the Cape Town airport. We surmised that Bandar was trying to inject himself into the Clinton-Mandela one-on-one meeting, and Washington instructed us vehemently to tell the South Africans that we would not stand for such a thing. We did our best. But when the big moment arrived, Bandar was there! Disaster! Madiba had done it again! [17]

Our National Security Adviser, Sam Berger, normally a jovial soul, emerged from the meeting looking furious. So did Susan Rice, then Assistant Secretary of State for African Affairs. We were shocked and I was personally alarmed. Who was going to get blamed? Well, they wouldn't go after the ambassador, a prominent black political appointee; that was for sure. Who else but his Deputy, who, after all, was charged with managing "details"? As soon as possible, I drafted a long telegram to Washington explaining how "we" had done our best to keep it from happening. Days went by without a reply.

Clinton addressed the South African Parliament on March 26, and after that Ambassador Joseph hosted a reception for the MPs at his Residence, just down the hill from us. Among other duties, Barbara and I were in charge of a choir from the Simon Estes Music High School[18] in Cape Town; the students would gather at our house before singing at the event. But what to do with Barbara's sisters, who were visiting? They had no security clearances, but Mary Beth Leonard, an old friend who was the relevant "event officer" and one of a crowd of FSOs who had been brought in from other posts to help with the visit, said don't worry, no problem, your sisters can help out as needed. Our unbiased

---

[17] At least one reporter, Lynne Duke, figured out that something had gone awry although she didn't know quite what; see Lynne Duke, "Clinton Visit: Mandela Sets the Tone," *International Herald Tribune*, March 30, 1998, in scrapbook 8 with much other press coverage of the visit.

[18] Initiated by and named for the same American opera singer also famous in Durban, as mentioned in the previous chapter.

opinion of Mary Beth was "This lady will go places," and she has; she is currently (2017) US Ambassador to the African Union in Addis Ababa, her second ambassadorship after . . . Mali! (our old home).

And help the sisters did, mainly by making zillions of sandwiches for the young choristers, who had come directly from school, and later making sure they walked down to the Residence on time and in order. Then Jane decided to take personal charge of making sure that the Simon Estes High School guest book, which they had brought along, was signed by *everyone* at the event. That of course meant POTUS and FLOTUS, so Jane, carrying the book, got to chat with both of them. Later Barbara and her sisters were photographed with Bill in the middle, looking devilish, with his hands disappearing behind their backs—an appropriate memento to wave at husbands back home. All in all it was a lovely, relaxed event and I think everyone there enjoyed it.

On March 27 the South Africans put on a state dinner at Vergelegen,[19] a famous, early eighteenth-century wine estate east of Cape Town, known for its magnificent old camphor trees imported from the Dutch East Indies (Indonesia) three centuries previously. It had recently been purchased by the Anglo-American (De Beers, etc.) combine, and its neglected winery was being rehabilitated with money to spare. On an advance tour, Barbara and I were shown around by the wine master, who explained among other things that screw caps are by far the best closing devices for fine wine; artificial corks are next best, and real cork is the worst, because it rots with age, and is the major cause of wine spoilage. When you taste a wine, he told us, it should be to see if it is "corked," i.e., spoiled by a bad cork, not whether you like the kind or quality of wine it is—you should know that already (Department of Life Lessons Learned in the Foreign Service).

The sisters were not invited to this one, but Barbara was.

---

[19] *"Vergelegen"* means "located far away," from Cape Town, on a hill where Dutch East India Company ships approaching its port, possibly with prying officials on board, could be seen well before they arrived. The story has it that the governor-general who built it was notoriously corrupt, and wanted plenty of advance warning so he would have time to hide evidence of his wrongdoing. It is not *that* far away by modern standards.

So they helped the visit another way—by being fashion advisers as she picked out an appropriate outfit for the big bash. It was a silky black skirt with a spaghetti strap black top and a purple sueded top—with great big shoulder pads. I have worn it perhaps twice since, but I felt very elegant then.

The dinner, hosted by Mandela for 650 guests, was unforgettable. It was held in a huge tent, near the camphor trees, and the Cape Doctor did his windy thing:

It was really fun, much more so than often dry official functions. The ceiling of the tent had stars painted on it and a light machine was projecting more stars. Sounds corny, but was really very effective. Behind the head table was a huge mural on canvas of African wildlife. Each table, rather than having a floral centerpiece, had three crossed spears (à la Zulu) with a lantern hanging from them. That was a help the three times the power went out, due to the wind, which caused the tent roof to groan and flap against the poles and made us all wonder whether it would stay up. I assume that the Secret Service was having fits, but inside, people just laughed and Clinton even made a joke about the tent during his toast. . . . Among Mandela's invited guests were all the Misses South Africa during his term of office and their escorts, so we had some fancy outfits and long bare legs to ogle—this was not a staid affair.

The menu, decorated with an artist's impression of a khoi (Hottentot) herder, featured "Duo of Karoo beef medallions with Ostrich fillet and Kalahari Truffle Mousse enhanced with a Rooibos and honey infused jus" and was designed to reflect the style and ochre coloring of the region's famous rock art.[20]

The invited Misses South Africa were a reminder that our hosts were well aware of the Monica Lewinsky imbroglio, news of which had broken only weeks previously. The more raucous press coverage suggested that the Clintons were visiting Africa to escape all the "Zippergate" fuss, but it got

[20] Barbara e-mail to Dear Family, "Update on Pringle News," April 14, 1998.

worse. One cartoon showed a distraught official exclaiming, "Oh No! Please . . . No traditional Dancing" as Clinton leers at bare-breasted maidens oscillating in the background.[21] The worst was from Zapiro, showing "Air Force One," drawn to resemble a giant flying penis, and a voice coming from inside it, "Trust me, Hillary, our African trip will divert attention from all that other stuff."[22]

Low comedy aside, it was a useful and well-executed visit, but its complexity and extravagance were absurdly excessive. The President's total entourage numbered almost 1,000 and required Air Force One plus two more big aircraft just for the VIPs. There were three Cabinet members, sixteen members of Congress, a large business contingent, civil rights activists, prominent donors, and of course hordes of press. Five helicopters for internal travel (to Robben Island, for example) arrived in giant C5A transports, the presidential chopper plus four identical decoys, to confuse and hence foil any would be-attacker. In flight they resembled a swarm of giant metallic bugs.

At least eighty sorties of USAF aircraft were required for the South Africa stops alone. Bits and pieces of equipment remained for weeks after the captains and kings had departed—a communication console of some kind in the ambassador's driveway, and a broken down USAF plane at the Johannesburg airport awaiting a spare part. The whole show cost tens of millions of dollars.[23]

A week later we still hadn't heard anything from Washington about the Bandar episode. Finally I called Johnny Carson, the principal Assistant Secretary of State for African Affairs, and asked him what was going on. He replied " Oh that . . . Bob, you don't have to worry. We knew that Bandar was going to

---

[21] Newspaper unclear, "Saturday Focus," March 28/29, 1998.

[22] It is not clear from our copy which of the several papers that Zapiro drew for ran this.

[23] Many details of the cost of presidential travel are still classified—Why? A 2015 report in the *Washington Post* discussing the cost of Obama's travel said that the Government Accountability Office had reported the total cost of Clinton's 1998 trip to Africa as "at least 42.7 million." ("When Presidents Travel Abroad," *Washington Post*," Outlook, January 25, 2015.)

be there before the visit."

Well!! Who might "we" have been? Why the very convincing public display of anger by people not noted for their forensic skills? I did not want to press him for details, but it seems that the Bureau of Near Eastern Affairs was in the know, but hadn't told anyone else, at least certainly not the Africa Bureau (headed by Susan Rice, Carson's boss) or the White House (Sam Berger). It was the most bizarre event of my official career, bar none, happy as I was at the outcome. The icing on this comic cake came much later when I was told that the Mandela-Bandar "meddling" had, in fact, contributed significantly to reaching a settlement with the Libyans.

Family Milestones

The period following the Clintons' visit was busy for us personally. Not exactly personal, but an echo of the Cade extended family story, was our accompanying ex-President Jimmy Carter and Mrs. Carter on a one-day visit north of Pretoria to visit a grandson who was an education volunteer in the second Peace Corps group to be sent to South Africa.

Volunteers came from miles around and it was hard to tell who was more proud, the young grandson or his grandfather. Susie and Jane had told Barbara about a video Mrs. Carter sent to Kathy's surprise 50th birthday celebration, and Barbara told her how much that gesture had been appreciated. After that, Mrs. Carter seemed inclined to follow her as a guide and Barbara had to make a real effort to be sure that she was introduced to as many other guests as possible.

In mid-April, 1998, just after the Carters had left, Annie called us with the news that Bob's mother Helena had developed a urinary tract infection and was gradually losing strength. The State Department paid for Bob's trip home to see her, but by the time he arrived she was in a near coma, and there was no telling when the end would come. She would have been one hundred years old in December. He finally had to return to South Africa, and she died not long afterwards. By this time she had become quite comfortable at the Woodbine Nursing Home, although she would no doubt have been irked at not reaching the century mark. As of 2017, three of her books on Western History—*We Pointed Them North*, *A Bride Goes West* and *War on Powder River* remain in print, and the first two are likely to remain so indefinitely. We still receive small royalty checks from permissions to use excerpts in other books, primarily history textbooks.

The next month we were both back in the United States for a grand family occasion. On May 9, 1998, Anne Pringle and David Johnson were married in the old town of Beaufort, NC, not far from the family summer house on Bogue Banks. Our early lobbying for a ceremony at Christ Church in Alexandria, before Barbara came out to South Africa, had never gotten off the ground due to the exigencies of David and Anne's academic schedules. But the wedding in the Ann Street United Methodist Church in Beaufort and reception afterwards in a courtyard between several historic houses was a smash hit, with friends and family attending from far and wide. Annie's wedding dress was made from hand-woven silk we had purchased in Kelantan, Malaysia, in 1965, and the get-away car was an antique Packard belonging to David's family.

The happy couple didn't get away immediately, because they wanted to say good-by to their many out-of-town guests.

Anne and David, just married, preparing to leave their wedding reception in the antique Packard that was the getaway car.

They did so at a lovely stop-by-before-you-have-to-leave-for-the-airport brunch on the deck of 105 Pecan Court the day after the wedding, and from there they left for Tuscany. Annie's reaction to the trip was "I understand the point of a honeymoon better now. It's a space and time apart from anyone else and away from the mundane realities of home (no dishes to do)." They visited Florence, Siena, "the countryside filled with olive groves and grapevines," Pisa, the Cinque Terre, and Assisi. And, since the groom has a strong interest in math and the bride is a botanist, "[we] had a good time when we discovered Fibonacci's monument in the adjoining cemetery—apparently he was from Pisa. Fibonacci was a big mathematician, but his formulas are also used by many plant pathologists."[24]

The family, except for us who couldn't make another trip back to the US so soon, convened again in June when Jamie was awarded his PhD in physical oceanography at MIT. The most important of his guests was his Grandfather Cade. Probably influenced by long years of watching scientists at work at the Taft Sanitary Engineering Center, in which he had held increasingly senior administrative positions all his working years in Cincinnati, he had always hoped that one of his daughters would be a scientist. Kathy came nearest, but finally wound up graduating from Radcliffe with a degree in history of science. Jamie's older cousin Heidi had become a science teacher, but now here was a genuine research scientist for the first time in the family.

For Jamie, Grandfather's presence was special, because Jamie and Christopher are the only grandsons, and Jamie being the first and much older had long enjoyed a special closeness to him. Kathy and Annie completed the family cheering section, and all had to endure an especially long wait before the actual commencement because of security for President Clinton, who was the main speaker on the occasion.

A few months later, ensconced at Scripps Oceanographic Institute near San Diego for a post-doc year, Jamie wrote us about the work he was doing, presenting a good snapshot of what research in his field means today:

---

[24] Anne Pringle e-mail to Robert Pringle.

The numerical model I have been refining [from] last June til the travels started has progressed to the point that I trust the results have some bearing on a real ocean, maybe even Georges Bank, which it is supposed to resemble—so now I have to start doing science with it. I have been studying how the little copepods, cod larvae, and other wee beasties get swept on and off the bank by the tides, and how they can be clever in their sinking and floating to get on or off the bank, as their needs require—they are much too weak to swim horizontally the many miles needed to move off the bank, but they can float and sink without great effort, and thus can play the same games as a balloonist. This will result in two papers, a physical paper and a biological paper. . . . The bio paper will be harder—I will have to introduce some mathematical techniques that are old hat to us physics types, but are less familiar to biologists.[25]

Anne, majoring in botany and genetics, and preparing her thesis in mycology, was not far behind him. Still in the throes of doing her research, she faced a major challenge: Her thesis adviser abruptly decided to move to the University of Virginia, leaving Duke University, so it thought, free to plough up a field which had been his for long-term botanical experiments in order to begin construction of an art museum on the site. But Anne was near finishing a multi-year project in that very soil, and suddenly her lifetime training by example in diplomatic skills became as important as her scientific knowledge.

She called on the University President, Nan Keohane, who was "gracious to me, wanted to know what I needed to finish my work, seemed willing to delay the start date of the museum for a few months if it meant saving my dissertation, etc." A post-doctoral student accompanying her, who had hoped to use the site for many years, angrily announced that not doing so for a longer term in her case would ruin her whole career and left the room in a huff. Our daughter "shook Nan's hand and thanked her ("Being the daughter of a diplomat, I'm finding out, has MANY advantages. . .)."[26] And she asked for, and got, Bob's help

[25] Jamie Pringle e-mail to bbpringle, October 15, 1998.
[26] Anne Pringle e-mail to Robert Pringle, "Re: bulldozers," November 17, 1998.

in composing the perfect letter making her formal request to President Keohane for extension of the museum construction start. She ultimately presented the results of her experiment as her dissertation. So it was already clear that we, historians both, had hatched not one, but two professional scientists, for reasons that are a bit too complex to unravel, maybe and maybe not including the stimulus of life in the Foreign Service.

Visiting and Helping Neighbors:
Lesotho, Swaziland, Mozambique and Namibia

In the months ahead there was time for more visits to the embassies we served in nearby countries, including Lesotho and Swaziland, both almost totally surrounded by South Africa, plus Namibia, Mozambique and Botswana. The first two countries, as well as Botswana, owed their existence to pressure from Christian missionaries eager to protect their flocks, often weakened by the impact of Shaka Zulu's expansion, from the evils of ruthless Boer control. Namibia, previously German Southwest Africa, was another story, as was Mozambique, a former Portuguese possession.

On such visits, I normally spent a day consulting with embassy staff, making sure that they were satisfied with the ministrations of Big Brother Pretoria. I would also check into the state of relations between their country and South Africa, which usually resembled in varying degrees that between Mexico and the United States. I always left time to explore the local countryside. All of these countries could be reached by road or short flights, and getting to them was often instructive.

Lesotho (population about two million, area slightly smaller than Maryland) was the most accessible. You could reach it by driving for half a day straight south from Pretoria, as I had done seventeen years previously.[27] Or you could proceed east from Cape Town along the "Garden Route," then angle north paralleling the Indian Ocean coast until you encountered the Drakensburg mountain massif, with which Lesotho is more or less coterminous. It is supposed to have the highest low elevation of any country in the world. Economic dependence

---

[27] See Chapter 8.

on South Africa is symbolized by the location of its capital, Maseru, on the border between the two countries. We stayed there with old friends from our Philippine days, Jack and Carol Urner.[28]

Maseru in 1997 was a mess, overcrowded and smothered in coal smoke. To escape it and see something of the interior, we went on a horse trek up through the rugged countryside. Our mounts stumbled on the narrow rock trail and although they never fell, this mode of transportation did not amuse Johannes, who was clearly yearning for his Toyota Camry. We climbed to a point where it was possible to stare down from the escarpment into South Africa, and we stopped at a weaving coop to buy nice handicrafts along the way.[29] Lesotho was already becoming less dependent on labor exportation, thanks to new income from selling the water originating in its mountainous heights to South Africa. But at the time of our visit trouble was just around the corner. I wrote home:

The political situation has been quite unstable and, like Swaziland, Lesotho suffers from the fact that it no longer gets a lot of outside help just because it's surrounded by wicked South Africa; instead, bright young Lesothans are now drained off into a South African labor market which is insatiably thirsty for educated blacks.[30]

Not long after our visit there was a coup d'état led by opposition leaders after their party lost an election. This precipitated a badly botched South African intervention early

---

[28] Jack was killed not long after our visit in an accident on the road to Pretoria; Carol survived. Their car was hit head-on by a car speeding toward them in the wrong lane. As we kept telling our embassy employees, South African roads were more dangerous than the much-hyped crime problem, precisely because they were good enough to encourage reckless driving.

[29] This coop had been set up by Carol Cassidy, whom we later met again at another workshop, in Laos, where she was training weavers, this time in silk, not wool, to revive a local handicraft. The covering on the rocking chairs in the living room and two silk hangings on our walls come from that enterprise. The long narrow wool hangings with African scenes on them come from the Lesotho workshop.

[30] E-letter home, n.d., but at the time of our visit to Grahamstown.

in 1999, resulting in chaos and extensive damage. As bullets flew, our young ambassador, Kathy Peterson, got to spend quality time under her dining room table with our Army Attaché, who had been sent down to figure out what was going on, leading to a widely rumored if possibly imagined romance. Later the country enjoyed some success by remaining one of the few still to recognize Nationalist China, thereby attracting a fair amount of Taiwanese investment.

Swaziland, an absolute monarchy with a population of less than a million, is the other country surrounded by South Africa, except for an area bordering Mozambique. It was a pleasant, peaceful place with a respectable tourism sector encouraged by excellent handicrafts (*inter alia*, the glass animals which Annie now has) and a pocket-sized game park where you could approach the elephants on foot, however unsafely. In addition, for those lucky enough to be there at the right time (we never were), there was the famous "Reed Dance," in which the well-born young ladies of the realm danced for the Queen Mother clad only in reed skirts, so that she could decide if they qualified to become royal wives. (This may have been the "native dance" referred to by the irreverent cartoonist during the Clinton visit as something to keep Bill away from.)

There were also a number of factories and big sugar cane plantations. Any diplomat dying of boredom while assigned to Mbabane, Swaziland's capital—as our friend, Alan McKee, the ambassador, did not seem to be—could get to Pretoria or Durban in half a day's drive over good roads, not to mention Kruger Park, just to the north. But the political situation was not entirely healthy:

Beneath the formal parliamentary façade, the king and his family still run everything. He is a nice young man but was installed at the age of fifteen before he had a chance to get much education. His mother is still very much the eminence grise behind the throne. He has twenty-two wives and the extended royal family is a substantial proportion of the population.[31]

Political parties were not allowed, but labor unions were.

---

[31] Bob e-mail to Family, "Latest Travels," no date but during June, 1998.

They had problems with the royal family and were being supported by their South African counterparts, which would lead to trouble later on.

We continued to Mozambique after our first trip to Swaziland. It was back to the big leagues: Mozambique is large (the size of California) and was getting more important by the minute. However, as soon as we crossed the border, the scars of decades of anti-colonial struggle and civil war were everywhere visible, in the form of overgrown and abandoned Portuguese plantations, ruined small towns, and apparent depopulation.

For the moment attention was focused on the country's mineral wealth:

Mozambique is now in the throes of a major minerals rush, mainly from South Africa. It has just about everything—gas, probably oil, huge amounts of hydro power, high-quality coal deposits, emeralds, probably diamonds (not that South Africa needs more of them), endless beaches made of sand full of minerals like titanium, even timber in the north, and vast agricultural potential. It's about two-thirds the size of SA with less than a third (twelve million) of the population. Politically things have pretty well settled down although the Renamo and Frelimo factions still control their respective territories at the local level. And economic policy is very much on track. South Africa is all abuzz about development of the "Maputo Corridor" to Pretoria-Jo'burg—since it is by far the closest port to the SA metropolis, only five hours by road straight east.

We stayed at the grand old colonial hotel, the Polana, this time full of white South Africans on a motor rally. Indeed, South African capitalists are back in full force along with tourists, yachties and beach-seekers. The unfinished buildings which dotted the downtown area on my previous visit eighteen years ago [in 1980] are mostly finished and many of the lovely old colonial buildings like the grandiose railroad station (designed by the same architect who did the Eiffel Tower) have been refurbished. The famous local seafood is quite cheap, notably the prawns, known in SA as "L.M." prawns, for Lorenzo Marques, the Portuguese name for Maputo. But the currency is still the metical, at 1200 to one rand, delivered in filthy notes ranging down to 50 meticals [less than one-half US cent]. Johannes tried his hand at the [Polana's] casino, but being used to other neighboring countries (like Swaziland) whose currency is at par with the rand, he was defeated by the complexity of the money and came away convinced that he was being cheated. (He is Pedi, and speaks Northern Soto, close to the Southern Soto spoken in Lesotho). I managed to catch scabies at the Polana. [32]

South Africa's growing economic presence led to an April Fool's joke in a South African newspaper to the effect that Pretoria had bought Mozambique for $12 billion, which fooled at least one wire service into running it. [33]

At about the time of our visit, President Mandela married the widow of the former Mozambican president, Graca Machel, with whom he had been living for some time. Bishop Tutu, holy jokester as always, said, "She made an honest man out of him." Mandela retorted, "Now you won't shout at me and say I am setting a bad example."[34]

Namibia (population two million, about half the size of Alaska) was another requisite stop, partly because Embassy Windhoek had been having staffing problems. Our good friend Peter Kaestner was the DCM there and his wife Kimberly was an embassy communicator. The country itself was doing well, although unrest continued in the Caprivi Strip, a peculiar relic of German rule,[35] and we couldn't go to that region.

During their long and much denounced occupation of German Southwest Africa, as it was until World War I, the South Africans had tried hard to rule respectably, and never dared to introduce apartheid. The Afrikaners who subsequently fought there against Sam Nujoma and his SWAPO freedom fighters adored the place for its vast open spaces and beautiful scenery. Since the country achieved independence

---

[32] Bob e-mail, "Latest Travels."
[33] Ibid.
[34] Bob e-mail to Dear Family, July 19, 1998.
[35] The Caprivi Strip is the narrow extension of Namibia between Angola and Zambia in the north and Botswana to the south, which the Germans controlled in the colonial era. See "A Southern African Interlude" in Chapter 13.

in 1990, they have continued to go back to Namibia, as it now is, on vacation, as have the Germans, who arrive in swarms every August.[36] Namibia's rich diamond sands have helped to keep the country relatively prosperous. After serving as Namibia's founding president, Nujoma, no doubt influenced by the Mandela model, settled in as a benign elder statesman, a role he is still playing at this writing (2017).

We wanted to see Namibia's famous coast and Peter advised us to take an unpaved, more direct, but less-traveled route than the main highway, which we did. Our rental car, picked up at the Windhoek Airport, came with no gas gauge, but a stern warning about going too fast on slippery gravel roads. After hours of driving through increasingly arid but beautiful country, we had yet to see a filling station or any mileage signs, and feared we might be running out of gas. Finally we saw a building under construction and pulled in to ask for help. It was a German-owned game ranch being expanded, and its owners were happy to sell us lunch as well as fuel, and to assure us that we were nearing our destination.

When we finally reached it, a small port town called Walvis Bay, we had one of the most memorable evenings of our traveling career. "The highlight of our stay was a delicious dinner at a picturesque restaurant, called The Raft, built on pilings over the ocean. The management turns on floodlights, which attract tiny fish, which attract hundreds of gulls and pelicans to float just outside the dining area and entertain guests while they eat. And to our delight, our place to stay for the evening, called The Courtyard, turned out to be a small private guest house, not a Marriott."[37]

The Skeleton Coast of Namibia, stretching both north and south from Walvis Bay, features spectacular sand dunes bordering a rough, cold, almost harborless ocean. The inhabitants of this apparently waterless terrain are amazing. As fog rolls in at night, the Tok-tok beetle crawls to the top of a dune and points his chitin-encased posterior in the air. Water condenses on it and rolls down into his mouth. Even more

---

[36] At one minor game park, the dining hall had a large portrait of Kaiser Wilhelm on the wall. A German tourist noted to us admiringly, "That is something we are not allowed to do in Germany!"

[37] Barbara e-mail to Kathy Cade *et al.*, November 3, 1998.

extraordinary is the Welwitschia plant, which Anne had told us not to miss. It resembles a large, hotel lobby-type plant with only two long, sloppy, spiny leaves, that has been hit by a bomb. But it can live to be 2,000 years old in the desert sand, and it is on the Namibian coat of arms (and banknotes) as a symbol of survivability.

Proceeding north from Walvis Bay, there are a few other picturesque German coastal towns, great seafood, and, further up the coast than we went, some famous desert-dwelling elephants, bigger than most elephants but with short, stubby tusks. As noted earlier, they are similar to the desert elephants of Mali, and like them migrate seasonally, but over even longer distances.[38] Southward along the coast, one encounters the now ghost town of Kolmanskop and a restricted area where diamonds are still mined, which we never visited, but wish we had. Travel in these places in slow.

Namibia has many other attractions, including Etosha, a park to rival Kruger. In its dry, sub-desert topography, game clusters around a huge natural salt lake as well as numerous water holes. The most famous rest camp there is Okaukeujo, with a waterhole right in front of the cabins, so that overnight guests can emerge and observe game all day and in the shadows of the night, especially if the moon is near full.

We would return there in 2011 when we visited Marilyn Mattke and traveled with her to the Caprivi Strip and Botswana as well. Marilyn scored a coup, and reserved us an A-frame with a second-story porch during our 2011 trip, and we spent a lot of our time going in and out to that porch, checking out, among the more common zebras, springbok, and gemsbok (aka oryx, the horse-sized ones with long, swept-back horns), black rhinos, a nursery herd of elephants with cute small babies, and elegant giraffes—all coming in to drink. Later, when the rains start, the animals spread out across the park, especially in the direction of the large seasonal lake, and are harder to see.

---

[38] See Chapter 11, "Desert Elephants."

A Whiff of Terror: the East African Bombings

On August 7, 1998, terrorists bombed our embassies in Dar es Salaam, Tanzania, and Nairobi, Kenya. Pretoria was the nearest US Embassy that could send immediate help, including a team of medical and security personnel, and the South African Air Force ferried them to Nairobi on one of its aging Boeing 707s. Ambassador Joseph was away, so I represented the embassy at its departure. What a scene! The Air Force was still all white, and reminiscent in its rough-and-readiness of something out of the Boer War. When the crew couldn't get the plane started by conventional means, they affixed a wad of oily rags to a long pole, set it on fire, stuck it into the engine, and (I guess) hit the starter switch. Notwithstanding loud coughs and clouds of smoke, this worked; they took off and got to Dar several hours before any other American help. We were all very proud, as were the South Africans, even though only a few wounded were ready to be moved on this early evacuation flight.

Just a few days later, the new Planet Hollywood restaurant in Cape Town was bombed, apparently by a local group, killing one person and injuring twenty-four. The perpetrators claimed it was in retaliation for US actions in Afghanistan and Sudan. This immediately led to an internal embassy debate over the extent to which the South African Muslim community, in Cape Town and elsewhere, was a growing security threat. Our Consul General in Cape Town, April Glaspie, thought it was, differing strenuously from others in Pretoria. I do not recall that this sudden injection of the not-yet War on Terror into our midst caused us major concern, certainly not as much as the old, familiar crime problem.

At almost the same time as the East African bombings, we received nine badly shaken Peace Corps evacuees from Boma, a town on the lower Congo River in Zaire, now Congo. They had been working on a vaccination project as part of a small experimental program which sent experienced volunteers into difficult places for only six months. Difficult it certainly was, and before long rebel Tutsis, at this point fighting the Congolese, flew in from the east and captured the city. When the hotel where the Peace Corps evacuees were staying was occupied by troops hostile to everybody, the volunteers took a local riverboat downriver to rendezvous with a Caltex oil company barge, but it wasn't there, so they were stranded in the jungle. Eventually an oil company helicopter appeared and took them to Angola.

But since Angola's own civil war had just flared up, they ended up with us, in South Africa, with nothing but the clothes on their backs. We invited them to a welcoming barbecue (*braai*) for newly arrived families, featuring big steaks which they loved, causing even the vegetarian PCV to break her own rules.

This was on a Friday, part of a fairly average week. On Wednesday we had gone to a diplomatic dinner for Yasser Arafat. On Thursday, we heard future president Thabo Mbkeki expound on one of his favorite subjects, the African Renaissance. On Saturday, it was an opera, *Don Giovanni*, at the Pretoria State Theater. The following Monday we hosted a reception for sixty-five South African "young leaders" selected by USIS for an exchange program; the Wednesday after that was a farewell for a couple that had done a fine job in our administrative section, and then (on Sunday) a dessert and coffee plus slides in honor of our friend Bruce Beehler, author of *A Naturalist in New Guinea*, for the Pretoria Bird Club. [39]

Even Fidel Visited Cape Town

In September, 1998, Fidel Castro addressed the South African parliament. According to our guidance from Washington, the US Ambassador could not attend, but nothing was said about the DCM. It was an opportunity not to be missed. The galleries were packed with communists and other radicals, many of them wearing red scarves. On the floor, members of the Nationalist Party, mainly white Afrikaners, assumed positions of acute boredom, many of them pretending to sleep.

Fidel surprised everyone. He appeared older than anyone expected and somewhat frail. Instead of the

[39] Barbara e-mail to Dear Daddy and Newell and Kate, n.d., but also late 1998.

expected revolutionary war cries, he launched into a long, seemingly whimsical recitation of South Africa's economic accomplishments, and how well it had done compared to other African countries. Much of this had of course been accomplished by the former regime, and after a few minutes the snoozing Boers stopped pretending to sleep and started calling out, "Hoor, hoor!" (Hear, Hear!) after each new positive statistic cited. The young radicals in the galleries must have been sorely disappointed.[40] Meanwhile a couple of my diplomatic colleagues asked me if my presence meant we were about to recognize Cuba.

Combining Travel with Reporting

Traveling to Cape Town we often chose a route to learn about a specific issue of growing official interest. A case in point was the onset of HIV/AIDS. At first everyone had assumed, or hoped, that the disease was primarily a Central African problem. But by this time it was casting a shadow over our most important aid project in South Africa, a $30 million, seven-year effort intended to create a model for the improvement of health services in previously ignored, black-inhabited rural areas, especially the former "Bantustans." The project was located in the Eastern Cape, Mandela's home province, and as we drove there through some of prettiest scenery in the country we were constantly reminded of Alan Paton's *Cry, the Beloved Country* and the road from Ixtopo (which we drove through) into the hills, "lovely beyond any singing of it."

The official US assumption had been that a relatively well-off country (compared to most in Africa) should be able to carry much of the financial burden of the project. So USAID offered no bricks and mortar, nor significant cash, only technical support, training and equipment. Most victims of AIDS were dying, technically, from some "ordinary" disease, in many cases tuberculosis, but in unprecedented numbers.

[40] "Family Letter" e-mail, October 17, 1998. My admission pass for the event, dated September 4, 1998, is for an address by Fidel Castro Ruz. I had no idea that "Castro" was not his only last name; "Ruz" is his maternal family name and his use of it, in addition to Castro, his paternal family name, follows Spanish custom.

A rural school and its staff, flourishing in part because of assistance from the Peace Corps volunteer in the middle of the photo.

Fearful of the mass stigmatization that would result, the South African authorities refused to publicize the extent to which the real cause was AIDS. In a rural clinic, the only evidence we saw that they were aware of it was small boxes of free condoms, discreetly displayed in secluded corners. In fact the relevant health budget was already on the way to being overwhelmed. A section heading in the report I wrote read "HIV/AIDS: The Telephone Pole that Could Break the Camel's Back."

The problems of this Xhosa [Khosa] heartland are symptomatic of South Africa's transformation and not unique to this area. Perceived from this local level it is hard to see how the government will be able to meet the challenge without devoting more resources to its reform efforts.[41]

---

[41] March 18, 1999, "Eastern Cape Health Project Trip—Context and Impressions" Pretoria 3797, [unclassified], sensitive." (This was a standard unclassified cable; the addition of the informal "sensitive" caption was simply to alert readers to the fact that it was just that, although not sufficiently so to be classified.)

The HIV/AIDS danger was not fully recognized for several more years, thanks in no small part to the delusional policies of Mandela's about-to-be successor, Thabo Mbeki, and the scourge was to become much worse.

At about the same time, I wrote another report based on a visit to Peace Corps volunteers working to improve math and science teaching in farm schools, meaning schools for black laborers living and working on white, Afrikaner-owned farms like the ones we had seen in Wakkerstroom. We visited five such schools around the towns of Piet Retief, Ermelo and Volksrust in Mpumalanga Province, northeast of Pretoria. Guided by the PCVs who worked in them and accompanied by the Peace Corps Country Director, Moses Turner, we found stunning variations.

In one, both the farmer/land owner and his wife enthusiastically supported the school. He had worked for a development NGO and his wife was a teacher at the school, which had a science facility equipped by the Swedish government. Another school we visited had such a good reputation that students were flocking to it from the conventional government school in a small nearby town (Perdekop).

In yet another, the farmer felt that school had gotten too big, resented not being able to control it, and had successfully blocked the construction of badly needed teachers' quarters. He was a white-mustachioed caricature of an evil Boer. When he heard of our visit he came down in his "bakkie" (pickup-truck) to check us out. At another school, a volunteer told us he had had to leave three schools because of hostile farmer-owners.

All the farm schools we saw were primitive by western standards—one we described as "a wattle and daub physical wreck with broken windows and no water or electricity"— probably above average for sub-Saharan Africa generally. The report concluded:

Peace Corps Volunteers working with these schools face highly variable if always daunting conditions. Physical conditions, quality of staff, community support and the attitudes of landlord-farmers—all range from hope inspiring to downright depressing. The volunteers, deeply appreciated by their

*communities, reflect great credit on the US as they bike along
rural tracks, bringing hope and change to the most neglected
sector of South African education.*[42]

Only a small minority of South Africans attended farm
schools; thanks to the vast relocations of earlier years, the
majority were in conventional government schools. Had this
not been so, the continued dominance of agriculture by white
farm owners as late as 1999 would have posed a far more
immediate political problem.

Barbara's Two Interesting Jobs and Our Last Visitors

I had begun tutoring three American sixth-grade girls,
who were attending a local school in Pretoria, in American
history almost as soon as I arrived, with periodic vacations
for them when we were in Cape Town or otherwise traveling.
Using a textbook recommended by Potomac's lower-school
teachers, I enjoyed this biweekly task and learned more about
the education scene in South Africa, as well as keeping my
professional skills honed and earning a pittance.

Two more challenging jobs materialized in the second year.
The first was teaching our Marine security guards American
History, part of a program administered by Central Texas
University (CTU) whereby they could earn credit toward
a college degree. The first attempts of the then current
detachment of Marines had been something of a disaster, due
to an unreasonable requirement set by CTU that any teacher
must have, as the minimum qualification, a Bachelor's degree
with a major in the subject being taught. Hence, they had had
to reject an engineer who volunteered to teach a beginning
Algebra course and a journalist who was willing to teach
English composition.

So they had hired the local girlfriend of one of the Marines,
who had majored in English at a local university, to teach them
English Composition. Unfortunately, she brought with her all
the rigidity of European educational practice. She flunked the

---

[42] "South Africa: A Farm School Journal," Cape Town 000726, June 10,
1999, unclassified, marked "not for internet distribution."

brightest student in the detachment because he was too often late to class, a complete misunderstanding of the duties and obligations of Marine watch standers, and the detachment did not know where to find their next "professor." Bob asked how I, with my BA and MA both in history, would like to take on an American History course.

My work was complicated by great differences in aptitude on the part of my eight students, in addition to which all of them worked ten to twelve hours a day or night. As I explained in a letter home:

In these circumstances, I decided exactly what I wanted them to learn, taught it to them in class (which we tape recorded for the two who had to be on duty during each class), reviewed it with sample questions on review days, and tested it on the tests. No tricks, no sneaky questions that we hadn't covered in class. They said they wished their high school teachers had been like me.[43]

I enjoyed it, got slightly paid for it ($500 for a theoretical forty hours of work) and the Marines obviously enjoyed being taught by a real teacher. The first course, from the founding until about 1820 was so successful that they talked me into doing a second course on the Civil War period, hardly my specialty. It helped that each unit in the syllabus was accompanied by an illustrated lecture on videotape.[44]

That second course took quite a while to finish, because we had to deal with the consequences of the Nairobi embassy bombing described above. For the Pretoria detachment, that meant one Marine seconded to Nairobi and another to help out in Namibia, which was short after sending someone to Nairobi. This, of course, meant even more missed classes and make-up exams. It also meant that, as had actually been happening for a while, I often had a stinky bunch of students just in from the afternoon exercise run in class, with two of them wolfing down an early supper so that they could take

---

[43] Bob and Barbara e-mail to Dear Family, October 17, 1998; also Barbara letter to Dear Daddy, Newell and Kate (i.e. the non-e-mail users), n.d., but also late 1998.

[44] Barbara e-mail to Dear Family, October 17, 1998.

the night watch on time. In the end, Central Texas University gave me a long extension of time to finish the course, and everyone passed.

My second project was a good deal more complex. As the embassy grew in size, many parents, assuming that adequate English language education facilities for children with special needs were available, sought assignments to Pretoria or one of the consulates. That impression, only partially true, had been encouraged by the American International School, located between Pretoria and Johannesburg. The result in some cases was severe disappointment and broken assignments, which could be extremely expensive both financially and in terms of reduced efficiency and damaged morale. My job, paid for by the State Department's Office of International Schools, was to find out exactly what "special education" facilities existed in the South African system, beyond the American International School.

To do so, I traveled all over the country for several months looking at schools for children of all ages with all levels of disabilities, from mild to crippling. My report, which was made available to all US Government employees contemplating an assignment in South Africa, described exactly what they could expect in Pretoria, Johannesburg, Durban and Cape Town.[45]

Whenever possible Bob let me use his official car and driver, Johannes. Because Johannes had one learning disabled son, he was fascinated by the project and was very helpful beyond his ability to navigate from school to school, doing his own research among the drivers and gardeners who worked at the schools and sharing the results with me on the way home. I wrote:

What I have been finding is that many good schools exist for children with all sorts of disabilities. However, about half are in Afrikaans [medium], so that puts them out of range of American families. Of the English-language schools, most are overcrowded now that color-blind education has come to South Africa. . . . So getting into the appropriate school is the problem.

---

[45] There is a copy of this report along with the remaining research items in my school files in the basement.

There is also a fundamental difference in the philosophy of special education in the US and South Africa. In the US, we are happy to alter curriculum and methods, and to be much more informal in the classroom. Here the big goal for all but the most severely handicapped children . . . is to prepare them to enter regular schools, in regular classrooms, and to cope with all the notebooks, neat handwriting, perfect spelling, etc., etc., that it entails. . . . So classes at schools for learning disabled children, for example, are far more formal and fussy than American ones would be. Jamie would not have thrived in them.

The American International School is growing so fast that it hasn't been able to keep up adequately with the children who have special needs who have enrolled there, which is in fact the genesis of this project. I've had to use some diplomacy in my interaction with the guidance counselor/admissions officer there, who is also in charge of special education and who tried to capture the project when it was proposed. But she was the source of the unhappiness of families here with LD children, and she also proposed to postpone the project until she had more time after the school year started, whereas the information was needed in September to help families bidding on posts here for next summer. I've succeeded in maintaining civil, even good, relations, I think.[46]

In general, I found that the more disabled the child, the more likely it was that facilities existed to provide adequate education/training for him or her. There was, for example, an impressive facility in Pretoria for daily care of severely retarded children, who might not even have been able to speak and who required help in eating and taking care of other bodily needs. In that situation, compassionate adults, not language, made the difference.

On the other hand, American sign language for the deaf is totally different from any other sign language used in the world, including South Africa. The School for the Blind in Johannesburg said that it would be willing to accept a blind American child if one applied. The situation for children with learning disabilities was also positive in Johannesburg, but the best school in the country, which was in Pretoria, was

[46] Barbara letter to Dear Daddy and Newell and Kate.

usually full at the beginning of every South African school year in February (i.e. not a good bet for a child transferring on the North American school calendar).

For years, the booklet I produced was available for consultation at the Foreign Service Institute, but apparently no longer is, and no replacement is evident. Maybe the Internet has changed things.

The last of our family visits, from Kathy and Fred, occurred late in November 1998—just in time for Kathy, who wrote shortly before coming:

I can't tell you how ready I am for this trip. As I am sure you read every day, the financial markets have been in total turmoil for the last six weeks. My business is actually one of the few making money, but every day is like being on a roller coaster.[47]

Still living comfortably in a land where a restaurant meal with wine set us back about $20 and enjoying our lovely government provided housing, we were blissfully ignoring whatever that total turmoil was, but we were happy to put together a trip that was total distraction for Kathy and Fred. We showed them around Cape Town (wine country, Table Mountain, Kirstenbosch, District Six, Cape Point—including a car break-down on the way back—Robben Island, etc.). Then they flew north for a side trip to Victoria Falls and Chobe (Botswana) before rejoining us in Pretoria, where we rented a Toyota van for our trip together to Wakkerstroom and various game parks in Kwa-Zulu/Natal.

As Barbara reported, the trip started with a bang because . . .

"we lucked out when the Wakkerstroom bird expert, who is also a part-time ranger for the Mpumulanga Parks Board, had a cancellation and was able to take us on a day-long tour to see such special birds as the blue crane (South Africa's national bird), crested crane, bald-headed ibis, and various small larks and pipits which we never could have figured out without assistance."[48]

This was John McAllister, whom Bob already knew from

---

[47] kcade@bkb.com e-mail to Robert Pringle, 10/9/98.
[48] Barbara e-mail to Kathy Cade *et al.*, very end of November, 1998. Following quotations about this trip are from this e-mail also.

previous trips to the region.

After that we headed to the St. Lucia Wetlands Park[49] on the Indian Ocean coast near the Mozambique border. The high point was "a wild after-dinner drive at low tide up and down the beach [where] we saw several loggerhead turtles in various stages of egg-laying," but nary a glimpse of human activity along many miles of beautiful, deserted beach. We would have loved to come back in February to see the baby turtles hatch, but it was not to be. A second stop near the coast was made at Ndumo, famed for both birds and elephants. We saw both.

Finally we visited the premier game park of Kwa-Zulu Natal, Hluhluwe-Imfolozi[50], once a hunting preserve of the Zulu monarchs, where Bob got his first-ever photo of a black rhino in daylight, shown on the back cover of this volume. We had stopped the car when we saw him coming up a slope toward us, and he just kept coming, chewing on a leafy branch and obviously not seeing us until he got quite close. (Black rhinos have notoriously poor eyesight.)

The parks we visited are operated by the Natal Parks Board, a unique provincial operation with a long history. From them we obtained a poster entitled "47 Rhino [sic] Seek Good Grass," advertising a forthcoming game auction. Obviously at the time (1998) there was a surplus of white rhinos, not to mention giraffes, kudu, warthogs (guaranteed swine-fever free) and many other species being put up for sale. It seems bitterly ironic in retrospect. Sixteen years later, more than sixty rhino, from an estimated Kwa-Zulu Natal population of about 4,000, were killed by poachers in 2014 alone.[51]

The final stop of the trip for Kathy and Fred was Durban, where, it being late in November, we had Thanksgiving dinner with Fred Hassani, the Consul in Durban, and his family. Then Kathy and Fred left for home, while we went on to explore the Drakensburg Mountains, most notably the Ardmore Pottery. It was founded by a South African woman, Fée Halsted-Berning, in partnership with a young polio victim, Bonnie

---

[49] Now the Isimangaliso Wetland Park.

[50] The first word is pronounced "Shoe-shoe-lway."

[51] Internet article: "expert – rhinos extinct in our lifetime," http://www. iol.co.za/news/crime-courts/rhinos-extinct-in-our-lifetime-expert-1.1737197#.U_ZZI0hieYc, accessed August 21, 2014.

Ntshalinshali. The pottery had become internationally known for its fanciful representations of wild animals executed by local artists, mainly Zulus, who had never seen a giraffe or elephant until Fée took them all to the Durban zoo.

By the time we left South Africa, Ardmore's gifted artists were being decimated by HIV/AIDS, but the pottery, as of this writing, seems to have survived and prospered.[52] We ordered a set of cups with bird designs and handles, but the administrative end of things being less talented than the potters, it had not been fulfilled by the time of a return visit six months later. So we bought the set of animal themed cups and saucers, plus the teapot and sugar bowl and creamer that we display in the breakfront in the dining room.

Signs of Change, Large and Small

It was at about this time that our driver, Johannes took us out to see *his* farm, outside Pretoria, of which he was immensely proud. It became apparent that he was the only, or almost only, black person in a small development. It was no secret that he had been invited to live there by the mostly white landowners because they felt that having at least one black person would safeguard them against possible legal action under future land laws aimed at achieving more equity between the races.

There were other signs that South Africa was changing fast. The Brooklyn primary school, just around the corner from where we lived, had been overwhelmingly white when we arrived. Now, three years later, it was at least one third black or colored, and the proportion was growing fast, as educated blacks obtained jobs in government, moved into the neighborhood, and sent their children to the local school. Apparently, also, some parents who lived elsewhere but commuted to work through Brooklyn simply transferred their children to the school and dropped them off on the way to their jobs.

There was no obvious anxiety about this change among our Afrikaner neighbors. There was, however unhappiness in

---

[52] For a recent (2014) account of Ardmore see http://www. ardmoreceramics.co.za/world-of-ardmore/about. Our book on the subject is Gillian Scott, *Ardmore: An African Discovery*, Fernwood Press, Vlaeberg, 1998.

at least one of the very large, Soweto-like black "settlements" outside Pretoria, whose inhabitants felt that their best and brightest citizens were moving away into formerly all-white areas, depriving them of badly needed community leadership.

Mandela's term as President expired in June, 1999. He had long since declared that would not run again. His deputy, Thabo Mbeki, anointed by the ANC, was expected to win easily, and did. The US Embassy, along with others, was invited to field election observers, and Barbara and I participated, equipped with T-shirts labeled "Embassy of the USA – Election Observer." We were given a list of things to observe, including: "Presence of women and youth? Checking of voters' ID and voter rolls? Presence of police/army? Security [in certain areas where the race was expected to be tight]?" The five polling places we observed included Wadrif, Johannes' home area (modest turnout); Deerdepark (mainly black, at least 500 people in line) and the very upscale Cullinan Rugby Club (all white, lunch provided, steady stream of voters, no line). We saw no major problems.

As part of this experience we finally were able to see the Cullinan diamond mine, famous for producing very high quality gemstones, but not enough of them to keep it from being closed for a time shortly before we arrived in South Africa. Portions of its original miners' quarters are incorporated into a historic village and tourist center, huddled under the huge headworks towering over the mine itself. Its most famous product is the Cullinan Diamond, weighing over 3,000 carats (one and one-third pounds), pieces of which, including the Star of Africa, are incorporated in the British Crown Jewels. It was found in 1905 by a supervisor who noticed a large rock protruding from the side of an underground shaft and thought at first it was a shard of glass put there as a practical joke. According to *Wikipedia*, Cullinan is also the only significant source of blue diamonds in the world.

We had expected Margot to visit in January, 1999, for a trip to Islandwana and Rorke's Drift, site of the battle so similar to the Battle of the Little Bighorn, which she knew so well. However, her partner broke up with her just before she departed, and she collapsed totally in London, unable to finish the trip to see us or indeed to get on a plane in any direction without help. For the first time in his career, Bob had to ask

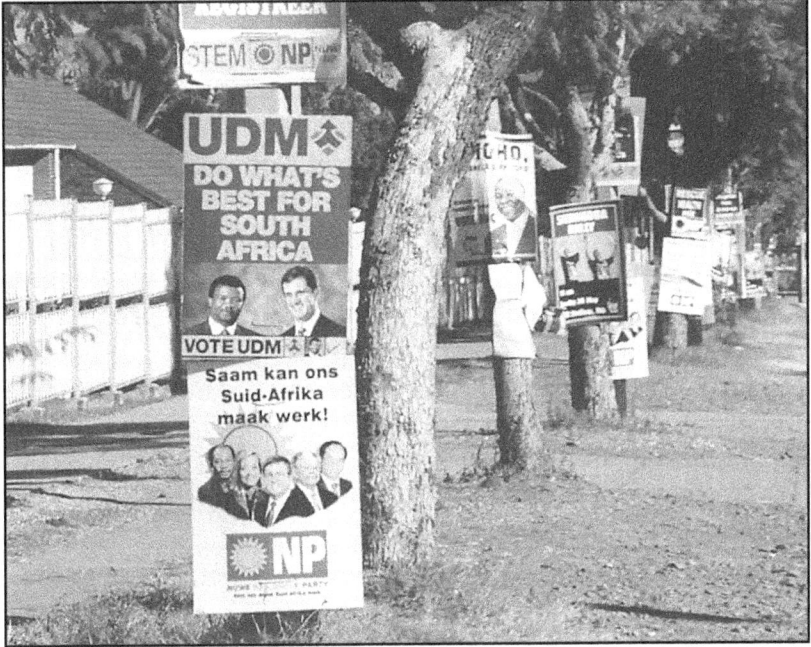

Mandela served one term, but after his long political/political prisoner life he announced his intention to retire. So there was a presidential election near the end of our assignment in South Africa, and it was hotly contested with campaign signs everywhere.

a Citizens' Services consular officer, at Embassy London, for help. That officer very efficiently got Margot on her way back to Sheridan, Wyoming, leaving Bob to feel that he had never previously appreciated fully the work done by these, usually very junior, Foreign Service officers.[53]

Preparing to Say Farewell

It was time for us to think about leaving. Bob wrote a long, dull memo to his successor, John Blaney, explaining the nitty-gritty of the DCM's job: the management of Official Residence Expenses

---

[53] Barbara letter to Dear Daddy and Newell, January 23, 1999. This letter mistakenly states that Margot never left Sheridan when in fact she got as far as London. She had been planning to visit her old friend Mulik, an Israeli anthropologist, on the way. I wrote the best thank-you letter I could concoct to the consular officer who helped us, with a copy to his Ambassador.

(ORE); where and how to order servants' uniforms; how to get to Cape Town and back with your two paid-for servants; whether you could allow other US Government officials on vacation to stay in your Cape Town house when you weren't there (you couldn't, unless they paid "fair market value" to Uncle Sam for the privilege); how the Residence alarm system worked; details of the six official committees the DCM chaired or attended, and finally notes about what was being done or could be done to alleviate the embassy's morale problem, as recommended by our recent inspection.[54]

I also wrote a farewell cable assessing the understandable anxiety about South Africa's future, especially among whites. I asked the ambassador's permission to do so because it was the sort of message that ambassadors normally write, although it was captioned as representing my personal views. Growing fears of "creeping Mugabization," a reference to the turmoil in nearby Zimbabwe, including the confiscation of white-owned farms by a black dictator, were, I thought, exaggerated:

South African history has been brutally detraditionalizing, primarily through the forced dislocation and conversion of farmers and herders into an industrial labor force. . . . "Westernization" in admittedly perverse form has happened to an extent unparalleled elsewhere on the continent. One symptom: self-sufficient villages in the classic African sense hardly exist here. This is primarily a country of "locations" and "settlements" inhabited by farm laborers and other largely urban or peri-urban populations ultimately dependent on industrial wage earning rather than subsistence farming. . . .

Today most South Africans do not aspire to return to traditional rural existence. Were it not so, pressure for land reform and dispossession of the white farmers who still own most of the good farmland would have been immediate and irresistible. Rather, the majority aspires to share in the broader national economy through access to better education and job creation.[55]

---

[54] Robert M. Pringle to John Blaney, "Transition Notes," 1999.
[55] "South Africa has Nothing to Fear but Fear Itself," Pretoria 009302, C; paragraphs quoted were unclassified, slightly edited in places.

The US should, I concluded, continue to assist South Africa in every way possible to achieve its goal of economic and social transformation, while refraining from efforts to persuade South Africa to divert its own resources to support our global and regional agendas. I noted George Washington's advice, at a similar stage of our own development, to avoid foreign entanglements. I failed to make the point that South Africa's development problems were already being exacerbated by the fact that it is not an island. The more the welfare of its own black population improves, the more new waves of poor migrants flock to it from countries to its north. This was already happening by the time we left.

I also attempted a bit of personal public diplomacy by writing an article for our local newspaper, the *Pretoria News*, dwelling on what we saw as the bright side of things:

> We are getting ready to leave South Africa after three years, and I can assure you we will miss it greatly.
>
> As I drive to work now on a sunny winter morning, I think of Washington, to which I am returning, with its congestion, its summer heat and humidity, its winter cold and slush. I think, "Am I going to miss this!"
>
> What more will I miss? To begin with, there is the climate. It is not original to think that sports and the climate are among the most potent unifying forces in South Africa.
>
> We are outdoor people. Kruger National Park is one of the features of South Africa we would like to take home with us.
>
> We will miss Kirstenbosch Botanical Garden and everything it stands for. Lots of other countries in Africa have the Big Five, but only you have the Cape Floral Kingdom.
>
> We will miss the mysteries of South Africa, beginning with cricket.
>
> I can't say that we will miss the aggressiveness of South African driving, but we will miss topping a hill on a country road and being able to see 15 km ahead with hardly a vehicle in sight.
>
> We will miss good and affordable food and wine,

fabulous fresh produce, restaurants, theater and much more. . . .

We will miss the daily fulfillment of being present at a creation.[56]

The piece ran with a slightly ridiculous photo of me holding crossed US and South African flags, the idea of the photographer. It got a warm reception, and one Pretoria preacher used it in a sermon.

British-origin whites were doing most of the worrying. This was curious because all of them either had British passports or could get them. If things got all that bad, they had a ticket "home."

The Afrikaners were not whiners. Either they were still vocally hostile and bitter, a tiny minority, or they tried, sometimes enthusiastically, to help make things better. They could not, as the British-origin South Africans could, "go home." They usually preferred to think, with Dutch stubbornness, that South Africa was their home. And to an extraordinary extent, many of them pitched in and did their best to make the Rainbow Nation a reality.

This viewpoint was also true of many apartheid-era institutions, notably the Afrikaans-medium universities. The University of Pretoria, right in our back yard, was one of them. By the time we left, it had evolved from lily-white to almost majority black, although admittedly many of the blacks were to be found on a new campus studying vocational subjects. However, it is also true that many of the white, largely Afrikaner farmers were inhibited from leaving by the fact that although they could sell their farms, they could not take the proceeds out of South Africa, so they might as well stay and keep plowing.

Always Time for One More Trip, to Madagascar

We had time for one last, purely recreational trip, to Madagascar. I had been there briefly on a visit while I was working for the Africa Bureau's Economic Policy Staff. Now Barbara and I could see more of this curious outlier of Malayo-Polynesian expansion, much bigger (twice the size of Arizona with twenty-three million people) than it looks just off the east coast of Africa. We

---

[56] Robert M. Pringle, excerpt from "Things We'll Miss as We Prepare to Go," *Pretoria News,* July 21, 1999.

availed ourselves of a cheap charter flight from Johannesburg to Antananarivo, stayed there with Ambassador Shirley Barnes, a friend from the Senior Seminar, and used what turned out to be a first-rate tour service which she recommended to visit portions of the island, concentrating on its southern half.

Jamie came with us and produced a splendid letter about the trip, proving that whatever his learning disabilities might once have been, he had become an excellent writer. His missive is full of perceptive glimpses of this unique island:

It's a low-wage country—a month of their wages will buy a small fraction of a dishwasher, or hire a man to do their dishes and laundry, while a month of my wages would easily buy an entire dishwashing machine, but not even hire a person to dust once a month. . . . The whole country is testimony to just how much labor you can substitute for capital.

[A] sisal plantation: Sisal is the fiber in a brown doormat, and used to be important before nylon. A hybrid agave plant, it is a five-foot hemisphere, sword shaped leaves a meter long tipped by a natural nail. The plantation is a parachutist's hell, and not that friendly to walkers either.

Madagascar takes graves seriously. . . . There might be a cross (most people are Christian), and there are definitely the skull and horns of the cattle sacrificed at the interment. . . . I have a picture of a large grave, in the center a mausoleum topped with a large plaster plane,[57] and on the end a spooky painted picture of a man with one eye closed, one eye watching the road. . . . Other places have crosses, wooden carvings of cows and naked people, and stone menhirs. In many regions they take the bones out every several years, have a huge party, wash the bones, and re-inter them. Syncretic it is.

Of all the things we saw, even better than lemurs, chameleons,

---

[57] Pride of place for a plane on the mausoleum somewhat negates Jamie's previous observation, commenting that scheduling confusion ("Yeah your flight is leaving, is not leaving, is leaving in 10 minutes, tomorrow, now, in two hours, why should we know, we're only the airline . . . ? I know this sounds like an American airline . . . it is, but much more so.") caused one trip to take "all day for a one-and-a-half hour flight, . . . It probably isn't a good way to run a country, to tax the poor farmers to subsidize an underperforming airline that they'll never fly, but discourages rich tourists from visiting & spending money." Foreign visitors do come in droves, and some local citizens do travel in them.

handicrafts, textiles, great birds, etc., none made a more lasting impression than the sapphire rush at Ranohira, first perceived as crowds of people and shacks in the middle of rolling grass country. As reported by Jamie:

Four months before our visit—nothing. Then someone found a placer deposit of sapphires. 15,000 people later, a Wild West boomtown, just like the pictures of California in 1849. Desperate people living in meter-cubed hovels, built of leaves next to shallow mine diggings, panning for sapphires in the river. All the land is covered with pits and yellow sand tailings, the town (which was nothing four months ago) filled with fast money, loose women and bars. We saw a restaurant with table, stove and customers, and four posts where the walls and roof will be, if they can be built before it all plays out. The town government (? or something) charged us about two bucks to drive into town. In the real town up the road, and in the luxury hotel, seedy looking Thai and Mauritian buyers traded little plastic bags of sapphires, holding them up to the light of the sun or those little silver Tiger brand flashlights. You could smell a cartel forming, just [as] in every other gem strike. All the small people want to be the next DeBeers; all the traders want to be the next Cecil Rhodes.[58]

Then there was "the raining forest," as our guide called it, at Ranomafana. As Jamie said, it seemed churlish to complain about rain in a rain forest, but really! My two Leicas got soaked, one of them fatally. There were, withal, neat beetles, birds, moths, fungi and leeches, and of course, lemurs, and, all kidding aside, Madagascar is a great trip well beyond this brief mention of it. The French have always been crazy about it, with good reason.

Kalahari-Gemsbok

By this time the rites of passage that mark any departure from a Foreign Service assignment were well underway or had already happened, in Cape Town as well as Pretoria. But our spiritual farewell was a trip to Kalahari-Gemsbok Transfrontier Park.[59] Most tourists skip it because it has

---

[58] "Madagascar," Jamie e-mail to friends and family, June 16, 1999.
[59] Kalahari is now spelled Kgalagadi and the full name of the park is Kgalagadi Transfrontier Park.

no elephants, so you can't see the Big Five there. It is also nowhere near any beaten path. These same defects make it splendidly uncrowded, a place where you can drive all day and have its glorious natural features to yourself. It is also the best place we've ever been in Africa to see cheetahs.

And there is a lot of it. From the southern gate near Twee Rivieren, a road winds northwards over 150 kilometers, then crosses the border into Botswana, where there is a lot more, but in 1999 you needed a four-wheel-drive vehicle to do that, and with only four days available we had plenty to see on the South African side. The setting is very dry, almost desert. Much of it is covered with ancient, fixed sand dunes, now immobilized by desert scrub, that run for miles. The road crosses them in places—great for seeing ostriches and sand grouse—but mostly follows dry riverbeds. In addition to cheetahs, the most famous attractions are black-maned lions, numerous gemsbok (oryx), and tons of birds.

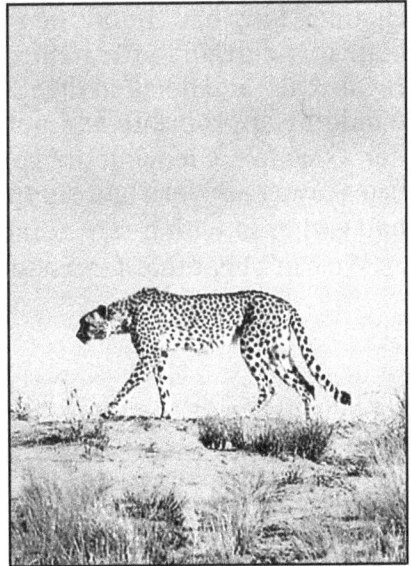

(Left) Barbara and Khoisan (aka "Bushmen") residents of Kalahari Gemsbok National Park (as it then was), who were selling small handmade souvenirs, several of which she bought. (Right) Cheetahs were one of the main attractions of this almost desert park; the others were black-maned lions and spectacular gemsbok (horse-size antelopes).

We spent a couple of hours watching a big male lion that

never deigned to get up and really show himself. But early the next morning we got close to a group of females that had just, probably before dawn, killed a big gemsbok and dragged it across the road and under a tree where they were having it for breakfast. The hunt must have been terrifying—gemsbok are as big as horses. Camp facilities were simple but attractive, mostly built of stone with thatched roofs. All of the labor force was local, either San or Khoi, who look unmistakably different from the broader population of black South Africans.

We spent two nights at Nossob, well into the park. The first morning Barbara discovered that the sapphire in our engagement ring was missing.[60] The soft, 22K Malian gold prongs of the ring had bent so that they were loose. We looked everywhere, to no avail, then set off to find birds and animals, having asked the staff to keep an eye out for it, never dreaming that anyone would ever find it and give it back.

When we returned tired from a wonderful day of game watching (both the cheetahs on that year's Christmas card and the lions eating the gemsbok), it turned out that our cleaning lady had found the blue stone, perched on the very edge of the drain in the bathroom floor. We discussed how to reward her and decided that 200 rand (slightly less than $30) would be appropriate and not too extravagant. We gave it to her as we were leaving the next morning and by the time we drove away all work had stopped; the whole camp labor force had gathered with her to admire and discuss this windfall.

We can't beat that for a happy ending.

---

[60] When I belatedly gave it to her to commemorate our 25th anniversary, well before the end of apartheid, South African diamonds still seemed wicked, so we bought a sapphire in Brussels. Who knows, it might have been found in Madagascar, which has been very slow to market its own gemstones, allowing them to be sold as being from Burma or Sri Lanka.

16

Assignment Washington and Retirement

We returned from South Africa in the fall of 1999, in time for Barbara to resume her teaching at Potomac, and for me to begin my final Foreign Service assignment, which was at the National War College. The children were on the verge of professional careers with Jamie completing his post-doc at Scripps, and Annie in the final years of writing her PhD thesis at Duke.

As if to signal "We're all on the same continent again," Annie and Kathy organized a special holiday celebration for the

A few years after the reunion in the Blue Ridge, the family gathered at Jane's house in Cincinnati to celebrate the patriarch's 90th birthday. Here he sits with six of his seven great-grandchildren: Scott Strong, Charlotte and Gaby Thurston, Great Grandfather, Zoe Pringle Johnson holding baby Penelope Pringle Johnson, and Sam(antha) Strong.

extended Cade family, from Grandfather Clarence and Newell to the first of his great-grandchildren, Heidi's daughter Sammy and son Scott and Heather's daughter Charlotte, in the Blue Ridge. We took over a small hotel near Ashville, did our own cooking, and enjoyed several days of fun—hiking, visiting the Biltmore Estate to see the Christmas decorations, presenting the new trophy for winners of the Super Bowl pool, with names of previous winners inscribed on it (and room for more) to Clay, and just catching up with each other's news.

We dispersed on New Year's Eve, Bob and Barbara to celebrate the new millennium in a very special way that linked our overseas career with our new situation as permanent residents of Alexandria: we went to welcome in the Year 2000 at a gala service at the National Cathedral. There was a huge choir, as well as several musical groups and numerous ecumenical clergy. Most important, the sermon was delivered by Archbishop Desmond Tutu, who was admired and honored for his leadership of the Truth and Reconciliation Commission, then in the midst of its proceedings to try to reunite South Africans after years of apartheid. It was an uplifting beginning to the next thousand years, which so far is not living up to his fondest hopes.

Bob Teaches at the National War College

The National War College (NWC) was not my first choice. With strong support from Ambassador Joseph, I sought an assignment as Diplomat in Residence at Howard University. However, the powers-that-were in the senior assignments office at State were determined to save that position as a possible parking place for a high-level political appointee, in case the need for one arose. I was annoyed that I was not selected, given my long family connections with Howard going back to the 1950s, and my father's interest in Negro (as it was then called) education.

But teaching at the National War College proved to be a good fallback. Aside from my Army service in the early Sixties, I lacked experience with the military and thought it would be interesting and useful to learn more. The NWC was founded in 1946 as a replacement for the Army-Navy Staff College. Later it became the hub of a National Defense University, co-located with the NWC at Fort McNair in Washington. The NDU had no independent teaching responsibilities that I could detect, but it had a superb library that served all its components. In addition, the services—Army, Navy, and Air Force—had their own War Colleges, all part of an impressive system of military higher education, in other parts of the country.

Many Foreign Service Officers, myself included, were envious of the military's seemingly endless resources for training of all kinds, not to mention for seemingly unlimited senior staff positions. The problem (or opportunity) flowed both from the ever more complex nature of the threat faced by our military and from the need to keep the standing force busy in peacetime. Foreign Service Officers had difficulty getting time off for training even when it was available, because the State Department had trouble filling real jobs with available personnel. (My year off to write a book in 1977-78, described in Chapter 8, was not typical, and I never could have obtained the necessary grant without a PhD.)

The mission of the NWC was to teach "grand strategy," meaning how to use all the resources available to our national government to achieve its national security objectives, with the emphasis on *how*. These resources included foreign aid, diplomacy and information (once crudely labeled propaganda), as well as military force and much more. So while most of the faculty at the NWC were military officers, there were quite a few civilians and at least one State Department officer (me). I could use the title "Ambassador," considered almost more important in Department of Defense circles than it was in the State Department itself.

My job consisted of helping to teach the NWC core curriculum, focused unrelentingly on strategy. Many students found this quite easy, because they were already familiar with such famous strategic practitioners as von Clausewitz and Sun Tzu from earlier bouts of training, but since I was not, it involved some real work to teach it.

The faculty also included foreign area specialists, and I would have been a natural for the Southeast Asia slot, but there was a career Civil Service civilian entrenched in it, so I was quite happy to be the Sub-Saharan Africa specialist instead. I enjoyed teaching an elective course on Africa, and another on Environment and Security, drawing on my OES experience. Each foreign area course ended with a trip by NWC students to the relevant region.

As one might have expected, the students were disciplined, polite and almost always hard working. They were already senior officers, meaning lieutenant colonels in the Army, or the equivalent in the other services, on their way to becoming full colonels. They often came from positions of grave operational responsibility, and from that perspective a year at the War College was for them almost a year off. It was not automatically a pass to being a general or the equivalent, but if a student did well, it would certainly help him or her along the way.

Students did not linger at Fort McNair after class, largely because almost all of them had horrendous commutes to return to their families each evening. Although they were by no means solemn or uncritical, there was nothing resembling adolescent fooling around, except on the athletic field. There they tended to forget that they were in their forties, and quite a few managed to hurt themselves by playing too hard. The College encouraged sports and especially a faintly silly rivalry with the Industrial College of the Armed Forces (ICAF), a major part of the NDU located right next door to the NWC. It was similar to the War College, but had been established to provide training in procurement, logistics and other aspects of industrial support for national defense. It was serious business, but the NWC looked down on ICAF as an inferior rival, sometimes to the point of resisting academic cooperation with them.

This was despite the great strides that had been made toward integrating the services, or, at least, making them learn to work together. The relevant terms were "Joint" and "Goldwater-Nichols." "Goldwater-Nichols" was the law that required the services to cooperate, at least far more than in the past, and even in peacetime. "Joint" was the adjective applied to any such work or agency. One had to learn all this special language. One of my favorites was "interagency," often used as a noun. "The interagency" was the ill-defined world of other agencies that the military was now being trained to work with, like it or not.

The State Department was seen as an important if somewhat mysterious component of "the interagency." It was criticized for not doing enough to resolve the endless political and even cultural issues which the military thought we were better equipped to handle than they were, and should be addressing more vigorously. One could only reply, endlessly, that we didn't have the resources to meet this expectation, and Congress was not about to provide them.

Getting to Fort NcNair was a breeze, but it required a second car, since Barbara needed our Subaru, by now a green one, for her longer commute to Potomac. So I bought a second-hand Ford Escort, which doubled as a garden car, for lugging plants and tools down to my communal plot on National Park Service land near the Wilson Bridge. To get to work, all I had to do was drive into Washington on the Fourteenth Street Bridge across the Potomac and head south for a few blocks. Security was quite relaxed when I began my two-year stint at the NWC, but it would get much tighter after 9/11.

The National War College building is a historic property, designed by the famous architect Stanford White, a pioneer of the Beaux-Arts style. He is known for his many famous landmarks in New York, including the arch at Washington Square and the Century Club, of which my father was so proud to be a member. White was equally famous for having been assassinated in 1906 at the garden-theater on the roof of Madison Square Garden. The deed was done by the husband of his former paramour and noted courtesan, Evelyn Nesbit, at a performance of a show entitled *Mamz'elle Champagne*.

Not many of our students were aware of this bit of history, but they did know that George Kennan, a God in the pantheon of strategic thinking as taught at the NWC, had served in Stanford White's building. Kennan was a senior foreign policy advisor, assigned to what would become the NWC, when he wrote a famous article on the need to contain Soviet expansion. It was entitled "The Sources of Soviet Conflict," published in *Foreign Policy* magazine in July, 1947, under the byline "Mr. X," and is regarded as the basis for the Truman Doctrine.[1] If

---

[1] In fact, as today's NWC students are taught, Kennan's article argued that the Soviet Union could be contained without provocation, through a policy that was "patient but firm and vigilant," one goal of which should be the removal of US forces from Europe as soon as possible. However this nuance was dropped before Truman announced his doctrine. For leads to some of the scholarship on this subject see http://en.wikipedia.org/wiki/George_F._Kennan.

I did anything permanent at the NWC, it was to draft the text of a large bronze plaque entitled "Mr. X Sat Here." It hangs in front of the office where Kennan worked, still the office of the NWC's senior State Department representative.

It was no surprise that the NWC bore almost no relationship to my previous army experience. For one thing there was only one enlisted man in the whole place. All those student-colonels had to do their own clerical work. At one time there had been a pool of secretaries, but it had been abolished after the advent of computers, and the space allocated to additional senior staff.

The NWC was a superb place to learn about the cultural differences among the four services. For example, scuttlebutt had it that the Navy did not volunteer its best officers for senior training, supposedly because it considered that anyone destined to be an admiral should spend as much time as possible "driving ships." Yet, paradoxically enough, the Navy War College, in Newport, Rhode Island, had what was widely considered to be the most talented faculty of all the service staff colleges.

The Air Force students were varied, from leader-of-men types (aka fighter pilot jockeys) to virtuoso techies. The Army cohort was intellectually dependable and even more diverse. The Marine Corps students were consistent high achievers without being flashy, and were personally dependable, the kind of people you would want to serve under. There weren't enough Coast Guard officers to make a comparable sample, and no one seemed interested in gossiping about the civilian agencies (including the State Department) that also sent students to the NWC. Of course, like all such stereotypes, these were of questionable validity, but no one could resist talking about them.

There were not many field trips or other off-post activities except sports competitions with the other war colleges. One exception was a project to tutor students at a supposedly disadvantaged high school in Northeast Washington, in which I participated. The faculty of this school was largely uninterested in us (except for a struggling principal), and its students were seriously undisciplined. NWC students had expected them to be impoverished, which few if any of them were, and had collected warm clothing to take them in preparation for winter. The visits were not well organized, and the ones I experienced did not include any attempts at teaching or even explaining what it is like to be a military officer or how such a goal could be achieved. That said, we all learned that good will alone is not relevant to the problems of education in the District of Columbia.

The most important NWC excursion was a traditional one-day outing to Gettysburg at the beginning of the school year. The students, who organized it, were passionately interested in the Civil War and did a terrific job of making the three-day bloodbath comprehensible. Our text was Michael Shaara's *The Killer Angels*. We came away accepting that Joshua Chamberlain of the 20th Maine Regiment was the ultimate hero of the battle because he led the defense of Big Round Top, its turning point.

On the Confederate side, James Longstreet, Robert E. Lee's deputy, who was long blamed by Southerners for the loss they could not bear to blame on the sainted Lee, emerges as an honest soldier who did his best to persuade his commander to withdraw to higher ground and let the Union attack *him*. Had this advice been followed, it might have changed the course of the battle, if not of the war. For the first time I understood what Gettysburg was all about, and like most of the students present, I found it an unforgettable experience.

The electives included lectures (some by guest speakers), required readings, and student briefings on assigned topics. Students took the area course for the regions they would be visiting. For the Africa course, everyone had to write a short book review of an African novel, a selection of which I had assembled at the NDU library, based partly on the list created by Barbara for Annie's independent study with Valerie Vesser during her final year at Madeira. In addition, everyone had to read Chinua Achebe's great African novel, *Things Fall Apart*, and we all visited the Smithsonian Museum of African Art.

My other elective, "Negotiating for Survival? The Environment and National Security," was not required for anyone and was not wildly popular, but it was the first time such a course had been given at the NWC and the idea of doing it attracted support from the faculty. The introduction to the course read as follows:

Reducing environmental threat is now officially part of our national security strategy. This course will analyze our efforts to achieve this objective. It will differentiate between vital but long-term threats, such as global climate change, and more immediate issues, such as the inequitable sharing of Middle Eastern water resources. It will sort through the impassioned rhetoric that surrounds most environmental issues, and strive for a balanced viewpoint. It will look carefully at the concept of "sustainable development," defined as using resources today in a manner so as not to deny their use by future generations.[2]

In the course we examined conflict case studies (Did overpopulation contribute to the Rwandan genocide?) and country studies on Russia, China and several other nations. We looked at the tangle of treaties flowing from the 1992 Rio Earth Summit. We surveyed NGOs and government agencies engaged in the environmental struggle, "from Greenpeace to DOD." To conclude, we assessed the efficacy of the US global environmental strategy. (At the War College, you could never get too far away from the word "strategy.")

The Area Studies Trips

The area studies trips were the highlight of the spring semester, although the days when the students got to fly everywhere by military air were gone. I led two such trips, in 2000 to West Africa (Ghana, Nigeria and Mali) and the following year to Southern Africa (South Africa, Swaziland and Mozambique). Most students signed up for European destinations, or places that were otherwise important or attractive. Predictably, only a handful picked West Africa. When that happened, higher authority urged students from the courses which had

---

[2] Elective Course 5964 Syllabus, "Negotiating for Survival? The Environment and National Security," Academic Year 2000-2001 (Spring).

attracted more than their quota to volunteer as needed for the less popular ones, in the time-honored "You, you and you" military tradition. On the first trip, I ended up with nine students of whom three were black. It was pretty clear that most of the black students had wanted to go, while many of the others had "volunteered."

Our first stop was Ghana, barely overnight, but a pleasant surprise to nearly everyone, including me, because Accra was bustling with economic activity and the shorefront hotel was excellent. There had been nothing like that in the early 1980's, during our time in Ouagadougou, just north of the Ghanaian border. At that time, conditions in Ghana were so bad that Peace Corps volunteers had to be evacuated from the rural areas because of acute food shortages. The next stop was Nigeria, including Lagos (mainly to call on the ambassador), Abuja (the new capital), Kaduna and Port Harcourt.

West Africa's biggest country was one teachable moment after another. The first eye-opener was the machines that counted the largest denomination banknotes (worth well under a dollar) and assembled them into "bricks," which were necessary for payments of any size. No one in the class had ever seen anything like that.

Then there was the trip to Kaduna along a largely deserted superhighway through what had once been actively farmed land. But since the oil boom, much of it had been deserted in favor of importing food. I explained that at one time, pre-oil, USAID had spent many millions developing a world-class agricultural faculty at the University of Ibadan. Some day, after the oil runs out, someone may do it all over again.

Then we spotted a column of smoke, visible for miles, where a gas tanker had skidded off the interstate-style road and caught fire in the median strip, a common occurrence we were told. It was surrounded by villagers scooping up the highly inflammable fuel to take home in whatever containers they had. Having taken photos of all this, the students concocted a tale to tell classmates who had gone to Paris or Tokyo, about how the wreck had been the work of the Central Nigerian Liberation Front whose ambush we had narrowly escaped.

Kaduna itself had a big new mosque, and its architect

had volunteered to show us around the interior. It was near noon and very hot, and quite a few men were napping in cool dark corners. When they woke up and noticed our female contingent they asked our guide to please ask those *women* to leave; didn't he know the rules? The women both happened to be black, but that of course was not the reason why they (and us with them, of course) had to leave.

Then we flew down to the "oil patch." The embassy recommended an airline which went anywhere in Nigeria for $50 a passenger; they all used it, they said; it was the safest one. There we met with Chevron and other oil company officials and flew over the coastline and several offshore rigs. We heard all about the ongoing quasi-warfare between local villagers, who routinely hacked into pipelines, etc., and the oil companies. At the end of the flight, having started with the opinion, as reflected in the western press, that the constant violence was mostly the fault of Greedy Big Oil, we were not so sure; there seemed to be plenty of greed and blame to go around.

Later, at one village, we saw belts of ammunition left behind by attacking Nigerian troops. We were told that they had killed 500 inhabitants in retaliation for attacks on local police, who had gone after them for their anti-oil activities. At another, we met its ruler, identified on his stationery, a copy of which I kept, as "His Royal Majesty King J.G. Egba, Olei X, Obanohan of Olei-Oloibiri 1st Class," wearing his official top hat. On the edge of his village, children tried to sell us roasted sago grubs impaled on sticks, another eye-popper.

Then came the best part. We flew back to Lagos, and for some reason our plane landed in a weedy corner of the airport, far from the main terminal. It turned out that the terminal building had burned down while we were away! Food stalls had already sprouted among the weeds, and as we sat waiting for our van to find us, a woman running one of them told us that a corrupt Nigerian businessman who owned a local airline had set fire to the terminal to destroy evidence of his corruption.

Ding! It just so happened that among the optional novels I had assigned for my students was another by the great Chinua Achebe, *Anthills of the Savannah*. In that tale, a crooked airline operator burns down the Lagos airport to destroy evidence of his wrongdoing. My reputation as a prescient teacher soared.

On to Mali. Due to an airline snafu we couldn't go to Timbuktu, as the class had dearly hoped. There wasn't time, because the military's European Command (EUCOM) had forbidden its people to fly on Air Afrique, the French-run regional airline, leaving us with an arguably less safe as well as later connection on Air Ghana. We did have time to drive from Bamako to Mopti, stopping at my and Barbara's favorite Lebanese coffee shop in Segou on the way.

Down the road, we decided to take a lunch picnic break, in the maximum midday heat, under a big tree; I wanted the class to savor the way ambassadors and their spouses in West Africa travel. One of our hyperactive students, Lt. Col. Marty Francis (Air Force) decided he had to go for a run, whereupon he met a procession of Peuhl ladies with calabashes of fresh milk on their heads, *en route* to the nearest village market. Two of them were young and typically flirty, and their mother, who was with them, decided on the spot to marry at least one of them to Marty, resulting in much hilarity and photos to prove his narrow escape. One almost universal attribute of Africans is that they know how to laugh.

Although we didn't get to Timbuktu, the students did see the great Mosque of Jenné, really more interesting than anything in Timbuktu, as well as the Mopti waterfront, with its hundreds of big pirogues and slabs of Saharan salt. They also met two of our old friends, Peace Corps Baba and Dr. Noumou Diakité, of Gourma elephant fame. Back in Bamako, in addition to seeing where I used to work and meeting my successor, we were able to call on Alpha Konaré, who as a journalist had often been a guest at the Residence, and was now Mali's democratically elected President.

By the end of the trip the students' opinions had shifted on both sides of an obvious division. Those who had been told to do it, and stepped forward as good soldiers, had concluded that Africa was a much better and more varied place than they had expected. Those who saw it as a romantic rejoining with the ancestral homeland had backed away considerably from their original rose-tinted perspective. Everyone had learned something they would never forget.

By this time I had known for some time that my War College assignment would be my last in the Foreign Service, as the indirect result of my insistence in South Africa that our law enforcement officers could not carry arms when they went out crime-busting with their South African counterparts without host government approval.[3] The fact that the necessary agreement was obtained in a timely fashion should, I thought, have redounded to my credit. But when a State Department team came to inspect our embassy in 1998 the affronted officers, especially the DEA representative, complained that I had been unfriendly and obstructive, and the leader of the inspection, who had previously worked with law enforcement programs in embassies, cited their criticism as evidence that I had not sufficiently supported this important work and was more generally aloof from my subordinates.

Such overseas inspections were not uncommon, although I had experienced only one other during my career. And the fact that this one took place just before the Clinton visit when we were frantically busy led me to treat the result less seriously than I should have, and I did not demand the excision of the criticism, although success would have been anything but certain. The fact was that *any* criticism on record was sufficient to have an officer "low-ranked," meaning that I would probably be passed over for further promotion in 1999, as indeed I was.

While I felt that this was galling and unjust, the American Foreign Service Association (AFSA) legal staff advised me that I was unlikely to get the bad language removed. Even if I did, I would have to retire for age in November 2001, when I would be 65, barring another presidential appointment, meaning another ambassadorship. I also felt that 34 years of government service was arguably enough, and that it was time for Barbara and me to enjoy a taste of freedom. As a result of all this I retired on September 29, 2001.

I was already thinking about the "post season," to borrow a term from baseball. I had once asked my Australian friend Milton Osborne if he knew of anyone who might be interested in supporting a book on the history of Bali. During our

---

[3] See Chapter 14.

frequent visits to Bali in the 1970s, it had occurred to me that although there were shelves of books on Balinese art, dancing and culture generally, there were virtually none in English on Bali's equally interesting and very long history. Milton responded that such a book might fit into a series of "short histories" that he was editing for the Australian publisher Allen and Unwin, and so it did.

But how would I do the necessary research? I was not associated with a university equipped with a library with decent holdings on Southeast Asia, and anyway there was none in the Washington area. I could use the Library of Congress to be sure, but I knew that it was anything but a model of customer service. Closer at hand, and very customer-oriented, was the library of the National Defense University, whose staff I knew well. They were not overworked and were expert at procuring books and more exotic materials online and via inter-library loan from other universities. So I decided to extend my stay at the War College beyond my Foreign Service retirement, continuing to teach my elective on national security and the environment under a contract with them.

Meanwhile, in May of 2001 I took a second student travel group to Africa, this time to Southern Africa. In the past, the NWC's Southern Africa trips had ended with a purely touristic flight to Victoria Falls. I replaced that with Mozambique because I wanted my students to experience a more typical but important African country, one that was in the midst of a critical transition to democracy. Kruger National Park was another addition, partly for its charismatic mega-fauna to be sure, but also to give the students a glimpse of how well the South Africans were managing their labor-and-income-generating tourism sector.

We flew to Johannesburg for a variety of embassy and other briefings there and, mainly, in Pretoria. Following that, we drove for six hours to Maputo, the capital of Mozambique. We made only one call, but it was a gem, on the witty and well-informed Foreign Minister. He did a splendid job of explaining the opportunities and challenges of a potentially wealthy country just emerging from years of murderous civil strife. Then we drove back across the border into South Africa to Kruger for a day and a half of game viewing, plus an expert briefing by a park official on the growing problem of elephant and rhino poaching.

At this point things almost got embarrassing for me, supposedly the expert guide. Our next stop was Durban, and my planned route was to head directly south from Kruger through bite-sized Swaziland, where we would stop for lunch with our Deputy Chief of Mission in Mbabane, its capital. The problem was that while this route looked logical on the map, I had never been on it, and the road turned out to be mountainous and barely paved in places. We made it only because youngish military officers were doing the driving, but it still took more than twelve hours on the road, not counting the lunch stop, where we heard all about the travails of governance in a tiny, traditional African state.

Fortunately the last stretch of our long day was over excellent roads, although it was too dark by then to see the endless sugar fields or the Indian Ocean beaches. After a quick look at Durban we flew to Cape Town, where my successor, John Blaney, lent us my old house, Fiesole, which had lost none of its charm, so I could host a big reception on familiar ground.

On this trip I had a military co-leader, Col. Bob Eskridge, a somewhat taciturn, old-school fighter pilot. The life of the party was one of the students, Lt. Col. Maggie Woodward, an air tanker pilot. At this time, women could not aspire to fly fighters or any other combat aircraft, which resulted in a significant cohort of very smart ladies flying tankers. Maggie was also very good looking; she had once been sent by the Air Force to be an aide to Senator Strom Thurmond, who in his dotage was still famously chasing women, and she entertained us with stories about being pursued by him around his big office table.

She loved to tease the more straight-laced Eskridge, and when I told her about the renowned Afrikaner-Jewish-gay satirist Pieter-Dirk Uys, she immediately started plotting to get him on our schedule, thinking it would probably annoy Eskridge. I told her it wouldn't work; Pieter-Dirk Uys was usually out of town, at his home-theatre in Darling. But I was wrong; he was going to be performing at the University of Cape Town theatre, playing Evita Bezeidenhaut as usual, and Maggie got us all tickets. If Eskridge was upset, he certainly did not show it. Maggie also managed to get us all accommodations, within our budget, at my old favorite, the very luxurious Cape Grace Hotel.

The trip was certainly a success. The students got an extraordinary exposure to the accomplishments and ongoing challenges facing South Africa, while both Swaziland and Mozambique brought home the diversity and importance of the whole southern African region, although as a total learning experience, it was perhaps not quite as dramatic as the West Africa trip the previous year had been.

9/11

On the morning of September 11, 2001, I was back at the National War College, organizing my research notes on the Bali book. It was a beautiful day in Washington, as in New York. My first inkling that anything was wrong came when a colleague across the hall called my attention to television coverage of the first plane to hit the World Trade Center. By mid-morning we could ourselves see smoke rising from the vicinity of the Pentagon, not far upriver. I remember someone speculating that there might have been a helicopter crash there. By early afternoon, as news of what was really going on spread, the NWC had largely closed down as it became increasingly obvious that for most students this might be a difficult trip home. I waited until a little later, and had no trouble driving to Alexandria on my usual route via the Fourteenth Street Bridge.

Barbara's memory is equally dramatic, but from the perspective of someone in charge of other families' children at Potomac School. As I finished teaching my first period class, I learned from a school administrator about the first plane crash into the World Trade Center. I agreed with other teachers that classes should continue, but we decided that high school students were sufficiently mature so that those who had a free period could watch the coverage of the crash (in the pre-cell phone era) on the big TV in the student lounge. Barely had that plan been implemented than the second plane hit the second tower, and then followed the plane which ploughed into the Pentagon. By that time the rumor mill was in full swing, suggesting among other hypotheticals that the nearby CIA headquarters would probably be the next hit, and the TV was turned off.

In addition, several school pupils did have parents who worked at the Pentagon. Mothers and Dads began arriving and collecting their sons and daughters, and, with the best of intentions, others of their children's friends who wanted to go home. In the Upper School, the result was total chaos, as there was no record of which pupils had left school, with whom, and when.

I, with no children in the area to be concerned about, decided to stay at school and help deal first with parents who did not know where their children had gone in the rush of families taking students home from school. For several hours after that, I remained to supervise other students who were still at school because their parents had to stay at their own jobs. We played board games. School busses did not run that afternoon, but at last arrangements were made for every child to get home somehow, and when I finally left, I too had clear sailing to Alexandria because the exodus from downtown and northern Virginia had finished.

Back at Potomac School

That never-to-be-forgotten day occurred right at the beginning of our third year back from abroad. Ann Scott had begun her retirement and I had returned to Potomac School in the fall of 1999, just as we had agreed when she joined the history department in my place after I left for South Africa two years earlier. While I was gone, World History had morphed into a two-year, globally inclusive Ancient and Medieval, then Modern History sequence, divided roughly at the year 1450.

I had what I thought was a brilliant idea for the freshman program in this new scheme, and I worked hard, even going to several weekend seminars on Central Asian history and contemporary affairs at Georgetown University, to expand my background knowledge. I then worked out an end-of-year term paper in which each student chose one area in one time period along the so-called Silk Road to study. Then, each would make an oral presentation based on his or her term paper, and in theory, the whole class would acquire knowledge of the Silk Road in its various geographical and chronological aspects.

It was a bridge too far in complexity—names of people and places were totally unfamiliar, as was Asian geography; in largely nomadic cultures, kingdoms had no borders, or at least unstable ones; and political units came and went too fast to keep track of. I realized only much later when Bob and I traveled in western China and five of the "Stans" how little of the whole convoluted history and geography of the region I myself had really understood when I was trying to teach about it. That was undoubtedly part of the reason I could not make lessons that really taught my students what I hoped they were learning.

My forays into teaching African history were more successful. A beloved English teacher, David Civali, offered a course in African literature, including works written in English and others in translation. He asked me to co-teach the course, and to provide historical and sometimes cultural background for the books read. I found a collection of primary sources and another of background essays as bases for discussion of such topics as the slave trade, inside Africa as well as to Europe and the Americas, and the differences among French, English, Portuguese and Belgian colonial practices and their effects on subject peoples.

Sadly, David died from AIDS in the era before the disease could be successfully managed. My additions had apparently been appreciated, because several students who had taken David's course were the ones who persuaded me to teach a senior seminar on African history the semester before I retired.

AP Modern Europe was no longer offered (too much pablum in easier senior elective course offerings in my opinion), but strong students in the tenth-grade Modern History courses were allowed to take the exam. I offered a series of review sessions to those who were willing to do extra skills work to practice answering the famous DBQ's (document-based questions), and almost all my candidates scored 3 or higher, a sizable minority each year earning 4s or 5s, the top scores.

In my absence, the Model Congress program had flourished to the point where I now had an assistant chaperone, a great improvement in regard to getting adequate sleep. With almost a decade of experience, our delegations were regularly earning individual gavels for their performance in committee work. However, the Model UN program, never strong, still only limped along, and soon after I left, a teacher experienced in debate formed a popular and successful debate team that replaced it.

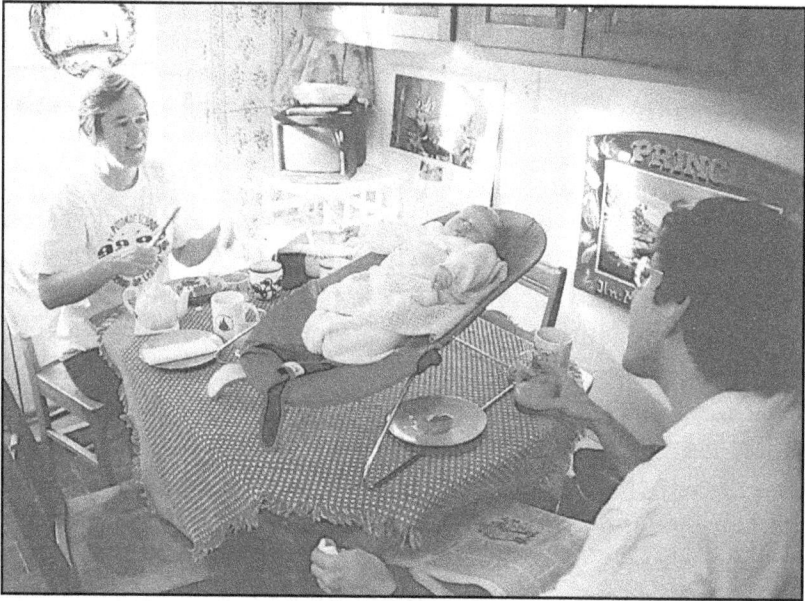

While all this was going on, our first grandchild, Zoe Charlotte Pringle Johnson, arrived. She came to Alexandria for her first Thanksgiving, but spent mealtimes on the table, not at it.

Life without Work?

As each of us retired, which Barbara would in 2003, our initial concern was how to keep busy. The second was having enough money to live interesting lives, while saving enough to help grandchildren with their college educations, as we had been helped with Jamie's and Anne's. Thanks in part to luck and in

Later, Zoe attended her proud mother's PhD graduation from Duke University. Here she poses with David, Anne, who is holding her, and Anne's close friend and fellow newly minted PhD, Janneke HilleRisLambers.

part to Kate and to Char and Clay, we need not have worried about either one.

Bob's Foreign Service pension was generous, enhanced as it was by his contributions to the government's Thrift Saving Plan, the equivalent of a 401(k) account. These would be supplemented by Social Security, and Barbara's TIAA/CREF savings after she stopped working. Our mortgage on 216 Wolfe Street was almost paid off, and we had no other significant debt. We had excellent government health insurance.

In addition, when Kate died in March, 2002, as the result

of a fall at her home near Carmel, she bequeathed to Margot and me money realized from the sale of the small house she had bought at 2911 O Street in Georgetown after my father's death, with the proceeds from selling their residence at 3319 N Street. Char had left Sears stock to her daughters and grandchildren, and Clay's estate would make another welcome contribution to our inheritance. So while we did not feel rich, we were certainly financially comfortable, and we wondered how on earth people far less fortunate than we, but still undoubtedly "middle class," could make do.

Our last visit to Kate was a reunion with the Massel side of the family at Big Sur, south of her home outside Carmel, California, to celebrate her 90th birthday. In this photo besides Barbara are Mario and Joan Soncini on the left, and then Paul Sedway, Kate, and Lynn Sedway.

Bali and its History

After leaving the National War College, I continued working on the Bali book. It turned out that the island's long history fell into nice, chapter-amenable segments. There was a long but little-explored animist prehistory, followed by a rich and quite well documented Hindu, pre-colonial period, including a time when Bali was linked dynastically with its big neighbor, Java. It was a revelation to me that inscriptions on copper plates left by the old Balinese monarchs a thousand years and more ago, often containing intriguing insights on how they governed, were still being discovered in local villages.

Dutch colonizers had been initially too busy trying to control Java to worry much about its little neighbor. They intervened in the 1840's on the north side of the island because its principal port was on the trade route between Java and the Spice Islands. But the Bali visitors know best today consisted, not of the whole island, but of eight little kingdoms isolated on its south side. They were continually fighting with each other, which did not bother the Dutch. However, their rulers had a habit of plundering foreign ships that ran aground on Bali's coral reefs. This annoyed the ship owners and the Dutch feared that, if it continued, it would give the British, based in Singapore, an excuse to intervene and establish themselves in their backyard.

That fear was almost certainly unwarranted, but the Dutch finally decided something had to be done about these unruly Balinese kinglets, so out of line with modern norms. Therefore, in 1904 they invaded Bali again, this time on the south side, with troops and artillery. Ironically, they landed at Sanur, which was to become the site of Bali's first modern hotel. The Dutch were astonished and horrified when the local ruler and his soldiers, dressed in full ceremonial regalia and wielding only krisses, marched into their gunfire and committed ritual suicide, apparently hoping to attract divine intervention. A total of over 1,000 Balinese were killed in this and similar episodes as the new rulers consolidated their control.

It was a bit late in the game for that sort of thing, and the massacres provoked an international human rights uproar, not least in Holland. After the smoke blew away, the Dutch realized they had a cultural gem on their hands, and began thinking about preserving it, above all against the encroachment of Islam, to the point of trying to tell the kinglets how to be more correctly Hindu. They were forbidden, for example, to use images of fierce Europeans wearing top hats to scare away evil spirits; the images had to be of proper Hindu demons. The Balinese of course mainly ignored such rules.

Other fascinating topics included the beginnings of tourism.

By the late 1930s Bali had become a destination for handfuls of globe-trotting glitterati, and a painting of a Balinese temple procession by Miguel Covarrubias ran on a full page of *Life* magazine in 1937, at about the same time as he published his book, *Island of Bali*. Balinese art started to be influenced by expatriate taste and a debate began over whether these stylistic changes were actually dictated by Europeans (they were not). My wonderful editor at Allen and Unwin, Rebecca Kaiser, initially doubted that this topic would make an interesting chapter, but when all was done, she concluded that it was probably the best part of the book, as did many readers. Other chapters covered Bali's experience during the anti-Dutch Indonesian Revolution, its bloody involvement in the anti-Communist killings of 1965-66, the question of why Bali has remained Hindu in a sea of expanding Islam, and the profits and challenges posed by a massive growth of tourism, just beginning during our time in Indonesia (1970-74).

My research included a visit to Clifford Geertz, a famous anthropologist whose writings on Indonesia, including Bali, have been very influential, and his wife Hildred, a scholar of Bali in her own right. Geertz was by then head of the Institute for Advanced Studies at Princeton, the first social scientist ever to hold this post. I was particularly eager to ask him about one of his more famous writings on Bali, *Negara: The Theater State*.[4] In it, Geertz concluded that traditional Balinese kingship had one objective and one only, ritual display, because all other governmental functions were carried out independently by irrigation associations and other non-state actors.

Surely, I asked Geertz, you can't have meant that? Surely all the lavish royal ritual and expenditure must have had a political objective? No, he answered, I meant exactly what I wrote. I asked if he could cite an example of something similar from anywhere else in the world. He thought a minute and cited the late medieval Dukes of Burgundy, known for their magnificent funerals.

But no one else thinks that the pomp of the Burgundian funerals was independent of the royal power they were

---

[4] Clifford Geertz, *Negara: The Theater State in Nineteenth Century Bali*, Princeton University Press, 1980.

clearly intended to demonstrate and reinforce during a long struggle with other noble families for primacy in France. I had posed the question because a Dutch scholar, Henk Schulte Nordholt, had written a book that depicted in detail how the pre-colonial Balinese lords of one kingdom, Mengwi, were real rulers, protecting clients, fighting wars, clearing new lands (which still existed at the time) for cultivation, and certainly not obsessed with ritual for its own sake.[5]

The problem seems to have been that Geertz had focused on the Balinese kingdoms as they functioned during the time he did his fieldwork in Bali, decades after the Dutch had stripped them of all real power. Being entranced by what he saw, and like many anthropologists of his time not much interested in history, he came up with the sociological concept of the Theatre State. As I later learned, once this great man of his profession had proclaimed a good idea, he was typically uninterested in debating it with others. That didn't mean that he had necessarily rejected what you were saying, just that he was moving on to his next great thought.

How to handle this? I did a chapter on the Balinese state, based largely on Nordholt's work, with his permission, and then explained, at the end of the chapter, the contrast between Nordholt's account and the more widely known Geertzian version, making clear which one was obviously correct.

I was able to spend a couple of months in Bali, thanks to a travel grant of $2,000 from the US-Indonesia Society (USINDO). This allowed me to gather first-hand material on recent history, especially the increasingly massive impact of tourism, including domestic tourism, on Bali's beautiful but delicate landscape. I stayed at the Puri Kelapa (Coconut Palace), a small hotel in Sanur, now part of a strip of development stretching down the coast, including dozens of hostelries large and small, where in 1974 there had only been a handful. Still, local culture persisted in the interstices of fast food joints, evident in the daily floral offerings scattered around ATM machines, and the jingle-crash-*boinggg* of Balinese percussion orchestras rehearsing for the next festival.

---

[5] Henk Schulte Nordholt, *The Spell of Power: A History of Balinese Politics*, Leiden, KITLV Press, 1996.

Within walking distance down the road was the Sanur Pillar, with an inscription written on it in 914 AD by an otherwise mysterious Balinese King, Sri Kesarmi Varma. It celebrates his campaign against an unknown enemy somewhere; scholars don't know where. The pillar is now well below ground level, where few tourists notice it.

I hired a part-time research assistant, I Nyoman Wijaya, to help me identify informants, analyze current issues, and navigate the side streets of the provincial capital, Den Pasar. This was hard because, although Den Pasar's streets were named, addresses were not even close to being numbered sequentially; you just had to know where they were. (A typically Balinese numerical challenge?) Fortunately there were plenty of cheap taxis, some of whose drivers were experts at this task.

Wijaya also helped me to find a cartoonist, working for a small magazine, who was satirizing issues like the encroachment of supermarkets and golf courses on rice fields and temples, exactly what I needed for my chapter on the impact of tourism. Other than helping a foreign scholar now and then, Wijaya made a living mainly by writing lengthy, posthumous biographies of ordinary local citizens, paid for by their families, another interesting Balinese custom.

Barbara was able to join me for the last several weeks, and this visit got her started thinking about the possibility of retiring too. Why let Bob travel the world alone? We drove around the island, taking photos for the book and visiting important sites, such as the temple on the north side of the island with whimsical reliefs showing circa 1930 tourists in a touring car being held up by pistol-wielding Balinese bandits (a wishful myth—it never happened), and another relief with one of the first Dutch scholars of the island in Balinese dress, riding a bicycle with wheels made of flowers.

One evening, when we needed cash for further travel, I set off from our hotel in Sanur toward the local ATMs. Since they could dispense only fifty dollars (in Indonesian money) per transaction, this took over an hour, and by the time I returned, Barbara was quite anxious. The totally cheerful Puri Kelapa staff was teasing her. "This is *Baliiii*, not Jakarta!!" they chorused; "You don't have to worreee!!" But that was March,

2002; in November Islamic extremists bombed a nightclub not far away, in Kuta, near the Bali airport, killing over 200 people, mainly Australian tourists. The Indonesians brought in a top-notch police officer, a native of Bali himself, to help catch the perpetrators and restore confidence. He was later elected Governor of Bali.

Near the end of our stay, Barbara and I headed for Karangasem, the easternmost of Bali's kingdoms. A Balinese acquaintance, anthropologist Degung Santikarma,[6] had recommended a beachside restaurant newly established by a friend of his. Although we thought that any fish it served would have been recently caught in the sea lapping at our feet as we ate our meal, the one used for our lunch was apparently several days old and had been not been properly frozen. Barbara came down with a serious case of food poisoning. Luckily we were returning via Bandung to visit old friends, Mary and Filino Harahap, and Filino was able to hunt down an antibiotic (available only by prescription in the US) which started her on the road to recovery and enabled her to survive the long flight home.

Our trip home via Jakarta is worth a mention, because it was then that we really discovered how vast the twenty-first-century capital had become. We already knew that traffic in the city was horrible, often completely stalled. As transport during our few days there, we were privileged to use a fancy car and driver loaned to us by Rukmini Abidin, who with her husband Zainal had founded the premier pharmaceutical factory in Indonesia, and with whom Barbara had worked on museum preservation issues more than two decades previously (see Chapter 6 above).

Still under the weather, Barbara asked permission to use the car to go to Bandung over a holiday weekend; the answer was, "Yes, but we advise against it. Despite suburban

---

[6] Degung was a talented anthropologist who had worked as staff assistant to Clifford Geertz at the Institute of Advanced Studies before returning to Bali to study the killings of 1966 as they had occurred in his home village near Den Pasar. He and his American wife, Leslie Dwyer, were editing an Indonesian magazine, *Latitudes*, which unfortunately did not long survive Degung's severe illness after our visit. I do not know if he ever completed his study of the killings on Bali.

development almost to Bogor, halfway there, the road through the mountains to Bandung has never been widened, and what used to be a two-hour drive at most might now take the better part of a day." We took the train, buying our tickets at the last minutes from scalpers, and sure enough, through the train window we saw horrendous lines of totally stationary cars trying to get to Bandung. It turned out that the city had become famous for its numerous outlet stores.

The Bali book was published in 2004.[7] Its timing was fortuitous: I was able to cover the initial impact of Indonesia's decentralized democracy on Bali, as well as the shock of the Kuta bombing. Knowledge of Bali's history enabled me to end on an optimistic note: having survived so many previous challenges the Balinese would, I felt certain, survive terrorism, as New Yorkers had after 9/11—and indeed they have.

A Short History of Bali is dedicated to granddaughters Zoe and Penelope, using their Balinese names, dictated by birth order: Ni Wayan Zoe and Ni Made Penelope, "to read before they visit Bali," which they did a decade later. The book remains in print as of 2018, without as yet a need for major revision. My mentor and constant source of support and encouragement, Australian Indonesianist Jamie Mackie, wrote a heartwarming review for the *Sydney Morning Herald*:

> This beautiful little book is a gem. Its striking cover photo entices you in; then Robert Pringle's engaging style takes over with crisp, well-informed accounts of Balinese society, politics, culture, agriculture and ecological conditions that add up to something far more than a conventional history. Like Sir Stamford Raffles's *History of Java* (1817), it covers virtually all aspects of life on the island, relating the Bali we see today to the various changes and continuities there over the past 500 years.[8]

---

[7] Robert Pringle, *A Short History of Bali: Indonesia's Hindu Realm*, Sydney, Allen and Unwin, 2004.

[8] Jamie Mackie, "Bright Flash in a Volatile Island Chain," *Sydney Morning Herald*, August 5, 2004.

Being compared to Raffles by someone as qualified as Mackie more than made up for all the virtually unpaid work and bouts of frustration that go into most books.

Barbara Retires: From Teaching to Volunteering

Barbara was in her ninth year of teaching at Potomac School and at least umpteenth of teaching anywhere when she took that extra few days of Christmas vacation to visit Bali at the end of Bob's research stint there. She was also about to reach her sixtieth birthday, and teaching salaries, while they had kept up with the inflation of the past two decades, were still modest. And she already had one grandchild. Time to retire. And so I did, in June, 2003.

While I was teaching in the US, I had had very little time for extra community activities, either to help others or to indulge artistic interest, other than the Brownie troop when Annie was little and our Washington Opera subscription tickets. The latter provided magnificent entertainment with as many as eight performances a season while the great tenor Placido Domingo was artistic director, and we were home for much of his tenure, from 1996-2011. So I decided to occupy my time outside family and the house with two major projects: the Lazarus Ministry at Christ Church and the Bead Museum in DC, founded in about 1998 by the Bead Society of Greater Washington (BSGW).

The Lazarus Ministry had been started several years before I became involved as a small-scale effort to help some of Alexandria's growing population of people living on the margin with emergency financial needs. In those early days, that meant bus tokens, coupons to get free clothing (mainly work clothes, including work boots or business suits) for those with new jobs or the potential for obtaining one soon, a few canned goods, or a $100 payment toward an electricity or gas bill. The program has since become a powerhouse in Alexandria's efforts to support its poorer citizens, and it now deals in larger financial payments on behalf of families threatened with utility cut-offs or eviction from their apartments.

From an almost secret ministry relegated to the basement

of the Parish House, it has morphed into a program which the church is proud to run in the main hall of that building, right next to staff offices and the rector's suite. There is now a large food distribution program once a week, and Bob regularly helps with that effort. I continue to participate in the financial assistance program.

I undertook my other new activity purely for my own enjoyment and continuing education. For years since our Africa postings, we had both been members of the Bead Society of Greater Washington, originally founded in the 1980's to focus on the history of beads and the craft of making jewelry with them. Very soon, besides monthly meetings, it began having semi-annual bead bazaars, at which its members could sell the jewelry and beads they created. To qualify as a 510c(3) organization, the society also donated some of the money earned at these bazaars to various scholars for research projects on bead history and ran outreach programs for local Girl Scouts and others interested in beads. It also sponsored two very successful International Bead Conferences, the second of which, subsequent to the one we attended upon our return from Mali, generated well over $100,000 in profit.

Using that nest egg, Hilary Whittaker, our friend and former Peace Corps director in Mali, led the initiative to found a small museum, initially in one second-floor room of a renovated office building on the corner of 7th and D Streets, NW, downtown. By the time we returned from South Africa, it had moved downstairs into a larger space, created a 30-foot long "Timeline of History through Beads," begun to put on major exhibits, and even established a small store as another source of income. Members had donated hundreds of beads for the Timeline and were continuing to do so, but the record-keeping for the donations lagged way behind the number of beads donated.

So I took on the task, one day a week and later more frequently, of entering data into a database, in the process learning just enough to be dangerous. I was not very efficient at using the complicated computer data-entry program; luckily, the sellers of the software had a great support system. Most important to me was the opportunity to examine hundreds of

Barbara and Hilary Whittaker in front of the Timeline of History through Beads at the Bead Museum in DC.

beads close-up, thus learning about them as I was cataloguing. My official title was "[volunteer] collections manager," though I had none of the training or expertise which that fancy title implied.

For several years in the early 2000s, just as I started working at the museum, it flourished, doing blockbuster (for us) shows on such topics as *Venice, Beadmaker to the World*; *Silver Speaks: Traditional Jewelry from the Middle East [with special emphasis on Yemen]* and *Naga Tribal Adornment: Signatures of Status and Self.* However, the profits generated by two bazaars a year plus the museum's little shop proved inadequate to the task of supporting even such a small museum. Every single year the society treasurer had to dip into the nest egg to make ends meet, and in 2008, after ten years, a board which had refused to admit the obvious had to close the museum precipitously just before Barack Obama's inauguration (during which it managed to rent the premises to a souvenir T-shirt seller to help pay one month's back rent).

As my final and probably most important contribution to the museum, I worked for a whole year trying to find an institution that would accept the Bead Timeline, which after a decade was a treasure trove of beads displayed in chronological sequence, with a guide to the exhibit that contained background information about each one.

At last I discovered that Rod McIntosh, the archaeologist whom we knew from his excavations near Djenné in Mali, had become a professor at Yale University and was a member of the board of directors of the Peabody Museum of Natural History there. Beads, Roman Empire era beads in particular, had been important in dating his site, and he jumped at the chance to acquire the Bead Timeline and attendant records, such as they were, for Yale.

Several years later, when a portion of the Timeline was put on exhibit in the Archaeology Department office building, I had the great satisfaction of learning that another professor had been able to use information from the Timeline to further his research—with the help of Jim Lankton, the anesthesiologist turned bead scholar who had helped create it originally.

A New Addition to the Family

A big new addition to the family arrived in 2004. Our first hint of change occurred when, back from a trip, Bob called Jamie to check in and get some computer problem-related advice, for he was now paying us back with interest for all those years of supporting his education. But this time when I asked him how things were, there was something different in his tone. "Everything is fine," he said, *"just fine."* "Hmm," I wondered, "what is going on?"

Jamie was now a professor of physical oceanography at the University of New Hampshire at Durham. Professionally all was going well; he was not far from tenure. Socially, we were beginning to wonder, as parents do, whether he would ever move on from bachelorhood. Short answer: he did. He had met the lady in question online, which we later learned was by this time not at all unusual.

Kathy was the first of us to meet Zorana Ivcevic, while working a phone bank for Al Gore, then running for president, not far from Jamie's home. When she called Jamie to tell him she was on her way to see him, Zorana, already a stalwart

Zoran and Dragana Ivcevic, parents of the bride, the wedding couple, and Barbara and Bob. The Ivcevices made their first visit to the US to attend the wedding, and they visited us in Alexandria before the great event.

Democrat though not yet a citizen, overheard her and introduced herself. Could Kathy give her a ride there? She was Croatian and a graduate student in psychology.

Jamie and Zorana were married on May 13, 2006, at the Durham Community Church. The wedding was attended by a full panoply of family and friends, midway through a tremendous, days-long rainstorm. Among the most honored guests were Zorana's parents, Zoran and Dragana, who stayed with us at the Three Chimneys Inn, a hostelerie dating to the 1600s. On Jamie's side, the special invitee was his beloved grandfather, Clarence (Clay) Cade. As he had at Annie's wedding, Clay gave a passage from scripture, now reading rather than reciting it from memory as he had six years previously. The reception was at the visitors' center of a nearby state park, once a coastal gun emplacement protecting the Portsmouth harbor. Because many of the wedding party

Bob and flower girl Penelope, the latter not quite sure what was going on—but it is fun.

and other guests had small children, Jamie hired several UNH students to take care of them in the children's section of its small nautical museum so the adult guests could enjoy the reception as storm-whipped waves crashed on the nearby beach. Penelope, a tiny flower girl, had such a good time that, memorialized in a photo we treasure, she finally drifted off to sleep in a box of toys.

The next day there was a post-wedding brunch at Jamie's condominium in Newmarket before most guests dispersed to drive home in the continuing rain. The condo was located on the bottom floor of an old mill building, facing a wide tidal pool, and although none of the wedding party noticed, the

Jamie's beloved Grandfather taught him to ride a bike, took him on fishing trips, went to Parents' Days at Milton and helped him and his sister in countless ways while their diplomatic parents were far away. After Charlotte died, it was Jamie who drove Clay around England to finish his genealogical research on the Cade family. Then, Grandfather, proud of the new scientist in the family, attended his elder grandson's PhD hooding at MIT. Here he reads the passage from Scripture at Jamie and Zorana's wedding ceremony.

river that had once powered the mill was still rising.

The following morning, Jamie and Zorana went to the Town Hall to take care of the next most important thing on their minds—getting civil registration papers of their marriage, so that Zorana could begin the process of becoming a citizen. Only then did the town clerk tell them that the ancient dam holding back the waters of the river was close to breaching, possibly with catastrophic effects, although it had held during a similar flood in 1936. They retrieved Zorana's parents from the Three Chimneys Inn a day early for a planned visit to New York, and let us know what was going on via our first clamshell cell phone as we drove home: "We're all fine," Zorana said, "and our computers and cars are both safe." In the end, amid much deployment of sandbags, the dam held. Jamie wrote, "In time, the water receded. A dam that does not break is not a dramatic thing, but waiting was tense." [9]

---

[9] Jamie and Zorana, e-mail of May 20, 2006.

A word about Zorana's parents: Zoran and Dragana are both engineers and former employees of state companies manufacturing fiberglass products. Later, in 2007 and 2008, we would enjoy their hospitality in Croatia, both in Split and at their second home in Komiza (population 1,500), a fishing village turned yacht anchorage on the Island of Vis, halfway across the Adriatic between Croatia and Italy. Dragana was a superb guide to the endless cultural attractions of Croatia, as well as a terrific cook. There is nothing quite like visiting the Ivcevics in their beach-front home on the island (part of which they rent to tourists during the summer) and going fishing with Zoran just offshore in the early morning.

Through the Ivcevices, we have come to understand better the trauma of post-Yugoslav Croatia. Both of them lost their jobs and their pensions in the transition. Zoran in particular laments the passing of Tito, the downfall of Yugoslav nationalism, and the recrudescence of toxic ethnic politics. He still belongs to the Titoist party. It is a big struggle for them to raise enough money to come visit their suddenly far-flung family.

Alexander Clarence Pringle, our third and their first grandchild, was born on August 19, 2009. So far, he is bilingual and, taking after both his father and his maternal grandfather, intrigued by anything mechanical or electronic.

"Freedom of Information"

I still felt a need for some sort of part-time employment, so after the Bali book was done I thought about part-time work—known as WAE, for "while actually employed"—at the State Department. There was a demand for experienced retirees to help fill staffing gaps, especially at embassies, not least in Africa. Many of my friends had done such work and enjoyed it, and the pay, roughly half one's old salary, made it worthwhile. But by the time I got around to trying it, the Africa Bureau at the State Department had a new policy of employing only administrative officers and secretaries for such work, despite a growing need for experienced ambassadors and DCMs like me.

Moreover, the only way to get into the WAE program was through the office that processed requests to declassify documents under the Freedom of Information Act (FOIA). I decided to try it, on the assumption that, after getting my security clearances reinstated and onto the WAE rolls, I could somehow, and despite the Africa Bureau's unhelpful policy, switch over to more interesting work with a regional bureau. It didn't work.

The FOIA process is a classic case of good intentions run amok. Under it, anyone can request that a classified document be released before the normal thirty-year period, when declassification happens automatically. However there are volumes of regulations, varying for the many agencies concerned, which specify why this may not happen at all, or can happen only after sensitive material has been "redacted," meaning deleted. To administer FOIA, dozens of retired State Department officers were employed at two locations, one for recent material which was computerized, and one for older paper documents where excisions of still-sensitive material, or outright denial of release, had to be done by hand.

In addition to enabling retired government employees to supplement their pensions, FOIA nourished a well-meaning non-profit organization, the National Security Archive[10] located in the library of George Washington University. For a fee, the Archive would help scholars, reporters and others to mine systematically a still-classified database, looking for nuggets to enhance their research. At the time I was there, the 1994 genocide in Rwanda, and especially whose fault it had been, was still a hot topic, and so it was that I found myself declassifying and releasing (or not) memos and cables that had crossed my desk in AF/C—and that in some cases I had written—almost a decade earlier. The ones I had drafted were all excellent, needless to say, so reading them made an otherwise dull day more enjoyable.

Joy of authorship aside, some people liked doing this work for the camaraderie of working with old colleagues, as well as for the money. But these pleasures did not compensate for the dullness of the work, and I stayed there only as long as necessary to compensate for the considerable bureaucratic effort that my employers had made to bring me on board. It

_____
[10] http://www2.gwu.edu/~nsarchiv/nsa/the_archive.html.

did not seem to be leading to other, more interesting, part-
time work.

The declassification process, in addition to being
depressingly tedious, was also bizarrely insecure. Our
huge electronic database, which included relatively recent
material, was clearly not leak-proof. Of course you needed a
security clearance to get inside the building, but once there
you could read anything in the database. Although the most
sensitive material was not supposed to be there—and much
material generated by the CIA and other intelligence agencies
was automatically exempt from declassification—mistakes
were possible. I once came across a State Department cable
from our ambassador in an important developing country
describing the entrenched chief of state and his growing
mental problems with a degree of candor that would have
generated real trouble had it been released or leaked. Chiefs
of mission and other diplomats are paid to do no-holds-
barred analysis of this kind, with reason, but such documents
should, indeed must, be kept classified until the individual
being discussed is safely out of office.

A Glimpse of the World Bank

It was mainly the boredom that convinced me to look for
something else.

In 2003, someone told me about an opportunity for part-
time work at the World Bank which sounded interesting. It
involved the evaluation of about-to-be-implemented Bank
projects by a reviewing staff not directly involved in their
design, the Quality Assurance Group, or "QUAG." The objective
was to determine if the projects would succeed. The pay was
attractive--$775 per day for a limited number of days per
year. So I accepted several jobs in QUAG.

There were two problems. Most of the people working
there, myself excepted, were World Bank retirees, so although
they were theoretically removed from the policy process, they
were, as in the case of FOIA, part of a robust old boy network.
The other and more serious drawback was that, although
the reviews were supposed to be corrective, they were done
only when implementation of the project in question was

imminent, after a long and complex design process. This meant that truly serious criticism entailed annoying, if not enraging, a bevy of one's ex-peers. Inevitably most QUAG reviews produced no more than feeble nitpicking leading to no serious revisions.

One of the biggest projects that came before QUAG when I was there involved a controversial oil pipeline from Chad through Cameroon to the Atlantic. It was controversial because critics thought the World Bank should, especially in Africa, be funding rural development, not helping oil companies. So, in return for Bank financing of the pipeline, President Idriss Deby, a battle-seasoned old fox if there ever was one, agreed to set aside ten percent of the resulting revenues for development projects. Deby promptly broke his promise in 2003 when he needed the money to buy arms to combat the latest would-be coup maker, causing the Bank to cut off most of its projects in Chad. [11]

The ill-fated deal had been pushed hard by then World Bank President Paul Wolfowitz, against the fervent disapproval of most Bank professionals. QUAG offered no serious criticism of it, although not without internal hand wringing. Given Deby's background, it should have been obvious to everyone that he would not hesitate to break his word if he felt sufficiently threatened. Wolfowitz was obviously willing to take the risk involved in trying to use an oil-related project to leverage economic development. He lost the bet, but I admired him for being willing to take it.[12] The critics simply didn't want

---

[11] For a summary of this episode see the UN publication IRIN: http://www.irinnews.org/report/58775/chad-idriss-deby-a-president-under-siege. Deby's earlier role in the displacement of Colonel Haftar's ex-Libyan rebels from Chad, while I was AF/C's office director, is discussed in Chapter 13.

[12] As noted earlier, Barbara and I knew Paul Wolfowitz at Cornell when he was an undergraduate at Telluride, and years later I unsuccessfully applied for a job as his DCM when he was Ambassador to Jakarta, where I think he did a good job, despite his notion that Indonesia's moderate Islam could help us in our struggle against Middle Eastern extremism. George W. Bush appointed him to the World Bank in March, 2005, and he was unpopular there mainly because of his role in promoting the Iraq War and his status as a leading neoconservative. I never had any contact with him at the World Bank. To be clear: I always lamented his tragically successful effort to promote a war in Iraq.

to sully the Bank by getting involved with Big Oil. Indeed, they were uncomfortable about discussing politics at all, as if African leaders were all unsullied technocrats, and there was such a thing as a development project that was not to some degree political.

Democracy in Mali

Perhaps because it was not producing anything of value, QUAG sputtered to a halt, and I did not work for it after 2007. By this time I realized that I could do more interesting work writing about issues in countries where I had served, which could be financed by seeking grants that would at least cover major expenses, in contrast to the pittance I had received for the Bali book.[13]

So I tried to find support for a study of the unexpected evolution of a real democracy in Mali. Serving there from 1987 to 1990 had been a wonderful experience, but at the time I never dreamed that this impoverished autocracy would become, as it had by 2004, a country which would hold three free and fair elections in ten years (1992, 1997 and 2002). Given the rarity of real democracies in Africa and the desirability of more, it seemed worthwhile to explore how this had come about. I made the rounds of potential donors and obtained support from both the newly founded US Institute of Peace and the USAID mission in Bamako. Research included two trips to Africa, one in the summer of 2004 and the other in early 2005. The latter dovetailed nicely with a trip to Uganda to be present at the dedication of a new Dental Clinic at Mengo Hospital in Kampala, partially financed through the efforts of a committee at Christ Church on which we had long served.

That extension of the trip also included fulfillment of a wildlife-viewing dream, as we visited the Bwindi "Impenetrable" National Park, the Ugandan section of a tri-national reserve which includes areas in the Ruwenzori Mountains in Rwanda and Congo. There we climbed a steep

---

[13] In the longer run, the Bali book has been the most financially productive of my books, with the possible exception of the *Rajahs and Rebels* reprint, which generated over $400 in 2015, less than half my (brief) daily rate at the World Bank.

mountainside and spent a half hour viewing a troupe of Mountain Gorillas in the high brush of an old farm. Tourists in the other two countries apparently have clearer views of the gorillas in mature forest with less understory, but our close proximity with a group of energetic juveniles climbing vines and swinging down them, plus a nursing mother and finally a silverback were satisfaction enough. A final plus was a successful early morning birding expedition from Kampala to Lake Victoria, where we were able to see a remarkable Shoebill up close.

As a result of the two research trips, I concluded that a major factor in Mali's apparent success was its long history of multi-ethnic statehood prior to colonialism, which had led to a culture of self-confidence and ingrained ethnic tolerance.[14] Because of it, Mali has a degree of national coherence which, in the springtime of its democracy, seemed poised to help solve a long list of problems, most of them relating to poverty. My optimism, however guarded, was at best premature. Mali stayed poor despite the growth of modern gold mining and floods of aid from donors eager to reward its democracy. Population growth stayed high and as a result, a dangerous cohort of unemployed youth emerged in Bamako, just what the country didn't need.

Most important was the growing handicap of the never-integrated Saharan north, where the Tuareg rebellion of 1990, which had commenced during my ambassadorship, had never really ended. This northern rebellion was revived by a weakening of Mali's democracy under Amadou Toumani Touré, the second president, who had been one of its founding heroes.[15] The army proved incapable of dealing with growing desert-based disorder, hijacked by non-Malian Islamic extremists and fuelled by growing income from trafficking in drugs, arms and people.

The result was a military coup in Bamako in 2012 and eventual French intervention, which brought short-term

---

[14] Robert Pringle, "Democratization in Mali: Putting History to Work," Peaceworks no. 58, Washington, United States Institute of Peace, 2006, http://www.usip.org/publications/democratization-in-mali-putting-history-work.

[15] See the end of Chapter 12 for Touré's role.

stabilization and new elections. But it is not clear as of 2017 whether Mali's democracy can truly be revived, despite its strong cultural foundation. Nor is it clear how long it will take to solve security problems in the Saharan north without a major international policing effort that includes Algeria, Niger, Libya, Chad and other bordering countries. Nothing of that scope is in sight, not surprising given the degree of turmoil demanding attention in other areas of North Africa, the Middle East and elsewhere.

Meanwhile, in the middle of all this, the grandchildren grew into their preschool years.

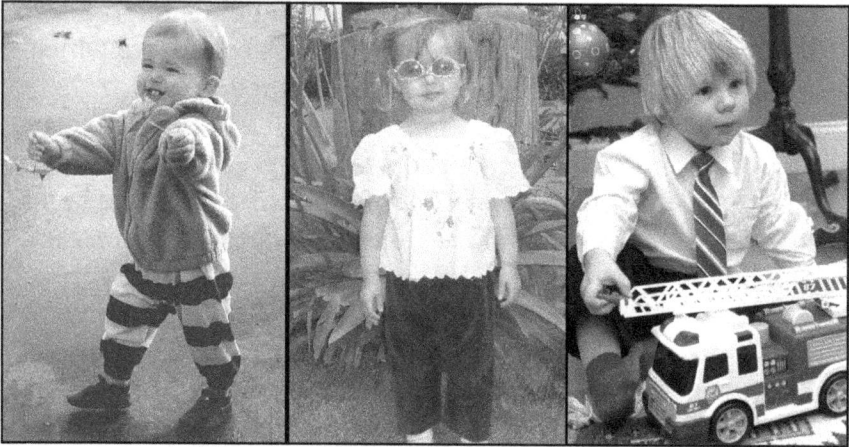

Zoe ...   *Penelope ...*   *and Alexander.*

Islam in Indonesia Observed, and a Return to Sarawak

My next project was a book on Islam in Indonesia, intended for generalist leaders worried by the possibility of violent Islamic extremism in the world's most populous Muslim-majority nation. The idea was to present the historical facts about Indonesian Islam, in the context of the country's profound cultural diversity. The goal was to produce a kind of desktop guide and primer for generalist readers. I hoped that it would enable anyone going to Indonesia for the first time not to be misled by unduly scary headlines, at a time of growing and often irrational global concern about Islam in general.

The US–Indonesia Society provided crucial support, even more so than in the case of the Bali book, but no money. For that, Al LaPorta, its president, steered me toward a foundation I had never heard of, Smith Richardson, knowing that its staff included Alan Song, an Asia specialist interested in Indonesia. It was excellent advice. I was also applying to several much better known Washington think tanks. By the time I had finished struggling through their bulky application forms, in October, 2006, Smith Richardson was ready to give me a grant of $125,000, almost as much as I had applied for.

H. Smith Richardson was the son of a rural North Carolina druggist, Lunsford Richardson, who developed the formula for Vicks VapoRub, an over-the-counter treatment for stuffy noses and the aches and pains of colds and allergies. The guidelines that he established for his foundation were vague in the extreme, something like "Do anything that will benefit our great country." Later, however, the managers of the foundation, still financed by the VapoRub fortune, embarked on an increasingly right-wing trajectory, leading some people to wonder why I was getting money from *them*. But by the time of my grant, centrism and sanity had been restored, and Smith Richardson was donating mainly to organizations like Harvard, Yale and the Council on Foreign Relations—but also, it must be confessed, to the American Enterprise Institute.

The book organized itself around some obvious questions. How did Islam arrive at a place so far from Mecca? Did the global growth of Islamic extremism pose a special threat to a nation that had always had trouble achieving unity? Was Indonesian Islam the real (read "Arab") thing, or some watered-down, tropicalized version? To the extent that it was relatively moderate, could the religion of this largest Muslim-majority nation have a benign impact on more "fanatical" variants elsewhere? This idea had already attracted the attention of policy makers in the US, including, as mentioned earlier, our old acquaintance Paul Wolfowitz.

It seemed obvious to me that generalist readers did not need or want to know about the doctrinal minutiae of Indonesian Islam. That was just as well, because I am no expert on Islamic law and I don't speak or read Arabic. But there are some major theological issues that the lay reader does need to comprehend. One is the meaning of "Sharia Law," or, more correctly, just "Sharia," widely interpreted by non-Muslims as a universally accepted, rigid code based on literal interpretation of Muslim scriptures and applicable to all Muslims.

In fact, and most importantly, it is none of the above. Sharia has always been subject to debate, and many Muslims believe it is as much about religious values as it is about "law" as we comprehend it. You have to understand this to understand why Muslims, just like Christians, are prone to lethal doctrinal disagreements—and why some want a universal authority figure, a Caliph, even more powerful than the Pope in Roman Catholic Christianity.

Another critically important doctrinal subject is Sufism, or Islamic mysticism, which is a lot more than whirling dervishes and holy men in caves. It is both a conservative and a liberal force in Islam. Sufism bears importantly on the broad difference between two major categories of Islam in Indonesian political culture. One has been influenced by the latest trends in Middle Eastern practice, often transmitted by Islamic pilgrimage to Mecca. The other is rooted in the need to coexist with traditions and mindsets dating to pre-Islamic times in Indonesia, plus the imperative to establish and maintain national unity. This dichotomy is just as important as the US distinction between "red" and "blue" politics. It's a subject clear in its essence but regionally complex; do read the book—or many books—if you want to know more.[16]

Already retired, Barbara was able to accompany me to Indonesia in January, 2007, for several months of fieldwork. In addition to Jakarta, we visited Central and East Java, West Java (Bandung), West Sumatra and Aceh, in that order, mainly to interview Indonesian students of Islam, and to take photographs for the book. Each place has its own styles of Islam and Muslim politics. Aceh, for example, is the only province in the country which has seemed bent

---

[16] Robert Pringle, *Understanding Islam in Indonesia: Politics and Diversity*, Singapore and Honolulu, Didier Millet/University of Hawaii Press, 2010.

on establishing its own Islamic State at the local level. But, a typically Indonesian twist, not all Acehnese are agreed on this aim, and even Aceh's red-hot Muslims never supported the Islamic extremists operating elsewhere in the country who brought a plague of violence to Indonesia after the establishment of its democracy in 1999.

In Bandung we visited a well-known Acehnese artist, A.D. Pirous, who is anything but fundamentalist in his political views. From him, we learned that there is no universally accepted ban in the Muslim world against representational art, as we should have known from the obvious example of classical Persian (Iranian) art.

Back in Jakarta we benefited from the hospitality of the embassy Public Affairs Officer, Mike Anderson, with whom we stayed, and from the help of many old friends, including Barbara's Ganesha Society friend, Rukmini Abidin. She, like many others, was interested in hearing about my work. The Abidins were, moreover, classic examples of the Minangkabau culture of West Sumatra, with its well-rooted thirst for education, entrepreneurial talent, and, still visible, a matrilineal, even matriarchal social structure which coexists with devout, but not fundamentalist, Islam. One must never forget people like this when attempting to generalize about Indonesian Islam.

Obama's presidential candidacy stirred a flurry of interest in Indonesian Islam in the US. Shortly after our arrival in Jakarta, international media reported that he might have attended a "radical *madrasah*" there. Reporters fanned out in search of it. What they found was a public school, not a private Islamic school, which is what "*madrasah*" usually means. It was located in the city's toniest neighborhood, within walking distance of the American Ambassador's Residence and our old house on Jl. Mangunsarkoro. Obama had attended this school after his mother could no longer afford a more expensive Catholic school. When a wide-eyed American reporter asked the principal if there were many Muslims there, he explained calmly that of course there were, Indonesia's population being more than three quarters Muslim.

Barbara had several opportunities to learn more about beads during this extended stay in Indonesia. We took the opportunity to renew contact with Sumarah Adhyatman, who had headed the Indonesian wing of the Ganesha Society volunteers at the National Museum when we lived in Jakarta. During that period, Marah's husband was special assistant to Adam Malik, the Foreign Minister. Later, she became curator of Malik's extensive collection of Chinese porcelain, which she probably helped him acquire. Years later, he sold it all, and she was crushed. But she had remained interested in all aspects of Indonesian and Southeast Asian art, and with her family's considerable financial resources had collected many fine works for herself.

By the time of our visit, her house was an exquisite museum. Not only had she bought a few pieces of the Malik ceramics collection and many beautiful examples of Balinese carving and painting, but she had acquired a small collection of old beads either traded to or made in Indonesia, including perfect examples of the so-called "Majapahit" beads, which at that time still remained mysterious as to their time and place of manufacture. She said that when she saw expatriates buying up the beads, she decided she needed to collect some too, in order that this interesting component of Indonesia's heritage not be lost to foreign collectors. That had been her philosophy in assembling Adam Malik's ceramics collection years before, and also in translating catalogue records in the National Museum from Dutch into Indonesian to help stem alleged illegal sales from that collection.

With a friend, Marah had written, in Indonesian and English, the only work available today on Indonesian beads and beadwork.[17] When we called on her, she not only showed us her bead collection, but gave us a guided tour of other objects in her house. In addition, she introduced us to her "cousin" (meaning a close relative), Yekti Kusmartono, a younger woman from Central Java who had moved a whole traditional Javanese house to Jakarta, where she reconstructed it as an addition to the family home and was using it as a studio for her flourishing bead shop and jewelry workshop.

Yekti became a good friend, and I bought several beads from

---

[17] Sumarah Adhyatman & Redjeki Arifin, *Manik-manik di Indonesia/Beads in Indonesia*, Jakarta: Penerbit Djambatan, 1993. Sumarah Adhyatman is also the author of various other volumes about the history of Asian art.

her. Just as important, she gave us directions to Jombong, the village in East Java, just beyond the Central Javanese border, where a flourishing glass bead making industry had grown up over the past several decades. The bead makers there worked only with the lamp-wound (now gas flame) technique, and relied heavily on scrap glass as a raw material, but they could imitate the appearance of any bead made by another method.

Some "Majapahit" bead copies were straight out of that village, but from the local beadmakers' point of view, their whole operation was totally legitimate: if you wanted a particular bead, they would make you one that was exactly the same in outward appearance. Dayaks came regularly from Borneo to order "heirloom" beads, and in fact we later saw modern beads with heirloom designs in our Sarawak friend Stephan Wan Ullok's collection, though he knew what they really were. In addition, several wholesalers were commissioning strings of thoroughly modern, often original beads from the various workshops in the village. Savvy Indonesian shoppers knew of the village, and came there to shop.

The sequel to this story is that, a few years later, I put bead researcher Jim Lankton, an early member of BSGW and major donor to the Timeline at the Bead Museum, into contact with Yekti. Jim had left his flourishing anesthesiology practice to study the chemical composition, and thus the origin, of ancient beads. With Yekti's help, he finally located a small village on the extreme eastern tip of Java which makes beads by the drawn bead technique and may well be the successor to the site where several centuries ago a small settlement of immigrant Chinese artisans created the so-called Majapahit beads.

The continuation of the East Java visit itself was equal parts interesting and astonishing. In Malang we visited Moertini, the Kenney's long-term nanny beloved by our whole family because she had traveled across the Pacific to the US with us in 1972. We were delighted to find her happy in a modest, but new and well-appointed house, close to her children and grandchildren, who were flourishing on property that her US wages had enabled her to buy for them.

Then came the astonishing part of our East Java visit. What

should have been a straightforward bus trip, then flight, to take us back to Jakarta, morphed into a two-day adventure due to a "mud volcano" which had suddenly erupted outside Surabaya and completely blocked the main road between that city and Malang.[18] The trip to the airport was suddenly going to take more than half a day. Then we learned that no flights were going to Jakarta anyway, because torrential rains had flooded its major airport. We ended up getting seats on a new branch of the national airline called "City Link" that aimed to connect major cities without going via Jakarta, and we went directly to visit the Harahaps in Bandung.

On our way home, we stopped in Singapore for a glimpse of how its small Muslim minority was faring. Our friend from Cornell days Chan Heng Chee, by then Singapore's Ambassador to the US, had assisted Bob with references and provided introductions to local scholars. After that we revisited Sarawak, for the first time since we had been there with Jamie and Annie more than thirty years previously to introduce them to friends at the Sarawak Museum and show them Benedict Sandin's new home at Karanggan Pinggai.

We had not been eager to come back to this place that we loved, knowing how despoiled it had become by ruthless logging and dam building. We decided it was time to stop being squeamish and go back, if only to see old friends, including Stephen and Brigitte Wan Ullok, with whom we stayed. Trade beads being for us an interest sparked much later during assignments in West Africa, we had hardly noticed their importance when we lived in Sarawak in the 1960s. But Stephen came from a long line of Kenyah chiefs, and this time we were fascinated by his excellent collection of glass and stone beads, many inherited from his ancestors—and some modern ones that may well have come from Jombong, the East Javanese village we had just visited. Both his home and his hotel were decorated with the scrolling designs and fanciful animals of the Kenyah people.

We were surprised by strong interest among our Iban friends in *Rajahs and Rebels,* the book based on Bob's PhD

---

[18] By 2016 when we were writing this, it was still spewing forth mud and had completely altered the topography of the land southeast of Surabaya.

dissertation. They did not like the fact that it was out of print, even though used copies were available online. Their interest was clearly related to growing political restiveness on the part of the Ibans and other non-Muslim indigenous peoples, accompanied by a desire to know more about their own history. Early in our stay we met with Leonard Linggi Jugah, a friend from our 1965-66 stay in Sarawak, now director of a foundation and a first-rate museum of Iban culture, and he gave us a dinner attended by several of our other Iban friends. One of them pulled me aside and asked, referring to the book's title, "Where are the *Rebels* now?" I was startled, but this sentiment probably had something to with the subsequent approval of a new edition of the book, published by the University of Malaysia Press (Sarawak).

The effort to create a new edition began with an electronic copy of the original, riddled with typos due to crude scanning; this first try was so poor (all footnote numbers were transformed into asterisks, for example) that it was unusable. However, a bright, energetic University Press employee, Resni Mona, took it upon herself to produce a better scan, and she and Barbara spent months, communicating over the Internet, to restore the original text and notes. I added a new introduction, explaining how the book had come to be written, plus a few thoughts on what I might have said differently if I had written it in 2007.

As many among the departing British had feared in 1966, Brooke rule left the Ibans, the largest indigenous group in Sarawak, with very little education and a state-sanctioned addiction to internal strife. As a result, the creation of Malaysia found them utterly unprepared to resist rampant exploitation by the new rulers and their local allies, a truly tragic flaw.[19]

The Malay Pirates Strike

Just as the new edition was struggling to be born, a Malaysian string of bookstores (Synergy Media/MPH Books/S.A. Majeed & Co) decided to print another new edition, without asking

---

[19] "Author's Introduction to the New Edition, *Rajahs and Rebels: The Ibans of Sarawak under Brooke Rule, 1841-1941*, Universiti Malaysia Sarawak, Kota Samarahan, 2010, pp. xv-xvi.

me, as part of a twelve-volume "Malaysia Heritage Series."
When I contacted the company to protest, one of its managers
claimed to have written to Cornell University Press for
permission to proceed, without receiving any answer. He said
he then concluded that I was probably deceased.

He did not deny copyright infringement, and the book
included a peculiar note admitting that, deceased or not, I
had a "moral right to be identified as the author of this work."
On the same page, it showed me as the copyright holder and
included the normal "all rights reserved" notice. In a way,
it was flattering to be a victim of piracy, an old tradition in
Malaysia; one chapter of the book is after all about Malay and
Iban "pirates" in the nineteenth century. But I feared that the
pirated version would put the kibosh on the legal reprint,
since it seemed to be selling quite briskly at MPH bookstores,
which were in every airport in the country.

So I wrote the US Embassy in Kuala Lumpur about this
infringement of intellectual property rights, and the embassy
sent a "Cease and Desist" order to MPH, via the appropriate
Malaysian minister. That resulted in a very sad-sounding
letter to me from Peer Mohammed of MPH saying that he was
ordering the recall of all the books and inviting me to come to
Malaysia (at my expense) to watch them being "pulped." No
thanks. Or I could have hired a pricey lawyer to pursue the
case, seek damages, etc., which would have taken years and
cost far more than any possible reimbursement. Meanwhile
friends in Malaysia, plus daughter Anne when she went
out one summer to lead a natural history seminar in North
Borneo, kept telling me that copies of the pirated edition had
survived the probably mythical pulping and were still on sale.

Undaunted, we ploughed ahead with the legitimate new
edition, and it came out in 2010. Initial sales were good,
producing about $US 500 in royalties in the first two years,
paid in Malaysian currency. I am donating all royalties to
Leonard Linggi's non-profit organization, the Tun Jugah
Foundation, named after his father, a famous Iban leader,
partly because bank charges to transfer the funds to the US
in dollars would eat up about forty percent of the amount in
question.

I went to Australia for more research on Indonesian Islam

in the summer of 2007. Jamie Mackie set up a series of very useful appointments and cheered me on at times when I wasn't totally sure of where I was going. In Canberra, Jim Fox, whom we had helped with his research in Indonesia three decades previously,[20] was now head of the Australian National University's Research School of Asia and the Pacific, which he had helped develop it into what was arguably the world's most important center of Indonesian studies. It was noteworthy for its talented faculty and an unmatched array of Indonesian graduate students, many of whom were deeply knowledgeable about Indonesian Islam, and I profited greatly from interviewing them.

Curiously, I had trouble finding a publisher for the book. It was perhaps a little too specialized for a trade publisher, yet not specialized enough for a university press. The University of Hawaii Press agreed to publish it, but it would have taken what seemed to me an excessive length of time and there would have been little room for photographs. Jamie Mackie suggested Didier Millet, a French-origin, Singapore-based publisher with a good reputation, and it was willing to produce a better illustrated product faster. Once Didier Millet agreed to publish, the University of Hawaii Press was happy to put out an identical "American" reprint edition legally marketable in the US, something that Didier Millet could not do.

Didier assigned me an editor I had never met, Ibrahim Tahir, a Singaporean and a Muslim. Although very pleasant, he was sometimes inclined to be fussy about my treatment of matters relating to Islamic doctrine. I didn't blame him for that, but I did remind him that the book was about the history and politics of Islam, not a treatise on Islamic law. It is not easy working with an editor you have never met. But *Understanding Islam* in Indonesia appeared in 2010, thanks in no small part to Ibrahim.[21]

The book turned out as planned, including a good range of photos and footnotes at the bottom of the page, not in the back, something few if any American publishers would have

---

[20] See Chapter 6.

[21] Full title: *Understanding Islam in Indonesia: Politics and Diversity*, Singapore, Editions Didier Millet and Honolulu, University of Hawaii Press, 2010.

agreed to. It also has many tools to aid non-scholars: a detailed table of contents, a glossary, and a very select bibliography, including online sources.

Most academic specialists on Indonesia accepted the book, but with some important exceptions they regarded it without great interest—after all, it is *their* job to interpret Indonesia to the world. As for the generalist readers for whom it was written, they certainly did not buy the book in great numbers, and to this day (2015) Amazon shows only one serious reader review, written, as such reviews often are, by an on old friend, Judy Bird. The book has, however, been extremely useful to me in my own occasional teaching about Indonesia.

17

Looking Back, Looking Forward

The publication of both *Understanding Islam in Indonesia* and the new edition of *Rajahs and Rebels* in 2010 were the culmination of my career as an author of books about history of the great world outside our family. Since then Barbara and I have settled into retirement, focused on family, friends, travel, house and garden, photography, bird watching, glass beads, civic and charitable endeavors, art, music, exercise and, this

Christmas, 2009, celebrated with the whole family, including Jamie and Zorana's son Alexander, three months old, who with Zoe and Penelope has completed the next generation.

family history. We continue to live in our old house at 216 Wolfe Street in Alexandria, wondering how we ever survived its narrow confines with two children, fortunately pre-adolescents. With them gone and the lovely new third floor, why should we not pretend we are on a yacht, and continue to thrive here? We have plenty of room to host children and grandchildren who come to visit and also to welcome far-away friends who occasionally find their way to our nation's capital.

Globetrotting and Bird Watching

With the global expansion of tourism and relatively cheap airfares, we have been able to do a lot of travel in our retirement years. Some of our earlier trips (to Mali, Indonesia, Sarawak) were associated with writing and visiting old friends. More travel has been to interesting places we had studied but never visited (Vietnam and China, and much earlier Russia) or ones we knew less about (Mongolia, Guatemala, Egypt, India [Gujarat], Central Asia, Ethiopia and Mexico). A bit has been primarily for bird watching (Panama, Costa Rica, Cuba, and Trinidad and Tobago).

Twice we have paired visits to Zorana's parents in Croatia with other trips, once to a bead conference in Istanbul and once with a Harvard 50th reunion trip to Greece. We have sometimes stayed with Foreign Service friends and asked them to recommend itineraries or local travel agencies—this tactic has worked well in countries like Mongolia, Ethiopia, Vietnam and Italy—but more often now we are going with small tour groups.

We've learned that a lot of luck is involved in modern tourism. Our fantastic tour of the Silk Road countries (Eastern China plus five "Stans") was greatly enhanced by its small size—due to dropouts, not planned that way. Good leaders are, of course, another key ingredient of a successful trip. Mark Kenoyer, a mix of native son (of missionaries) and deeply experienced scholar, who took us to see Indus River civilization sites and much more in Gujarat, was an unbeatable example of what tour leadership should be. Our recent guide in Mexico combined deep knowledge of his own country with English language fluency that made his explanations instantly comprehensible and always interesting, and he was fascinated by Barbara's knowledge of European history relevant to Mexico (think Emperor Maximilian).

We know that if you don't record it, you don't really learn about it. So we take notes, write trip reports, assemble photo albums and digital slide slows, even hard-cover photo books on Central Asia, Ethiopia, Costa Rica, Cuba and Mexico, thanks to *mycanvas.com*, a spin-off from the Mormon genealogy website, *ancestry.com*.[1] These albums, especially the privately published ones, have been almost wholly Barbara's work (with a preponderance of photos by Bob). Yet all our travel has made us realize that when it comes to learning, no tour, however well documented, can begin to compare with actually living and rearing children abroad. If you have ever done so, it will make you wince to hear others announce that they have "done" Mali or Malaysia.

Having said that, even short-term travel certainly does educate. The best places for learning were the countries we knew little or nothing about, beyond the detritus of good educations. Central Asia was a good example. We knew the Silk Road as a series of dots across the Eurasian steppes, with Borodin's symphonic tone poem swelling and fading in the background and the golden peaches of Samarkand somewhere out there. We did not know that Kyrgyzstan has 8,000 glaciers, or forests of wild apple trees, or that nomadic herding still flourishes across the region because it makes economic sense, or that Turkmenistan has what is probably the looniest dictatorship in the world next to North Korea.

Most importantly we got an indelible glimpse of Han Chinese imperialism in Xinjiang, and began to appreciate why the Stans, for all their problems, are lucky to have been buffered against the expansion of China by a modern history of Russian/Soviet rule. Despite their dictators and other problems, they seem to have some chance of surviving and even flourishing while doing business with both Russia and the Eastern colossus.

---

[1] [M]ycanvas.com is great because it allows more sophisticated layout than less expensive sites AND excellent technical support (talking with real people).

(Left) Visiting the grandchildren where they live: Zoe and Penelope took us to see The Nutcracker ballet during a Christmas visit in 2017.

(Below) We were joined by Aunt Kathy, who has meant so much to her Pringle niece and nephew, for lunch at Wentworth-by-the-Sea near Portsmouth, New Hampshire, sometime the same year. Left to right: Barbara, Jamie, Kathy, Zorana, and Alexander. As usual, Bob was behind the camera.

At home, Washington's museums, art galleries and operas have been a never-ending fantasia. For a time, we made a plan to reserve one day a week to visit a new museum exhibit, but we have never quite adhered to it. Plus we began going to the fine museums in Richmond (the Virginia Museum of Fine Arts) and Baltimore (the Walters Art Gallery), despite the terrors of I-95. We usually go to New York by train, sometimes on the way to visit children further north. We have a special relationship with the Smithsonian's Museum of African Art, because Bob donated to it many of his photographs of Burkina Faso and Mali (while retaining copies). So we get invited to parties at the Museum, excellent in almost every respect, even though no drinks are allowed, sensibly, in the exhibition area.

We never get tired of visiting the Shenandoah and hiking its trails, a tradition that began when our children were young, and continued with Kate during her visits at dogwood flowering time. And we have a very special relationship with Huntley Meadows, a nature preserve in nearby Fairfax County. Once a wooded wetland; then, after the land was drained, a farm; then a military communications site; then, during the Cold War, an anti-aircraft missile site, it was eventually sold to Fairfax County for $1. Beavers soon multiplied and the old wetland plus fringing forest came back; today it is a green oasis completely surrounded by city.

We participate every Monday, year around and almost regardless of weather, on an organized bird walk through this place. The birds are counted and the results reported to Cornell University's Lab of Ornithology, which maintains a national statistical base, as well as a large educational program on the Internet for birders. The commander and soul of the Huntley birding operation is Harry Glasgow, an army veteran. He still barks commands at us despite worshiping Aldo Leopold and Henry David Thoreau.

Attendance at the Monday walk, which has been going on since 1985, is amazingly diverse in terms of socio-economic status and bird-watching skills. We include an ex-reporter, a hospice nurse, a retired statistician, a pastry chef, a former Deputy Director of the Voice of America (who chirps in many languages) and several kinds of scientists, one of whom is the Official Huntley Counter of Canada Geese. Regular attendees include Stuart and Pam Davis. Stuart is a former colleague of Barbara's from the history department at The Madeira School, and they are the ones who introduced us to the Huntley group. They, along with three others in the group, Barbara and John Perry, and Dixie Sommers, are also among our most helpful travel advisers—as we are sometimes theirs.

Novice birders up to octogenarians with weak eyes can see and learn about birds well beyond their skill levels thanks to the help (and spotting scopes) of others. After an hour or two of walking and neck-craning, Harry yells "I'm going to go fix the coffee!" and this entrancing assemblage gradually retires to a Denny's restaurant on nearby Route 1 for breakfast, where the bird count is compiled. Our large group is attended at a long row of tables specially set up for us by a priceless waiter named Mo, for Mohammed. He is Moroccan, although most of the customers at Denny's are Hispanic, and many of them plus some of our colleagues probably assume he is also. On Monday holidays the place is mobbed, and one of us hosts a potluck brunch at home instead.

Monday morning birding group at Huntley Meadows. On this occasion we were guests at a holiday potluck at the home of Stuart and Pam Davis.

In compiling the count, Harry frowns on unlikely sightings. If someone says he saw a Count Raggi's Bird of Paradise, both white eyebrows go up, because such a report would get him in trouble with those higher up the ornithological chain of command. Even a Marsh Wren (rare at Huntley) may be redacted in favor of a Winter Wren (tiny but slightly more common in cold weather), but certainly not a Carolina Wren, too loud and familiar to be confusable.

Part of Huntley's appeal is returning to the same place week after week throughout the whole year and noticing the seasonal changes, both plant and animal. Question: In which season would you guess that Huntley has the most birds? Answer: probably fall. Seasonal migrants visit in spring and fall, and winter is rich in waterfowl. In summer, Congress is out of session and everyone else leaves the region as well.

Joking aside, the birds that remain tend to be staying close to nests, which are generally hidden, at least until they prepare to migrate south. Mysteries abound. Question: How can ducks bear to swim around in icy water and even walk on ice with nothing on their webbed feet? Answer: I have no idea.

Since we first started watching birds in Ouagadougou, birding has become unexpectedly and enormously popular in the US, and is today an important force in the conservation movement. Not long ago we walked out to the Hunting Creek inlet immediately south of Alexandria, mainly to take a walk and not expecting to see any unusual birds; I did not even take my camera. Among the usual seagulls, Mallards and Canada Geese, I saw something different swimming across the inlet in full view. "It looks like a domestic goose has escaped," I told Barbara. Wrong. A few minutes later a man with a spotting scope approached and asked us if we had seen "It." It turned out to be a White-fronted Goose that had strayed off its normal migration route from Greenland to the Texas coast, and e-Bird was spreading reports of its presence and location.

The birders who showed up due to this notice were mainly middle aged or elderly, like us, but most of them seemed to be novices. Several were grateful when we could show them the rare goose; however, by the time they arrived it was almost concealed in a confusing group of common Canada Geese and presented only an obscure rear view. But a sighting is a sighting, and one eager novice thanked us for helping add a 200th bird to his life list.

Strife on the Alexandria Waterfront

In 2010 a proposal to rezone the Alexandria Waterfront got us involved in local politics. In all our comings and goings, we had hitherto paid little attention to City Hall. But now the Greater Washington area was booming as never before, and inevitably developers were agitating to rezone our waterfront to allow more and bigger buildings, both commercial and residential, plus hotels. Their eagerness increased when the state of Maryland promoted new, multi-story development, eventually including a big casino, at National Harbor, well within sight across the Potomac. The result has been a permanent frisson of envy among some city officials and developers on our side of the river.

Alexandria has an Old and Historic District, including many solid blocks of pre-Civil War buildings like our own house. Its current waterfront has few historic structures, with the exception of some great old warehouses like the one we lived next to at 103 Prince Street. However, we and many other Alexandria residents believed (and still do) that misguided overdevelopment would affect the adjacent historic district badly in many ways, and would forgo a great opportunity to do something truly worthwhile with an inherently beautiful and historical river vista.

A major target of the developers was a pair of newsprint warehouses owned by Robinson Terminal, a subsidiary of the *Washington Post.* Looking toward the river from our house, located on a natural dike deposited by past floods, we could until recently see the superstructures of ocean-going freighters bringing newsprint from Finland and Canada, docking beyond the trees just below us. But the *Post* was hemorrhaging money (this was before Amazon mogul Jeff

From our house on Wolfe Street, we used to see ocean-going cargo ships like the one in the distance behind the snowplow bringing newsprint for the Washington Post. Now condominiums are being built where the warehouse was, and the future of the docks is uncertain.

Bezos bought it) and anxious to cash out. So its management lobbied hard for rezoning to allow greater commercial and residential density, which would raise the price of the warehouses the *Post* wanted to sell, and they succeeded.

Neighborhood sentiment favored a mixed development model emphasizing open space plus art and history features that would have complemented the old houses of the adjacent historic district, which had narrowly escaped obliteration by "urban renewal" during the 1960s. This was, after all, George Washington's waterfront and the major town on what is in many ways our national river, located at the junction of its upstream and tidal portions. Some of us suggested a Museum of the Potomac River, illustrating historical topics such as the river's critical role in the negotiations that led to the Constitutional Convention in 1787, and its later importance as a massive logistics base for Union forces during the Civil War.

Other displays might have addressed the entire range of river-linked environmental issues exemplified by the Potomac, from pollution to the disappearance of the massive sturgeon, now on the edge of extinction due to overfishing and upstream dams. The northernmost of the two *Post* warehouses, which has a commanding view of the river and a dock capable of handling big ships, would be an ideal site for such a Museum.

Our organization[2] did extensive research on other cities which have invested in riverfronts worthy of their respective heritages. It demonstrated that while such efforts require long-term planning and sophisticated fund raising, most of them become better for businesses in the long run, and more profitable than simply accepting high density, mediocre architecture, and maximum profits from fast turnover of real estate. Notable examples are common, including our neighbor Baltimore and even inland municipalities like San Antonio and Oklahoma City, accomplished in the latter case under a staunchly Republican mayor.

However, the solid Democratic majority controlling

---

[2] Our unwieldy title was CAAWP, (Citizens for an Alternative Alexandria Waterfront Plan). Later, after the battle was largely lost, it was changed to Friends of the Alexandria Waterfront.

Alexandria's government, largely in the pocket of out-of-town developers, has been uninterested in an expensive, long-term effort. Just before the waterfront debate erupted, they had succeeded in rescheduling the next City Council election to 2012, so it coincided fatally with the presidential election, in which Barack Obama headed the ballot. In heavily Democratic Alexandria, enough citizens voted a straight ticket to give its solidly Democratic City Council and Mayor free rein to approve a wall of hotels, condominiums and office blocks along the waterfront from Prince Street to Wolfe Street, adding little new park space or educational features.

The battle for the properties south of King Street seems to be over. The big newsprint ships are no longer coming. Robinson Terminal South has already been razed, and construction of modern glass and steel condominiums is already underway. But Robinson Terminal North, where we had dreamed of a Museum of the Potomac River, with its lovely upriver view of the Washington skyline, is in limbo due to the discovery of severe pollution in the underlying soil. It might end up as a park or even a museum after all.

Looking Back at the Foreign Service

We have not forgotten the Foreign Service. We have been able to keep up with it through contacts with friends of our generation, younger colleagues still on active duty, and Bob's teaching, mainly about Indonesia, at the Foreign Service Institute.

We have mixed feelings about the future of our diplomatic service. There is no question that impressive people are still joining the Foreign Service,[3] but increasingly few of them are committed to a lifetime career in it. Many are just dipping their toes in the water to see what it's like. Others may be thinking

---

[3] The Foreign Service is legally defined to include three other agencies besides State: USAID, the Foreign Agricultural Service (part of the Department of Agriculture) and the Foreign Commercial Service (part of the Commerce Department). It does not include the CIA except, *de facto*, when its employees are serving under State Department cover, or the military, or the myriad other agencies that now have employees assigned to US embassies.

about serving for twenty years, after which, according to current law, they qualify for a minimal pension.

The attractiveness of a Foreign Servicer career has been dimmed by its increasingly shoddy treatment at the hands of the Congress. Ambassadors go unconfirmed for months on end, victims of partisan conflict. As this is written the Foreign Service, like the Civil Service, has gotten no raises for the past two years, and the erosion of salaries, in real terms, is likely to continue. These negative trends have been accelerated by the Trump administration. Stagnant or declining pay may be acceptable in the short term as long as inflation rates are low, but no one can be sure if things will change when (not if) high inflation returns. [4]

The traditional assumption has been that no matter how much the Civil Service suffers, the Foreign Service, legally defined by its own statute, will be sheltered by its similarities with the military. Among these similarities is the requirement for Foreign Service Officers, unlike Civil Servants, to serve abroad, at destinations decided by the government. This of course involves inconvenience, financial sacrifice and some risk. It used to be said that, since World War II, more US ambassadors than generals have been killed in the line of duty, despite the much greater size of our military. True or not, the fact is that no federal benefits, even including military, seem totally secure as this written.

As will be apparent from previous chapters, the value of the Foreign Service, when it works well, is heavily dependent on the insights and professional contacts gained through *living* abroad. Only by living in a country does one begin to understand it well. Most people cannot "live" in this sense without family. The alternative of military-style, six-month unaccompanied tours would save some money and partially solve the trailing spouse problem, but it would be almost as damaging to the profession as dependence on Skype. Analytic reporting based on area expertise is one of the most important things that the State Department does and the only one that no other agency is mandated do.

---

[4] It is too soon to estimate more serious damage being done by Trump throughout the Federal Government.

George Kennan's "long cable" written in February of 1946, which created a framework for contesting the Cold War, is the most famous example of such reporting. It is true that today few FSO's serve in countries comparable in importance to Kennan's Soviet Union. But however unimportant, these places have a way of suddenly blowing up. Then they became important (or notorious) overnight, sometimes, as in the case of the Rwanda crisis and its aftermath, generating endless trouble and heavy defense spending. Arrayed in regional clumps, such places have come almost to dominate our foreign policy concerns. We need to understand them better in advance, before the need becomes painfully obvious, and good reporting is critical for such understanding.

The central fallacy about State's reporting function is the notion that our job is simply to load a Washington-bound conveyor belt with reports for officials and politicians who will cook them up in a big pot to produce Policy. In fact, reporting has a second function as valuable or more so than conveying information: the generation of deeper understanding, otherwise known as expertise.

Because of this, Foreign Service Officers overseas need to do two kinds of reporting. The first is factual, aimed primarily at Washington-based specialists whose work demands data, not necessarily opinions, on all kinds of topics. The second is analytic and judgmental, usually "big picture" oriented. It addresses such issues as the quality of national leadership, economic viability, the potential for conflict and crisis, internal tensions, and the nature of threats to the US—and it often proposes policy to deal with these issues.

Both kinds of reporting require diplomats to travel within the country to which they are assigned, to have adequate language skills to read the local media, to identify and talk with host country experts, and to form friendships. But the act of writing is equally important. Writing forces the author to think through the topic at hand, in other words to master it and thereby become expert. Such expertise is the basis of analytic reporting, but that is not all. Expertise also informs decision-making in time of crisis. In that respect it is like money: it must be earned in advance of being spent.

Expertise is also an important component of classic

diplomacy. Your official counterpart in country X is more likely to listen to your efforts to enlist his or her support if you demonstrate that you understand his problems and his country, however poor and backward it may seem. Otherwise you are may end up knocking on a closed door.

Others actors besides the State Department, both public and private, analyze foreign countries. The best journalists do it superbly, as do think tanks like the International Crisis Group. But is hard for them to shape their product with US Government requirements, interests and limitations in mind. They do not operate in every country, and they often lack the perspective which only extended living and travel in a foreign country can instill.

Formal academic expertise or training (like my own) is certainly valuable, but not essential for good field analysis. The best Foreign Service practitioners have more similarity to newspaper reporters than to professors, who, especially in today's social sciences, are too often inclined toward narrow overspecialization with minimal relevance to public affairs. Having said that, FSOs will always need to know what academic experts are writing and thinking about the regions and countries they are specializing in.

The intelligence agencies have their own limitations. They operate largely in secret and typically pay their foreign sources for information. This activity is crudely known as spying; it is illegal, dangerous, and not conducive to friendly relationships. Those caught at it customarily risk execution; not for nothing is a statue of Nathan Hale, executed by the British for spying in 1776, in the main lobby of the CIA. With rare exceptions, its end product is "raw intelligence," which is returned to Washington for analysis. By contrast, in the case of State Department reporting, the analyst and the author are the same person or persons, and the entire process is field-based.

I have no doubt that excellent Foreign Service reporting of this kind is still being done, but it is under grave threat. Security concerns are inhibiting diplomats from traveling, and they increasingly live in American-only compounds and work in fortress-like embassies. Monumental congestion in many capital cities is an almost equally powerful constraint; often one does not know how much time a routine call beyond the embassy's walls will take. Required reporting, personnel and administrative concerns, floods of official American visitors, attention to e-mail and ever-proliferating social media are all important, but they are crowding out work which is a fundamental reason for having a Foreign Service—and which, by its very nature, is dependent on individual insights and initiative.[5]

It is hardly surprising that ambassadors are sometimes part of the problem. My own failure to push harder for systematic analysis of Mali's desert unrest is a good example of how easy it is to neglect the need to understand an obscure problem before it turns into a money and attention-grabbing crisis.

Barbara Sums Up

As I have observed Anne pursuing her 25-hour-a-day upward climb through graduate school, post-doctoral fellowship, exciting but ultimately exasperating experience trying for tenure at Harvard, and current new beginning at the University of Wisconsin, concurrent with demanding roles of wife and mother, all without the benefit of any household staff, I often wonder how my life would have turned out had I been born a generation later.

Certainly, Anne has already had professional rewards that I never did. The most satisfying part of my teaching career

---

[5] After I wrote this, Stephen G. McFarland published "A Roadmap for New Hires: 30 Rules to Survive and Thrive," in the July-August 2016 issue of *The Foreign Service Journal*. The first on his list of thirty rules was "Geographic, Policy and Language Expertise," worth quoting in full: "Keep learning about the host country—find a part that interests you and become as interested in it as possible. Read its literature, listen to its music, discuss its politics, history, religion and economics; attend cultural and sports events. Within your security constraints, travel widely outside the embassy 'bubble.' (Carrying a nine-pound two-year old girl from a farm to a USAID child malnutrition feeding station in Guatemala, for example, and listening to her parents' survival strategy—feed the older brothers, not the baby girl—taught me what no briefing paper could.) Figure out what makes the society work the way it does, and what its contradictions and dynamics are."

came at The Madeira School, where my colleagues taught me more about really effective teaching and testing techniques than I ever learned anywhere else, including Cornell and my stint studying special education at George Mason. Discussion with them, members of the history department especially, about historical subject matter and current affairs was at a higher level than in any other faculty room, perhaps because we were still pre-Internet and pre-cell phones. When we relaxed over coffee, we really did have the time and inclination to chat.

So I did not move up an ever more challenging professional ladder, but seesawed along a path that sometimes offered other rewards. My teaching at the Ateneo de Manila helped to introduce Bob and me to a group of University scholars whose friendship and company enriched our stay in the Philippines. At Port Moresby International High School, lots of experience enabled me to cope with an inflexible curriculum and bone-headed administration and still offer classes that benefited my students. Potomac School was an extraordinarily nice place to work, but by the time I taught there, both subject matter and social milieu were repetitious, not challenging and mind-stretching. Given my split tenure, I could not consider moving up into administration, either as academic dean or college counselor, both of which I think would have been new and interesting.

Instead, the most intellectually broadening part of my school life came in the contacts I had with students, parents, and colleagues in various countries of which I knew very, very little before I set off with Bob for his various Foreign Service assignments—and that first doctoral research stint in Sarawak. I think it is safe to say that I have taught students from nearly ten percent of the world's countries in their home countries or the ones where their parents were working.

Had I not married, I would not have stayed a high-school teacher my whole life; of that I am sure. So I might have figured out how to go abroad in another career. But as it was, in our foreign postings, whether or not I was employed, with large, and generally competent household staffs, I had plenty of time to explore and learn about my exotic surroundings. And in Indonesia and the Philippines, I was blessed with childcare any time I needed it.

Activities like the Ganesha Society in Indonesia, or the course in Melanesian Prehistory at the University of Papua New Guinea, plunged me into the history and culture of the places where we lived. The natural history of such countries was an aspect which we always made time to explore. Whether Ujung Kulon and the reefs of the Thousand Islands in Indonesia or the birds and animals of Africa or the interlocking human and natural diversity of Papua New Guinea, we enjoyed them all—and incidentally, perhaps, influenced in some degree the careers of both Anne and Jamie. It was, in general, much less expensive and more rewarding to take advantage of these attractions in depth as residents than it would have been as tourists. From accompanying Bob on reporting trips in Indonesia and the Philippines to working intensively with Kady Sanogho of AMALDEME as she built a clinic and school for disabled children in Mali, there were generally many opportunities to learn about the social and economic issues in each country—and usually to help, in small ways, to improve the lives of some of the people we met.

Then, for sheer fun, there was the introduction to the arts and crafts of the countries in which we lived. In Sarawak we marveled at the intricacy of the tie-dyed (*ikat*) blankets (*pua*) which Iban women wove. We brought several home, as well as several small examples of the exquisite Kayan, Kenyah, and Kelabit beadwork. When we got to Indonesia on a Foreign Service salary, we lashed out a bit and bought several paintings in Jogjakarta and Bali, and various high quality batik sarongs, still done with traditional dyes in traditional patterns. We were even able to commission our living room drapes from Iwan Tirta's workshop.[6]

In Bali, we purchased painted cloths and intricate carvings, and various other items of art—but no beads yet. Because the

---

[6] Iwan Tirtaamidjaya had studied at Cornell, and though we never met him there, we introduced ourselves in Jakarta. Still living in the family home in Jakarta, while experimenting with new fabrics for batik there and in Central Java, he was glad for our large order in heavy cotton to try out that new product. I bought a lovely scarf on silk, an example of his finer work, affordable because it had one small flaw, and we enjoyed the curtains in two houses in Jakarta and one in Manila. Now Anne and David have some of them in their living room.

economic woes left over from the end of the Sukarno era were still forcing some families to sell furniture, we also brought home with us the huge bookshelf made from a Javanese Chinese bed, a small Chinese altarpiece, the desk which has graced our living room ever since, the heavily carved table upstairs and a scattering of fascinating but hardly priceless ceramics imported to the Indies from China, Vietnam, and Thailand.

Our collection of objects too large to fit easily into 216 Wolfe Street continued in Burkina Faso with the acquisition of masks and pottery, and then in PNG with shields and carvings. Often we were able to photograph our treasures and their makers in situ. Especially in the Philippines and in Africa, we rode home from upcountry trips with baskets or pottery in our laps. Fortunately, in Mali our main artistic interest was beads. The cost of all this was minimal because the Foreign Service shipping allowance provided more than enough weight to send home our acquisitions. We bought items that we liked aesthetically, that displayed amazing craftsmanship, and that reminded us of interesting people we had met and places we had visited. Each piece in our house holds memories for us.

A final benefit both Bob and I took home from our lives abroad was fluency, now a bit rusty, in two foreign languages. Both of us had studied French at various levels in grade school and high school, and I had continued in college as well as spending that Girl Scout summer in France. But what really consolidated our ability to handle the language on a conversational level and to read it easily were the five years living in francophone West Africa. Parisian accent, maybe not. A few extra colloquial words and usages, definitely. But we will be able to handle a French conversation for the rest of our lives.

Bob learned Indonesian in graduate school. Though I learned a bit of Malay, which is essentially the same language as Indonesian, at SOAS in London before going to Sarawak, I mastered it to a conversational and simple reading level at the Foreign Service Institute before going to Jakarta. Bob has followed up more than I have, and always had the larger vocabulary, but I operated in markets and with the household staff in spoken Indonesian the whole time we lived there, and I have plenty of speaking ability left, especially when we visit Indonesia.

The Trailing Spouse Dilemma

The dilemma of the unemployed spouse, male or female, was serious in our time and has now evolved into a potent threat to the future of the Foreign Service. Today many, if not most, American families depend on full income from both spouses, and increasingly few families can afford to lose it. The problem increases as women are treated more equally in the US workplace, acquire equal or greater professional credentials, and can earn as much or more than their partners.

For years the State Department has tried to employ spouses at embassies, but the work available is hardly ever well paid and even more rarely compatible with the skills of professional spouses. Doctors, lawyers and engineers are often barred from practicing abroad by licensing requirements. We remember the situation faced by one of our friends who was a junior partner in a big Washington law firm when her husband was posted to Israel, where lawyers are not exactly in short supply.

In our case, Barbara was willing to follow me and take what teaching jobs materialized at each post, if they did, and the Foreign Service got two employees for the price of one. She enjoyed sharing my work because, as noted earlier, it was interesting and rewarding intellectually. Suppose she had been able to find serious, equitably paid, full time employment at the embassy? It might have been practical at first, but as I advanced up the career ladder there would have been the same kind of conflict-of-interest issues that plague many of today's "tandem couples," the term for officers married to each other, especially when one is more senior in rank.

Teaching being a portable career, she was often able to work professionally abroad, usually part-time. But she did so at wages that were derisory by American standards. During the sixteen years we served abroad together[7] the "opportunity cost" to us was probably at least several hundred thousand dollars, according to our rough estimate. That includes lost wages and pensions but also, and probably more important, forgone ability to advance up career ladders—as things stand, a foreign posting typically means a job lost and a ladder kicked away—or to pursue an additional degree. What is clear is that this situation is one which few modern families, unless they are independently wealthy, can afford, particularly in cases where the spouse can earn as much or more than the officer.

In our case, I was able to benefit substantially from my "trailing spouse's" skills and experiences working outside the embassy and interacting with elements of society different from the ones that I got to know. Her experiences and friendships contributed powerfully to our shared knowledge of the country where we lived, and which I was paid to know well.

The only way out of the unpaid spousal dilemma that we can imagine, aside from eliminating accompanied tours abroad, would be to pay the non-working spouse a compensation commensurate with what he or she could earn at home or to supplement a local salary if he or she found a job at post. It would be worth it if the value of expertise-based diplomacy is taken into account, and a pittance measured against what we spend on other instruments of national security—the military, intelligence services, and foreign assistance, to name just the largest. The fact that spousal payment is thought to be a non-starter politically[8] is bound to keep on raising persuasive questions for bright young Americans weighing the merits and demerits of a Foreign Service career.

---

[7] Four years in Indonesia, three in the Philippines, two in Burkina Faso, two in Papua New Guinea, three in Mali, and two in South Africa (where Barbara remained at home teaching at Potomac School for one year of a three-year tour).

[8] I am told that the idea of spousal compensation would never be supported by the Congress, if only because Congressional spouses are not paid. Nevertheless, opportunities for adequately recompensed and professionally satisfying employment for spouses are far greater in Washington, DC, than in many overseas capitals.

How Fortune Smiled on Us

Well, you may ask, it sounds as if you had a fine time, even
if you did have to pay something for it. You got to live in nice
houses in fascinating places like Cape Town (and Ouagadougou)
at government expense, with servants to wait on you hand and
foot, while renting your house at home. In the really tough
places where adequate schools were lacking, the government
even paid for your kids to attend prestigious boarding schools,
like Milton and Madeira, in the US. Living abroad, they endured
a bit of trauma here and there, but also received a powerful, if
informal, education outside formal schooling.

It is true that we enjoyed our experience in the Foreign
Service, and were recompensed in the ways listed above, but
as noted earlier, times and circumstances have changed. And
we were in several ways very lucky.

The timing of our foreign tours in relation to our children's
needs is one example of how we lucked out. Many Foreign
Service parents decide that the best time to be abroad as a
family is when the children are small and the focus of their
lives is still within the family, and that the time to return is
sometime about seventh or eighth grade. The trouble is that
adolescents are at a stage in life when having a few close
friends and fitting in with the crowd are very important.
Especially for children coming home from postings with
small, super friendly overseas schools, reinsertion into a big
US high school or junior high can be overwhelming.

Contrary to this conventional wisdom, our children were
abroad with us from babyhood until the middle of grade
school. They were at home in Alexandria through (or almost
through) junior high, and then spent their high school years
in US boarding schools, where everyone was a new student
in ninth or tenth grade. Our nomadic existence was certainly
not without difficulties for them, but they never had the more
serious problems of identity and alienation from peers that
were all too common among the children of our colleagues
who moved with uprooted teenagers in tow. This issue was
not well understood at the time; we were just fortunate in
our timing.

Although we were almost always in "hardship posts,"

we usually managed to arrive just after a coup d'état (e.g. Ouagadougou) or leave just before one (Bamako).[9] As in Indonesia, the various ructions we experienced rarely hurt foreigners as long as they stayed indoors until the shooting or rioting stopped. The "rascals" didn't get us in Port Moresby, nor were we hurt by South Africa's vicious crime problem or, even scarier, its hair-raising highways.[10] And, no question about it, the salary increase ("hardship differential") we received for serving in these places—the "sticky" countries where political appointees rarely set foot—was significant.

My professional track in the Foreign Service was also more a product of luck than of strategy, as is often the case. I began prepared to an unusual extent for work in one region, Island Southeast Asia. My transition to a second specialization on Africa was largely serendipitous, based on my personal feelings about the leadership of the Asia regional bureau in 1977, as explained in Chapter 8. This followed two years of leave without pay to write a book and acquire some badly needed economic training. Taking a break to write and study was invaluable, but it would be much more difficult to do today, especially if, as in my case, it involved writing based largely on Foreign Service experience.

Geographic specialization is important for Foreign Service work, especially for the kind of field-based analysis described earlier, but it can be overdone. After I embarked on a second specialization on Africa, in 1979, I found that the experience actually helped me think better about Southeast Asia, by giving me an in-depth basis for comparison between two major developing areas. Since two of our three African postings were French-speaking, they also allowed both of us to polish our French language skills, and to see a lot of the French themselves, both in Africa and during later postings in Washington. Our children, especially Anne, who attended the *lycée* in Ouagadougou and was later able to join us for a year in Bamako, were beneficiaries of this career shift.

---

[9] What we missed in Bamako (1990) was less a conventional *coup d'etat* than a democratic insurgency supported by the army, but bullets flew nonetheless.

[10] Except for the quasi-comical pick-pocketing which took place when we were there on vacation in 1990, before being posted to South Africa.

In general, both children, now in their forties, look back on their Foreign Service experiences with pride and pleasure, not withstanding hard landings in Conakry and some lonely moments without parental support. Fortunately they had Aunt Kathy, plus on occasion Uncle Ron and Aunt Jane, and the Grandparents Cade back home to act superbly *in loco parentis*. Meanwhile they developed a degree of self-reliance no longer deemed acceptable by modern helicopter parents. In short we were lucky again, and so hopefully were they, although that is for them to say.

On balance, the Foreign Service was great for us. Would we recommend it to others? The answer is "Yes," but with some big provisos attached. Anyone contemplating a Foreign

Bob and Barbara Pringle, in front of the Alexandria Athenaeum, where they celebrated their 50th wedding anniversary with family and friends in October, 2014.

Service career today should be truly interested in living abroad as a family and should understand clearly the constraints it imposes on other family members. The State Department has no doubt lost influence over policy-making in a sea of newer agencies, partly because it has progressively lost (or shuffled off) vital functions, from intelligence to foreign aid. In addition, there are now many alternative ways of experiencing life and work abroad, both in the private sector and with non-profit organizations.

Nonetheless, we remain confident that the need to understand the rest of the world will remain with us, and that our government, whatever its follies of the moment, will always require a cadre of specialists to fill this need. Some potential Foreign Service recruits will appreciate the interest and fun of such careers, despite the sacrifices involved, and see the difference between a long-term commitment to service abroad and sporadic visits to complex countries, however assisted by the latest technological tools.